Out-of-Control Criminal Justice

Out-of-Control Criminal Justice shows that our system of criminal justice is broken; it is out of control. The author writes that a research-based strategy is needed that builds on the insights of those who work within criminal justice or are affected by it. Such a strategy must entail continuous evaluation and improvement, so that what works can be expanded and what does not can be eliminated. *Out-of-Control Criminal Justice* identifies how systemic problems plague our criminal justice systems. It then presents a comprehensive strategy for bringing these systems under control to reduce crime, to increase justice and accountability and to do so at less cost. The strategy can be used, too, to create greater responsiveness to victims and communities, effectiveness in reducing racial and ethnic disparities and understanding of the causes and consequences of crime. After describing this new approach, the book identifies the tools needed to implement a systems solution to create a safer and more just society.

Daniel P. Mears is the Mark C. Stafford Professor of Criminology at Florida State University. He has published widely, with more than 100 articles and two books, including the award-winning book, *American Criminal Justice Policy*. His research studies and federally funded projects have examined a diverse range of crime and justice issues. His views have been cited in such media outlets as the New York Times, Los Angeles Times, and USA Today. Previously, he served as a Senior Research Associate at the Urban Institute's Justice Policy Center and as a Peace Corps Volunteer and a program counselor working with adolescents.

Out-of-Control Criminal Justice

The Systems Improvement Solution for More Safety, Justice, Accountability, and Efficiency

DANIEL P. MEARS

Florida State University

CAMBRIDGE
UNIVERSITY PRESS

CAMBRIDGE
UNIVERSITY PRESS

University Printing House, Cambridge CB2 8BS, United Kingdom

One Liberty Plaza, 20th Floor, New York, NY 10006, USA

477 Williamstown Road, Port Melbourne, VIC 3207, Australia

314-321, 3rd Floor, Plot 3, Splendor Forum, Jasola District Centre, New Delhi - 110025, India

103 Penang Road, #05-06/07, Visioncrest Commercial, Singapore 238467

Cambridge University Press is part of the University of Cambridge.

It furthers the University's mission by disseminating knowledge in the pursuit of education, learning and research at the highest international levels of excellence.

www.cambridge.org
Information on this title: www.cambridge.org/9781316614044
DOI: 10.1017/9781316676578

First published 2017

A catalogue record for this publication is available from the British Library

ISBN 978-1-107-16169-6 Hardback
ISBN 978-1-316-61404-4 Paperback

For Eli and his generation

Contents

Figures and Tables

TABLE

Preface

America's criminal justice system – what amounts to a series of federal, state and local systems – has much to recommend it. Yet, this system operates like a tanker with no captain: it consumes large amounts of resources, fails to reach its destination, and wreaks havoc wherever it goes. More specifically, criminal justice in America wastes taxpayer dollars, creates uncertain benefits, and consistently misses opportunities to reduce crime and improve justice. In many instances, our criminal justice systems contribute to the very problems that they are supposed to address. We end up with more crime and less justice and accountability, and we quite literally pay for these "benefits." It is both tragic and avoidable.

In this book, I argue that we need to improve our *system* of criminal justice. Systemic change, not piecemeal change, provides the path toward greater public safety, justice, and accountability at less cost. To advance this argument, I first step outside the realm of crime and justice and focus on such policy arenas as health care, education, environmental protection, manufacturing, and the War on Terror. This detour is purposeful. It illustrates the importance of understanding systems to the creation of better outcomes. It serves, too, to show that systems problems are real and are not specific to criminal justice. The book then turns to the failures of criminal justice and how inattention to systems contributes to these failures. These observations form the foundation for presenting a systems-based approach to reducing crime and improving justice.

This approach – what I term a Systems Improvement Solution – will not magically solve all problems. It is, however, essential for diagnosis of what is wrong in criminal justice and what we need to do to create a safer and more just society. It is essential, too, for increasing accountability and cost-efficiency. How? The approach can help policymakers and criminal justice officials and practitioners to enact better policies, programs, and practices. It can help them to make better, empirically based decisions. Continuous attention to improvement, generation of better research to understand crime and justice, revised policy based on this research, and engagement of multiple stakeholders – these steps all are central to the proposed solution. They are critical, I argue, for any effort, whatever name we might give to it, seeking to create large-scale improvements in criminal justice and, in turn, more safety and justice.

The Systems Improvement Solution offers more than an opportunity to increase the effectiveness and efficiency of policy for crime and justice. It also provides an opportunity to apply, modify, and test theories of offending, crime rates, criminal justice policy, and justice. Such work can benefit scholars in developing stronger theories. At the same time, it provides a critical platform for creating a feedback loop that can contribute to more-effective crime and justice policy. In short, the book seeks to provide an approach that can be used to create a safer and more just society and, at the same time, to advance our understanding of crime and justice.

Myriad factors inspired this book. First and foremost for me has been a long-standing concern about crime and injustice. A second factor was a trip to Disney World with my wife and son. We toured "Spaceship Earth" and, by the end, had been asked several questions through a computerized kiosk on the panel in front of our seats. Our answers were analyzed then and there, and led to an instantaneous forecast about what our future might look like. This moment made me aware of what I should already have known – collecting and analyzing data in "real time" is technologically possible. That possibility opens the door to generating data in "real time" and answering questions of critical relevance to understanding and improving safety and justice. Yet, at present, this possibility remains just that – a possibility, one largely untapped by contemporary criminal justice policymaking and decision-making.

Yet another contributing factor has been my experience of evaluating crime policies and programs, writing books and articles on crime and justice, and seeking to illuminate public views about crime and justice. In the course of undertaking that work, one thing has been clear: several decades of unrelenting growth in corrections (including probation, jails, prisons, and parole) has created a pressing need to prevent crime and promote justice in more cost-efficient and less harmful ways. A piecemeal approach to reducing crime and meting out justice does not and will not work. A large body of theory and research underscores that point. A "way out" – a solution – requires a systematic approach, one grounded in theory, research, and evidence about what works, and in the insights and education of the diverse actors, including citizens, who contribute to and implement crime and justice policy.

Other factors that have contributed to this book are more eclectic. In examining criminological scholarship on crime and justice, one can become convinced that somehow the problems in criminal justice greatly exceed those in other policy arenas. I certainly hewed to that view for many years, until I considered the problems that plague other policy arenas. The medical system in particular stands out because it can seem that advances in medicine necessarily mean that our health care systems are exemplary. Nothing could be further from the truth. Criminal justice and health care, in fact, share much in common. Both face intensive case-processing pressures and rely on largely unexamined assumptions about the need for or benefits of various interventions. These and other problems greatly undermine their effectiveness and efficiency.

A direct prod in developing the book came from my training in sociology. As an undergraduate, I was exposed to the work of Talcott Parsons, credited with helping to found sociology and establishing a systems perspective on society. I did not understand a great deal of his work at the time. I did come to understand, however, that his approach to "grand theorizing" antagonized many scholars, perhaps rightly so. In subsequent years, I undertook work that might be likened to the "middle-range" theorizing and research advocated by Robert Merton, a student of Parsons, which arguably represents what most social scientists do in their day-to-day work lives. Even so, years later, the insight that systems matter continued to resurface in my own work and in the literature on crime, justice, and a broad array of policy arenas. It also resurfaced as I watched prison populations dramatically increase, which led me to write a book about prisoner reentry in the era of mass incarceration. The insight about systems did not mean that recourse to Parsonian "grand theory" was necessary. It did mean that a systems approach to understanding and improving safety and justice might be helpful, and perhaps even necessary.

Advances in research on cognitive decision-making provided an indirect prod for the book. This research, including work by Nobel Prize winner Daniel Kahneman has identified many ways in which intuition, unchecked by relevant information, leads us astray. Policymakers, judges, prosecutors, and the many individuals who work in criminal justice are no exception. This phenomenon can lead to a great deal of bad policy and practice. Advances in other academic arenas served as further prods. For example, economists have provided insight into ways in which systems crash because of incomplete, incorrect, or irrelevant information. Nassim Taleb's book on anti-fragility builds on that insight to argue for the importance of developing systems that build on the best available information, that are structured to adapt to changing landscapes, and that limit knee-jerk shifts based on ideology or unusual events. In a related vein, Nate Silver's popular book on "signal" and "noise" illuminates how efforts to improve policy require that theory and research identify patterns and not be distracted by "noise."

Yet another inspiration from the book came from chairing a local school board. I frequently felt the need for "systems information" about aspects of the school. At the same time, I experienced keenly the risk of drowning in too much good information and bad information. I think that the board achieved much, but I know, too, that a great deal more could have been achieved. To do better would have required, among other things, the ability to prioritize based on good information and an ability to sift through it quickly. A failure to prioritize translates into inefficiency. That insight guides us in many walks of life. In the medical system, it clearly is more important to help someone to breathe again than to salve a small wound. In our day-to-day lives, we all have many goals that we want to achieve, yet only so much can be completed in a given day. So we prioritize, even if unconsciously. We may not prioritize well, and when that happens we pay for it, sometimes dearly. For the criminal justice system, the failure to prioritize effectively has disastrous consequences: it results in more crime and less justice at great cost. However, prioritization requires data and an ability to sort through the data to identify patterns and, potentially, needed or effective changes. We need *research*, but we also need a *process* for improving research and ensuring that policy efforts are research based and well implemented. This observation provided no small impetus for this book.

Finally, students and their views about problems in criminal justice have provided a constant source of ideas that have helped to shape the book's arguments. Many students ardently advocate for solving social problems. They advocate as ardently for policies or interventions that they believe necessary to help society. Their energy and enthusiasm are infectious. In the hands of those students who seem to be headed for political careers, one can see how specific policies, programs, and the like come into existence. Some ideas simply seem to "make sense" and, well, we have got to do something, right? However, the fact of the existence of some social problem or the assumed or demonstrated effectiveness of a given intervention does not help us to prioritize problems and policies. We need an approach that can help state and local governments prioritize and produce cost-efficient improvements in public safety, justice, and accountability. That approach entails, as this book argues, a systems-focused solution.

I would not have been able to complete this undertaking without the support of colleagues and friends and without the insights of a broader community of scholars, policymakers, administrators, and practitioners. Their efforts are greatly appreciated. I especially thank Dean Tom Blomberg for his friendship and his support, not only to me but also to the College of Criminology and Criminal Justice at Florida State University, which has been my home for the past decade. His enthusiasm for the melding of theory, research, and policy has helped to put the College on the front lines of scholarship and practice. Thank you to Frank Cullen, Bill Kelly, and Brandon Welsh for their time, wisdom, guidance, and friendship. That one sentence does not remotely do the sentiment justice. I owe them each a debt of gratitude that words alone cannot fulfill. Thank you, too, to Robert Dreesen for supporting the book and doing so when it was but the first trace of an idea. Thank you to Josh Cochran for fun afternoons spent brainstorming several research projects; in indirect ways, the conversations informed the present book. Thank you to Sam Scaggs for tracking down helpful source materials. Special thanks go to my wife, Emily, and son, Eli – the world is, quite simply, a brighter, more sunlit place because of them.

Introduction: Out-of-Control Criminal Justice

Criminal justice has turned into a burgeoning, out-of-control industry. Prison, parole, and probation populations and the supporting apparatus – law enforcement and the courts – have dramatically expanded since the 1980s. This expansion has obligated large amounts of resources and tax dollars, with little evidence of benefit.[1] Worse, investments in criminal justice consistently ignore the "systems" nature of both crime and justice. In so doing, they almost guarantee that investments will be wasteful, will fail to improve outcomes, and may even worsen them. The problem stems in part from insufficient research infrastructure at federal, state, and local levels. Such infrastructure is necessary to systematically understand the causes of crime in particular places and how criminal justice can be configured to achieve greater public safety and justice. The problem also stems from a failure to carefully couple policymaking and research. Ideally, policymaking – including the design and implementation of various programs and practices as well as the day-to-day decision-making that occurs throughout the criminal justice system – would be informed by research. Ideally, too, research would accommodate and address the real-world constraints and challenges that confront lawmakers and those who work in criminal justice. These ideals have not been met. Indeed, they cannot be met without an institutionalized basis for doing so. The end result? Less government accountability, less cost-efficiency, and missed opportunities to reduce crime and to achieve more justice.

This book seeks to chart a better path. To this end, it proposes a "Systems Improvement Solution," or "Systems Solution" for short. Briefly, the solution consists of a continuous interplay between, on the one hand, research, and, on the other hand, a policy process focused on designing, implementing, and improving policy. "Policy" here refers to a wide array of laws, rules, programs, and practices, as well as decisions made by policymakers and criminal justice administrators and practitioners. The research component of the Systems Solution consists of continuously applying the evaluation research hierarchy *and* systems analysis to all parts of the criminal justice system and its subsystems. This hierarchy entails *needs* evaluations that assess whether a given policy is needed; *theory* evaluations to assess the integrity and credibility of a policy's design; *implementation* evaluations to assess how well and completely a policy is implemented; *impact* evaluations to assess how well a policy contributes to intended outcomes while minimizing harmful unintended outcomes; and *cost-efficiency* (or simply "efficiency") evaluations to assess the relative benefits as compared to the costs of a policy, especially in comparison to other policy options.[2] *Systems analysis*, by contrast, involves identifying the structures and dynamics that influence one another and contribute to or inhibit achievement of the target or "end" outcomes that we want for a given system. It serves, in particular, to assess how changes in one part of a system may affect other parts and, more broadly, to raise awareness about the ways in which crime and justice occur within and are affected by a systems context.

Research that occurs in a vacuum, however, will do little to provide relevant insight into crime and justice (or how to improve it). Policymakers and the stakeholders who work within or are affected by criminal justice must be involved. However, involvement without understanding – without good and relevant information – will not achieve much. It is for this reason that the emergence in recent decades of policymaker calls for evidence-based policy has been a positive occurrence.[3] As Brandon Welsh and colleagues have emphasized, "There is a growing consensus among scholars, practitioners, and policymakers that crime prevention and criminal justice programs and policies should be rooted as much as possible in scientific research."[4] This idea can be seen across many social policy arenas, as reflected in the enactment by Congress of the bipartisan Evidence-Based Policymaking Commission Act of 2016.[5]

The consensus amounts to a paradigm shift in discussions about what should guide criminal justice policy and practice. However, policymakers, administrators, and practitioners ultimately must be able to understand research if they are to know what constitutes "evidence-based" policy. That does not mean that individuals in these roles have to be researchers. But they *do* need to be able to evaluate the credibility and relevance of research. They need to be able to understand the systems nature of crime and justice. And then they need to ask for and use research. The only alternative is recourse to assumptions and ideology.

At the same time, researchers must be involved in policy design and improvement. Otherwise, they must guess at policymakers' intentions and the challenges that they, as well as administrators and practitioners, face. Researchers who are not part of efforts to design and improve policy typically lack the requisite access to the types of data that would allow for credible and timely analyses that could be used to improve policy deliberations.

Accordingly, the Systems Improvement Solution entails a multi-stakeholder policy *process*. This process brings together lawmakers, criminal justice administrators, front-line personnel who have on-the-ground experience with, and a "stake" in, the day-to-day implementation of policy, and, not least, researchers. In addition, it involves the "clients" served by the criminal justice system, including victims, affected communities, defendants, and offenders.

A lynchpin to the Systems Improvement Solution centers on the implementation of policies that are based on empirical evidence and that are driven by a multi-stakeholder policy process. It centers on continuous attention to evaluating implementation, impacts, and efficiency. It centers, too, on improving all aspects of the criminal justice system. Core priorities that guide the process include the following: Improve the system; focus on goals; avoid big mistakes (which by itself can create substantial returns for society); prioritize high-bet, low-risk minor changes or "tweaks" (if they do not work out, we have not lost much); maximize positive feedback loops and minimize negative feedback loops that create a vicious cycle and lock government into ineffective and inefficient investments; and continuously reevaluate and improve policies.

The Solution calls, too, for adherence to core principles to ensure the integrity and effectiveness of the process. For example, the process must be institutionalized into everyday decision-making and policy discussions. It must be non-partisan, deliberative, and research-informed. Stakeholders from throughout the system or who shape or are affected by it must be included, and discussions should be guided by research. Insights from those on the "ground floor," such as officers, community residents, public defenders, and so on, should be included, as should knowledge from scientists who study criminal justice. Insights from theory, data analysis, and new data are critical as well. In an era of "big data," numerous opportunities exist to identify patterns in crime and justice that can be leveraged to produce understanding about system operations and changes that could improve safety, justice, and other outcomes. At the same time, advances in data collection and analysis have created the ability to generate information that can be used to gain insights that go beyond what existing data permit. Not least, information from the Systems Solution process should be disseminated widely and frequently. Doing so helps to ensure that stakeholders and the public share a common understanding about crime and justice. In turn, it creates a foundation for identifying evidence-based policies that best reduce crime and improve justice, accountability, and efficiency.

I.I OUT-OF-CONTROL CRIMINAL JUSTICE

A starting point for understanding the need for a sea-change in how America addresses crime and justice begins with a short litany of the dramatic failures of criminal justice policy in recent decades. There assuredly are many bright spots on the policy landscape, and these will be discussed. The bar, however, should not be a landscape pockmarked by failure and a few offsetting bright spots. Rather, it should be a systematic focus on minimizing failures and maximizing success. At the least, it should entail limiting avoidable mistakes that fail to reduce crime and that potentially increase it, worsen justice, and leave taxpayers the poorer for it. Although not all scholars, and certainly not all policymakers, would agree with the list that follows, it consists of examples that many members of each group have identified as failures. Some examples, such as high recidivism rates, can be seen as end outcomes of failed policies. Others, such as racial profiling, can be seen as intrinsically problematic policies that, as a "bonus," may also worsen crime and perpetuate injustice. In many instances, the failures – such as an investment in an ineffective policy and a concomitant disinvestment in an effective one – compound one another. Here, then, is a small sample of criminal justice failures:

- *Increased crime rates in the 1980s and 1990s, followed by crime rates that, because of ineffective policies, did not decline as quickly as they otherwise might have.*[6] Both problems could and should have been avoided.
- *Failure to invest in effective crime prevention strategies and punishments.* Instead, during the punitive era of the past four decades, ineffective tough-on-crime laws and various examples of "correctional quackery"[7] were implemented that lacked, and continue to lack, credible social scientific support.[8]

- *Large-scale investment in "get tough" policies throughout the criminal justice system.* A prominent illustration: states have built expensive supermax facilities to house the "worst of the worst" inmates, yet have done so with little credible theoretical or empirical evidence that the facilities were needed, effective, or cost-efficient.[9]
- *Excessive use of incarceration, or what has come to be termed, "mass incarceration."*[10] No question, incarceration serves a clear purpose or, more precisely, multiple purposes, such as retribution and public safety. However, the lack of credible empirical research that documents consistent and large recidivism benefits, coupled with evidence that prisons may worsen offending and harm families and communities, indicates that incarceration should be used carefully.[11] The sheer expense of incarceration would seem to dictate a need for caution. Yet, precisely the opposite has occurred since the 1970s.

  Under the *best-case* scenario, this effort may have dramatically reduced crime, prevented some individuals from spiraling into a lifetime of offending, and helped families and crime-ridden communities. A few studies suggest in fact that mass incarceration may have contributed to upward of 25 percent of the crime reduction that occurred from the mid-1990s to the early 2000s.[12] These studies, however, are few in number and considerable disagreement exists about their credibility. At the same time, an emerging literature suggests that incarceration does little to reduce recidivism.[13]

  Under the *worst-case* scenario, mass incarceration has failed to appreciably reduce crime, may even have increased it in some places, increased recidivism, damaged the children and families of the individuals sent to prison, poorly served victims of crime, and harmed communities.[14] And it will have done so at considerable taxpayer expense.
- *Extraordinarily high recidivism rates.* It is estimated that over three-fourths of prisoners are rearrested within five years of release.[15] Were an accurate measure of actual offending used, we would see that the recidivism rate is much higher.
- *Persistent evidence of racial profiling and racial and ethnic disparities and discrimination in policing, court processing and sentencing, and correctional system (mis)treatment.*[16] Evidence of disparities and discrimination has accumulated annually. Little evidence exists that criminal justice processing has been is being

reformed in ways that will appreciably and measurably reduce these problems.

- *Intensive investment in a wide range of tough-on-crime sentencing laws that "bet the farm" on specific and general deterrent effects and ignored the social and financial costs of incarceration.* This investment occurred alongside of limited attention to addressing the many different causes of offending among those punished and among those who might offend. Not least, it ignored the many different, cheaper, and more balanced approaches to reducing recidivism and crime rates in communities that exist.[17]

- *Criminalization of drug use rather than treatment of it as a public health problem.*[18] Illegal drug use creates many problems. The simple but big question is how best to reduce demand and supply of it. Little credible evidence exists to suggest that incarceration substantially reduces national drug abuse or drug-related offending.

- *Harm to communities through "top down" approaches to policing, inattention to the causes of crime in high-crime communities, the removal of large numbers of individuals from these communities and their placement in prison, and the return of these individuals to these same areas.*[19] Instead of a careful assessment of the causes of crime and other problems in a given area and then systematic attention to them, the predominant approach has been a "get tough" one, in the hope that doing so would serve as a "silver bullet" solution to crime. It is not.

- *Enactment of wide-ranging reforms that sought to criminalize juvenile justice.*[20] The end result was expansion of probation, incarceration, and transfer of youth to the criminal justice system. That occurred alongside of little credible research to suggest that reductions in juvenile crime resulted or that the "best interests" of youth – the reason for having a separate system of justice for adolescents – were advanced.

- *Inattention to systematically monitoring and addressing the innumerable opportunities for abuse and mistakes in criminal justice decision-making.*[21] Criminal justice and corrections is a machinery, one that is rife with the potential for abuse and error. Harm and mistakes occur. Yet, their occurrence and causes are largely ignored, except when media accounts profile extreme cases. In the meantime, both good decision-making and poor decision-making throughout criminal justice systems go unacknowledged.

- *Public dissatisfaction with criminal justice.* Policymakers introduced tough-on-crime policies and dramatically increased criminal justice system expenditures, and did so based on the notion that they were being responsive to the public. Yet, public views did not call for extreme, narrowly focused responses to crime. They called for balanced approaches. Not surprisingly, public dissatisfaction with the criminal justice system was a persistent theme during the era of tough-on-crime lawmaking and remains so.[22]
- No *institutionalized apparatus for government accountability exists, despite persistent calls for greater accountability and reliance on "evidence-based" practice.*[23] The result? More such calls, no evidence of accountability, and no foundation for creating it.

Such critiques barely scratch the surface. Again, many bright spots exist. One can point, for example, to efforts that cities have undertaken to implement crime analysis, hot-spots policing, programs, and practices that have been well-evaluated, and so on. However, the unifying thread by and large is one of failure to plan systematically through the use of credible research, meaningful inclusion of diverse stakeholder groups, and a commitment to improvement. Another unifying thread is the adoption of well-intentioned policies that are undertaken based on personal beliefs and ideology rather than careful empirical assessment about the scope and nature of a particular problem, its causes, or the diverse options for addressing these causes.

Still another unifying thread is the vast disjuncture between policy and research. Policymakers and criminal justice administrators frequently reside in a universe far removed from the nuts-and-bolts realities of offenders, victims, and the communities and families from which these offenders and victims come. All too often, they also do not understand research. They do not know how to ask better research questions or how to consume study findings. Researchers are complicit; they, too, typically reside far from the realities of offenders and victims. Just as problematic, they rarely interact with policymakers and criminal justice administrators.

In defense of these different groups, however, lies a simple fact: No institutionalized arrangement exists that requires policymakers and administrators to interact with the targets of their policies or with researchers. At the same time, researchers cannot willy-nilly insert themselves into policymaking processes or criminal justice administrators' decisions, nor can they whole-cloth create data that address spur-of-the-moment crises in a timely, credible manner.

The failure of criminal justice policy – viewed here as encompassing criminal justice and corrections as well as the laws, programs, practices, and day-to-day decision-making of system actors – does not lie with any one group, organization, or agency. It results from multiple systems failures. There is a failure to require a systems-based approach to understanding and addressing crime and justice. There is a failure to require sustained and ongoing involvement of diverse stakeholders in guiding both policy and research. Not least, there is a failure to institutionalize continuous policy evaluation, reevaluation, and improvement.

1.2 HOW SAFETY, JUSTICE, ACCOUNTABILITY, AND EFFICIENCY ARE SYSTEMS PROBLEMS

Safety (Crime)

Criminal justice exists in large part to improve public safety and to do so by reducing crime. That is well and fine. Fortunately, many tools exist to combat crime. These include crime prevention efforts, policing, a variety of sanctioning options, rehabilitative programs, and so on. An effective and efficient approach to promoting public safety would be one that sought to use these tools when and where they are most helpful and least costly.

However, in America, crime has been conceptualized in recent decades as something to which government must respond primarily through punishment. The belief, if implicit, has been that a lack of punishment constitutes the most important cause of crime. Consider, for example, that few if any states or jurisdictions have a "Department of Public Safety" that systematically targets the causes of crime. Instead, criminal justice agencies almost uniformly center their efforts on policing and punishment, not a broad spectrum of activities that might improve public safety. To be sure, policing and punishment may reduce crime. They may introduce a general deterrent effect, for example. But they do not typically address the many different factors that give rise to crime among individuals, families, schools, or communities.

The fact that crime largely results from societal conditions does not absolve individuals from responsibility for their behavior and it does not mean that punishment should not feature prominently in our crime-fighting efforts. It also does not mean that individual characteristics, such as low self-control or criminogenic thinking, do not contribute to offending. It simply means that on an "aggregate," societal level, the *volume* of crime stems primarily from societal conditions. For example, a country that does not ensure that children are well parented will have a greater number of children who develop low self-control, which in turn will contribute to higher levels of crime relative to countries where children are well parented. Is the state supposed to be a parent? No. Should it usurp parental authority? No. At the same time, a country that, for whatever reason, allows high rates of poor parenting to occur likely will have more children with low self-control. Similarly, a country that fails to take steps to reduce criminogenic – that is, crime-causing – conditions will have higher crime rates, no matter the characteristics of its citizens. For example, all else equal, a country with fewer well-lit streets and communities where neighbors look out for one another will likely have more crime.

When individuals commit crime, they should be punished. There also should be interventions aimed at reducing their offending. However, the effectiveness of any such individual-focused punishments or interventions will pale in comparison to efforts that reduce *aggregate* rates of crime. That idea is not novel. To the contrary, policymakers almost annually proclaim that efforts should be targeted toward reducing crime in society.

The seemingly systematic inattention to the causes of crime is itself a cause of crime. A piecemeal approach may work here and there. Crime of one type or another may go down for a while in an area. Sustained reductions in crime, however, almost necessarily require a more careful and calibrated approach that targets *crime-causing factors*.[24] Here, I do not mean the causes of crime in general. For that, criminologists conveniently have identified a long list of possibilities. Instead, I mean the causes of crime in *particular* areas.

How can these causes be identified? There is no shortcut: Research must be regularly undertaken in these areas. To echo a theme that will reverberate through this book, we have here another indicator of an entrenched problem. Few states or jurisdictions invest sufficiently in research to arrive at an accurate assessment of the prevalence or causes of their local crime. Policymakers and administrators then go with their instincts, beliefs, and research from this or that study, and hope that a piecemeal approach will work in these places. In so doing, they enable criminogenic conditions to persist or worsen. When crime goes up (or fails to go down fast enough), they simply call for more punishment. Does punishment have a role to play? Yes. But it does not address the myriad factors that cause crime in general or in specific places.

Sustained inattention to the causes of crime in specific areas and overemphasis on sanctions and interventions that lack credible scientific evidence constitutes a systems problem. It amounts to the institutionalization of failure. Consider, for example, if individuals who would never commit crime again are placed in well-intentioned diversion programs, a mainstay of the juvenile justice system; here, we clearly are wasting resources.[25] The problem is worse, though. These same youth, by dint of being diverted, now are supervised by whoever runs the diversion program. Any misbehavior then will be more likely to be noticed. The youth may be no more delinquent than any other youth, but nonetheless they get caught, labeled as delinquent, and sentenced more harshly. Why more harshly? Because now the court sees a youth who seemingly has squandered an opportunity and needs a lesson. Here we have the juvenile justice system spending money on an intervention that may not be needed and whose effectiveness typically has never been established.[26] At the same time, that money is not being spent in more effective ways. Not least, the youth may suffer academically and socially. Once the youth penetrate deeper into the juvenile justice system, these problems reverberate even more strongly.[27]

This situation arises from a system of justice that allows diversion to occur without a careful empirical assessment of the risk that these youth present, the distribution and causes of crime in an area, the estimated costs and benefits of different policies, and so on.[28] It arises, too, from a system that can be easily pushed by a charismatic policymaker or judge who champions a special program or by a courtroom culture that thinks that certain "types" of youth should be diverted and others not.[29] Perhaps not surprisingly, those who promote special programs envision only that the interventions help. Frequently, however, the interventions do not. And to the extent that they divert resources from efforts that could address the root causes of crime, they contribute to more of the very problem that they were designed to address.

When, on a state or national level, we impose a sanction that may be criminogenic, we contribute to higher crime rates. Such likely is the case with mass incarceration. We have squandered opportunities to address root causes of crime and to impose sanctions that could be more effective at less cost. We continue to do so by relying heavily on incarceration and lengthy terms of incarceration, even though we have no empirically based foundation on which to justify specific uses or amounts of time in prison to reduce crime or recidivism or to achieve a satisfactory level of retribution.[30] Perhaps for that reason we have dramatic variation in incarceration rates and of time served; states essentially guess at what they think must be an effective amount of incarceration.[31] They simultaneously ignore known causes of offending.

Perhaps for that reason, too, we have depressingly high recidivism rates. In a national assessment of recidivism among prisoners released from 2005 to 2010 across 30 states, researchers found that 77 percent were rearrested for a felony or serious misdemeanor within five years of release.[32] They also found that more than half (55 percent) were reconvicted of a new crime. Not least, just over one in four (28 percent) were incarcerated for a new crime. If prisons effectively reduce recidivism, it is not evident from these statistics or extant research.[33]

A typical policymaker response would be to ask, "Well, what else should we do? Let crime go unpunished? Don't incarcerate?" The answer is at once simple and complicated. If we want more safety and justice, then we need to create empirically based approaches to determining how much any given punishment achieves in reduced crime and recidivism, as well as how much retribution we gain. We also need empirically based approaches to determining how much any of our policies, programs, practices, and decisions – not just our punishments – affect crime and justice. We then need to estimate the improvements that might arise through adjustments to these policies, programs, practices, and decisions or through the addition of new ones. Such an approach may seem pie-in-the-sky. It is not. Businesses undertake complicated assessments all of the time. They do so by investing heavily in research and they do so because it serves their bottom-line interests. Criminal justice systems can do the same.

Justice

Justice, like crime, is fundamentally a systems problem and phenomenon. In modern societies, a legal apparatus exists to mete out justice. In a very real sense, justice is defined by the way in which society responds to crime. Notably, then, America has a largely *offender-based* criminal system of justice. The focus centers on the offender as "criminal." Relatively little systematic attention attends to whether defendants receive fair hearings, victims of crime have their voices heard and are helped, or certain groups, such as minorities, receive fair treatment.

That indictment seems harsh. There clearly have been strides taken. Progress has occurred. For example, in the juvenile justice system, the federal government enacted disproportionate minority contact legislation that required states to monitor and address racial and ethnic disproportionalities in juvenile justice.[34] Many accounts exist, too, of efforts to supply quality defense counsel to minorities and to improve community conditions in high-crime minority neighborhoods. Victims today receive more support and attention than in the past.[35]

Yet, at the end of the day, there remains no systematic, ongoing empirical monitoring nationally or among states of the amount or quality of "criminal" justice, factors that influence the administration of justice or how to improve it. One prominent example involves policing. A way to improve policing effectiveness and to improve citizens' objective and subjective experiences with the police could include surveying citizens about their experiences with the police.[36] Doing so would inform the police about how citizens perceive them, alert law enforcement executives about successes and possible problems, and, possibly, what to do about them. This type of effort, however, requires that continuous research be undertaken on citizens' views. Also, continuous analysis and discussion of these views would need to occur. Not least, multiple stakeholders would need to meet to identify, develop, test, and reevaluate proposed solutions. Citizen experiences with the police, as with criminal courts, would seem central to documenting that justice occurs. Yet few if any jurisdictions in America systematically assess these experiences on an ongoing basis or demonstrate success in achieving "justice." Ideally, for example, we might compare multiple jurisdictions or states in the extent to which defendants and victims feel fairly treated by the justice system. No institutionalized research foundation exists to undertake such a seemingly basic comparison, not just for court experiences but also for experiences with crime prevention efforts, policing, and corrections.

Accountability

Accountability, too, is a systems problem and phenomenon. There can be no accountability without collection of relevant information on performance. Here, again, no institutionalized foundation exists within states or, typically, in local jurisdictions to collect information that documents how well various parts of the criminal justice system operate. A simple example illustrates the point. As mentioned above, diversion programs are touted as offering offenders a less severe sanction than they otherwise would receive. Yet, we know from research that individuals placed in diversion programs sometimes would have received no intervention but for the fact that the programs exist.[37] Because of these programs, they receive something rather than nothing, even though the motivating idea typically is to offer a milder sanction as an alternative to a more punitive one. How often does this phenomenon – termed "net-widening" – occur?[38] More generally, to what extent are these programs used appropriately? No one knows.[39]

Similar questions face us when we look at many aspects of the criminal justice system. How often do the police receive insufficient training or abuse citizens? How often do the courts face unreasonable caseload processing demands that almost necessarily translate into excessive delays in resolving cases? How consistent and fair are the courts in deciding whom to detain, convict, or send to prison? How much abuse occurs in prison, what are the causes of the abuse, and what has been done to reduce it? These and hundreds of other examples can be identified.[40] In most instances, little to no systematic empirical research, undertaken on a regular basis, exists to demonstrate accountability – that is, to demonstrate that the government ensured that criminal justice agencies and actors fulfilled their obligations and were sufficiently supported to do their jobs well.

The situation cannot be readily resolved through heavy-handed legal responses to this or that high-profile incident. Such responses typically fall into the same trap. A law is enacted. Then, absent a body charged with and funded to assess implementation and its impacts, the law remains "on the books" only. Or perhaps the law is applied appropriately here, inappropriately there, and so on. No systematic assessment of these uses occurs, nor, by extension, any evaluation of the law's impact. This situation, one in which the system is ignored and high-profile legislation or popular new programs receive priority, creates considerable leeway for abuse or for the government to fail to do what it is charged with doing – helping society.

Efficiency

"Efficiency" is a shorthand term for cost efficiency and refers to efforts to achieve policy outcomes, or benefits, at the least cost. Policymakers frequently call for cost-benefit analyses. The reason is clear – such analyses seem intuitive. We want the most "bang for the buck." Yet, the essence of any efficiency analysis boils down to a comparison of different policy scenarios. That creates complexity in undertaking and interpreting efficiency analyses. For example, we can change the results of an efficiency analysis simply by selecting those scenarios that we prefer or that we guess would be most likely. To illustrate, supermax prisons are costly, and so would seem like an obvious focus of a cost-benefit analysis.[41] What, though, is the proper comparison? That depends. What would the prison system have done instead? Nothing? Build another prison? Invest in rehabilitative programming? Would the legislature instead have invested the funds in community crime prevention programs? Each question entails a different policy scenario, and for each we need estimates of the expected outcomes.

No researcher can magically select the "correct" scenario. Doing so requires the engagement of policymakers and, in this instance, corrections administrators. Even then, a failure to consider the broader systems context can well result in largely meaningless results. For example, the analysis might show that, for the prison system, a supermax facility is "cost-efficient." Somehow, for example, it produces sufficiently large improvements in prison to offset the costs of building and operating a prison. The monetized benefits exceed the monetized costs, and so it is efficient.[42] What, though, would have been the benefits-to-costs ratio if the same funds had been distributed to officer training or to rehabilitative programming for inmates? For this scenario, we need a separate efficiency analysis. What if the funds were used to improve risk assessment of convicted felons and better individualization of their sanctions, supervision, and treatment? Here, again, we need a different cost-efficiency evaluation that places all results into a dollar metric so that we can determine which investment yields the greatest returns. Only state policymakers can really determine if a given scenario is realistic or might occur. Accordingly, generation of meaningful efficiency analyses requires policymakers to drive the framing or scope of a cost-efficiency analysis and dictate which scenarios get considered.

Such involvement or understanding is unlikely to occur without a systems-based approach to assessing efficiency. By extension, with no systems-level efficiency evaluation, we cannot demonstrate that taxpayer dollars are being used to the greatest advantage. Consider, again, policing and prisons. An assessment of crime might identify several factors, such as poverty or unemployment, that could be addressed to reduce crime. Most jurisdictions undertake no such assessment. Instead, they invest in police or prisons. Then they then fail to evaluate the impact of the police efforts or prisons. Even if they did, however, they would lack any insight into how much more crime might have been decreased through alternative approaches.

By contrast, a systems-based approach to assessing cost-efficiency would place crime and justice at the center of all decision-making.

It would require careful deliberation about the relative costs and benefits of diverse policies that might reduce crime and improve justice. What it would not do is default to hiring more police officers and building more prisons. Nor would it default to investing in a promising new policy or an evidence-based practice that was found to work in other places. Rather, it would proceed through a systematic, deliberate assessment of crime in a given area, the approaches in place to address crime, justice system processing, and the range of viable strategies that might be employed to reduce crime and improve justice.

1.3 THE SYSTEMS IMPROVEMENT SOLUTION TO CRIME, JUSTICE, ACCOUNTABILITY, AND EFFICIENCY

We have ample evidence of the problems associated with piecemeal approaches to criminal justice policy.[43] We have ample evidence, too, of the problems associated with a lack of research on timely, pressing crime and justice issues. Policymaker awareness of these problems can readily be seen in some of their statements and calls for action. In 2016, for example, the Charles Colson Task Force on Federal Corrections – which included Democratic and Republican legislators – issued a sweeping set of recommendations for improving the federal correctional system.[44] A central recommendation centered on the need to collect, analyze, and use information about correctional system operations to improve performance and accountability.[45] Unfortunately, states typically do not provide the research infrastructure or a deliberative process for regularly monitoring and evaluating criminal justice systems or improving them.

Absent such research and a process, policymakers and criminal justice administrators and practitioners of necessity lean on personal beliefs, ideology, and whatever information – no matter how questionable its validity – may be within reach. Beliefs and ideology no doubt form a critical part of policymaking. In a democracy, they should. Yet they are not a good substitute for credible information. Indeed, when applied to social problems and policies, they can serve to blind us. Worse yet, they cement a view of the world that may run counter to reality. Unchecked intuition is a dangerous tool, as decades of research on cognitive decision-making errors have revealed.[46] But intuition, when informed by a process that allows for careful consideration of new and relevant information, can lead to better decisions.

The trick, then, lies in tapping the intuition and insights of different groups of individuals, undertaking a research-informed process of deliberation, developing new and better information, testing policy changes, evaluating and improving policy, and repeating this process continuously. It lies, too, in ensuring that this process focuses on the *entire* criminal justice system. Doing so focuses attention on "big picture" goals – reducing crime and creating more justice, accountability, and efficiency – and how different parts of the system can be configured or changed to achieve these goals. It educates all stakeholders about the interplay between and within parts of the criminal justice system and about the assumptions involved when investing in various parts of the system or particular policies. Not least, it enables them to identify opportunities for the greatest amount of improvement and efficiency.

The Systems Improvement Solution takes heed of these observations. It places research and a multi-stakeholder process at center stage, and it emphasizes continuous analysis and discussion. The strategy boils down to seeking constantly to understand the operations and impacts of the criminal justice system, problems that exist, and opportunities to create the greatest improvements. The ultimate goals are to reduce crime and increase justice, accountability, and efficiency. To this end, research cannot be undertaken in piecemeal fashion. In addition, policymaking and implementation of various programs, interventions, rules, and the like should not be divorced from research. Instead, both activities must be combined and inform one another if appreciable gains are to occur.

Picking away at a systems problem with isolated efforts, especially ones that ignore the broader systems context, cannot and will not work. As Kathleen Auerhahn has emphasized, "one of the primary reasons that criminal justice systems are in the state that they are in is due to a lack of consideration of the consequences of policy from a systemic standpoint. This failure to consider the system in all its complexity results in simplistic policy choices that result in ever-more complex consequences."[47] What holds far more promise, I argue, is a systems-focused, research-infused, multi-stakeholder policy development, evaluation, and improvement process. If followed, this process holds the potential for substantially reducing crime and improving justice, accountability, and cost-efficiency. It holds potential, too, for shedding light on crime causation and the nature of "justice," and, in turn, for advancing criminological and criminal justice theory. This process and set of activities constitutes the Systems Improvement Solution.

1.4 SYSTEMS PROBLEMS ARE EVERYWHERE AND ARE NOT SPECIFIC TO CRIMINAL JUSTICE

Systems problems pervade society, not just criminal justice. Medical systems are replete with flaws that result in poor practice and less health as well as lost lives. Social service systems struggle to provide assistance or to intervene in a timely, effective manner. Schools often fail America's children. Economic systems fail and lead to housing market collapses and recessions.

In every instance, systems failures contribute to ineffectiveness and inefficiency. These failures stem from a set of causes that can plague any system. Consider a situation where no single entity oversees an entire system. For example, imagine a computer chip factory or the construction of a tall skyscraper with no one who oversees all operations. Failure is almost guaranteed. A captain of sorts is needed. Yet, oversight by someone with little to no accurate information about different aspects of the operations will not improve matters much.

Consider another situation: a school district invests heavily in a new technology that a small group of forceful, highly articulate individuals want. However, this investment may not address the most pressing needs confronting the school district. Indeed, it may amplify problems, such as disparities in the performance of students from different socioeconomic groups.

Consider yet another situation: more and more individuals default on their home mortgages. In response, legislatures enact new rules for bank lending. Such rules may be effective. Yet, in a highly complex universe of lending laws, rules, and practices, they may achieve little and may even provide cover for predatory lending or high-risk loans.

For criminal justice, these problems in one sense are good. They signal to lawmakers, practitioners, and scholars that they do not have to be concerned that safety and justice constitute isolated dysfunctional policy undertakings. At the same time, they may be able to glean insights from these other policy arenas about understanding and improving criminal justice.

After the tragedy of September 11, 2001, when terrorists attacked America, a complete overhaul of intelligence efforts occurred. One lesson resulted from the overhaul: predicting terrorist attacks entails sifting through large amounts of data, and yet, as became quickly apparent, no magic formula exists for doing so. Indeed, one can drown in too much data. There can be, as Nate Silver has highlighted, too little "signal" amidst too much "noise."[48] When someone whispers to us in an empty room, the words that they utter quietly – the "signal" – can be heard because no noise interferes with the signal. When, however, the whisper occurs in a room filled with many people talking, the "noise" overwhelms our ability to detect the signal. But if we can see the person and turn our head "just so," we might, if we are lucky, hear them.

What relevance does that situation have for criminal justice? Systems failures occur in part because too little attention focuses on paying sustained attention to using theory and insights, both from different stakeholders and from research, to know how to turn our head "just so." Analyses – *useful* analyses – do not occur by themselves. They require knowledge about the outcomes that matter, the forces that may contribute to the outcomes, predictable policy shifts on the horizon, and so on. This knowledge in turn can drive research and lead to greater insights into systems operations, potential problems, and their causes and solutions. Such analyses themselves require more and better data. The very fact of data alone matters little. True, we sometimes can mine existing data for insights. But we often are better off with less data and a clear idea of how to analyze it. It helps, too, if we can create data relevant to our questions.

Across many policy arenas, systems failures result from inattention to detecting relevant signals about system performance. They result, too, from insufficient research about the inner workings and effects of subsystems and how they affect one another. The failures result, not least, from a lack of an institutionalized process for combining the insights and experiences of diverse stakeholders in crafting useful research and creating effective policies and practices.

1.5 ARGUMENT AND STRUCTURE OF THIS BOOK

In *American Criminal Justice Policy*, I argued that institutionalization of an evaluation hierarchy framework – one focused on needs, theory, implementation, impact, and cost-efficiency evaluations – into policymaking and criminal justice operations could help to place crime and justice policy on a more evidence-based foundation, one that more cost-efficiently addresses crime and increases "justice."[49] Undertaking evaluations along these lines constitutes an essential approach to improving public safety, justice, and accountability. It does not, however, ensure that the entire apparatus of criminal justice operates effectively and efficiently. Systems analysis is critical for that endeavor. It ties together different types of evaluation activities and takes stock of systems. It also identifies needs, patterns, and opportunities for change that otherwise would go missed through narrowly focused, single-policy evaluations. Thus, institutionalization of systems analysis, along with the evaluation hierarchy, constitutes a key avenue along which to advance policy and practice. Even so, investment in research alone ignores an essential ingredient for reducing crime and improving justice: the policy process. Policymakers, criminal justice administrators, practitioners, and other stakeholders create and implement policy. They therefore need to understand and contribute to research to be able to base policy changes on an evidence-based foundation.

In *Prisoner Reentry in the Era of Mass Incarceration*, my co-author Joshua Cochran and I examined reasons why mass incarceration occurred and identified consequences of the unprecedented growth in the number of individuals placed into and released from prisons.[50] This undertaking underscored the need for better, more systematic integration of research and policy efforts. Time and again, we confronted scenarios in which states enacted well-intentioned policies that either did not work or backfired because they ignored the systems context of crime and justice. For example, as many states established laws that required lengthier terms of confinement they simultaneously employed more police officers and court personnel. Recidivism rates did not change appreciably. Instead, more police did what police do: they made more arrests. More court personnel did what such personnel do: they processed and convicted more individuals. More prisons did what prisons do: they housed individuals without, by and large, addressing the causes of offending. Not least, more parole officers did what parole officers do, especially when carrying heavy caseloads: they ceased to help ex-prisoners and instead issued violations when a condition of parole was not met. The individuals then went to the courts, which sent them to prisons, where, once again, few of the factors that contributed to their offending were addressed. The machinery of "justice" thus created, and continues to create, a vicious cycle, the main beneficiary of which is not society but the criminal justice system.

Here, then, I argue for a Systems Improvement Solution that addresses these problems – and, in particular, the vast disjuncture between research and policy – and serves as a central organizing framework for creating more public safety, justice, accountability, and efficiency. Research alone will not suffice. It simply creates the equivalent of "noise." Some of the information here and there may rise to the top or be heard; the "signal" gets through to a legislator or criminal justice administrator. However, no ongoing, systematic use of the information occurs because no institutionalized process exists to ensure that those who most need the information contribute to its creation and obtain it in real time. *For that reason, research needs to be coupled with a policy process.* Multiple stakeholders need to be involved. And scholars must be central to the process. They have much to offer: theories, knowledge of extant research, experience with different research methodologies. If included in a research-infused policy process, scholars can develop and test theories about crime and justice in ways that can inform policy and practice and contribute to science. In an effort to advance these arguments and make the case for the Systems Improvement Solution, the book is structured as follows.

Chapter 2 begins by drawing attention to systems problems that lie outside of criminal justice. I discuss different policy arenas – such as health care, education, environmental protection, the War on Terror, and manufacturing – to illustrate systems problems and the need to under-stand them and identify solutions. I point to different systems-related problems, such as decisions that flow from misprioritization or are driven by case-processing pressures. The message in each instance is that systems understanding and responses are needed to improve the aggregate out-come. Without such understanding, we have little ability to introduce minor or major policy changes that will appreciably and cost-efficiently improve society. This discussion, in turn, sets the stage for anticipating the arguments in favor of the Systems Improvement Solution.

Chapter 3 steps back to discuss more formally what is meant by a "system." Several core dimensions – including systems outcomes, elements (and subsystems), and dynamics – are identified as means by which to characterize, understand, and examine systems. The chapter discusses the central role of theory to the understanding of systems and identification of ways to improve them.

Chapter 4 turns to criminal justice and the myriad ways that crime and justice operate as a "system," one with many subsystems and constituent policies, including various programs, practices, and decision-making pro-cesses. Here, I begin by describing the contemporary criminal justice landscape and the stakes involved, and then describe different goals and outcomes relevant to the assessment of criminal justice system effectiveness. I also describe the different elements and subsystems (e.g., law-making, law enforcement, courts, probation, prison, parole) of the broader criminal justice system. Particular attention is given first to dynamics that occur within and between parts of this system and then to theoretical accounts of criminal justice. The chapter closes with the observation that a central flaw in contemporary criminal justice policy stems from a failure to implement policies in ways that reflect awareness of the broader, systems context. This observation provides the backdrop for the central premise of the subsequent chapter: that attempts to understand and reduce crime and justice require that attention be paid to the systems nature of criminal justice. Failure to do so will result in missed opportunities to reduce crime and improve justice. It will result, as well, in less accountability and less cost-efficiency.

Chapter 5 describes and argues for the use of a Systems Improvement Solution to aid in efforts to understand and reduce crime and increase justice, accountability, and efficiency. If used continuously and as part of a deliberative multi-stakeholder decision-making process, this approach can help prevent systems problems and improve crime and justice outcomes, as well as accountability and efficiency. The evaluation hierarchy and systems analysis together constitute one part of this solution. In the past, systems analysis was hampered by limited data and computing power. The advent of desktop computers, smart phones, mobile devices and apps, statistical software, and more have changed the equation substantially. Times have changed. Data for answering critical research and policy questions can be developed quickly, updated frequently, and examined in near-real-time to shed light on critical questions concerning all manner of social outcomes, not least among them crime and justice. However, the Systems Improvement Solution calls not simply for use of the evaluation hierarchy and systems analysis. It also calls for continuous involvement of policymakers and practitioners in creating and using data and analyses and in designing, evaluating, reviewing, and improving policy.

The proposed solution calls in particular for three activities, or steps: (1) Research that includes institutionalized use of the evaluation hierarchy and systems analysis; (2) a multi-stakeholder policy process; and (3) implementation of evidence-based policies, programs, practices, and decision-making. I argue that for these steps to be helpful, they must be institutionalized into a broader, policy-focused process aimed at understanding and improving public safety, justice, accountability, and efficiency. They must be guided by a commitment to improving the system, focusing on key goals, avoiding big mistakes, prioritizing high-bet and low-risk changes, leveraging feedback loops to maximize gains and minimize harms, and continuously monitoring and evaluating system activities. To be effective, the process must be guided, too, by core principles. These include institutionalization of the solution; reliance on a non-partisan, deliberative process; incorporation of insights from individuals on the "ground floor," such as prison officers or community residents, as well as from scientists; use of theory and data to understand system operations and impacts; and dissemination of research information and results to diverse stakeholder groups, including the public.

Chapter 6 describes the anticipated benefits of the Systems Improvement Solution as well as pitfalls that may arise when it is being implemented. The anticipated benefits include less crime and more justice, accountability, and efficiency. Other potential benefits include avoiding big mistakes and creating greater responsiveness to victims and communities, reducing racial and ethnic disparity, increasing public understanding of crime and justice, and improving understanding of the causes of crime and the nature of justice. After discussing these benefits, the chapter discusses potential pitfalls or problems that may accompany efforts to implement the Systems Solution, and how they can be avoided or addressed. It also highlights the existence of efforts to use systems analyses or systems-focused approaches to improve criminal justice. They illustrate not only that such approaches are feasible but also their potential to improve policy and practice.

Chapter 7 concludes by recapitulating the case for the Systems Improvement Solution – or a systems-focused approach that adopts similar strategies – to improving public safety and justice. I argue that its use can help advance theory and research on crime and justice, and, as importantly, that it can help localities, states, and the federal government to bring criminal justice "under control." That includes creating an evidence-based foundation for improving policies, programs, and practices – and criminal justice systems more generally – to achieve greater public safety, justice, accountability, and cost-efficiency. The time is none too soon to pursue this goal.

2

Systems Problems Are Not Specific to Crime
and Justice

The goal of this chapter is to convey the idea that systems matter. That
insight serves as a starting point for the subsequent argument that understanding crime and justice – and how we can improve public safety, justice
and government accountability and efficiency – requires a systems perspective. To this end, the chapter proceeds in a seemingly odd way.
We will turn away from criminal justice and focus on other social problems and policy arenas, including health care, education, environmental
protection, the War on Terror and manufacturing. These all have the
virtue of being interesting. More relevant is the fact that although they
at first blush appear to be completely irrelevant to a focus on crime and
justice, instructive lessons can be gleaned about the importance of systems
for criminal justice. This chapter thus establishes an important foundation
for understanding the basis of the argument for the Systems Improvement
Solution to crime, justice, accountability, and efficiency.

2.1 SOCIETAL PROBLEMS AND THE IMPORTANCE OF SYSTEMS
UNDERSTANDING AND RESPONSES

Health Care

Everyone gets sick or hurt at one time or another. The struggle for society
lies in preventing and treating illness and injury. Efficiency is critical.
We might spend millions of dollars to treat a person, but perhaps we
could save money through the use of cheaper and equally effective
approaches. Alternatively, we might achieve greater aggregate amounts
of health in society by spending the money in different ways. In a world of

unlimited resources, such concerns would fall by the wayside. That world, unfortunately, does not exist. All countries face the critical challenge of promoting the greatest amount of health possible using a finite amount of resources.

In the United States, health care challenges are compounded by highly divisive and politicized debates. For many decades, policymakers have highlighted the need to address rapidly escalating health care costs and have pointed to the need for large-scale solutions, not piecemeal ones. Even so, until the passage of the Affordable Care Act (ACA) in 2010, such solutions were not forthcoming. The ACA, however, was strongly critiqued and subjected to continuous legal challenges. That, in turn, ensured that implementation would be weakened.[1] In addition, the ACA's complexity created challenges in evaluating its impact.

Regardless of any gains that may have been achieved by the ACA, the fact remains that substantial health care challenges persist in America. Many examples illustrate the problem:

- The United States spends over $9,020 per person in health care each year, almost twice as much as the typical developed country, yet has health care outcomes that are worse.[2]
- Lack of access to affordable health care has been and remains a significant problem. For example, in 2013 – three years after enactment of the ACA – 42 million Americans were uninsured; just one year later, in 2014, over 60 million individuals delayed or did not seek health care because of concerns about costs, and over 60 million individuals struggled with medical debt.[3] The precise estimates change from year to year, but the common denominator has been that millions of Americans suffer from medical problems and either cannot obtain or afford health care or are saddled with debt after receiving treatment. Absent a large-scale change, tens of millions of Americans will remain uninsured or underinsured in coming decades, creating less health and more cost.[4]
- Half of Americans with private insurance do not go to the doctor when sick or when preventative check-ups are indicated, because of concerns about insufficient coverage.[5]
- Approximately 2 million Americans become infected while hospitalized; these infections then kill about 90,000 patients.[6] Medical errors in general are estimated to result in the deaths of over 250,000 individuals annually, making them the third leading cause of death in the United States.[7] (Heart disease is the top leading cause

and cancer is the second.) Many of these infections could be prevented by a simple intervention – washing hands. Yet getting physicians and other medical care providers to take this easy precaution turns out to be difficult, with only one-third to one-half of doctors and nurses washing their hands when they should.[8] This problem has been understood since the mid-1800s, but little progress has emerged, not only in making it easy for medical staff to wash their hands, but also in getting them to actually do it.[9] The same observation holds for a host of factors that give rise to medical errors in general.[10]

- About 20,000 Americans die annually due to unaddressed, treatable medical problems.[11]
- Many types of unconscious assumptions and biases result in physician misdiagnosis and mistreatment, yet they go almost entirely unmonitored and thus unaddressed.[12] Due to case-processing pressures, for example, doctors have to rely on "heuristics," cognitive shortcuts for processing a large amount of information quickly to arrive at a diagnosis. "They are the essential working tools of clinical medicine,"[13] as Jerome Groopman has emphasized, yet "medical schools do not teach shortcuts."[14] This problem is compounded by the fact that misuse of heuristics – such as the systematic misinterpretation of a set of symptoms due to privileging familiar diagnoses (availability bias) or to seeking to confirm an initial impression (confirmation bias) – can lead to decision-making errors that accumulate into misdiagnosis, mistreatment, health problems or even death, and, again, greater cost.[15]
- The large volume of cases that physicians see results in less time to meet with patients and review information, resulting in "inattention blindness" (missing what is right in front of us) and decision-making errors that compromise patient health.[16] Studies, for example, have found that "physicians interrupt patients within 18 seconds of when they begin telling their story"[17] and they frequently fail to tell patients about the proper dose of a medicine or its side effects.[18] "Assembly line" medicine takes a toll on specialists as well. For example, estimates indicate that up to 30 percent of medical images reviewed by radiologists are incorrectly interpreted.[19]
- Despite marked advances in scientific understanding of medical problems and disease, the vast bulk of treatment lacks a scientific, or "evidence-based," foundation.[20]

- Patient attributes and attitudes can greatly affect diagnosis, treatment and how patients respond to health care information. For example, patients are more likely to accept a treatment that has been framed in a positive manner (e.g., "You have a 40 percent chance of improved symptoms with this treatment") than when the treatment has been framed in a negative manner (e.g., "You have a 60 percent chance of failure").[21] How the framing of health care information affects patient decision-making is not systematically monitored, resulting in uninformed decision-making among many patients.[22]
- Malpractice lawsuits, pharmaceutical representatives who repeatedly visit physician offices, administrative paperwork for processing insurance claims, hospitals' enthrallment with and investment in the latest technology, differences in access to health care among different sociodemographic groups – these and myriad other factors shape clinical decision-making and health care practice. These forces, however, largely operate "in the background," with little to no oversight or management.[23]
- A process for prioritizing health care spending is absent, but desperately needed. To illustrate, since the late 1980s, the World Health Organization (WHO) has spearheaded a campaign to eradicate polio and has spent over $10 billion.[24] Eradicating polio is a critical and clearly beneficial undertaking. Even so, as Atul Gawande has observed, the question remains: how much greater might public health have been improved if the funds had been expended on "building proper sewage systems or improving basic health services"?[25] Determination of how best to use scarce resources requires assessment of the causes of health problems and the most cost-efficient and feasible ways to address them.

Juxtaposed against these examples is the fact that medical care costs continually increase and, at the same time, medical systems operate with little systematic monitoring of the accuracy of medical diagnoses or the appropriateness of prescribed interventions, the quality with which these interventions are implemented or health outcomes.[26] Gawande, a surgeon, has noted, for example: "Ask a typical American hospital what its death and complication rates for surgery were during the last six months and it cannot tell you."[27]

As the above examples illustrate, systems problems – that is, ineffectiveness and inefficiency that arise from a dysfunctional system – abound.

There may be pockets of effectiveness and efficiency; however, they occur within a larger context that all but precludes cost-efficient promotion of health. John Banja has written, for example, that

the commission of errors is only one piece of the mosaic of unwarranted or preventable harms. Just as important, if not more so, are system weaknesses or failures, which frequently appear as persistent and chronic deviations from practice standards or rule violations. As they occur in healthcare, these deviations or rule violations are rarely motivated by malice or greed, but often result from personnel feeling intense performance pressures.[28]

Improvements sometimes might arise within one part of the system. But these improvements are often offset by problems in some other part. For example, outreach efforts might result in more disadvantaged groups accessing health care. If, however, too few medical practitioners exist to provide services and treatment, these groups may receive inappropriate care or may cease seeking care unless an emergency arises.

Many analyses of health care point to the need for Systems Solutions. Notably, American political debates in recent decades emphasize this idea. Just as notably, models of national health care plans exist that provide a template for addressing the systemic problems in medicine that drive up costs while generating health care outcomes (life expectancy, infant mortality, recovery rates from major illness) far worse than those of other developed nations and democracies.[29] Yet, politicization of health care in the United States has resulted in such efforts being depicted as "socialized medicine." In lieu of large-scale changes, then, enactment of simplified, piecemeal reforms occurs. (The ACA, though broad and sweeping, does not entail comprehensive systems research or improvement.) Such reforms fail to address systems problems and so risk contributing to or escalating ineffective and inefficient health care.

Education

How to educate children and young people? It is a conundrum that has sparked ongoing national debates and led to considerable dissension. One consequence has been investment in testing students – lots of testing.[30] Indeed, school districts across America devote several weeks of the school year to preparing students for tests and then for administering the tests. The emphasis on testing permeates schools and has led to additional changes in education, including "teaching to the test." This problem, as it turns out, dates back to the nineteenth century. William

Reese found, for example, that by the late 1800s, educational reformers became enamored of statistical measures of educational performance. In 1878, during a presentation to principals, teachers, and education reformers, this situation led Charles Parker, an experienced Chicago high school principal, to criticize "testing zealots" for their "vanity and arrogance" and to urge "a little modesty among educators mesmerized by test scores."[31]

Advocates of performance testing point to potential benefits, such as holding schools accountable – so that schools actually do what they are supposed to do – and improving educational outcomes. Testing also can provide a way to identify the needs that specific students, classrooms, or schools may have, which in turn can allow for the tailoring of resources to address these needs. In addition, it may serve to motivate students. Not least, it can be used to evaluate whether particular curricula or modes of instruction improve student learning.[32]

Opponents of performance testing point to potential harms. Testing may provide an invalid assessment of learning. It "steals" time from the classroom that might be better used to, well, teach students. It also can serve to "rubber-stamp" existing inequalities. For example, better-performing schools have more resources and students who enter with more social capital, and so necessarily do better on performance tests, regardless of the quality of instruction. These schools then receive better "grades" from school districts and receive benefits, such as more resources and teacher raises, for their top performance; "underperforming" schools get sanctioned. Testing can be stressful for students, parents, teachers, and schools, and may ultimately benefit only the purveyors of tests and of accompanying instructional materials. It can serve to reinforce the dominant culture of society. Not least, it can motivate schools to "teach to the test," and yet may not ultimately create greater accountability or improved learning.[33]

Alongside of testing has been a call for and substantial investment in "charter" schools.[34] These schools ascended into prominence during the 1990s as part of a more general policymaker embrace of privatization efforts. The general logic was and remains that the private sector can do what government does better by being more innovative. Under a charter school arrangement, public school systems can create a "charter," or contract, with private-sector organizations to run a public school. The hope is that these schools improve students' educational outcomes and those of students in public schools.[35] These other schools, for example, may be induced to perform better by having to compete with charter schools. Under these arrangements, charter schools typically are exempt from many local and state regulations. They also cannot discriminate or "cream" and choose to select only the best students.

What has been the effect of the increased use of testing and charter schools? By and large, despite an abundance of studies, there is little credible empirical evidence that consistently demonstrates that they have produced the anticipated benefits or harms.[36] Why? One reason is that the target keeps moving. Schools, school districts, and state educational agencies continuously change the tests that they use to gauge performance. As for charter schools, a central problem is that they vary enormously and the populations and areas that they serve vary. In addition, any given school may change over time in structure and design and in the populations served, so the "intervention" itself is constantly changing. When assessing impacts on educational outcomes, it may be that initial implementation challenges create limited to no improvement, or even worse performance on tests. However, these outcomes may improve over time. In a related vein, a charter school might end up with a more disadvantaged group of students, which can occur if more advantaged parents withdraw their children from the school. The school might improve outcomes for these retained youth, but school performance levels nonetheless would show a decline. Such possibilities make it difficult to know whether a given impact assessment is valid or generalizable to other schools, populations, or places.

Still other factors confound efforts to assess the impact of testing and of charter schools. For example, the best measures of learning remain unclear. Standardized tests have many virtues; for example, they allow for comparisons across students and schools. At the same time, their utility in measuring higher-level learning, including critical reasoning skills, is limited. As importantly, testing does little to identify the *causes* of poor student performance. These can run the gamut: hungry students, family disadvantage, unmotivated teachers, a lack of or unequal access to resources, organizational bureaucracy, continuous leadership change and accompanying organizational change and so on. Similarly, charter schools operate in a context where the effectiveness or efficiency of public schools often is unknown. They vary greatly in design, student population, curriculum and more. In addition, the absence of systematic and comprehensive monitoring and evaluation of public school performance and charter school performance, respectively, means that little credible information can be generated that establishes the generalizability of findings about a given charter school. In short, for two of the most prominent changes in education in contemporary America – testing and charter schools – there exists little credible, systematic or consistent research foundation on which to evaluate whether the investments have created appreciable, aggregate benefits for society.

Juxtaposed against this situation is a lack of consistency in the quality of educational offerings in public schools. Testing, of course, has been designed to help change that problem. The idea is that low-performing schools can be identified and then sanctioned into performing better. A related idea is that insight is supposed to magically emerge about what produced differences in scores. Neither assumption has proven correct. In addition, substantial questions exist about whether student and school performance scores used by local jurisdictions and states provide a balanced assessment of impact. For example, a reading literacy program might well produce an increase in the number of books that students read during the school year and in their ability to answer questions about specific facts in these books. That would seem like a clear improvement. Yet, if these students have not improved in their ability to identify themes in books or to critique them from different perspectives, the benefit of the program is less clear.

It is not that testing serves no purpose. Rather, its purpose is limited and cannot, by itself, improve education. When we test students and evaluate schools, we want valid measures of learning across a range of relevant learning outcomes. For improvements to occur, however, we want insight into the causes of variation in these outcomes and how we might effectively target the causes to improve learning outcomes. Similarly, it is not that charter schools cannot be effective or that public schools should be presumptively viewed as such. Rather, the critical issue is that the absence of a coherent strategy for approaching education and of a systematic evaluation of any type of education leaves our schools and students floundering. No tests or charter schools can substitute for a clear and viable plan for educating all students. Indeed, without a clear plan for school systems and without empirical monitoring and evaluation of it, assumptions, ideology, and inequalities in education are likely to govern education. Whatever benefits may arise from these influences, improved education is not one of them.

In many respects, the situation is worse than that. For any given program, policy, practice, or intervention – as with any medical treatment – effectiveness hinges on ensuring that we get the "dose" right. Mix the ingredients of a recipe incorrectly, or forget one, and the resulting dish likely will taste terrible. Put the parts of a car together incorrectly and it will not run. Fail to take the correct amount of medicine each day and at the right time and you may not get well. Similarly, when we fail to implement a program correctly – the right amount in the right sequence for the right population – failure will likely result. With education, testing has focused attention on educational outcomes, but a prior question is whether schools "implement" education well. Put differently, to what extent do schools effectively and appropriately, and in the correct "dose," use teaching strategies that help students to learn specific ideas and information and to learn how to learn? Here again, we have little systematic, empirical monitoring of how schools operate.

Against that backdrop, consider a number of sobering facts about education. First, the purpose of education remains unclear. More precisely, education serves multiple goals, and some school systems emphasize certain goals more than others. For example, school can be viewed as a means by which to inculcate "proper" morals in children. In this regard, the origins of American public schools appear to share much in common with the origins of juvenile justice.[37] To what extent do schools achieve this goal? How much do efforts to reform education prioritize this goal over others? State school boards, for example, can and do battle over what "counts" as science and history in the curricula used in local school systems, and both religion and political ideology can loom heavily in the background in shaping these curricula.[38]

Second, despite growth in testing, charter schools and various other efforts to "reform" education, US college participation rates have steadily fallen and moved the United States far below the number-one ranking that it previously held.[39] Only about one-third of young people in the United States earn college degrees, while more than half of young people in European countries earn them.[40]

Third, inequality permeates American education. Indeed, racial, ethnic, and social and economic class disparities are endemic and persistent, in spite of (and perhaps because of) the focus on testing and inattention to the root causes of educational inequality.[41]

Fourth, although one purpose for education is to contribute to the ephemeral goal of having an intellectually engaged citizenry, another – and more pragmatic – reason is that it can help individuals gain employment and, once employed, helps them to be productive. Notably, then, "at least 70 percent of US jobs now require specialized knowledge and skills, as compared to only 5 percent at the dawn of the last [twentieth] century, when our current system of schooling was established."[42] The nature of work, and the preparation required for it, has changed dramatically in recent decades. Workers used to hold two or three jobs during their lifetime; now they may hold as many as ten jobs before they have reached middle age.[43] This situation creates a dramatic challenge for schools. They somehow must provide a general education for youth – simply because education for "education's sake" constitutes a central value in America – and an education that prepares them for an ever-changing employment landscape.

Fifth, schools are systems. They entail multiple layers or organization. Indeed, it is precisely the "multilevel" aspect of schools that makes necessary the use of sophisticated, multilevel statistical modeling to evaluate school performance and the factors that affect variation in performance.[44] However, only in recent years have such models been used to examine education. As Stephen Raudenbush and Douglas Willms have noted,

An irony in the history of quantitative studies of schooling has been the failure of researchers' analytic models to reflect adequately the social organization of life in classrooms and schools. The experiences that children share with school settings and the effects of these experiences on their development might be seen as the basic material of educational research; yet, until recently, few studies have explicitly taken account of the effects of the particular classrooms and schools in which students and teachers share membership.[45]

A central benefit of taking a multilevel modeling approach to understanding and evaluating school performance lies in the ability to estimate more accurately what happens in schools and what contributes to differences in student, teacher, school, and school system performance. Another is the ability to answer new and important questions, such as the influence of different parts of an educational system on student learning. The fact that multilevel modeling of school systems has not featured prominently in monitoring and evaluating education illustrates the limited empirical basis on which educational changes frequently rest. It also illustrates the tendency to ignore the multiple contexts – educational goals; student populations; families; communities; school structure and resources; and local, state, and federal laws – that shape education.

Many more facts could be enumerated, but the point would remain: piecemeal approaches to education will not address the above-identified problems or others. These problems, too, cannot readily be addressed through educational efforts that occur without careful, systematic and comprehensive empirical monitoring and evaluation. In writing about educational reform and racial and economic inequality, for example, Linda Darling-Hammond has observed, "A growing number of schools have disrupted the status quo by providing opportunities for low-income students of color ... Unless policy systems change, however, these schools will remain anomalies."[46] It is difficult to see how any large-scale, meaningful reform in education could occur without systems change, and without systems change guided by empirical research.

Environmental Protection

Environmental crises have persisted for decades. Some have not been visible, but others have, and they have garnered considerable attention. For example, in 1963, 406 people died due to air pollution during a weather inversion in New York City, and in 1969, pollution on Cleveland's Cuyahoga River was so bad that the river caught fire.[47] Such incidents led to the creation, in 1970, of the United States Environmental Protection Agency (EPA). Since that time, the problems confronting the environment have grown, though they are not always as visible as a burning river. As Alan Hecht and Joseph Fiksel have emphasized, these problems include "climate change; declining biodiversity; threats to vital natural resources, including water bodies, soils, forests, wetlands and coral reefs; and increased health risks to minority urban communities."[48] Climate change alone constitutes a paramount problem for the world.[49]

The problems, as well as their causes, are so diverse that the EPA's approach has evolved over time toward the use of "systems thinking" to help understand and address them and to do so in a manner that can be sustained over the long term. Initially, that was not the agency's approach. For example, the response in the 1970s centered on legislation, including the Clean Air Act (1970), Clean Water Act (1972), Endangered Species Act (1973), Safe Drinking Water Act (1974), Resource Conservation and Recovery Act (1976), and the Comprehensive Environmental Response, Compensation and Liability, or "Superfund," Act (CERCLA, 1980).[50] From this perspective, legislation – and the regulatory authority it created – would necessarily improve the environment. This approach was augmented by an emphasis in the 1980s on "risk assessment"; the idea was that a better understanding of factors that contribute to risks to the health of people, animals, and the environment would lead to changes that addressed these risks.[51] Then, due in part to passage of the Pollution Prevention Act (1990), the EPA turned toward efforts not only to control harms to the environment but also to prevent them.[52]

Whatever progress these different efforts achieved, they suffered from a lack of a coherent plan and infrastructure that would lead to an aggregate good: the various legislative Acts, for example, provided a regulatory framework but did not address the root causes of pollution and other environmental harms; risk assessment provided a better understanding of the problems, but did not provide a structure for addressing these problems; and efforts to prevent harms provided improvements here and there but did not create a foundation for systemic change. Rather, the various efforts left a "silos" problem in place: most efforts focused on specific delimited aspects of the environment or on activities that could be undertaken by one or another agency or organization. No coherent, systematic plan or infrastructure existed for preventing and reducing environmental harms. In turn, any improvements tended to be short-term and missed opportunities to create appreciable changes that would persist for many decades.

The problems associated with this situation are well recognized by EPA administrators.[53] They can be and have been illustrated in numerous accounts of environmental disasters and challenges.[54] One of the most compelling is Dan Fagin's description of New Jersey's Toms River, a seaside town where, unbeknownst to residents, local industry dumped tons of toxic chemicals into the ground, the local river and the ocean.[55] In our own homes, we typically would not pollute the living room or leave major structural damage unaddressed. When problems exist in communities, however, they can persist unless concerted action from different parties – including residents; industry; business; and local, state, and federal agencies – occurs. They can also persist unless laws exist to address the problems and unless information exists that documents the nature, location and causes of problems.

The dumping at Toms River occurred long before the EPA or various federal environmental protection laws existed. Industry clearly did not want information about its practices known. And local, state, and federal agencies clearly did not communicate well with one another. As a result, the dumping went on year after year. Complaints by residents had little effect. What finally turned the trick was an event that could not be ignored: in 1984, in the middle of Toms River, the road buckled. When a county road crew investigated, they found "that the soil underneath was deep black instead of sandy brown and saturated with a liquid that had a strong chemical smell."[56] Citizens thus were confronted with "a pollution problem in town that was literally impossible to overlook."[57] In turn, questions began to be asked about the source of the pollution. Residents came to learn that the pharmaceutical company, Ciba-Geigy, was on the federal Superfund list and "had been pumping its treated wastewater into the ocean for almost twenty years."[58] Even so, legal action would be unlikely to change matters. As Fagin noted, "in the 1980s, criminal prosecutions of polluters were so rare that in 1984, the EPA referred just thirty-one cases to the Justice Department for prosecution, while more than three thousand cases were handled administratively or in civil court."[59] In addition, a lack of coordinated action on the part of local, state, and federal enforcement agencies – coupled with limited empirical data on ground and water quality, and its determinants, over that time period – stymied an effective resolution to the problem. It contributed, too, to an indeterminate assessment of the extent to which the many decades of dumping contributed to a cancer cluster in Toms River. Instead, a series of legal battles and short-term, stop-gap measures occurred. Each one ignored the larger context and enabled pollution, and its harms to the environment and people, to continue.

The Toms River example and others like it serve to highlight several themes that cut across the other illustrations and much of what will follow in this book. For example, piecemeal efforts that do not consider the broader, systems context are unlikely to achieve much.[60] A focus on short-term solutions may be appealing, not least because they can be undertaken and one can point to "results." Yet the short-term gains frequently may be just that, short-term, and may be offset by the harms that arise from ignoring systemic problems. In addition, solutions that rest on weak information or none at all necessarily amount to stabs in the dark. They likely miss their mark and enable problems to fester. Not least, enforcement alone or the efforts of one or another agency can do little more than provide short-term gains, if any. The EPA's transition toward a "systems thinking" approach reflects a recognition of these issues. It has led, among other things, to an emphasis on promulgating information about environmental changes and doing so in an easy-to-access manner. It has led, too, to creating tools that facilitate local efforts to more effectively plan land-development strategies, promote government-government and business-government collaborations, and develop better forecasting tools.[61] The changing of systems provides the path toward creating lasting and large-scale improvements.

The War on Terror

On September 11, 2001, the Islamic terrorist group al Qaeda flew one airplane into the Pentagon and two planes into the North tower and the

South tower, respectively, of the World Trade Center; a fourth plane, headed for Washington, DC, crashed into a Pennsylvania field. Altogether, almost 3,000 people were killed.[62] Although the federal government anticipated any number of potential terrorist attacks on the country, an attack of such a scale was not predicted, not even by the then Secretary of Defense Donald Rumsfeld.[63]

In his account of 9/11, Nate Silver has identified one of the central problems that contributed to this situation: the challenge of sifting through large amounts of data to identify patterns, or "signals," that indicate the potential for an attack.[64] One critical approach to data analysis begins with theory. When we have an idea about what may happen, we know where to focus our attention. Absent such guidance, the likelihood of accidentally stumbling upon a pattern is near zero. In Rumsfeld's account, such a pattern constitutes an "unknown unknown," and results from a failure of imagination.[65] This failure featured prominently in the 9/11 Commission Report as a reason for the inability of federal agencies to anticipate the attack on the Pentagon and World Trade Center.[66] A "known known" is, by contrast, a pattern that we can imagine and that we have been able to document or describe empirically. In such cases, we can plan and take steps to protect against an attack. Between these two extremes are "unknown knowns." These amount to possibilities that we can anticipate, even if we do not have the data to determine whether, in fact, they exist. What we need first, though, is the ability to contemplate possibilities and thus to undertake analyses that aid us in describing the contours of what we do and do not know empirically about the "known" possibility.[67] Otherwise, we fail to appreciate what may be sitting right in front of us – signals that an attack may or will happen.[68]

The challenge, then, lies in knowing to anticipate a possibility. That allows us to collect and analyze data and assess its likelihood. How, though, to proceed? Ideally, there would exist a coherent strategy for organizing efforts to collect and analyze data. No such strategy existed. As the 9/11 Commission Report emphasized, the United States failed to anticipate the 9/11 attack not just because of a failure of imagination but also because of a failure of policy, capability, and management.[69] There was, for example, little ability to share information across the many different agencies involved in studying or addressing terrorism. In commenting on the "missed opportunities to thwart the 9/11 plot," the report noted,

Information was not shared, sometimes inadvertently or because of legal misunderstandings. Analysis was not pooled. Effective operations were not launched. Often the handoffs of information were lost across the divide separating the foreign and domestic agencies of the government. However the specific problems are labeled, we believe they are symptoms of the government's broader inability to adapt how it manages problems to the new challenges of the twenty-first century. The agencies are like a set of specialists in a hospital, each ordering tests, looking for symptoms, and prescribing medications. *What is missing is the attending physician who makes sure they work as a team.*[70]

Part of the challenge in predicting an event like 9/11 consists of being able to imagine different terrorist attack scenarios, to collect and analyze information about possible scenarios and to share the information with those who can act on it. Consider, then, the situation prior to 9/11. According to the then US General Accounting Office (GAO), "more than 40 federal departments, agencies and bureaus have some role in combating terrorism," with the National Security Council (NSC) serving to coordinate their efforts.[71] This report, undertaken at the request of the US Congress, was published in 1997, four years prior to the 9/11 attack. The difficulty in coordinating efforts across so many different departments and agencies was known. As the 9/11 Commission Report later would emphasize,

Responsibility for domestic intelligence gathering on terrorism was vested solely in the FBI [Federal Bureau of Investigation], yet during almost all of the Clinton administration the relationship between the FBI Director and the President was nearly nonexistent. The FBI Director would not communicate directly with the President. His key personnel shared very little information with the National Security Council and the rest of the national security community. As a consequence, one of the critical working relationships in the counterterrorism effort was broken.[72]

The NSC, in theory, could serve to effectively mobilize the efforts of different agencies. However, its effectiveness was undermined by limited access to information relevant to terrorist threat assessment. For example, NSC counterterrorism coordinator Richard Clarke and his staff "had extensive access to terrorism reporting, but they did not have access to internal, nondisseminated information at the National Security Agency (NSA), CIA [Central Intelligence Agency], or FBI."[73] It is difficult – impossible, really – to develop credible predictions without good information. It is difficult, too, to do so without the requisite institutional structure and capacity to analyze information. In the era of "big data," this limitation frequently gets missed. Data, or information, is but one ingredient for making predictions. Another is theory. Still another is the capacity to analyze data to identify possible patterns that might form the basis for a prediction about where to target efforts to prevent an attack. Even after 9/11, for example, the FBI "had no capacity to use intelligence as a weapon of national security. It was consumed by reacting to the events of the day, the hour and the minute. It could not see over the horizon."[74]

Would better theory, or imagination, have helped to prevent 9/11? It is possible. As Silver has argued, "If we had attached some prior possibility, even a small one, to the hypothesis that 'terrorists might highjack planes and crash them into buildings,' our estimate of its likelihood would surely have increased substantially once we came across this intelligence."[75] But we did not anticipate this possibility. And even if we had, the Byzantine bureaucracy of intelligence – and the dysfunction in sharing information within and across various agencies – might well have prevented this estimate from landing in the hands of individuals who could act on it. In 2002, the Department of Homeland Security (DHS) was created to help address these and other problems. As with the EPA's transition to a "systems thinking" approach, a central guiding motivation in the creation of DHS was the identified need for a more coherent institutional foundation on which to base the coordination of information collection and analysis and efforts to act on it.[76]

Manufacturing

As part of calls to create more efficiency, policymakers have promoted the idea of running government like a business. This notion surfaces in arguments for privatization efforts.[77] The idea reduces in large part to the notion that private markets have a way of weeding out inefficient companies and selecting on those that operate efficiently. How well this approach works in criminal justice remains highly disputed.[78] For example, questions arise about whether justice and punishment can best be achieved through a market economy.[79] Regardless, if the idea is taken seriously, then an obvious step involves considering how businesses operate.

So, how in fact do businesses operate? There exist many types of businesses. One large category is manufacturing. The very concept of manufacturing can be extended not just to the production of material objects – cars, phones, televisions, and the like – but also to analogous social service "products," such as health care, education, and so on. Accordingly, manufacturing provides a useful, final illustration and point of departure for thinking about systems.[80]

Any discussion of manufacturing almost necessarily requires thinking from a systems perspective.[81] An automobile factory, for example, has one primary goal: to produce as many well-made vehicles as possible and do so as rapidly as possible. It actually is not that simple, of course. When we look past the vehicle assembly line, there remain the challenging tasks of distributing cars across the country and even overseas, marketing and selling the cars, keeping up with vehicle recalls, fulfilling warranties responsively (so that customers keep coming back) and so on. Within a given factory, however, we can instantly appreciate, even if we have never worked on one, that efficient management of an assembly line requires collecting, evaluating, and acting on a large amount of information. Any slow-down in production costs money.

What, then, do we monitor? Inputs, such as procurement of supplies for the factory. A delay in delivery of even one part might impede production throughout the factory. Labor and production is another critical category. How many workers show up on time? What are the rates of turnover? What can be done to ensure more consistent performance across the assembly line? The relative efficiency of different units on the assembly line is critical as well. How well do certain teams work together? How does the productivity of one team affect another? Technology and equipment, too, must be monitored. What technology and equipment is working well? What needs to be repaired or replaced, and when and how can that happen without adversely affecting overall production? Demand constitutes still another consideration. What types of vehicle specifications – colors, specialized equipment, modifications, etc. – are most likely? What supplies, reorganization within the factory, shifting of workers from one area to another, and so on, will be needed to accommodate temporary increases or decreases in demand for certain specifications? Delays can play a critical role in company profits, which is why manufacturers work to prevent delays and to monitor factors that contribute to them.[82]

Thinking in a systems perspective is not, then, a nicety or a theoretical issue for manufacturers. They must do it to survive. Whether they do it well, and regardless of the way in which they do it, the end result remains the same: only efficient companies can survive in the long run. It is interesting, then, that policymakers frequently call for running criminal justice like a business. Why? Because few criminal justice systems in fact are operated like businesses. If they were, they would have much larger research divisions, they would collect much more data, and they would devote considerable attention to monitoring, evaluating, and improving all aspects of the crime and justice "assembly line" to improve effectiveness and efficiency.

2.2 TYPES OF SYSTEMS PROBLEMS

What are the lessons that can be gleaned from this brief tour through different policy arenas? What insights do they afford us in our efforts to understand and address crime and justice? The first and most important is that understanding the diverse causes of and solutions to many social problems requires a systems perspective. That is not to diminish theory and research that focuses on specific parts of systems. To the contrary, such work is the foundation on which many advances and improvements in society occur. However, such efforts do not hold much promise for identifying how different parts of a system interact with one another or how large-scale changes might arise. They also do not enable us to see how we might avoid large-scale problems or enact targeted changes that can generate large-scale improvements.

The medical system illustrates the point. Despite tremendous advances in understanding different diseases and how to treat them, translating these advances into affordable health care has proven to be extremely difficult. Case-processing demands, challenges in determining which health conditions should be prioritized, bureaucratization, changes in local, state, and federal law – these and many other factors drive medical practice in ways that create inefficiency. Within that larger, systems context, advances and improvements might occur. However, their ability to improve outcomes for large swaths of the population, or even to sustain improvements within a specific sphere of the health care system, has been limited.

Across a range of policy arenas, then, systems problems interfere with the effective and efficient amelioration of social problems. A wide range of such problems exists and can be manifested in different ways and caused by different factors. Here, I describe some of these problems and describe their salience for criminal justice. In the next chapter, I step back and more formally discuss the concept of a "system," how inattention to system structures and dynamics creates problems, and how, conversely, attention to them holds the potential to create substantial improvements for society. We then turn to the criminal justice system and focus on the ways in which it is a system and the problems that stem from a failure to appreciate or address them.

The No-Captain Problem

Systems problems derive in part from situations in which the captain is "asleep at the wheel" or where, worse still, there is no captain. For shorthand, we can refer to this situation as the no-captain problem. Imagine a manufacturing factory with no facilities manager, a director-less summer camp for thousands of children or a space shuttle launch with no individual or group overseeing all aspects of the take-off. In each instance, so many things can go wrong that some or many of them invariably *will* go wrong without someone in charge.

A central cause of the no-captain problem is bureaucracy. The decentralization of various tasks and functions can, no doubt, generate remarkable efficiency. Yet it also can leave an organization rudderless. A new director, president, chief executive officer or the like might serve as a true captain, one who takes charge of the ship and actively steers it to an intended destination. All too frequently, though, this person resides in the new position for a short period of time, has insufficient information about various aspects of the organization, and must respond to short-term crises and case-processing pressures that preclude the sort of careful planning, implementation and evaluation that could ensure the effective and efficient attainment of goals.

Robert Reich's account of his time as the Secretary of Labor under the first Clinton administration illustrates the problem. He arrived at the Department of Labor and knew little about various parts of the organization. His staff filtered for him the phone calls, letters, invitations and the like to which he would respond, because otherwise he would be buried in the minutiae. When he learned of this policy, he asked his staff, "How do you decide what I do and what gets through to me?" The response: "We have you do and see what you'd choose if you had time to examine all the options yourself – sifting through all the phone calls, letters, memos and meeting invitations." Reich: "But how can you possibly *know* what I'd choose for myself?" The response: "Don't worry. We know."[83] Reich spent the next several years learning about the department, and then left. What is the end result of these types of situations, ones where entire organizations and systems either have no captain or where the captain faces a steep learning curve and too little information? Critical goals are not achieved. These situations are the equivalent of a rudderless ship: almost invariably, it will miss its intended destination.

The importance of this problem cannot be understated. Without an informed "captain" who operates with relevant information and resources, a complicated undertaking simply cannot be carried out. Coordination of multiple activities, groups, agencies, and the like requires that someone be in charge. Accordingly, the no-captain situation constitutes a leading cause of systems problems. No one is in charge of identifying problems, monitoring how one part of the system is doing or how it affects another, searching for opportunities to improve the coordination of efforts and so on. This situation can readily be seen in the health care arena. As the discussion above highlighted, policymakers, medical practitioners and researchers all readily recognize that the medical care system is "broken" and requires a large-scale solution that includes better performance monitoring. That solution, however, will remain a distant possibility if efforts at piecemeal reform persist. Much the same can be said of education reform, environmental protection, the War on Terror, and efforts to improve other aspects of society. It can be said, too, of the criminal justice system: many different groups drive pieces of it, but no one ensures that the system operates efficiently to create greater public safety and justice.

The Emergency or Short-Term Thinking Problem

In the absence of an empowered "captain" – that is, one with the skills and experience, information and resources – to lead a system, many problems arise. One is the likelihood of focusing on perceived emergencies or short-term considerations. The system runs about like the proverbial chicken with its head cut off. This problem can permeate all aspects of a system, and case-processing pressures, as discussed below, amplify it. Politicians, for example, may become enamored of the idea that requiring more educational testing will somehow force schools to achieve better outcomes. The testing is concrete. It sounds good. And it may well help politicians to get elected. But it does little to nothing to address root causes of educational shortfalls among students or school systems. Simultaneously, it steers school districts into revising their curricula and teaching to align with testing requirements, or into expending considerable energy in efforts to circumvent the various requirements.[84]

Of course, sometimes real emergencies arise. For policymakers and administrators, these can almost be a relief because crises are so concrete and clearly warrant a response. If an oil rig, for example, breaks and spills oil into the Gulf of Mexico, we clearly need to fix the break and clean up the oil as soon as possible. Yet, as important as such an effort may be, it completely ignores the range of factors that created the emergency in the first place. In addition, we may find ourselves focusing only on the risk of this type of emergency rather than on a constellation of risks and issues that merit our attention. By responding to crises and thinking only about short-term consequences, we allow systems problems to persist and to drive our decision-making. In criminal justice, for example, legislatures in the 1980s enacted sweeping "get tough" legislation in response to real and perceived increases in crime. They largely ignored a wide range of problems in criminal justice or the systems context within which the legislation took effect. The end result? A dramatic growth in all parts of the criminal justice system and a concomitant indefinite commitment to expending taxpayer dollars to support such growth.[85]

The Squeaky-Wheel Problem

Another type that is akin to the emergency or short-term thinking problem is the squeaky-wheel problem. Here, though, it is not an emergency, but a mundane aspect of systems that draws disproportionate amounts of resources. Specifically, one part of a system directly or indirectly attracts attention. The adage, "the squeaky wheel gets the grease" aptly characterizes the problem. Consider a hospital where surgeons call for purchase of a state-of-the-art magnetic resonance imaging (MRI) machine. Several surgeons forcefully argue that it is "needed," and so one is purchased. MRI scans go up in the coming years. The increased use of scans contributes to the identification of more non-threatening medical problems that nonetheless – perhaps due to an effort to increase profits or to "defensive medicine" practices intended to avoid lawsuits – result in surgeries. These further drive the perceived need for even more investment in expensive diagnostic equipment. The investment might well be worthwhile. However, it is equally possible that it needlessly increases MRIs and surgeries. It is equally possible, too, that careful review of health problems in a community might highlight the need for investment of scarce health funds in other ways.[86]

The squeaky-wheel systems problem arises in many guises. One part of a system might "squeak" (or "yell") louder than another. However, another possibility is that a certain high-profile incident will attract attention. It may not rise to the level of an emergency, but it nonetheless seems to demand that something be done. Policymakers and criminal justice officials then clamor to address the problem, even though there may be no real problem or there may be other problems that warrant greater attention. No matter. Policymakers pass laws, new policies are crafted, funding for a program emerges, new policymakers get elected on a platform of addressing the supposed problem and so on. In such cases, it may well be that a problem does exist. Police shootings of minorities, for example, may indicate not only isolated officer misjudgment but also the existence of a pervasive problem in law enforcement. Alongside such instances, however, are those that simply do not warrant special attention. The axiom "bad cases make for bad law" illustrates the problem: we overgeneralize the extent or cause of a problem and ignore more pressing issues or relevant causes. Put differently, instead of a careful, thoughtful and systematic approach to addressing crime and improving justice – or some other social problem – we politicize one particular incident and ignore a broader set of issues.

Paradoxically, our crime theories may contribute to the squeaky-wheel problem. How? They typically focus on only one cause of crime. From a policy perspective, that is problematic. One wants to systematically and comprehensively reduce crime, not invest in an intervention that targets only one possible cause. From a scientific perspective it is problematic as well. We miss the opportunity to investigate how different causes may be related to one another.[87] Instead, we spend more and more time testing, elaborating upon and then testing again a particular theory. (Efforts to integrate crime theories exist, but these constitute the exception.[88])

One example can be seen in criminological research in the 1980s. The march toward tougher, more punitive policies in that era contributed to funding for deterrence studies that indirectly lent credence to a predominant focus on punishment. Criminologists could have diversified their theory and research portfolio. Instead, they concentrated on studies that mirrored national policy debates. That led to less attention being directed toward studying rehabilitation, and so reinforced attention to punishment-focused theories, research, and policies.[89]

The Misprioritization (and Missed Opportunities) Problem

If a house has multiple holes in the roof, all of them should be patched. Priority should be given to the largest, but leaving any holes in place will result in significant damage to the home. In this illustration, each hole amounts to one problem. Our task is simple. Patch the holes. Still, we must be mindful to address all of them, not just one. By extension, systems have many problems, some bigger than others, and they all may warrant fixing. But we here face a more daunting challenge. With the roof, there may only have been one cause (e.g., hail or excessive wear and tear), meaning that the cure is the same for all of the holes. With systems, however, we must identify a range of different problems as well as options that exist to address not just the problems, and any harms that stem from them, but also their causes.

Physicians must triage patients and, for a given patient, must focus on the most pressing problems first. This need extends, in fact, to all walks of life. We typically need to prioritize various goals, problems, and solutions. Resource limits constrain us and enforce the need to prioritize. Accordingly, the question is not whether to prioritize, but rather *how well do we prioritize?* For policymakers and administrators, the stakes should be clear: misprioritization of policy and program efforts means that we allow critical problems to fester or that we invest in costly solutions where cheaper ones might have sufficed.

The squeaky-wheel problem contributes to misprioritization of research and policy efforts, which can lead to the equivalent of a magic-show trick: we focus on one part of the stage and miss what happens on the other part. We focus, for example, on deterrence, and so think a great deal about punishment. In so doing, we ignore the potential for rehabilitation to create greater reductions in offending than might arise through punishment.[90]

A great deal of policymaking entails a form of "action bias" that leads to misprioritization.[91] Policymakers, for example, feel the need to take any action, as long it is immediate and targets a tangible, visible problem. They may do so because of the perception that something must be done quickly or because of political pressures; for example, only quick action likely will enable a politician to claim credit for being a change agent. The problem lies in the fact that the action taken may focus only on a surface-level cause of the problem. It may ignore a root cause or may focus on one problem that warrants far less attention than another.

Consider student test scores. A study comes out that shows that student test scores statewide declined by 5 percent over the past year. Clearly, something must be done, or so say policymakers. A quick and easy solution? Mandate that schools improve test scores or risk loss of funding. This approach might work. However, it ignores many potential root, or core, causes of test score declines. Root causes are the deeper forces that give rise to outcomes. They may be likened to tidal forces that ultimately influence water currents and waves. For example, a sustained downturn in the economy might result in more families working two and three jobs, with less time left to read to children or to buy books for them. In this case, penalizing schools for working with a higher-need population of students seems unlikely to achieve much. Conversely, providing support for working families or furnishing them with free used or donated books might achieve more and would not necessarily require large amounts of taxpayer dollars.

In criminal justice, action bias abounds and leads to over-prioritization of certain problems or solutions. It leads, too, to a failure to capitalize on opportunities to address important problems. Consider, again, tougher sentencing laws. Policymakers in the 1980s reacted to rising violent crime rates – while ignoring declining property crime rates – by assuming that sending more people to prison for lengthier prison terms would reduce crime.[92] There was, however, little empirical evidence that too little punishment existed. It was not clear then (nor is it now, in fact) exactly how much punishment for specific crimes constitutes an appropriate amount for achieving various goals, such as retribution, incapacitation, or deterrence.[93] There was also little evidence that more punishment would address the myriad factors that contribute to crime. Indeed, when one takes stock of such factors, it becomes readily apparent that more incarceration would at best constitute one small part of a larger strategy to reduce crime.[94]

The Intuition and Failure-to-Appreciate, -Model, and -Address Complexity Problem

Complexity is central to systems and certainly to the criminal justice system. A failure to appreciate or model the complexity dooms us to the creation of emergencies, which in turn leads us to focus on emergency responses and short-term thinking. It leads us as well to attend to "squeaky wheels" and, more generally, to misprioritize problems.

One response to complexity is to fall back on intuition, especially if that intuition leads us to a simple, "silver-bullet" solution. Unfortunately, intuition frequently is wrong. It also can distract us from thinking about a larger set of factors that influence an outcome or goal.

To illustrate this problem, consider the following question: if we placed a cord around the Earth's equator and then added 36 inches to it (making the cord 36 inches longer), and if we could magically levitate the cord equally across all points on the globe, how high would it rise up above the Earth's surface?[95] Our intuition tells us that it would rise up an imperceptible amount. Yet, as shown in Figure 2.1, the cord in fact would rise up about 6 inches. It would rise by the same amount if we substituted a golf ball for the earth or, indeed, any sphere.

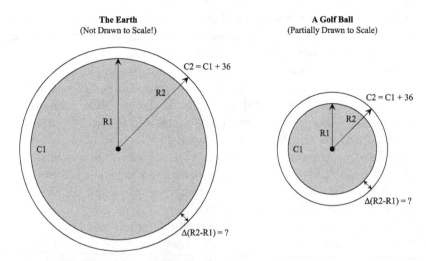

Question: How much does a levitating cord, bound to Earth's surface, rise if we add 36 inches to it? How much does it rise if instead we use a golf ball? That is, in each instance, what is Δ(R2-R1)? Intuition says that it will be infinitesimal in the case of the Earth and a lot in the case of a golf ball. That intuition is incorrect.

Answer: The formula for radius is C / 2π. So, the change in radius, Δ(R2 - R1), is equal to (C2 / 2π) - (C1 / 2π). This formula reduces to Δ(R2 - R1) = (C2 - C1) / 2π. Since π is a constant (typically approximated to be 3.14), the formula further reduces to Δ(R2 - R1) = (C2 - C1) / 6.28. Here, C2 - C1 is equal to 36. So, the solution then is Δ(R2 - R1) = 36 / 6.28. The cord thus rises 5.73 inches. It does so if the sphere is the Earth or a golf ball.

FIGURE 2.1 Intuition Can Lead Us Astray: An Illustration Using the Earth, a Golf Ball, and a Little Geometry and Algebra

How can that be? A little math will help. First, we add 36 inches to the cord, whose initial circumference, C1 (circumference 1), is that of the Earth's. This new circumference is C2 (circumference 2); it is equal to the initial circumference, C1, plus 36 inches. Second, we solve for the difference between R1, the radius of the Earth, and R2, the radius for C2. Here, R2 will equal the Earth's radius plus the additional amount of radius caused by adding 36 inches to the cord wrapped around the Earth's circumference. To figure out what the difference (Δ) is between R2 and R1, we rely on the formula for the circumference of a circle, C = 2πr, where C is the circumference, π is a constant whose approximate value is 3.14, and r is the radius. If we revise the formula to solve for radius, we get r = C / 2π, or r = C / 6.28. Accordingly, Δ(R2 − R1) = (C2 / 6.28) − (C1 / 6.28). Since C2 equals C1 + 36, this formula becomes Δ(R2 − R1) = (C1 + 36) / 6.28 − (C1 / 6.28). That reduces to Δ(R2 − R1) = 36 / 6.28 = 5.73.

In short, by adding 36 inches to the cord, the cord levitates almost 6 inches up off the surface of the Earth! Observe that we solved for this difference without knowing the Earth's actual circumference. That is because it is not needed – the change in radius will always be the same regardless of the initial circumference of any sphere.

Intuition can be a powerful thing. We trust it. Sometimes that trust is well-placed. But it can also lead us to incorrect beliefs.[96] The criminal justice landscape is filled with examples of this problem.[97] Programs abound that seem to be eminently reasonable – grounded in "common sense" – and yet constitute what Edward Latessa and colleagues have referred to as "correctional quackery."[98] Boot camps, "Scared Straight" and self-esteem programs and many policies, including mass incarceration and Project HOPE (Hawaii's Opportunity Probation and Enforcement program), fall into this same camp.[99]

The situation is, perhaps, one that is all-too-human. We target simple problems when more complicated ones seem too daunting or overwhelming.[100] Or we focus on simple solutions because they require less effort. In fact, simple sometimes may be best.[101] Yet, when problems and their solutions are complicated, we would do better to acknowledge – and then navigate – the complexity rather than ignore it.[102] The challenge with much policymaking and administrative practice, however, is that the incentives for leadership lie with quick assessments and action. That engenders a focus on piecemeal change, guided by intuition, rather than systematic assessment and a comprehensive long-term strategy for improving outcomes.

In prison systems, super-maximum – or so-called "supermax" – housing illustrates the point.[103] Such housing entails single-cell confinement of inmates, typically for up to 23 hours or more per day, for an indefinite period of time. The goals of this housing vary enormously.[104] One goal is the maintenance of order throughout the prison system.[105] Given their substantial financial costs, supermax prisons constitute a large investment in a hoped-for "silver-bullet" solution to order. The idea? Most prison disorder and violence results from a small number of inmates. Yet, that is not true. Indeed, a wide range of factors – the types of inmates admitted, the composition of inmates at a given facility, inmate culture, availability of rehabilitative programming, officer professionalism and culture, administrative managerial styles, and so on – can and do affect order in prisons. Supermax housing by and large address none of them.[106] Accordingly, the housing is unlikely to appreciably improve systemwide prison order. By contrast, conducting an assessment of the different factors that contribute to prison order and then making an effort to target them would hold much greater promise of improving order.

The importance of understanding and navigating complexity can be seen in other ways. For example, we tend to think in a linear manner, and that, too, can lead us astray. Evidence of that tendency can be seen, as Donella Meadows has observed, in our assumptions: "If we've learned that a small push produces a small response, we think that twice as big a push will produce twice as big a response. But in a nonlinear system, twice the push could produce one-sixth the response, or the response squared, or no response at all."[107] A personal story illustrates the point. I learned one day of a family friend whose daughter burned a batch of cookies. The cause? The daughter asked how to double the cookie recipe. Her mother told her to double everything in the recipe. So, the daughter doubled the oven temperature (or set it at the highest possible setting, since a typical oven can only go up to 400 to 500 degrees Fahrenheit)!

Many criminal justice policies follow this logic. Time in prison, for example, is assumed to have a constant effect – more of it, therefore, necessarily results in a proportional reduction in recidivism. Research in fact suggests that the effects of time served may be nonlinear.[108] More broadly, policies all too frequently ignore the nonlinearity inherent to systems. This nonlinearity is different from the fact that a given factor, like time served, may have variable effects at different "doses." This nonlinearity stems from dependencies. In these cases, a given factor's influence may vary, depending on some other factor. For example, the hiring of more police might increase prison populations in states with court systems that embrace a more punitive sanctioning approach. It may have little effect on prison populations in states with courts that embrace community-based sanctions over incarceration. A failure to appreciate such possibilities means that policies or interventions may not produce the effects that we want.[109]

The Case-Processing Problem

Systems handle cases. With a smaller number of cases, more room exists to consider each case individually. With a larger number of cases, less room exists, and the attention given to any one case becomes perfunctory. The distinction sometimes made between juvenile justice and criminal justice captures this idea. Traditionally, the juvenile justice system has been characterized as offender-focused, whereas the criminal justice system has been characterized as offense-focused.[110] How can the more individual-focused approach be sustained in the juvenile justice system? It typically handles far fewer cases and operates with much more per-individual funding. Consider Texas, which historically has taken a more punitive approach to punishment than other states. In 1997, during the peak of its "get tough" response to juvenile and adult crime, the daily cost of juvenile incarceration ($113) was almost three times that of adult incarceration ($40) and the daily cost of juvenile probation ($8.21) was almost five times that of adult probation ($1.77).[111]

The nature of case processing is that different individuals, units, divisions, or the like take responsibility for handling various decisions. David Heilbroner, a former Manhattan Assistant District Attorney, has provided an engrossing but also disturbing depiction of how individuals (cases) move through criminal court.[112] There are decisions made by police personnel, some of whom may make arrests late into a shift so that they can accumulate overtime. Then there are prosecutors, who initially write down brief descriptions of a case on a 3×5 index card. Next are other prosecutors who use these cards – without having met the accused – to inform the charging decision at the arraignment hearing. The defense counsel at this point may know nothing about his or her client. Even at this early stage, judges can and do weigh in heavily on how the prosecutor says the case will be handled. Additional decisions then must be made, and in each instance a different prosecutor may be involved. In virtually all instances, case-processing pressures influence every decision. We have, as Heilbroner captured in the title of his book, "rough justice," because too few resources exist to allow sufficient, devoted time for careful review of each case, collection of relevant information, a sorting-through of the facts and competing interpretations of them, and arrival at a "just" outcome.

Case-processing pressures create problems – and undermine service delivery and outcomes – across many social policy arenas. For example, it is one thing to individualize education for a single student. To do so for thousands of students is another, especially if funding for administration, teachers, buildings, equipment, and technology does not keep pace with student population growth. Similarly, large increases in the numbers of patients seen by doctors create less-individualized care. Physicians have less time to meet patients, collect information and reflect, resulting in ever-greater rates of misdiagnosis and mistreatment.

Systems either manage case-processing pressures or get managed by them. A failure to manage them creates large-scale harms because errors become institutionalized and applied to many "cases." When, for example, physicians or prosecutors must decide within minutes how to handle a particular individual, they must rely on cognitive shortcuts, or heuristics, which may well lead them to make mistakes and to do so consistently and frequently.[113] Court personnel, for example, may unconsciously view minorities as inherently more likely to be guilty, and may write case reports and recommendations that reflect that belief. Without case-processing pressures, such reports might be questioned; with them, recommendations are automatically followed and can result in "criminalizing" minorities.[114] When case-processing pressure distorts the decision-making throughout a system, it exerts an amplification effect: decision-making errors enhance the pernicious effects of other decision-making errors and contribute to still others.[115]

The Taking-Action-without-Good-Information Problem

When situations are complicated, people who work within systems frequently make seat-of-the-pants decisions about how to proceed. They become used to this approach. In many cases they must do so because they have little relevant information at their disposal. These two issues go hand-in-hand. Without relevant and accurate information, decision-makers may miss the mark. An institutionalized commitment to this fly-by-the-seat-of-the-pants approach then can emerge over time. The end result is a system where there may be some "evidence-based" policies or programs, but where in the main, these constitute the exception rather than the norm.

Even if evidence-based approaches were the norm – and they are not – there would remain the need to ensure that the entire system operates in an effective and efficient manner. A sports team, for example, that consists of nothing but star players will rarely win games unless the efforts of these different players are well integrated. Similarly, a system comprising excellent personnel and evidence-based interventions will be ineffective unless the different parts of the system are well coordinated, evaluated, and modified as needed to improve performance. Any such undertaking, however, requires relevant and timely information. A coach can look out on the field and take stock of how plays unfold as well as talk to players. Many systems, however, do not readily lend themselves to this approach: we cannot "see" them the same way as we can see a sports team playing. We therefore need a large body of information, presented in an accessible manner. Otherwise, no effective "coaching" can happen.

In criminal justice, this issue can be illustrated in many ways. One prominent example is the failure of most jurisdictions to collect or analyze information about front-end decisions made by the police and the courts.

Anne Milgram, who served as New Jersey's Attorney General, has described how, for example, she was stunned to realize that much of what occurred from arrest through sentencing occurred in the equivalent of a "black box."[116] Each part of the New Jersey system – police, jails, courts, and so on – created and used entirely different databases, and information was not shared or analyzed together. That meant that little systematic information existed about the profile of individuals at each stage of processing, the risk level of these individuals, rates of appropriate or inappropriate use of jail and various sanctions, and so on. Ultimately, then, it was not possible to know how well decisions contributed to public safety or whether safety and justice occurred in the most cost-efficient manner.

2.3 CONCLUSION

The central argument of this book is that systems matter. If we want to more fully understand crime and justice and to improve it, a systems approach is critical. Notably, though, this approach does not surface regularly in scholarship or in policy. Studies and policies typically zero-in on a particular topic, issue, or dimension. How is self-control related to offending? How does the perceived legitimacy of prison systems affect inmate behavior? How effective is a particular program or policy in reducing recidivism? These and many other questions are fascinating and important. They lead to insights that enable us to understand crime and what we might do to improve public safety and justice. Yet they also leave unexamined and unaddressed the myriad ways that systems contribute to and shape crime and justice. Systems processes and dynamics have a life of their own that can greatly contribute to crime and justice. They can facilitate or constrain the effectiveness and efficiency of specific activities, programs or decisions that occur within and throughout the criminal justice system.

To highlight the salience of a systems perspective, this chapter turned away from crime and justice and focused on other social problems and policy arenas, such as health care, education, the environment, and the War on Terror. It also discussed manufacturing, not because it constitutes a social policy area but because policymakers frequently call for running government like a business. Accordingly, it can be instructive to consider how a conventional business activity, such as manufacturing, can be thought about and managed as a systems undertaking. Across the different policy arenas, the main message is that, well, systems matter. Attention to systems problems is critical if we want to achieve large-scale improvements in such diverse goals as health, education, pollution, and protection from terrorist attacks.

We can see how systems matter by considering the variety of systems problems that exist and that cannot readily be addressed by a specific law or program. For example, with no "captain" overseeing health care, inaccurate or inefficient decision-making goes unchecked. Misdiagnosis occurs, preventative medicine opportunities are missed, physicians overprescribe medications, expensive surgeries are pursued without first determining whether physical therapy may resolve pain or discomfort, and so on. In such a context, a related problem arises: those who work within the system focus on addressing emergencies or become enmeshed in prioritizing short-term goals rather than strategies that will be sustainable and beneficial in the long term. When school test scores, for example, drop precipitously from one year to the next, the state responds by creating a new policy for punishing low-performing schools and rewarding high-performing schools. No sustained attention is given to the underlying causes of the changes in the scores or to the variety of strategies that might be most cost-efficient for improving school performance.

Still other systems problems exist. Many stem from or interact with one another. The no-captain problem can allow the squeaky-wheel problem to occur, for example. Here, some individuals within a system may be more successful in drawing attention to an issue that affects them. Policymakers and administrators then attend to that issue. At the same time, they ignore issues that may be more pressing or that, if addressed, would result in greater improvements. This problem is further amplified by a failure to institutionalize processes for prioritizing various issues and opportunities for creating improvements. It is also amplified by decisions made on the basis of intuition and by a failure to consider the larger system within which the proposed changes are to occur.

Policies, programs, and the like do not occur within a vacuum. Yet we frequently see policy reforms that contemplate a simple universe, one where a change in one area can be undertaken with little need for concern about how other areas may respond or may be affected. The failure to appreciate, model or address the complexity of a system constitutes a critical weak spot for many reforms. It accounts for why, in the long term, any putative benefits of particular policies or decisions may be offset by unexpected systems changes. This problem is enhanced by case-processing pressures and action bias.

The main take-away point is that undisciplined systems – those, for example, that operate with no "captain" in charge – lead to ineffectiveness (i.e., a failure to achieve intended outcomes) and inefficiency (i.e., considerable expense for little gain). Worse, they lock us into ineffective and inefficient policies. In so doing, they reduce our ability to seize opportunities to create large-scale improvements. It is not just the no-captain problem, however, that can create and amplify systems problems. Other systems problems exist that, if unaddressed, reduce the likelihood of successful outcomes in the aggregate for society. In this situation, even though success stories may be found here and there, society receives little overall benefit.

The importance of understanding how systems problems undermine effective and efficient policy cannot be overstated. What can be done? The possibilities for improvement involve addressing the dimensions that surfaced in the illustrations above, such as creation of the institutional equivalent of a "captain," better information collection, monitoring of system activities and outcomes and drawing on the efforts of multiple stakeholder groups to create changes that can persist not only in the short- or intermediate-term, but also over the long term.

These possibilities will be discussed in subsequent chapters (Chapter 6 in particular). Here, however, to illustrate the possibilities, mention of the Washington State Institute for Public Policy (WSIPP) is warranted.[117] WSIPP has been instrumental in providing empirically based assessments of different crime and justice issues in the State of Washington. WSIPP stands out because it constitutes one of the few examples of an institutionalized research process that serves not only the legislature but also the governor and public universities. In this way it resembles the Texas Criminal Justice Policy Council, which served a similar function until, in 2003, Governor Rick Perry disbanded it.[118] WSIPP's mission is to "carry out practical, non-partisan research at the direction of the legislature or Board of Directors."[119] It produces an abundance of annual and special-request analyses on a range of policy questions, issues, and considerations. In so doing, and because it responds directly and frequently to a diverse set of stakeholders, it produces work that regularly informs policy and practice in Washington.[120] This arrangement does not include formal systems analysis. However, WSIPP conducts a wealth of analyses that, because of its institutionalized role in policymaking, can help to avoid systems problems.

Before turning to a discussion of solutions, however, there is a need to turn to a simple but important question: What is a system? After that, there is the question of how criminal justice can be viewed as a system and what problems arise from not addressing the systems problems that are unique to it. Chapters 3 and 4, respectively, address these questions. With Chapter 5, we will zero-in on the Systems Improvement Solution; Chapter 6 will then discuss its benefits.

3

What Is a System?

The goal of this chapter is to describe the concept of a "system" and the salience of understanding systems to address social problems such as the reduction of crime and the improvement of justice, accountability, and efficiency. The chapter discusses several core dimensions necessary to describing and understanding a system. These include systems outcomes, elements and subsystems, external forces, and dynamics. In addition, the chapter describes the importance of theory to guide one's understanding of systems and how to improve them.

3.1 AN OVERVIEW OF SYSTEMS

Numerous accounts of systems exist. Systems theory, general systems theory, systems analysis, systems simulation, operations research: these and many similar undertakings all examine the same thing – systems – but do so with different terminologies, methodologies, and emphases. What unifies them all is the notion that the concept of a system is useful: it helps us to understand reality. Concepts are not typically "correct" or "incorrect," but rather are more useful or less useful. They help us to see the world in a different way, and ideally as it actually is. The concept of a system can be useful because it enables us to see how seemingly disparate and disconnected – or perhaps loosely connected – activities may be interrelated and, possibly, managed.

How, then, do we define a "system"? Donella Meadows has provided a simple and useful definition: "A system is an interconnected set of elements that is coherently organized in a way that achieves something."[1] An alternative definition from Anatol Rapoport: "A whole which functions as a whole by virtue of the interdependence of its parts."[2] Many other definitions exist, but all typically emphasize, as Tom Bernard and colleagues have noted, that systems are characterized by "the interaction of different units toward a common goal."[3]

Although the definitions seem vague, they capture an important idea – different units (e.g., parts of an organization or members of a team) may seek a common set of goals and interact in ways to achieve these goals. When we ignore this idea, we miss much of how the world operates. We view the world instead as if it is a set of independent pieces and activities.

One way to illustrate the usefulness of the concept of a system for understanding social phenomena is through reference to sports. For example, if we want to understand a soccer (or, for places other than the United States, "football") game, we need to know how the different elements (e.g., players) are interconnected (e.g., what rules they follow) and what goal is sought (e.g., winning). The game makes sense – it is intelligible – if we view it as a system.

In fact, the game makes *no* sense if we view it in atomized way, such that somehow soccer consists simply of the addition of each player or rule. It is not. Why players pass the ball, move it around the field in a particular pattern, rotate players out, and so on, all of that can only be understood, using Meadows' terminology, by considering the different elements, interconnections, and goal. In Rapoport's terminology, the game (the "whole") makes sense ("functions") through the different ways that players, rules, coaches, and other elements interact ("interdependence"). Or, in Bernard and colleagues' phrasing, the game makes sense only when we consider how the different units interact and work toward a common goal.

Systems are everywhere: families, schools, organizations, neighborhoods, and so on. What makes a system a system is the pursuit of a goal or set of goals and the interdependency of the different parts and their activities. Of course, many systems are not well integrated. A sports team with the best players, for example, will perform poorly if the players do not get along, or "play well with others."[4] Some teams perform so poorly that it can, indeed, seem a bit of a stretch to call them a "team." Similarly, various systems may be so poorly integrated that it can be difficult to see how they constitute a system. They do, but the system simply lacks much integration and so is unlikely to achieve its goals.

Perhaps the central insight to understand about systems is the fact that they have a life of their own, that the interdependency and the activities collectively amount to more than the sum of their parts. A soccer game is not, for example, simply the addition of players. Rather, it is defined literally by a set number of players and how they interact with one another in pursuit of winning a game. Put differently, a player cannot "play" "soccer" alone. The game requires multiple players, the coordination of their play, adherence to the rules, enforcement of those rules, and pursuit of a goal (or multiple goals, when possible!).

It is the nature of systems that the parts within them do not operate in isolation. By extension, when these parts "move," they can and frequently do affect other parts. A player who kicks the ball down the field sets into motion a cascade of movements among the other players on his or her team and among players on the other team. Similarly, when a change occurs within one part of a system, it may well cause changes elsewhere. When a law mandates that schools must test students and that schools whose students test well will receive more resources, other parts of the educational system "move" into action. When a hospital invests in an MRI machine, it simultaneously opens the door for physicians to order more scans and surgeries; in so doing, it also creates the need for more physicians or for cuts to other hospital operations. And when, as will be discussed in the next chapter, states build more prisons, the courts send more people to them, and perhaps, given the additional capacity, "lower the bar" for who they send to prison. If the incarceration experience improves offenders, then public safety goes up. Conversely, if it worsens them – for example, if it increases recidivism – then public safety goes down, and greater pressure emerges to incarcerate these individuals and thus to build yet more prisons.

A systems perspective might be cast as an intrinsically sociological view.[5] The whole is understood to be more and different than the sum of its parts. Cities, communities, and families, for example, cannot simply be understood as aggregations of individuals.[6] At the same time, individuals do not make sense in isolation. No individual, for example, magically decides that he or she must always face forward in an elevator. Rather, societal "norms" exist about the "proper" direction. (And, of course, it is society that provided the elevator in the first place.)

Even so, the salience of a systems perspective can be readily understood from work in psychology on how individuals see the world. For example, scholarship on cognitive decision-making highlights that humans appear to be "hardwired" to see patterns – that is, connections between seemingly isolated or unrelated bits of information.[7] We do that quite well in our day-to-day lives, noticing the barest hint of a path through the woods, tension that exists at a social gathering, the source of someone's voice in a crowded gym, and so on. Yet we do not do as well when it comes to "seeing" systems. That stems from the fact that only some parts of systems are readily visible. Criminal justice, for example, includes courts and prisons, but few citizens ever step inside either place. That can make it difficult to see patterns; nonetheless, they do exist. So, we need a different approach, such as research and stakeholder discussions, for the system to be "seen," understood, and then perhaps improved.

Systems logic can be seen in many walks of life. In tax law, for example, the "step transaction doctrine" states that a sequence of actions, all of which might individually be legal, is illegal if – when viewed together in their totality – they clearly serve to achieve an outcome that otherwise would not be legally permissible.[8] Systems feature prominently in the sciences as well. For example, scholars have highlighted ways in which evolution may occur differently for different units of analysis, such as the gene, organisms, and groups, in large part because of the unique interdependence of parts and the "goals" specific to each unit of analysis.[9] In the natural and social sciences, then, scholars have found that systems have properties and processes that are specific to them. These properties and processes cannot be readily derived by extending the logic of units of analysis "above" or "below" the system unit of analysis.[10]

Given the ubiquity of systems, we need a way to "see," understand, and analyze them. Many different approaches exist for doing so. Here, my goal is not to review each of them; as noted in Chapter 1, a wealth of sources exist that describe these approaches. Instead, my goal is to focus on the concept of a system and to describe some of the dimensions that can be helpful in identifying, describing, and understanding one. This discussion, in turn, sets the stage for the focus, in the subsequent chapter, on criminal justice as a system.

Figure 3.1 provides an illustration, using four dimensions, of a simplified system. First, a system seeks to achieve particular goals or outcomes, which can be viewed as desired end "products." The challenge for the system lies in how these goals or outcomes will be achieved. Ideally, it will be designed such that it efficiently achieves these goals. How good the design is, and how well implemented it is, are critical to the system's success.

Second, when thinking about systems, our focus – after identifying the critical outcomes – is on how the system is structured. The system may have many parts or elements. Indeed, some parts may be sufficiently complex that they can be viewed as subsystems. In the figure, for example, four subsystems constitute the core parts of the system and are depicted as

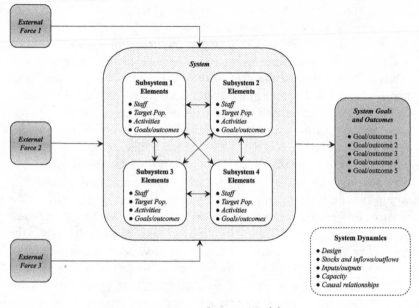

FIGURE 3.1 Systems Model

sufficiently complex and distinct to each stand alone. Each one includes many elements, including, for example, staff, a focus on a particular group (e.g., students, customers), activities, and subsystem-specific outcomes. (We could include additional elements, such as the physical buildings or court rulings that guide subsystem operations and goals.) One or more of the parts or subsystems may interact with one another, as depicted by the dual-direction arrows.

Third, a broader context, or set of external forces, may exist that facilitates or constrains system activities or that changes the system's goals. Systems do not exist in a vacuum. Indeed, external forces, or context, may greatly influence their operations and effectiveness.

Fourth, systems dynamics – captured in part by the arrows – exist that define the system and also influence its effectiveness. A car might be understood through examination of the schematics for it that show the location of various parts. However, an understanding of how the car moves requires more. It also requires knowledge of the ways in which various parts interact with each other and how they may interact with external forces (e.g., tires and road surface, cabin height and wind noise or resistance). Similarly, an understanding of systems requires knowledge of the system's design and how the various parts interact. It also requires knowledge of additional, related dimensions, such as stocks and flows, inputs and outputs, system capacity, and the causal relationships that may exist within and across the system and in relation to external forces.

Figure 3.1 is a simple sketch of a system, yet it serves the purpose of highlighting key features of a system and the dimensions necessary for characterizing it. The sketch also serves the purpose of highlighting a key insight from systems research: that any one person, group, unit, part, and so on, operates within a larger context that may inhibit or amplify their effectiveness and the achievement of subsystem or system outcomes. To facilitate discussion of the criminal justice system in the next chapter, each of these dimensions is described in more detail below.

3.2 SYSTEMS: GOALS AND OUTCOMES

Systems, like individuals, are oriented toward goals, or one might say, "outcomes." Goals and outcomes can be viewed as equivalent. Alternatively, we can view outcomes as examples or indicators of goals. We can be more precise with our terminology if we want. For example, we can refer to goals as the overarching guiding mission of a system, objectives as specific dimensions of each goal, outcomes as specific dimensions of each objective, and measures as empirically observable scores that gauge the extent to which an objective is met.[11]

These conceptual distinctions matter. They help us to clarify that individuals and organizations typically have large-scale aims. They clarify that if we want to demonstrate success, we need measurable indicators of success in achieving these aims. They clarify, too, that goals may be nested, much like a Russian nested ("matryoshka") doll. In these cases, we might refer to goals, sub-goals, sub-sub-goals, and so on. Such language is, however, cumbersome.

For simplicity's sake, I will refer to goals and outcomes interchangeably. A goal is a term that most of us intuitively understand and so is useful in conveying key points about systems. An outcome – a term used frequently in policy and program evaluation research – connotes a goal as well. At the same time, it reminds us that goals can be nested and that we want ultimately to be able to use empirical measures to show how well goals have been achieved. It also is a term that has entered everyday parlance in discussions about government accountability and performance monitoring.[12] (Again, we could use "goals," "objectives," "outcomes," and "measures" to achieve greater degrees of precision, but at the cost of excessive detail.)

To say that systems are goal- or outcome-oriented is not to say that they do so well. Indeed, systems, like individuals, may be unclear about their precise goals or the specific outcomes that they wish to achieve. They may lack a clear or logical plan for achieving their goals. And the execution of any given plan may be poor. None of this matters for defining a system. What matters is that goals or outcomes are, in fact, pursued.

For a system as a whole, then, we want to identify intended goals or outcomes. With businesses, the end goal or outcome may be profits. Success is defined as making money, and doing so consistently. It might be defined as well as steadily increasing profit. The logic of capitalism, for example, places an emphasis on ever-expanding growth and profit.[13] For social service agencies, the outcomes may be more varied and less easily quantified. For example, the child welfare system seeks to protect youth from harm and, at the same time, to promote their interests more broadly, such as by safeguarding or improving their mental or physical health and ensuring that they receive an education. Multiple outcomes thus may be relevant. In each instance, we must find valid measures for these outcomes. Unlike profits, however, "harm," "best interests," "mental health," "physical health," "education," and the like are not easily quantified. Even so, the child welfare system exists to achieve these outcomes. We therefore need to identify them if we are to understand the structure and organization of this system and its success – that is, how well its various structures and activities contribute to them.

In describing and evaluating a system, we should be cognizant of and model all goals or outcomes, not just select ones. That is an insight that should be easy to understand but that frequently gets lost in policy discussions and research. Many discussions and analyses of criminal justice, for example, focus almost exclusively on crime rates and recidivism. They give minimal attention to justice, including retribution or the experiences of victims. They also ignore a range of outcomes that criminal justice can affect.[14] The individuals who go to prison, for example, may be influenced by the incarceration experience in ways that go well beyond recidivism. They might be more likely – or less likely – to be employed, find housing, or obtain needed drug abuse or mental health treatment.[15]

One reason we can lose sight of systems goals and outcomes is because, as will be discussed below, systems can be fragmented or highly complex. A federal agency, for example, can be viewed as a system, and might well employ 10,000 or more employees.[16] Many companies employ thousands of individuals and seek to integrate the efforts of these individuals and the divisions within they work. Universities rely on many administrative offices and diverse academic colleges, schools, institutes, centers, and departments to achieve their goals. In each instance, we might well find ourselves focused on the "trees," that is, the activities and outcomes specific to a given division, office, unit, and so on. From a systems perspective, though, we do not want to lose sight of the "forest." We want to see clearly the broader set of goals and outcomes that the entire system and its various components are designed to achieve.

3.3 SYSTEMS: ELEMENTS AND SUBSYSTEMS

In addition to using goals and outcomes to define systems, we can refer, too, to elements and subsystems. A car is designed for driving: the goal is to use it to get somewhere. Description of that goal, however, does not suffice for understanding what a car "is." For that, we need information about the parts and configuration, or structure, of the car. What pieces go into the car? In what arrangement? With such information, we can begin to picture the car and, depending on the precision of the description, how the different parts work with one another.

In a similar manner, systems can be described through reference to the elements or subsystems that create them. Elements can be viewed as the organizations, divisions, units, parts, or the like that perform specific functions, the physical space through which the organization or its parts are manifest (e.g., a college campus and its buildings), and tangible or intangible conditions (e.g., values, court rulings, economic pressures) that shape the system.[17]

"Subsystems" can be viewed as a larger type of "element" that help make up some systems. They constitute clearly distinct organizations that interact with other organizations and do so within a larger systems context. A university system, for example, may have separate offices for undergraduate studies, graduate studies, student admissions, external grant funding, human resources, and so on. Each may operate somewhat autonomously and with distinct goals. Yet they also, by design or simply because they operate within the same larger systems context, may interact with or influence one another. Ultimately, the university system may be geared toward educating youth, creating a stronger labor force, advancing science, and other such goals. The different subsystems, and how they connect to one another, exist to help achieve these goals. At the same time, their relative autonomy means that each operates according to its own internal logic, with its own elements, linkages among those elements, and goals or outcomes.

To extend the car analogy, we might view vehicles as consisting of multiple subsystems. For example, they have seat safety systems, air-conditioning and heating systems, audio systems, and so on. Each of these subsystems has its own parts, internal logic, and function (another name for "goal"). Collectively, though, they serve to advance the overall goal of driving or, more specifically, of driving safely and comfortably. In a subsystem analysis, we want to identify how well the air-conditioning works and what contributes to its effectiveness. For a systems analysis, we want to identify how this subsystem's operations and effectiveness may interact with that of other subsystems. Perhaps, for example, an extremely effective air-conditioning system places too large a demand on the engine system, thereby reducing the car's ability to accelerate rapidly.

In short, if we wish to describe a system, we must identify the different elements and subsystem as well the outcomes specific to each subsystem and to the system as a whole. In addition, as discussed next, we need to describe how the system operates. That is, what are the system dynamics that characterize how various elements and subsystems interact?

Before proceeding to that discussion, several points warrant emphasis. First, it is the nature of many, if not all, social systems that they cannot readily be seen. We can see a car, but we cannot see educational, health care, or criminal justice systems. In some instances, we might be able to see a building within which a system (e.g., a company or some other organization) resides. Even then, we cannot literally see all elements or the interconnections among them. That does not make the system any less real; it simply means that we need clear theoretical and empirical accounts that enable us to infer, or "see," it.

Second, systems frequently may have "fuzzy" boundaries. That is, the boundaries of a system may be only vaguely discernable. Such is the nature of many systems. Here, again, that does not make systems any less real. It simply means that we need the conceptual tools – including theory and research methodologies – to define, describe, and examine systems.

Third, we can seek to describe in infinite detail a system, but doing so can lead one down a rabbit hole. We ultimately want to describe a system sufficiently well that we can discern how it operates, what effects it may have, what influences its effectiveness, and how we might modify it to be more effective and cost-efficient. No magic formula exists for what counts as "sufficient," any more than a specific number of brushstrokes suffices to draw a portrait that best "captures" a person, landscape, or event.[18]

Instead, we can be guided by utility. After some number of brushstrokes, do we start to discern the essence of a portrait? More specifically, given a level of systems description, how well can we discern and predict or explain patterns within and across the system? Even when we cannot predict accurately, we may find that a systems "portrait" better enables us to understand the variety of options that exist for achieving a "big" goal, such as improved education, health, environmental conditions, or criminal justice.

3.4 SYSTEMS: EXTERNAL FORCES

External forces are the conditions that affect a system. They can vary enormously. These forces might include the supplies to a system. Educational systems, for example, will be affected by the flow of students into them as well as by the available resources for buildings, renovations, equipment, books, technology, teachers, and so on. They will be affected, too, by political events or decisions, such as when a law mandates that certain courses must be taught or a number of days must be allocated to testing. Community context may influence them as well. Parents' expectations of schools might shape education policies and practices, for example.

Such forces or conditions can both facilitate and constrain system activities and, as importantly shape them. For example, a state might adopt across-the-board funding cuts to state-run agencies, thus necessitating cost-cutting measures that reduce or eliminate certain activities. A state, too, might change the mission of a given agency. In the 1990s, for example, some states revised their juvenile justice system goals to emphasize punishment more than rehabilitation.[19] In so doing, they created a situation in which system efforts needed to be realigned to correspond more closely with the new rank-ordering of goals. New political and economic contexts as well as changes in goals may affect any system. Accordingly, efforts to understand systems activities, impacts, and efficiency need to consider them.

3.5 SYSTEMS: DYNAMICS

Systems dynamics consist of the various ways in which parts of a system interact and produce outcomes. They consist, too, of ways that parts of the system interact with external forces. These dynamics are central to understanding systems. When a system is well designed and well implemented, the parts work well together, they interact efficiently with the external environment, and they result in achieved goals and outcomes. When poorly designed and implemented, systems fail to achieve goals and outcomes or to do so efficiently.

The word "dynamic" serves to draw our attention to the fact that systems do not exist in "blueprint" fashion. That is, they do not exist as the functional equivalent of a building. Rather, they entail constant movement, interaction, and change. To understand their operations and impacts requires, therefore, an understanding of these dimensions or "dynamics." When examining dynamics, it can be helpful to focus on several dimensions.

First, there is the *design* of the system – that is, the ways in which various parts and subsystems have been designed to work together to achieve particular goals or outcomes. No one person or entity may have designed the overall system, as is the case with criminal justice, but the logic of the system nonetheless is that it serves to achieve specific goals or outcomes.

Second, it can be helpful, too, to identify the *stocks* and *flows*, or what might be viewed as the interconnections within and across the system.[20] "Stocks are the elements of the system that you can see, feel, count, or measure."[21] They can be physical (e.g., supplies, individuals). However, they also can, and frequently are, not physical (e.g., information, willingness to help others). Flows are the "material or information that enters or leaves a stock over a period of time."[22] Meadows has aptly illustrated the idea of stocks and flows through reference to bathtubs. When we fill a tub to the brim and stop up the drain, the water in the tub can be viewed as "stock." If we remove the stopper, the water will drain out. If, however, we remove the stopper and turn on the faucet, the "stock" of water may remain level. Much depends on the rate of *inflow* from the faucet and the rate of *outflow* out of the drain. For example, water might overflow the edge of the tub if the rate of water inflow exceeds the rate of water outflow. Or the stock of water may slowly go lower if the rate of inflow is less than the rate of outflow.

Inflows and outflows all directly affect the stock at a given point in time, and both constitute a leverage point for achieving a desired level of stock. A company, for example, might maintain a particular workforce level by hiring just enough new employees to offset the rate at which existing ones leave (i.e., by ensuring that inflow matches outflow). Or it might undertake activities to reduce the rate at which employees leave (i.e., by reducing outflow and so reducing the need for increased inflow).[23] Similarly, and to anticipate the discussion in the next chapter, prison systems might maintain a given stock population of inmates through adjustment to inmate admission rates (inflow) or to average time served among inmates, which affects the release rate (outflow).[24] Of course, the ability of prison systems to adjust either is limited. Lawmakers, however, may do so through sentencing laws, parole policies, and funding for law enforcement and crime prevention.

Third, we will find it useful to identify *inputs* and *outputs* when describing system dynamics. Inputs can be viewed as "resources (i.e., expenditures or employee time) used to produce outputs and outcomes," while outputs can be viewed as the "completed products of internal activity."[25] An input might be the number of staff assigned to a task. The sufficiency of that allocation will determine how effectively the task is achieved, and thus the outputs. We can combine these two sets of terms to characterize dynamics in a system. For example, the inflow of various inputs may affect the outflow of outputs to other parts of a system.

Fourth, any description of system dynamics also entails identification of *capacity*. When capacity of any part of a system is too little or is exceeded, it can result in ripple effects throughout the system. Too few emergency room physicians will result in more death or injury. By the same token, an excess of emergency room physicians main drain resources away from areas where they may be more needed and better used. The capacity of any given part of a system may not necessarily be fixed. Indeed, it may be less than or more than what was planned. In general, when inputs (e.g., injured patients) exceed capacity (e.g., number of emergency room physicians), we can anticipate problems, or damaged "outputs," such as death or injury.

Finally, description and understanding of system dynamics can benefit from identifying *causal relationships* – that is, how various inputs and outputs, or inflows and outflows from and to various parts of the system, may be causally associated in a linear or nonlinear manner. Table 3.1 identifies some of the different types of causal relationships that exist.[26]

In general, the simplest situation involves a *linear*, or "straight line," relationship between a causal force, X, and some output or outcome, Y. Here, the effect of X on Y is constant. Additional "units" of X thus produce additive effects on Y. Many phenomena in life may be linearly associated. For example, if we plant twice as many seeds in a garden, there may well be twice as many plants that grow. When we examine the causes of offending, most criminological theories seem to contemplate linear relationships: lower self-control, more strain, weaker social bonds, and so on, all are thought to be positively associated with offending.[27]

TABLE 3.1 *Examples of Types of Causal Relationships*

- **Linear, or "additive."** Unit changes in X (e.g., an input or some other causal force) result in the same change in Y (an output or outcome), regardless of the level of X. Thus, changes in X result in additive effects on Y. For example, 3 unit changes in X produce 3 times as much change in Y as does 1 unit of change in X).
- **Nonlinear.** Change in X results in different changes in Y depending on the level of X or the presence of other factors. Different types of nonlinear relationships exist.
  - *Curvilinear.* Changes in X result in different amounts of change in Y, depending on the level of X. For example, an increase in X at low values of X may have little effect on Y, but the same increase at high values of X may have large effects on Y. Conversely, the increase in X at low values of X may have a large effect on Y, but subsequent increases in X may have little to no effect.
  - *Tipping point (or threshold).* Changes in X may not affect Y until X reaches a certain level. For example, water does not boil until it reaches a certain temperature.
  - *Interactive.* The effect of X on Y varies depending on the level of one or more other factors.
  - *Dose.* A specific change in X achieves a particular change in Y. Dose effects may be variable or may involve thresholds or interactions.
  - *Reciprocal or self-reinforcing causation (feedback loop).* Changes in X may affect Y, and a change in Y may affect X. This process may occur through intervening causal mechanisms. There may be stabilizing feedback loops (i.e., the feedbacks tend toward stabilization of X at a certain level) and amplification feedback loops (i.e., the feedbacks tend toward amplification of X).
- **Other**
  - *Direct vs. indirect.* Changes in X may directly affect Y or it may do so indirectly through intervening causal mechanisms.
  - *Proximate vs. distal.* Effects of X on Y may occur over different time spans or areas. Those that occur sooner in time or space may be said to be temporally or spatially proximate; those that occur later in time may be said to be temporally or spatially distal.
  - *Reversible.* A change in X changes Y, and the opposite change in X produces the opposite change in Y. For example, an increase in X increases Y and a decrease in X decreases Y.
  - *Irreversible.* A change in X changes Y, and the opposite change in X does not produce the opposite change in Y. For example, an increase in X increases Y but a decrease in X does not decrease Y. (The change in Y still may be reversible, but not through a change in X.)

However, "the world is," as Meadows has observed, "full of *nonlinearities*."[28] If we ignore them, we risk misunderstanding how society and systems work:

The world often surprises our linear-thinking minds. If we've learned that a small push produces a small response, we think that twice as big a push will produce twice as big a response. But in a nonlinear system, twice the push could produce one-sixth the response, or the response squared, or no response at all.[29]

Many types of nonlinear relationships exist. A few prominent examples will illustrate the range of possibilities. One is a *curvilinear* association between X and Y, the situation contemplated by Meadows. Here, the effect of X may be variable, depending on its level. The concept of diminishing marginal returns captures the idea. Our first pair of shoes may make us happy (and protect our feet). A second pair also may make us happy, but probably not nearly as much as the first pair. The added happiness we might feel with a third, fourth, fifth, and so on, pair of shoes may be negligible. Except for the rare few among us, a hundredth pair of shoes likely produces a barely appreciable dint in our happiness. Another type of curvilinear relationship entails the opposite situation: initial increases in X may not produce much of a change in Y, but changes at the upper end of the X spectrum may exert quite large effects. Curvilinear relationships may abound in systems. Their presence means that we need to be careful about how much we change some input or output or the inflows and outflows of a system.

Tipping points, or thresholds, constitute another type of nonlinearity. Here, no effect, or not much of an effect, on Y occurs until a tipping point is reached. Fatigue (X) may make us grumpy (Y), but it may not be until our fatigue reaches a certain tipping point, or threshold, that we become openly irritable with others. When children become sufficiently hungry, they cry. These and many other tipping points are ubiquitous. As with all nonlinearities, they warrant identification if we are to introduce changes that produce desired effects.

Interaction effects entail still another type of nonlinearity that affects systems. Here, the effect of a given factor, like hunger, may have a variable effect on an outcome, such as crying, depending on the level of some other factor, like fatigue. For example, a little hunger may not lead an infant to cry, and a little fatigue also may not cause crying. But increased hunger when an infant is tired may more likely result in a crying jag than when he or she is rested. Interactions can pervade systems. For example, the introduction of a standardized testing requirement (X) may improve student learning outcomes (Y), and the improvement may be especially large if it occurs alongside a process that provides needed resources to poorly performing schools (X2).

Dose effects can exist as well. Curvilinear and tipping point effects might be described as possible dose effects. Here the question is, how much of a given causal force is needed to produce a particular effect? The dose-effect relationship might be linear or curvilinear or it might entail some type of threshold. It also is possible that a given dose may exert a different effect on a goal or outcome, depending on the level of some other factor (an interaction effect). Specifying the correct "dose," or amount, of any given causal force is critical for ensuring that we achieve desired goals or outcomes and do so efficiently.

Reciprocal, self-reinforcing, or *feedback loop* effects – where X may affect Y and Y may affect X – also may influence systems. Robert Agnew has highlighted this idea through reference to criminal offending, noting that the causes of crime may themselves be caused by crime.[30] For example, if an individual commits a crime, he or she may be labeled a criminal, come to accept the label, and then act to fulfill that label by committing more crime. To use a more mundane example: If we are irritable, we may be more likely to be rude to others. When we act rudely to others, they act rudely back to us, and then we feel even more irritable and so become even more rude to those about us, creating a vicious cycle.

In systems, reciprocal causation can be viewed as a feedback loop, one that creates the equivalent of reverberation effects. These loops amplify outcomes and do so directly or indirectly, as when the effects ripple through a variety of intervening causal mechanisms.[31] Some feedback loops are stabilizing – that is, changes in X may lead to changes in other forces that, in turn, adjust X up or down to maintain the stock level. A thermostat operates in this way. Changes in room temperature trigger the thermostat to turn on the heat or air conditioning; when the temperature reaches a target, "stock" level, it turns off the heat or air conditioning. The thermostat (X) can be said to cause changes to the room temperature (Y) and the room temperature can be said to cause the thermostat to turn on or off. Other factors, such as the rate at which the warm or cold air leaves or enters the house, may affect room temperature and so affect the thermostat's operations. Feedback loops thus can involve multiple causal mechanisms or triggers.

Other loops entail amplification feedback processes. One example is when a part of a system acts as the equivalent of a resource magnet. Consider a situation in which a system grows rapidly. When some parts grow faster than others, they may dominate the dynamics of the overall system. Indeed, the system may become increasingly geared toward accommodating or adapting to that part. Then, if this part continues to grow, even greater imbalances occur that alter the entire system. For example – and to anticipate a critical point for this book – a criminal justice system might suddenly expand its capacity to incarcerate. As a result, prison operation costs escalate and result in increasingly greater resource demands. This change reduces the ability of the system to invest in alternative sanctions or in improved case processing.[32] If, in addition, laws encourage more and lengthier incarceration, then this incarceration-centered dynamic increases and so inhibits the system from initiating other policies.[33]

Additional types of causal relationships exist. For example, there may be *direct* effects of a given causal force on some outcome, or there may be *indirect* effects that arise through a simple or complex chain of intervening causal mechanisms. To illustrate, a high-profile oil spill might lead policymakers to enact tougher environmental protection laws (a direct effect) or it might first lead to community frustration, which in turn may lead to community calls to policymakers, which then leads policymakers to pass new laws (an indirect effect).

Some causes may be temporally or spatially *proximate* or *distal* to their effects. An oil spill might result in immediate policy action (a temporally proximate effect) or it might result in a chain of events that at some much later time leads lawmakers to act (a temporally distal effect). Similarly, the oil spill might result in new laws in the state or region where it occurred (a spatially proximate effect) or in far-distant states (a spatially distal effect).

Some causal effects are *reversible*, while others may not be. A reversible causal effect is essentially one where we can increase or decrease an outcome by increasing or decreasing the cause. For example, when rates of smoking increase in the population, lung cancer rates increase, and when rates of smoking decrease, lung cancer rates decrease.

An *irreversible* causal effect is one where an increase in X changes Y, but a subsequent decrease in X does not reverse the change in Y. When individuals smoke, their probability of lung cancer increases. However, decreasing smoking when they already have cancer will not reduce the disease. At the population level, then, the effect of smoking on lung cancer is reversible; at the individual level, it is not.[34] An irreversible causal process between X and Y does not mean that Y is irreversible. Some other causal force may be capable of reducing Y.

Many of these types of causal relationships and others may exist in systems. They can influence system effectiveness and efficiency and are relevant because they can help us to characterize, understand, and change systems. Not everything in systems can be changed. In addition, not all changes that can be made should be made or will provide much of a return. We may be able, though, to readily change some parts and produce large returns. What we need is the ability to identify those parts. We then may be able to leverage mechanisms to manipulate inflows and outflows throughout the system to improve effectiveness and efficiency.[35] Awareness of possible causal relationships can help us to better describe, explain, and predict system behavior and the current or likely effects of different parts of the system.

3.6 SYSTEMS: THEORY

Theory as Description and Understanding

"There is nothing more practical than a good theory."[36] Indeed, theory is indispensable for understanding the social world (a goal for scientists) and changing it (a goal for policymakers, government and program officials, and practitioners). The argument here is that a systems view of the world is, in and of itself, a theoretical perspective.

A starting point in advancing this argument begins with a question: What is theory? Scholars have long debated what theory is and how to construct and evaluate it.[37] A conventional view is that theories amount to generalizations or laws, or sets of interrelated propositions or axioms.[38] They help us to describe and explain or predict social phenomena. Description and explanation or prediction go hand in hand.

Accurate description requires some frame of reference – a theory – for understanding what something "is" or "means." Viewed in this light, theory helps us to characterize or apprehend a phenomenon. Clifford Geertz has provided an illustration of the importance of this task.[39] His starting point begins with the act of blinking one's eyelid. We might describe this act in considerable detail, including an account of the physiology of blinking. However, doing so would get us no closer to understanding when a blink is a "wink." To know when "winking" occurs, we need to know something about culture, or meaning systems, and how blinks can serve as "winks" and have variable meanings in different contexts. For example, a wink might be used to flirt with someone or to convey that one is "just joking." Without knowledge of how to describe something, we are left either missing that something entirely or mischaracterizing it. We miss that a blink was a wink and we classify a joking wink as a flirtatious wink. A systems theoretical perspective, like other theoretical perspectives, provides a lens through which to describe the nature and meaning of different phenomena.

Description alone does not suffice. Theory provides a *causal* account of how different factors combine in some way to produce other factors. Establishing causal explanations arguably constitutes the central goal of science.[40] To establish causality, however, requires first an ability to describe the phenomena and the various factors thought to influence it, and then an ability to describe the effects of the phenomena. A causal account thus is simultaneously a descriptive and an explanatory undertaking. We might view description and explanation as synonymous with prediction: to explain something is to describe and identify how it works and to predict something is to use a descriptive or explanatory framework to anticipate how one or more phenomena may give rise to others. When our predictions fall short, our descriptions or explanations do so as well. Conversely, if our descriptions and explanations are defensible – that is, if they describe reality accurately – they should be capable of predicting causal relationships.[41]

In short, theory guides how we describe particular phenomena and, indeed, guides us in what we can "see." At the same time, it provides the foundation for explaining the causal relations that produce these phenomena and their effects. Theory provides predictions that we can test, and if the tests support the theory, we feel more confident that perhaps we understand the phenomena accurately, if perhaps only in part. Viewed in this way, description, explanation, and prediction all are part and parcel of the same undertaking.

For scientists, a causal understanding of the nature of the natural or social world serves to advance knowledge for "knowledge's sake." For policymakers and practitioners, this understanding serves as the foundation for guiding their actions. The hope is that a given policy, program, or practice will contribute to particular goals or outcomes. For scholars and policymakers alike, then, theory and causality are of direct relevance to their respective goals.

A Systems View as Theory

A systems view of the social world can be viewed as a theory. First, at its most general, a systems view anticipates that systems exist and that they have consequences. Second, a systems view anticipates, too, that systems typically consist of a range of elements and subsystems. Third, these elements and subsystems combine – in interaction with one another – to produce outcomes. Fourth, the processes include stocks and flows, inputs and outputs, and linear, nonlinear, and other causal relationships within and across parts of a system. Fifth, a systems view anticipates that external forces will influence system activities and, in turn, anticipates how well the system achieves its goals. Sixth, and not least, a systems view anticipates that successful systems are hierarchical, self-organizing, and resilient.[42] Those that function at a high level – with effective integration of efforts across the system – are more likely to achieve their goals. These concepts are central to a systems view of social phenomena, and so warrant discussion.

Hierarchy refers to parts that are clustered within subsystems and to subsystems that are clustered within systems. This hierarchical arrangement creates efficiency by enabling higher-level organizational structures to coordinate lower-level structures. Such an arrangement, when designed and implemented well – with enough centralized oversight and control to ensure effective coordination of efforts but not so much as to interfere with subsystem operations – enables systems to better achieve their goals.[43]

Self-organization refers to the ability of a system to change its structure and design to achieve efficiencies or adapt to changing circumstances or goals. Self-organization contributes to resiliency and an ability to thrive. Any individual, organization, or system that can change how it works will be better positioned over the long term to adapt and succeed. Conversely, those that wait for circumstances to dictate change will be less likely to adapt or succeed.

Resilience here can be viewed as the ability of a system to adapt to and survive in the face of changing conditions.[44] That does not mean that such systems stay the same. Rather, they are sufficiently flexible so as to be able to adapt to, and possibly become stronger because of, changes in the external environment. Nassim Taleb has described systems that are designed to become stronger in the face of change as "antifragile."[45] Such systems do not simply "survive" or do passably well, which the notion of resilience suggests: they become stronger. They thrive.

Consideration of these dimensions can be used to anticipate conditions under which systems fail or succeed. Many systems, in fact, do not perform well. Such systems may have hierarchical arrangements that are incomplete or poorly designed and may be limited in their capacity to self-organize.

By extension, they are unlikely to be resilient or to thrive. They may, for example, be vulnerable to external forces and to a situation in which subsystems dictate overall system functioning. In short, they may operate "suboptimally."[46]

Other systems operate at a "passably performing" level. A hierarchical arrangement exists, but it may be incomplete, and within-subsystem and between-subsystem efforts likely are not well-integrated. In addition, the ability to adapt to external forces is limited. Bureaucratic rigidity may further limit subsystems' ability to change and may institutionalize inefficiency.

Still other systems operate effectively and efficiently. These successful systems typically have clearly and logically integrated hierarchical arrangements. They have the flexibility to adapt to circumstances. They can and do reorganize their structure and activities to achieve their goals. Those that can withstand sudden change might be said to be "resilient," while those that proactively plan and adjust to create substantial improvements might be said to be, in Taleb's language, "antifragile," or thriving.

Figure 3.2 illustrates these three conceptually distinct situations: systems that fail or barely survive, systems that passably perform, and systems that are resilient and/or that thrive. The figure serves to highlight the importance of system functioning. Improvements in functioning should, as a logical matter, generate improved outcomes and goal achievement, and thus, success.

An important theoretical and empirical question for scholarship and policy is how system functioning and success are related. The figure portrays several possibilities. First, improvement in functioning, when proceeding from very low-level functioning, might result in markedly higher levels of success. Similar levels of improvement, however, at higher levels of functioning, may produce small improvements in outcomes. This situation is reflected in the top line, designated "rapid improvement initially." Second, returns on improved functioning might plateau and result in "passably performing" success. Achieving high levels of success in this situation may require very high levels of functioning. This situation is reflected in the second line. Third, and as shown in the third (straight, or linear) line, returns on improved functioning may be constant: each additional amount of improved functioning generates a constant and proportionate amount of increased success. Fourth and finally, improved functioning may not generate much system success until a high level of functioning is achieved, which can be seen in the bottom line.

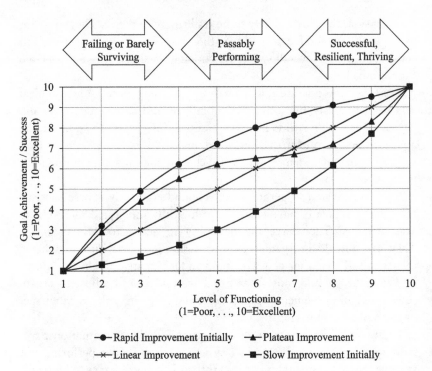

FIGURE 3.2 System Goal Achievement or Success and Level of Functioning: Failing or Barely Surviving vs. Passably Performing vs. Thriving

In all of these situations, improved functioning leads to improved system success. Yet they reflect highly different levels of success. For scholars, identifying the "functional form" of the X-Y relationship – that is, precisely how Y (success) is related to X (functioning) – and what explains it, is of theoretical and empirical interest in its own right. For policymakers and practitioners, the relationship matters for more pragmatic reasons. If, for example, the "slow improvement initially" pattern (the bottom line) characterizes a system's operations and effectiveness, then improving functioning will achieve little until and unless a relatively high level of functioning is attained. Much the same holds for the "plateau" situation.

Knowledge of how system success and functioning are related thus can provide critical insight into the potential returns, including cost-efficiency, of improving system functioning and, conversely, the costs of allowing system functioning to worsen.[47] From a policy perspective, an important insight that emerges from awareness of such possibilities is the risk of assuming that poor system functioning will achieve high levels of success and that the simple boosting of one part of a system (e.g., prisons) will somehow compensate for poor system functioning.

A benefit of a systems theoretical perspective is the ability to conceptualize and anticipate just such a problem. The toolkit for adopting this perspective entails consideration of system hierarchy (including elements and subsystems), self-organization (including interactions and dynamic processes, such as stocks and flows, within the system and in interaction with external forces), and resilience and the ability to thrive. These dimensions all inhere in the very notion of what a system entails. A systems view leads us to focus on these dimensions and to identify the conditions under which systems succeed. It also leads to a focus on system integration, or functioning, and the consequences for policy of focusing on only one or another delimited aspect of a system without consideration of the broader, systems context.

Theory sometimes is equated with a variety of terms: "perspective," "model," "conceptual framework," "paradigm," and so on. I do not seek here to debate the merits of different views or approaches to theory. Rather, I want only to highlight that a systems view of crime and justice provides a unique vantage point from which to describe and explain both. Many accounts of crime ignore systems entirely. They focus on this or that causal variable alone. For example, a theory might examine a particular causal force, such as self-control, and how it contributes to offending, or how structural inequality contributes to higher crime rates. Alternatively, a theory might focus on explaining why social control, such as incarceration-as-punishment, is applied more to some groups than to others. These approaches have much to recommend them. Yet, they leave largely unexamined the way in which crime and justice are intertwined within a larger context. A focus on this context – the criminal justice system – and its structure and dynamics provides an opportunity to provide a different, and potentially powerful, account of crime and justice. A systems focus, too, provides a foundation for understanding how public safety and justice may be increased, and how such benefits might be achieved more efficiently.

The Importance of Not Committing to a Particular Theory

What is advocated here is a systems approach to understanding crime and justice – that is, an approach that involves thinking about systems and their many parts, how they work, the conditions under which they do not work well, and how they might be changed or improved to achieve the goals that society sets for them. What I do not advocate is a commitment to a particular theory or approach to theorizing. Why? One reason is that debates about how *best* to theorize ultimately are unlikely to be resolved. A second is that critical insights about systems can and do come from those who work within them, and these individuals or groups are unlikely to hew to a particular theoretical perspective, at least not one that scholars have formally articulated and published in books and journals.[48] A commitment to a particular theory or even an approach to theorizing thus risks imposing blinders that forestall generation or inclusion of important insights. Finally, no one theory would suffice for examining an entire system and its parts. For example, one theory might be useful for understanding police relations with residents in high-crime neighborhoods, another may be useful for understanding how prosecutors make decisions, and still another might be useful for understanding why inmates behave in certain ways in prison. Accordingly, an understanding of systems requires that we draw on theories that help us to describe and explain the different parts of a given system.

A systems view has the benefit of leading us to consider how different structures and activities interact with one another to produce a variety of outcomes through a series of causal chains. This view takes seriously the insight from a large body of social science that finds that much of social life entails multiple causation.[49] Indeed, little in life appears to operate "net" of other factors.[50] Disorder in a prison system, for example, does not likely result from any one facet of individuals, groups of individuals, or officers, but rather from how these individuals and groups interact, and the larger prison, and prison system, contexts within which they reside.[51]

This benefit comes with the cost of creating complicated models about how the world may work. That means relying on multiple theories about different parts of a system as well as its overall operations. Such complexity is, however, necessary for shedding light on important issues and dynamics if the world itself is complicated. The benefit also comes at the cost of simplifying much of this same world. As with all social scientific endeavors, simplified renderings are necessary to apprehend how the world works.[52] A systems analysis, for example, requires honing in on the parts of this system that interact to produce outcomes. Any accounts, then, of the structures and activities of systems necessarily "are simplifications of the real world."[53] Much as directors must do when they turn a book into a movie, scientists must zero in on aspects of a system that likely are essential. No cookie-cutter methodology for doing so exists.

Theory ultimately entails a good-faith effort to identify patterns and phenomena and to identify what gives rise to them and what their effects are or may be. It does not entail a commitment to a particular theory or a particular approach to theorizing.[54] This view neatly accords with evaluation of policies and programs. One of the first steps in any evaluation entails trying to describe the causal logic of these efforts:[55] what are the critical parts of the policy or program and how do various activities contribute to particular goals? A similar mindset is central to a systems approach. Indeed, a systems view of crime and justice can lead us to think about how a seemingly diverse set of activities and conditions may in fact be related.

3.7 CONCLUSION

Systems affect the world around us, and yet are difficult if not impossible to "see." We must infer their existence indirectly. That does not make their existence less real. It simply means that we must look for and identify them. As a starting point, we must know to do so. That accords with how science proceeds: when we look at the world from a certain angle, we gain insight into it.[56] Among the core dimensions that guide our ability to detect and analyze systems are identification of goals and outcomes as well as the elements, subsystems, and structures, or parts, that combine or interact to achieve these goals and outcomes. Stocks and flows, inputs and outputs, and the multifaceted dynamics among the various parts – these, too, help us to characterize a system and how well its operations function and lead to system success.

Many approaches exist to describe and examine systems. All of them, though, emphasize a core idea: systems follow an internal logic, one that involves hierarchical arrangements, some level of self-organizing, and a need to respond to external forces and adapt to change. Systems have a life of their own and are more than the sum of their parts. That does not mean that they are well-designed or operate well, or that they achieve their goals. Indeed, all too frequently they do not. For society, systems problems ultimately are societal problems.

This insight has long been, and continues to be, recognized by some scholars, policymakers, and practitioners. Yet, paradoxically, it also has gone largely unaddressed both in studies of many social phenomena and in policy efforts. That may be due to a variety of factors, such as the complexity that inheres to studying and changing systems.

If, however, we are to understand better the world around us and to create large-scale improvements, we need to prioritize a focus on describing, understanding, and changing systems. Failing to do so opens the door to a continued situation of the "tail wagging the dog" – that is, a situation in which the lack of a captain and the presence of many "squeaky wheels" vying for attention leads to gross inattention to critical problems and excessive attention to others. This misprioritization results in insufficient attention being paid to changes in systems that could prevent harm and increase benefits. In short, systems and their management matter for achieving societal goals.

4

The Criminal Justice System

Scholars, policymakers, and practitioners seemingly understand that criminal justice operates as a system. Yet efforts to reform and examine this system typically have focused on isolated parts, not the system as a whole.[1] One exception to this pattern is the work of a few criminologists, such as Alfred Blumstein, in the 1960s. They used operations research to describe, understand, and evaluate criminal justice systems.[2] However, that approach fell by the wayside in the 1970s. It recently has begun to resurface, as evidenced by scholars' calls for comparisons between countries and states to highlight the systems nature of criminal justice.[3] A prominent illustration comes from David Garland's Sutherland address at the 2012 American Society of Criminology. In it, he featured David Downes' work, which identified ways in which criminal justice systems in Wales and England, respectively, created differences in rates of imprisonment. In Wales, the criminal justice system was more tightly coupled, with checks in place to impede unsustainable prison growth.[4] By contrast, in England, sentencing decisions were largely uncoupled from the rest of the criminal justice system. According to Downes, that enabled growth to occur largely unchecked. The analysis showed that *systems* vary greatly in ways that do not neatly correlate with crime rates.[5]

Despite such work, the fact remains that research, as Sheldon Messinger emphasized in his analysis of the California prison system, has tended to focus on bits and pieces of the criminal justice system.[6] That is understandable. A focus on discrete aspects of crime and justice lends itself more readily to empirical study. This emphasis is important because criminology views itself as a science and in so doing places a premium on quantitative analysis.[7] This approach, though, puts the field in the position of ignoring tidal forces because they are difficult to assess with precision, and prioritizing the study of eddies because they are easier to study with methodological rigor. Researchers focus, for example, on the analysis of sentencing decisions, desistance among a particular cohort of individuals, or the effectiveness of a particular program in reducing recidivism. At the same time, they largely ignore the ways in which system dynamics affect public safety, justice, accountability, and cost-efficiency.

A similar problem attends to policymaking and practice. Policymakers hold office for brief stints of time and may understand little about the criminal justice system or its parts. Even so, they may discern, and indeed frequently argue, that "the system" needs to be fixed. The resulting "reforms" they pass, however, focus on narrowly construed changes that ignore "the system." Consider shifts in sentencing laws. Legislators might decide to enact some form of "mandatory sentencing." It seems simple and reasonable. Why not ensure that specific crimes result in specific types of punishment? Such a change, however, involves a critical leverage point within the criminal justice system: the prosecution, and along with it the plea-bargaining, of large numbers of individuals. All at once, an entire system can be shifted by this seemingly small "reform." The end result? More expense, little to no clear progress toward safety or justice, and expansion of the criminal justice system. It is analogous to allowing a plane that leaves a particular city to veer off a degree or two after takeoff. It will not likely reach its destination and more likely will wind up far off course.

The goal of this chapter is to describe how criminal justice *is* a system, one that in turn involves several subsystems. Along with the previous chapter, it lays the foundation for anticipating the contours and justification of the Systems Improvement Solution. This chapter begins first by discussing contemporary crime and justice trends nationally and the critical stakes involved for society. It discusses the goals of the criminal justice system and the different structures, parts, or subsystems – including law-making, law enforcement, courts, probation, prison, and parole – that it comprises. It discusses, too, the external forces that can affect each subsystem and the system as a whole, as well as different dynamics that occur within and across this system. Not least, it discusses the importance of theory to understanding how criminal justice is a system, with parts and subsystems that operate independently and interdependently.

The primary purpose of these discussions is to highlight how criminal justice operates as a system. Another purpose is to highlight the consequences of ignoring this fact, which include flawed policy and practice and missed opportunities to reduce crime and improve justice, accountability, and efficiency. A solution to this situation is sorely needed. Of necessity, it must, I argue, be systems-focused if we want substantial and sustainable improvements.

4.1 CONTEMPORARY CRIMINAL JUSTICE AND THE STAKES INVOLVED

The criminal justice system consists of different activities or domains. These include law-making, law enforcement, the courts, probation, and the administration of intermediate sanctions, jails, prisons, and parole. They collectively serve to promote public safety and justice. If our criminal justice system is ineffective or inefficient, then society suffers, whether through more crime, more injustice, wasted expenditures, or some combination of these harms. To set the stage for discussing this system and how its effectiveness and efficiency may be improved, we start with an overview of the contemporary context of American criminal justice and the financial and human stakes at play. We then will zero in on specific goals and outcomes that provide the basis for determining whether criminal justice as a system is effective.

Our initial context begins with the dramatic shift in policy in the 1980s that greatly raised the stakes for offenders and society. Historically unprecedented "get-tough" legislation in this era stemmed in part from the view that violent crime and property crime were out of control.[8] In fact, as can be seen in Figure 4.1 – based on estimates from the National Crime Victimization Survey (NCVS) – violent crime consistently ranged from between 40 and 50 per 1,000 persons age 12 or older throughout the 1970s and into the 1980s, and property crime steadily declined from the late 1970s onward.[9] There was no historically remarkable crime wave.

Indeed, if anything was remarkable, it was the steady, continuing decline in property crime. That alone might have been taken as a basis for substantial confidence in the criminal justice system. However, any such inference either was ignored or offset by concern about a short-term trend from 1986 to 1991, when violent crime rose from 42 to 49 victimizations per 1,000 persons age 12 or older. Policymakers reacted as if this trend was unprecedented and would continue indefinitely. They ignored the fact that the violent crime rate at its peak was consistent with violent crime rates throughout the 1970s. In addition, they seemed to assume that the short-term increase stemmed from social changes in America that

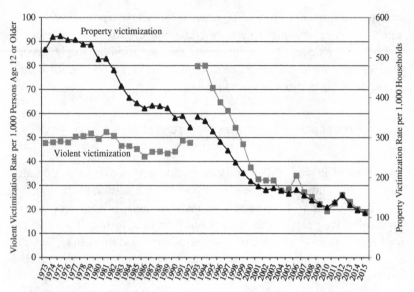

FIGURE 4.1 Violent Crime and Property Crime Victimization Rates, 1973–2015

reflected a dramatic weakening of the social fabric. Society somehow was coming apart at the seams. These changes included an apparent rise in drug abuse and drug-related offending as well as rapidly rising homicide rates. Such trends were viewed as a result of the failures of past criminal justice policies, including rehabilitation, and the failure to send a clear signal to would-be law violators.[10] Highly publicized news accounts that pointed to a rise in "super-predators" reflected and fueled such thinking.[11] These views proceeded from incorrect assumptions. Among the more prominent such assumptions was the belief that violent crime increases were historically unusual, that they would continue indefinitely, and that past policy efforts were uniformly ineffective.

One response is to say that crime actually was out of control, by historical standards, and that the NCVS failed to capture that fact. It is true that crime trends identified by the NCVS provide a less-than-fully accurate view of crime. Even so, the NCVS provides the best national estimates that exist of crime. As importantly, crime trends identified using the NCVS correlate with trends identified using the Federal Bureau of Investigation's (FBI's) Uniform Crime Reporting (UCR) data. Some differences exist between the two sources in estimated crime, and they reflect a number of methodological differences in the measurement of crime. The UCR program, for example, relies on police reports, and so, only on what citizens bring to the attention of law enforcement; the NCVS asks citizens about their experiences with victimization. The UCR includes crimes against businesses, the homeless, and institutionalized populations; the NCVS does not. The UCR program excludes simple assault; the NCVS includes it. These and other methodological differences create divergent estimates of crime in any given year and of crime over time.[12] Yet, the *trends* that they identify are similar. Homicide rates, for example, which the UCR tracks but the NCVS does not, increased from 1986 to 1991 – from approximately 8 homicides to 10 homicides per 100,000 residents – and then steadily declined thereafter.[13] That pattern reflects the broader trend for violent crime identified by both the UCR and the NCVS.

There was, in short, no clear crime-based need to dramatically alter punishment policies and practices. What, though, about drug-related crime? Given the pronounced attention by lawmakers to such crime, perhaps a new problem in fact existed. There is no question that from 1986 to 1991, violent crime increased (while property crime decreased) and that drugs were "implicated." They somehow were part and parcel of some of the short-term increase in crime. However, their causal role was and remains unclear.[14] Consider homicide, which garners more policymaker and media attention than most crimes. In 1991 – the peak year in the rise in violent crime – the percentage of all homicides that were drug-related was 6.2 percent, only about 2 percent higher than in previous years and only slightly higher than what occurred in subsequent years as homicide rates declined.[15] Yet, policymakers viewed crack cocaine and other illegal drugs as a cause of a violent crime "epidemic." They framed drug use as a criminal rather than public health problem, and they enacted a plethora of policies that penalized illegal drug possession and use. When coupled with substantial increases in funding for police, the courts, and corrections, the end result was dramatic growth in arrests, convictions, incarceration, and lengthier prison sentences for drug-related offending.[16]

Guns, too, were thought to have contributed to crime. However, consistent and strong evidence to support this claim also is limited. No question, guns may be "implicated," or somehow associated with, criminal activity. But their causal role remains far from clear. For example, guns can facilitate some crimes and impede others, and they may result in more injury or, possibly, less.[17] Also, crime can occur regardless of the availability of a gun or some other weapon. More relevant perhaps is the fact that guns are widely prevalent in America and were so *before, during,* and *after* the temporary spike in violent crime in the late 1980s.

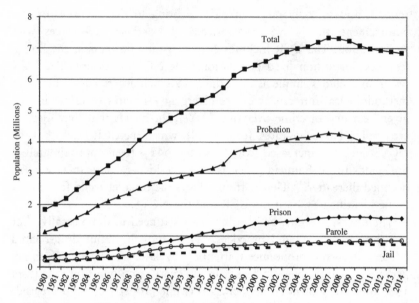

FIGURE 4.2 US Adult Correctional Supervision Populations, 1980–2014

There was, then, some cause for alarm in the late 1980s: even though property crime was declining, violent crime was increasing and lawmakers did not know if it would plateau. More precisely, they assumed that it would not stabilize or decline and that instead it would escalate. (Crime in fact dramatically declined, beginning in the early 1990s.) That led to historically unprecedented increases in get-tough legislation and expansion of criminal justice, a shift that continued through subsequent decades and was facilitated by Democrats and Republicans alike.

The growth can be illustrated by focusing on corrections, including probation, parole, prisons, and jails. As shown in Figure 4.2, from 1980 to 2014, the total population under correctional supervision grew from 1.8 million to 6.9 million, a 270 percent increase that well exceeded national population growth.[18] The increase was steady and sustained. It began several years before the late-1980s violent crime increase, it continued throughout the 1980s and 1990s, peaked in 2007 at 7.3 million, and then stabilized at approximately 7 million.[19] Although considerable attention focused on the increase in incarceration – and contributed to an emerging literature on "mass incarceration" and prisoner reentry[20] – probation and parole populations dramatically increased as well and greatly expanded the web of formal social control.

The use of corrections, however, was not and is not evenly distributed across regions or states.[21] In absolute numbers, the correctional population, as of 2014, is much greater in the South (2.8 million), followed by the Midwest (1.4 million), the West (1.3 million), and, last, the Northeast (almost 1 million), as shown in Figure 4.3. In addition to regional differences, there exist marked within-region differences. For example, among southern states, Texas and Georgia stand well above the others; Texas, Georgia, and Florida collectively account for 59 percent of the total southern correctional population. Texas and Georgia supervise roughly the same number of individuals (45 percent) as the 14 other southern states combined, Florida included. The most marked within-region difference is the west. California, for example, supervises almost half (46 percent) of all adults under correctional supervision in the 13 western states.

These variations partly reflect total state populations. Maine, New Hampshire, and Vermont have small correctional populations because they have relatively few citizens. Even so, after adjusting for population size, states still vary greatly in their use of corrections. Indeed, the range in the use of corrections, after adjusting for population size, is remarkable, as can be seen in Figure 4.4. It includes a low of 940 adults on supervision to a high of 7,580 adults on supervision per 100,000 adult residents. Georgia clearly constitutes an outlier. Its rate of correctional supervision (7,580) exceeds that of the next closest state, Idaho (4,010), by over 3,000 per 100,000 adult residents. What explains the variation in these rates? Differences in crime may account for some of it, but not most of it.[22] The bulk of variation likely stems from variation in the effectiveness of state and local efforts in reducing crime and recidivism and in philosophical views about appropriate approaches to and amounts of retribution and justice. Garland, for example, has written, "Whereas in other nations, and in earlier periods of American history, probation and parole aimed to promote rehabilitation and resettlement (or 'reentry' as it is now known), in America today they are oriented toward surveillance, policing and risk management."[23]

A clear and simple consequence of criminal justice and correctional system growth is cost. States, including local jurisdictions within states, spend a great deal on criminal justice and corrections.[24] Nationally, in 2012 (the latest year for which national statistics are available), states, including the District of Columbia, spent over $212 billion on corrections. They vary, however, in their expenditures. As can be seen in Figure 4.5, California's spending on corrections, $37 billion, greatly exceeds the spending of other states. And five states – California, New York, Texas,

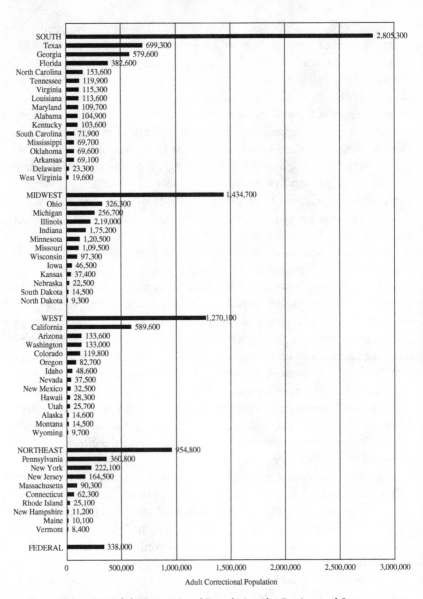

FIGURE 4.3 US Adult Correctional Population, by Region and State, 2014

Florida, and Pennsylvania – collectively spent $93 billion on corrections in 2012, or 44 percent of all state corrections spending nationally.

The investment in corrections as a percentage of state spending provides additional context for understanding the stakes at play and the need

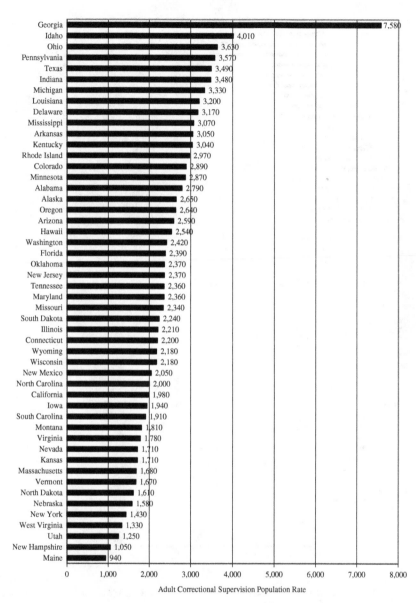

FIGURE 4.4 US Adult Correctional Supervision Population Rate, per 100,000 Residents, Age 18 or Older, by State, 2014

for examining systems, not just their parts. As shown in Figure 4.6, a considerable percentage of state budgets goes both to criminal justice (police and courts) and to corrections (probation, parole, jails, and prisons). The percentage varies from a low of 4 percent in Maine to a high of

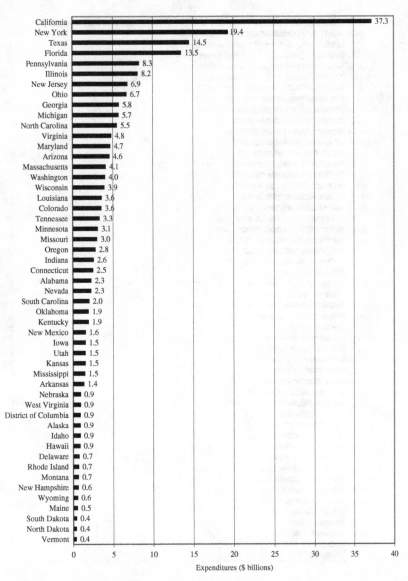

FIGURE 4.5 US Criminal Justice (Police and Courts) and Corrections Expenditures, by State and Washington, DC, 2012

10 percent in Nevada, in 2012. In larger states such as California and Florida, the relatively large percentage of the state budget that goes to criminal justice and corrections obligates disproportionately greater

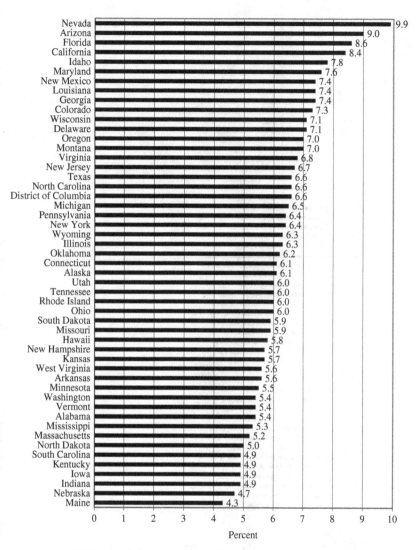

FIGURE 4.6 US Criminal Justice (Police and Courts) and Corrections Expenditures as a Percentage of Total State Expenditures, by State and Washington, DC, 2012

amounts of funds than similar percentages do in states such as Nevada and Idaho that are much smaller.

Population differences among states do not explain this investment difference. Nationally, states spent 7 percent of their total budgets on corrections, and per capita spending on corrections was $676 per person. State-level variation around this average is considerable. As can be seen in

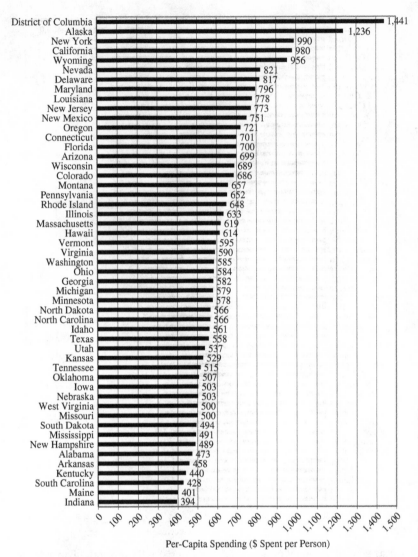

FIGURE 4.7 US Criminal Justice (Police and Courts) and Corrections Per-Capita Expenditures, by State and Washington, DC, 2012

Figure 4.7, the range entailed a low of $394 per person (Indiana) and a high of $1,441 per person (the District of Columbia). Nevada devoted 10 percent of its budget to corrections, placing it at the top among states that devote a large percentage of their spending to the police, courts, and the correctional system. In addition, its per-capita spending, $821 per person, well exceeded that of the national average. By contrast, Alaska, which spent 6 percent of its total budget on corrections – placing it near the middle of percentage spending among states – had the *highest per-capita* spending ($1,236 per person) of any state. (The District of Columbia, which had the highest per-capita spending nationally, spent 7 percent of its budget on corrections, the same percentage as was spent nationally.) Maine, which devoted the smallest percentage of the state-wide budget to corrections, had the second-lowest per-capita spending on corrections ($401 per person); Indiana had the lowest per-capita spending. California, which spends the most on corrections annually, had a per-capita expenditure rate of $980, as compared to Texas, which was among the top five states in total expenditures on corrections, yet had a per-capita expenditure rate of "only" $558 in a context in which the national average was $676.

Investments in corrections also vary across functions. Nationally, 46 percent of all justice expenditures among states and the District of Columbia in 2012 went to support policing, 20 percent supported court (i.e., judicial and other legal) activities, and 34 percent supported corrections. Among states, however, the allocations by function vary greatly, as depicted in Figure 4.8. Some states invest proportionally more in policing. For example, Illinois and Missouri spent 56 percent of their justice funds on policing. By contrast, seven states – Alaska, California, Kentucky, Pennsylvania, West Virginia, Washington, and Wyoming – spent 40 percent or less of their justice funds on it. Conversely, some states invest proportionally more in corrections than do other states. For example, four states – Arkansas, Georgia, Pennsylvania, and South Dakota – invested 40 percent or more of their justice funds in corrections. By contrast, some states, such as Hawaii and Illinois, invested 25 percent or less in it. Most states spent between 18 and 22 percent of their justice funds on judicial and legal activities.

States thus devote dramatically different amounts of their budgets to crime and justice efforts. They do so over and above differences in population or crime rates. And they allocate their funds to police, court, and corrections functions differently. The end result is what amounts to 50 state experiments (51 if we include the District of Columbia) in addressing crime and justice. Yet, states by and large do not systematically justify these variations on evidence-based grounds.[25] They instead follow past practice, making modifications to these practices as they go along under the rubric of "reform." Reliance on research, much less assessment of the

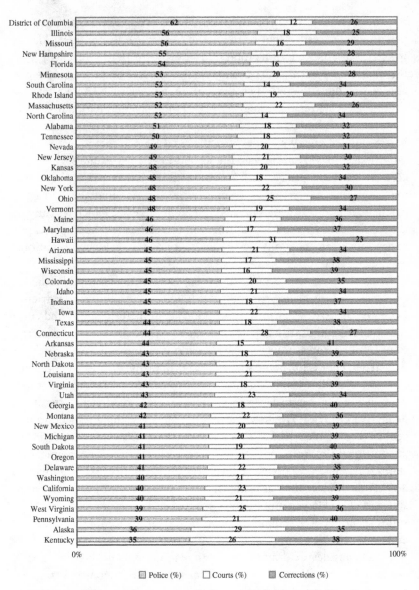

FIGURE 4.8 US Criminal Justice Expenditures, by Function (Police, Courts, and Corrections), by State and Washington, DC, 2012

systems context of criminal justice, typically is minimal and focused on narrow dimensions of crime and justice or, conversely, on broad, sweeping changes, such as hiring more police or toughening sentencing.[26] Whether these efforts improve public safety or justice, or do so in ways that minimize collateral consequences and harms, goes largely unmonitored and unchecked.

4.2 SYSTEMS: GOALS AND OUTCOMES

The entire reason for having a criminal justice system is to achieve societal goals. No one part or subsystems achieves these goals; rather, they do so collectively. What are these goals? As depicted in Figure 4.9, a number of system goals and outcomes exist.

One is public safety. An effective criminal justice system is one that reduces crime. This reduction can come through several pathways, or changes in specific outcomes. It can arise through reduced crime rates; for example, punishments might create a general deterrent effect. It can arise through reduced recidivism of sanctioned individuals, whether through rehabilitation, specific deterrence, incapacitation, or some combination of these and other mechanisms. And it can arise through reduced opportunities for crime to occur; for example, police and crime prevention efforts might result in more guardianship of individuals and places. We seek greater public safety in each instance. A highly cost-efficient

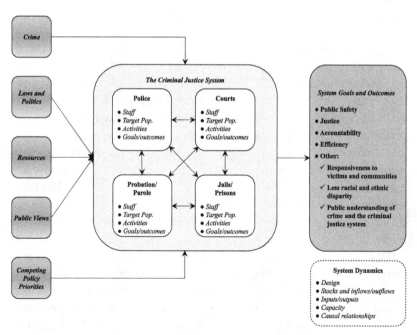

FIGURE 4.9 Criminal Justice Systems Model

system of criminal justice would invest in the balance of these different approaches that realized the most safety at the least cost.

A second important goal is justice. Citizens expect that the courts generate "just" outcomes. Offenders should be sanctioned, sentences should be "just," victims should be compensated, and errors of justice should be minimal to non-existent.[27] "Justice" may seem more tangible than crime, but it is no less important. Even so, it rarely gets assessed in studies of criminal justice policies and programs. Crime and recidivism instead get "top billing" because they seem more tangible and can be measured using police and court data.

Consider, for example, that while philosophers, policymakers, and the public all agree that justice is essential, they disagree about what exactly it is.[28] The very concept of "justice," for example, raises many complicated questions. What types of punishments result in an "appropriate" amount of retribution?[29] Even if we had an objective metric for calculating "retribution," how much would be appropriate for particular crimes? What punishments should be imposed when their effects may vary among different individuals or groups?[30] Is it "just" to invest less in prevention and more in punishment? Is it "just" to do so when the impacts of this investment may result in disproportionately more minorities being incarcerated?[31] Is a prison term for a parent "just" when it may adversely affect the parent's children? Is it "just" to impose punishments, such as housing and employment restrictions, that may adversely affect individuals and their families? How "just" is punishment that simultaneously may worsen an individual's physical or mental health? How much compensation to victims – including individuals and communities – of specific types of crimes is "just"? Whose opinions about what counts as "just" matter more, given that individuals and groups may vary in their views about such dimensions as appropriate crime prevention spending, punishments, emphasis on victims' rights, the extent to which we should invest in rehabilitation or crime prevention vs. punishment, and so on?[32] Not least, when criminal justice system goals, such as public safety, can be achieved through diverse strategies, which strategies would be most "just" to implement?[33]

Despite the importance of justice to any appraisal of our criminal justice system, few of these questions get answered in studies of this system. In addition, despite significant policy shifts in recent decades aimed at providing services to victims, the criminal justice system remains, by and large, focused primarily on offenders.[34] How well the criminal justice system accords with public preferences and views about "justice" remains largely unknown. We do know, however, that polls and studies typically find the public to be dissatisfied with how just or appropriate this system is its treatment of suspects, offenders, victims, families, and communities.[35]

A third goal is government accountability. Here, again, no clear consensus exists about definitions or criteria for determining the amount of accountability achieved by any governmental agencies or systems. However, accountability has been and remains a core feature of what policymakers and the public expect of agencies and systems.[36] A commonsense view of accountability sees government as being required to show that it has done what it is supposed to do and that it invests in effective policies. A broader view, one still grounded in common sense, is that government is accountable when it invests in policies, programs, and practices that accord with the evaluation hierarchy. That is, they are (1) needed, (2) grounded in credible theory, (3) implemented fully and well, (4) effective in achieving their intended goals and minimizing unintended harms, and (5) cost-efficient.[37]

The very notion of a hierarchy connotes accountability. The logic, for example, is that one should not target a problem that is not actually a problem or is not one that merits attention. If there exists a need for a policy, we should not implement one unless it rests on credible theory. If there exists a need for a policy and it rests on sound theoretical grounds, we should ensure that the policy is well implemented. Then and only then should we evaluate its impact. Not least, we then should assess whether the impact produced benefits that exceeded the costs of implementing the policy and whether the benefits-to-costs ratio exceeded that of other possible policies. From this view, government is not accountable when it invests in policies that are not needed, rest on weak theoretical grounds, or are implemented poorly, or when it invests in policies that could be effective but are implemented poorly or are less cost-efficient than others.

A fourth goal is efficiency. This goal is part of the emphasis on accountability. Policymakers and the public place a premium on the notion that taxpayer dollars should be used sparingly, carefully, and to the greatest effect. It is not enough that criminal justice policies, programs, and practices be effective. They should be the ones that maximize benefits and minimize costs. Despite the centrality of cost-efficiency as a goal, criminal justice by and large operates in an information vacuum. Although studies exist that examine the cost-efficiency of specific aspects of criminal justice, such as the costs and benefits of drug courts, they are not undertaken on a widespread basis across all aspects of criminal justice or for the system as a whole.[38] Regardless, it constitutes a core goal of criminal justice. An evaluation of any criminal justice system that ignored it would provide an imbalanced portrait of system performance.

There are still other goals that society expects criminal justice to achieve. Figure 4.9 identifies several, but its list is by no means exhaustive. For example, we want criminal justice systems to be responsive to victims and communities. That includes addressing citizen perceptions of safety and their satisfaction with the police, courts, corrections, crime prevention efforts, and policymaker efforts.[39] It also includes assisting victims and communities in recovering from the negative impacts of crime and injustice.[40]

We also want criminal justice systems to not adversely affect some racial and ethnic groups more than others – that is, we want *less racial and ethnic disparity*. A system that achieves other criminal justice goals and does so without producing racial and ethnic disparity, or discrimination, is, all else equal, the more effective system. Sustained concerns about disparate treatment of minority offenders and communities and the disparate impacts of this treatment put this goal at the center of any evaluation of system performance.[41] Disparities may exist along other dimensions as well. Females and immigrants, for example, may experience disparate treatment. An effective system identifies and seeks to reduce any such disparities.

In addition, we want a criminal justice system that the public understands. Ideally, for example, the public accurately understands the amount and causes of crime as well as the operations, costs, and effects of the criminal justice system. To illustrate, when the public knows little about the practices and activities of the police, the courts, or prison system, there is the risk that this system will operate in a manner that does not comport with the public will. Similarly, if members of the public mistakenly believe that sentencing severity has lessened or if they underestimate the costs of incarceration, they may call for tougher punishment when they would not do so if they had correct information.

These possibilities do not exhaust the range of goals and outcomes relevant for evaluating the effectiveness of criminal justice. However, they capture those that are central. And their existence highlights the limitations of policy discussions and evaluations that narrowly focus on a particular outcome, such as recidivism, and ignore others that may be as or more important.

We should do the opposite. We should focus on the goals that matter, weight them, and then evaluate the success of our criminal justice systems in achieving each goal, especially goals that matter the most. Instead, what happens? Policymakers and criminal justice officials tinker. Sometimes they may be forced to do so. A police chief, for example, may be limited in how much and in what ways he or she can change in a department. Regardless, the end result is tinkering: small changes here and there in the eddies without appreciably affecting the tidal forces that govern the criminal justice system and its ultimate costs and effectiveness.

The stakes for society of having an ineffective and inefficient criminal justice system could not be higher. Crime goes up or does not decline as fast as it could. Errors of justice occur. Little accountability exists. And all the while, society pays for it. What is needed is a way to ensure that criminal justice systems are maximally accountable, effective, and efficient. A starting point is to focus on all relevant goals, monitor relevant outcomes within and across parts of the system, and then work to improve them efficiently.

4.3 SYSTEMS: ELEMENTS AND SUBSYSTEMS

In describing, analyzing, or changing a system, we want to identify core elements, including subsystems, that make up a given system. No set formula exists for doing so. When we can literally see a system, the task is easier. For example, if we view a car as a system, the task we face consists of identifying each particular element, or part, of the car. Even then, though, as discussed in Chapter 3, we face interesting challenges, such as determining which parts form their own coherent "whole" within the car. Some parts may serve to support air conditioning, other parts may constitute an engine, still other parts may make up the cabin, and so on. Collectively, they operate as a system of sorts that we view as a vehicle, one capable of transferring us from place to place in varying degrees of comfort, speed, fuel efficiency, and the like. When describing and analyzing a system that cannot be directly observed, we confront more challenges in "seeing" the system. But that does not make any given system less real.

Criminal justice systems have been described in many textbooks, scholarly books, journal articles, research reports, and more. Their core elements consist of an interrelated set of systems, which, in the context of the broader criminal justice system constitute subsystems. They include (1) law enforcement, or police, agencies; (2) courts; (3) probation and parole, sometimes termed "community supervision," as well a wide range of intermediate sanctions; and (4) jails and prisons. Figure 4.9 provides a simplified rendering of these four core subsystems and how collectively they make up the criminal justice system.

As can be seen in the figure, each subsystem itself can be viewed as a system in its own right. A police department, for example, constitutes a system, one comprising various elements, such as buildings, support staff, detectives, street officers, etc. Courts typically operate under administratively distinct arrangements and then are configured to handle a variety of cases. Here, again, various elements – including facilities, personnel, judges, and the like – come together to constitute a court system and simultaneously enable it to operate. Probation and parole may operate as distinct entities or may operate under a broader organizational arrangement, such as a department of corrections. In either scenario, there is, again, a distinct set of organizational and staffing arrangements that exist. Not least, jail and prison systems exist that operate independently of the police, courts, and probation and parole.

Each system has unique and sometimes overlapping goals. Broadly, they all seek to promote public safety, justice, accountability, and efficiency. Yet, they each do so in different ways or through different activities and through targeting different populations or areas. For example, prisons serve entire states, and their primary focus centers on incarcerated individuals. By contrast, the police might investigate specific crimes or patrol various neighborhoods. Prison staff might contribute to public safety by helping to reduce recidivism, while police might do so by helping contribute to the punishment of particular individuals (catching them and then letting the courts determine how to proceed) or by deterring would-be offenders in certain areas. The police also might be envisioned as problem-solving agents who identify potential causes of crime in certain areas and help community residents to address them.[42] Courts contribute to public safety and justice through the processes that they follow and decisions they make about guilt and punishment. In addition, they seek to process as many cases as possible. A failure to do so would result in a concomitant failure to promote public safety and justice. Notably, though, case processing pressures confront each subsystem, and one subsystem's failure to manage case processing well will affect other subsystems and, in turn, overall system performance.[43]

The criminal justice "system," then, really is in many respects like a car "system" that has different stand-alone components. When configured in a certain way, the car "works." It can be driven. When the different components of criminal justice work together well, they enable public safety, justice, accountability, efficiency, and other goals to be achieved.

But these goals cannot be achieved by one subsystem alone. Public safety, for example, will be minimal if prisons rehabilitate inmates and then these individuals return to communities that lack any appreciable police presence or opportunities to work and that have high crime rates. Likewise, justice cannot happen without the police and the courts doing their respective "jobs" and without some degree of coordinated activity. It is at once trite but no less relevant to observe that the courts require cases, and cases can only arrive at the court's doorsteps if the police make arrests. By the same token, if the police routinely make arrests in marginal cases – ones that perhaps may pass legal muster but provide no appreciable foundation for convictions or sanctions – they can clog the courts up to the point that they can barely do more than process paperwork.[44]

As detailed at the outset of this chapter, criminal justice expenditures across parts of the criminal justice system vary greatly, and this variation itself varies at regional, state, and local levels. There has been, in essence, a national and ongoing experiment in how to design, fund, and operate criminal justice systems.[45] Some states and localities invest proportionally more in policing than others (net of any differences in crime), others invest proportionally more in the courts, and still others invest proportionally more in corrections. In each instance, how the investments are allocated may vary. For example, one state might invest more in community supervision while another might invest more in prisons. The salient point is that system design, funding, and interactions among subsystems create the larger criminal justice system.

A related point is that the subsystems warrant attention in their own right. To understand how any given subsystem operates, it helps to know something about the larger systems context. Indeed, knowledge of the criminal justice system is paramount. At the same time, efforts to improve subsystems require description and understanding of these subsystems. Why? Each subsystem operates according to its own internal logic and is structured and operated differently.

Consider probation. Many accounts of criminal justice system ignore probation, even though it serves as the "workhorse" of the correctional system.[46] The rise in awareness about mass incarceration has led some observers to focus primarily on imprisonment. However, during the era of get-tough crime policy that began in the late 1970s, increases in the total number of individuals placed on probation greatly exceeded that of increases in the number of individuals incarcerated. The reason is simple. Prison cells are finite. Only so many individuals can be housed in them. By contrast, individuals can be, and are, added to probation officer caseloads ad infinitum.[47] Probation, as well as a variety of intermediate sanctions, may not seem like "tough" punishment. But in many cases they may be perceived by offenders as tougher than incarceration.[48] Regardless, the criminal justice system relies heavily on probation (and various intermediate sanctions) to achieve public safety, justice, and accountability. One reason is that they seemingly hold the promise of doing so in a cost-efficient manner. Probation costs less than incarceration, for example. If it can achieve comparable, or even near-comparable reductions in recidivism, then marked efficiencies arise. This potential explains why states and localities rely so heavily on probation and why almost three-fifths of the correctional population in the United States is supervised by probation departments.[49] Estimates indicate that probation costs roughly $3 per probationer per day and that incarcerating an individual costs almost $80 per day.[50] Of course, if the public sees probation as insufficient punishment or if probation fails to reduce recidivism any more than no sanction at all, then when probation occurs in lieu of no punishment we pay for something that gives us nothing in return. That amounts to a net loss.

Probation thus constitutes a critical part of the criminal justice system, one that affects this system but that also operates independently.[51] It serves a less serious and violent population than what one typically finds in prisons. It relies on supervision, support, referral for services, and a variety of conditions that individuals must meet, and it is used by courts for a range of purposes. For example, probation may serve as an alternative to no sanction, which in turn might reflect an appropriate use of probation as punishment or an effort to appear tough on crime. Probation also might serve as an alternative to prison. Here, then, it might be viewed as more cost-effective or appropriate for purposes of public safety and justice.[52]

The probation subsystem differs greatly from other parts of the criminal justice system. It has different staff, rules, procedures, and the like, and typically operates under its own administrative auspices. In addition, it may veer in different philosophical directions than other parts of the system. For example, it might emphasize rehabilitation more than do prisons. To illustrate, in a study I undertook of juvenile court sentencing in Texas, the chief of juvenile court probation in one large county steadfastly emphasized rehabilitation. He instructed officers to avoid recording minor violations that probationers committed. Why? The District Attorney hewed strongly to a different philosophy, one that emphasized retribution above all else, and so would likely seek stiff punishments of violators.[53]

All of these differences create a subsystem that stands on its own and follows its own logic. Even so, it is a system whose goals and operations affect and are influenced by other parts of the criminal justice system. The same can be said for the other major subsystems. Each emphasizes or pursues public safety and justice, yet does so through different means. Each also consists of elements – that is, organizations, divisions, units, and the like. Each, in turn, features prominently in creating something bigger: a criminal justice system.

4.4 SYSTEMS: EXTERNAL FORCES

Any system operates in broader contexts that can be likened to external forces. These forces can and do affect the system and its ability to achieve the goals that society sets for it. Criminal justice is affected by many such forces. As depicted in Figure 4.9, these can include crime, laws and politics, resource allocations, public views, and competing policy priorities. They may affect the entire system or specific subsystems in varying ways.

Crime would seem to be the most obvious force that affects criminal justice. Its role, however, is unclear. Emily Durkheim long ago observed that crime serves diverse functions in society.[54] Society needs crime, for example, to delineate boundaries of authority and the importance of collective adherence both to formal rules and laws and to informal, unwritten norms of conduct. If serious or violent crime entirely ceased, society then would focus on minor offenses. According to Durkheim, society "will become more sensitive to these minor offenses, which up to then had had only a marginal effect on them."[55] Durkheim wrote in the late 1800s and early 1900s. Had he lived in the era of the internet, he might well have emphasized this point even more. Today, regardless of how crime may be trending, a single crime can be covered instantly in hundreds and thousands of media outlets. For those who consume any news on a daily basis, it would be difficult, through the course of a year, not to read about a horrific crime that occurred somewhere in the United States or the world. Crime can feel to the public like a ubiquitous force that constantly threatens the social fabric.[56]

Such factors may explain why crime does not appear to be a primary determinant of the criminal justice system's activities. To be sure, if a clear surge in violent crime occurs, as was the case in the late 1980s, we can expect that states will take action. Even then, the course of action they take can and does vary. Nationally, the pendulum swung toward a tough-on-crime response. That response reflected disenchantment with rehabilitation and the dominance of conservative Republican leadership over a period of twelve years, beginning with President Ronald Reagan's tenure (1980–1988) and running through George H. W. Bush's presidency (1988–1992). The response nationally might well have been different had the same crime increase occurred during an era in which rehabilitation was embraced or during an extended period of rule under Democratic leadership.[57] Regardless, state-level variation can be seen even during large-trend shifts in policy. During the 1980s and 1990s, for example, states adopted many different strategies for preventing and responding to crime. Many of the strategies comported broadly with being "tough on crime." These, though, varied in design, scope, timing, funding, and more. Other changes did not neatly fit the broad-based trend. The emergence of drug courts is illustrative: states and local jurisdictions that adopted them sought to provide an approach that balanced rehabilitation and punishment and that simultaneously might improve the efficiency of the criminal justice system.[58] Similarly, although juvenile justice shifted toward a more punitive stance, a wide panoply of other changes emerged. These reflected a trend toward finding diverse ways to provide a more balanced set of strategies for reducing delinquency.[59]

Changes in laws and politics, including sentencing practices, constitute what may be the largest external forces that shape the criminal justice system. When legislators enact policies that provide for lengthier prison sentences, for example, they place pressure on the system to respond. If the policies empower prosecutors – as many sentencing guidelines do – then the dynamics throughout the system shift. Police may prioritize crimes that they know prosecutors will aggressively pursue. Public defenders may plea bargain more quickly because of the threat that a prison sentence presents to their clients. And judges may have less discretion in how influence cases, and prison systems may have to build more capacity. In short, the change may seem minor or straightforward, but, as a large body of research on sentencing has established, it is anything but that.[60] Similarly, when, as occurred under President Clinton, Congress allocates funding to hire 100,000 more police officers nationwide, ripple effects throughout the criminal justice system can be anticipated. More police translates into more arrests, for example, even if crime rates are falling. When prosecutors decide to automatically prosecute certain kinds of cases, such as domestic violence incidents involving victims who do not want to press charges, we can expect that there may be delays in processing cases and reductions in the percentages of cases successfully convicted, given that the victims may be unwilling to participate in the proceedings.[61] Many more examples could be given. But they would bring us back to the fact that the politicization of crime may drive criminal justice system policies, practices, and operations to a greater extent than crime rates or than what the public wants.[62]

Resource constraints and opportunities, too, may greatly influence criminal justice. When economies decline, taxpayer revenues do so as well. States and localities then must operate with smaller budgets. That can lead to across-the-board budget cuts or to targeted cuts. Crime and justice may get a break if policymakers prioritize them, as they typically did during economic downturns that occurred throughout the tough-on-crime era. In some cases, though, the declines dictate that cuts occur. Then, regardless of crime trends, the criminal justice system has to operate either more efficiently or produce less safety and justice than otherwise would occur. Funding opportunities, too, can shape the system. A case in point: in the 1990s, drug courts become increasingly popular. Federal funding was made available to support this growth. By the end of the decade, and persisting thereafter, drug courts proliferated throughout the country. As federal funding for these specialized courts dried up, local jurisdictions scrambled to find alternative funding sources.[63] In so doing, they of course had to make decisions about the allocation of scarce resources across all parts of the criminal justice system.

The influence of public opinion on the criminal justice system is at once obvious and, yet, not so obvious. America is a democracy. Citizens speak through their elected officials. In that sense, all criminal justice policy and practice reflects the "will of the people." At the same time, public opinion research clearly establishes that the public often does not understand basic facts about crime, the police, courts, jails, or prisons, that policymakers misread public sentiment, and that, contrary to typical lawmaker accounts, the public wants balanced approaches to reducing crime and improving justice. During some eras, there may be more public support for, say, the death penalty. Even then, however, public views favor balanced approaches. Selecting responses to only one question or another from a public opinion poll will not reveal that fact. Presenting responses to a wide range of questions will and does.[64] Such issues aside, how, or under what conditions, public opinion influences public policy or government agency practices remains unclear.[65] For example, which voices do legislators listen to the most? Do they react primarily to those views with which they agree? Few answers readily exist in response to such questions. Studies suggest that policymakers and government do respond to public opinion; it simply is unclear when or under what conditions they do so.[66] What can be stated unequivocally is that policymakers typically must rely on inferences about "the" public will. Why? States and local jurisdictions do not conduct regular public opinion polls about crime, the police, courts, prisons, and crime and justice policy. Legislators' inferences, not surprisingly, likely say more about their own views and political goals than they do about public views.

Finally, and not least, the criminal justice system can be shaped by competing policy priorities within and external to the system. Budget crises, educational reform, war, health care, welfare – these and many other issues compete for policymaker and public attention. In so doing, they can affect funding to criminal justice, the politicization or depoliticization of crime, attention to reforming various parts of the criminal justice system, concern about victims or racial or ethnic disparities, expanding or contracting corrections, and so on.

External forces can extend well beyond these examples. In each instance, our concern centers on the need to understand how they affect the criminal justice system. Failure to do so can result in a concomitant failure to understand the very design of this system. It can lead, too, to a failure to appreciate the factors that drives its internal operations and how these may affect public safety, justice, accountability, cost-efficiency, and other related goals.

4.5 SYSTEMS: DYNAMICS

As discussed in Chapter 3, systems consist of different elements, or parts, that interact. They do so in ways that affect one another and that result in "emergent properties" – that is, properties that go beyond the parts and do not result simply from the addition of them.[67] A car, for example, does not move through the accumulation of windows, seats, tires, axles, and the like. Rather, the interaction of all these parts (and, presumably, an engine and fuel tank) – when combined in the right way – results in a car that has the "emergent property" of being able to move when the accelerator is pressed.

Criminal justice is, likewise, a system that, by design, has "emergent properties." Many such properties can be identified. For example, public safety is supposed to result not from the actions of any one part of the system but from the effective interaction of all parts. To illustrate, the police make arrests, prosecutors prosecute, courts sanction, and corrections "corrects." Public safety then results, whether through reduced recidivism, rehabilitation, general deterrence, or other mechanisms. Of course, one might examine one subsystem, such as prisons, and conclude that a particular program is effective. That may be true. However, it obscures the fact that any such program itself exists only because the police make arrests and the courts process the individuals who are arrested. The criminal justice system is designed to improve public safety, and no one part serves to achieve that in isolation. Nor does public safety somehow reflect the addition of cumulative effects of isolated parts of the system. Subsystems may have discernible isolated effects, but broader public safety benefits accrue from how the system as a whole operates. Conversely, a poorly functioning criminal justice system may produce no public safety. Indeed, it may worsen it, and in so doing render largely insignificant any micro-level gains that particular subsystem programs achieve.

Similarly, justice cannot readily be achieved by the actions of only the police or the courts. It instead requires coordinated efforts. The police must be sufficiently present in a given community to respond to calls, investigate, apprehend suspects, and so on, and they must do so in a manner that is at once professional and responsive to citizen concerns and needs. Courts then must have the capacity to process cases fairly and, to the extent possible, accurately. If they receive "weak" cases from the police and operate with little capacity to do more than provide cursory reviews of these cases, then injustice to alleged offenders and to victims almost assuredly will result.[68] Those individuals who are placed on probation or sent to prison, too, have a right to anticipate equitable and humane treatment. And society has a right to expect that individuals who are under community supervision or are released from prison pose less of a threat than they did prior to criminal justice system intervention. Here, again, if correctional systems receive "weak" cases – that is, ones where individuals may not be guilty or may not warrant a formal sanction – they may amplify injustices to these individuals. They may amplify, too, other types of injustices, such as racial or ethnic disparities in arrest, convictions, and imprisonment.[69] When the individuals who are subject to these cases return to society and offend at higher rates than they otherwise would have, society pays for it. In short, justice, like public safety, constitutes an emergent property that emanates from the way in which the entire criminal justice system operates.

Numerous scholarly accounts document the "systems" nature of criminal justice.[70] The unifying theme across them is the emphasis on the system's design and on how processing decisions and activities influence one another. They do not occur in isolation. Rather, they are shaped and constrained by larger contexts and other parts of the criminal justice system as well as by external forces in society at large. Systems involve *stocks and flows*, so it is not surprising that many scholarly accounts focus on case-processing pressures. For example, they focus on how, when left unaddressed, these pressures distort decision-making and create errors, harms, and inefficiencies. Such results can, but need not necessarily, arise from deliberate actions on the part of any one individual or organization. They instead can result from the systems context in which decision-making occurs.[71]

As but one example, consider that slight differences in the processing of minorities may not be readily discernible at any one stage of criminal justice processing, but they can amplify differences that arose at prior stages of processing and ultimately result in large disparities in rates of imprisonment.[72] Another example: in prison systems, no one person may be responsible for the emergence of a poor or unprofessional officer culture. It might arise from limited monitoring of officers, a reliance on inexperienced hires, an influx of especially dangerous inmates who are forced into overcrowded facilities and who pose threats to staff, signals from administration that rules can be bent, and so on. And yet another example: among law enforcement departments, the police may come to focus primarily on arrests rather than on helping communities to identify and address crime-causing problems in their community, a dynamic that can arise when departments respond to lawmakers' pressures to demonstrate accountability. Problem-solving can be more difficult to evaluate; arrests are easier to count and may seem more clearly to reflect effective policing, even though they may constitute only one part of an overall strategy to promote public safety.[73]

In addition to the design and the stocks and flows of the criminal justice system, there are *inputs* and *outputs* that both define and shape the system. Recall that inputs are resources, such as the number of staff or available rehabilitative programs, that are used to create outputs, which can be viewed as the products of activities undertaken by individuals or units within a system. Any system requires inputs to produce outputs. Insufficient inputs affect system activities and thus outputs. For example, when too few police patrol streets, they cannot effectively monitor communities or deter would-be offenders. When insufficient funding exists to train officers, they will be less likely to effectively interact with residents. In turn, the residents come away dissatisfied and the police subsequently garner less cooperation in fighting crime or conducting investigations.[74]

Likewise, when prosecutors face unrealistic caseloads, they may dismiss cases that they should not, plea-bargain more aggressively than may be appropriate, and have little time to respond to victims' concerns.[75] And jails and prisons that lack rehabilitative programs, perforce, must limit provision of those that do exist to a relatively small proportion of inmates.[76]

The *capacity* of the system to function smoothly is another factor that defines and shapes the criminal justice system. The ability of this system to operate efficiently depends greatly on available inputs, the ability of sub-systems to generate outputs, and the ability for stocks and flows to and from different parts of the system to occur unimpeded. One of the most interesting dynamics to arise in American criminal justice was the hiring of 100,000 police officers nationwide during the Clinton presidency. This initiative instantly provided considerable capacity for departments to patrol streets, undertake community policing efforts, and make arrests. Court processing capacity had to increase and, in turn, so, too, did correctional system capacity.[77] They did not occur in lockstep fashion. Shortfalls necessarily, and predictably, arose at some stages of processing and caused logjams. Jails became overcrowded, case processing times in courts lengthened, and caseloads of community supervision officers increased.

Chapter 3 discussed different types of *causal relationships* that can exist in systems and that affect overall system effectiveness and efficiency. Similar types of relationships can and do arise in the criminal justice system. They are important for characterizing the operation of the system and how to improve it. Consider the following examples, which focus on law enforcement but have parallels in the courts, community supervision, and corrections. First, there may be a linear association between the number of police and the number of arrests. That is, the greater the number of police, the greater the number of arrests. Whether that relation-ship holds regardless of crime rates would be, of course, an interesting question for scholars to investigate and an important one for policy-makers to answer in seeking to achieve efficient returns on investment.

Second, the association might be curvilinear. As the ratio of officers to citizens gets larger, there may be disproportionately fewer arrests that occur. Why? Perhaps the more serious cases already have resulted in arrests. Accordingly, the police focus their efforts more on other activities. Monitoring the association between police-to-citizen ratios and arrest rates may provide insight into anticipating and understanding changes in police activities.

Third, there may be a tipping point. At some level of police presence, for example, there may be no appreciable deterrent effect on offending. Or at a certain level or presence, arrests may exceed the capacity of the local jail to house individuals, an effect that could arise if the police were making arrests in questionable cases. Regardless, overcrowding at the jail may cause the courts or jail administrators to take action, whether by increasing capacity, changing decision-making, or advocating for changes in how the police undertake their work.

Fourth, interaction effects may exist. Police efforts to patrol certain communities may provide some general deterrent effect. However, this effect may be more pronounced in areas where citizens simultaneously adopt opportunity-reducing strategies, such as increasing the lighting along their streets or yards or monitoring neighbors' houses.

Fifth, there may be dose effects. For example, sudden and large targeted police presence in high-crime areas might effectively disperse gangs and inhibit gang-related activity. By contrast, small, incremental additions to police presence in such areas might achieve little.[78]

Sixth, reciprocal effects – or what can be termed self-reinforcing effects of feedback loops – might arise. The police may view residents in a high-crime area with suspicion and hostility. Their attitudes and demeanors toward residents may engender ill will, especially among crime-prone groups and individuals. In turn, these groups and individuals may engage in more crime or may act aggressively toward the police, thereby contributing to greater police suspicion and hostility toward citizens. A vicious cycle of negative police-citizen interactions ensues.[79]

Seventh, direct or indirect effects might exist. For example, a community policing program might lead citizens to more frequently call the police for assistance. That is a direct effect. However, it may be that the presence of the program results in citizens having more interactions with the police and trusting them more. They become more likely to call the police for help. Here, then, we have an indirect effect, one that would be important to identify in efforts to enhance the effectiveness of community policing.

Eighth, police actions might create effects that arise instantaneously or that take many days, weeks, or even months to arise (temporal effects), and the actions might be concentrated in certain areas (spatial effects). Community policing efforts, for example, may not result in changed citizen perceptions for many months. Improvements might center primarily in areas where crime rates were only moderately severe and where the police presence was visible. Higher-crime areas or those that lie more spatially distal may experience no benefits.

Ninth, reversible or irreversible causation may result from police actions. For example, the police might not readily identify that crime has rapidly escalated in a particular area. This oversight may cause crime in the area to escalate even more rapidly. If the police then discern that a "hot spot" of crime has emerged, they may target it for intensive patrolling, which in turn might drive down crime. The causal effect was reversed. In some cases, however, a causal effect may not be reversible, or perhaps may not be easily reversible. Racial tensions in communities can intensify after instances in which video footage showcases what appears to be egregious police misconduct. If law enforcement agencies or the courts do not find cause to dismiss or convict the involved officers, riots may occur. Citizen mistrust of the police then may create little to no willingness to cooperate with law enforcement for months or even years, regardless of efforts that administrators and officers take to remedy the situation.

These examples all center on law enforcement, yet the identified types of causal relationships can be found in court, probation, and jail and prison subsystems as well as between them. Consider feedback loops. Perhaps because of get-tough laws, communities invest more heavily in hiring police officers. More arrests result. The courts convict more and send greater numbers of individuals to prison. Once there, individuals receive little rehabilitative programming or preparation for release back into society. Simultaneously, they face barriers to housing, employment, and participation in civic society. They recidivate. In turn, lawmakers perceive that crime is out of control and step up investments for aggressively policing communities. At the same time, probation officers and the courts toughen their stance toward offenders. Each part of the system contributes to a feedback loop that generates ever-greater growth in the system and, typically, in unknown public safety benefits.[80]

Another example: interaction effects. These permeate the criminal justice system and its subsystems. For example, at least three distinct sets of factors – individual-level characteristics of inmates, officers, and wardens; facility-level characteristics; and community-level characteristics – may interact to influence inmate behavior.[81] Similarly, success during reentry can be affected by many factors, including individual characteristics, family context, community context, and the quality and amount of supervision.[82]

In short, efforts to describe, understand, and predict how systems operate and what their effects are or will be require that attention be paid to system dynamics. Systems research is critical for devising ways to improve public safety, promote the most justice, create greater account-ability, and achieve these goals at the least cost. If, for example, one part of a system operates willy-nilly with no regard for other parts, it might seem effective. However, any success comes at the cost of impairing other parts of the system and quite possibly creating more harm than good.

By the same token, if system relationships are identified and monitored, opportunities arise for creatively leveraging parts of the system. For example, monitoring efforts might identify that some counties avail them-selves of the state prison system more than others. Officials could use such information to explore whether allocating set numbers of prison beds to districts, or incentivizing non-incarcerative alternatives, might reduce demand for prisons while simultaneously promoting more equitable use of a state resource.[83] Monitoring, too, can allow for the equivalent of manufacturing quality-control checks. For example, and as Thomas Bernard and his colleagues have observed, an increase in inputs that is not matched with an increase in capacity can lead to system overload and thus "defective" "products" that may be returned to the system for correction and that in turn may further overload the system.[84] Identifying such dynamics constitutes a critical step in being able to introduce appreciable improvements. Conversely, failing to do so – and failing more generally to oversee how the entire system contributes to public safety and justice – constitutes a critical misstep and missed oppor-tunity. In order to leverage a system, we must understand it. That includes knowing how different parts influence or interact with one another. It requires, in turn, that we know where and how to target our efforts to create the greatest gain at the least cost.

4.6 SYSTEMS: THEORY

A wealth of theories exist to explain individual-level offending or macro-level (e.g., neighborhood, city, state) crime rates. Alongside such work exists an even larger range of theories that seek to explain all manner of criminal justice system phenomena.[85] These include theories that seek to understand the operations and effects of subsystems as well as the system as a whole. An obvious parallel is to medicine. Theories and research exist to explain why individuals have certain diseases or medical conditions and why rates of diseases or conditions may be higher in some places than in others. Theories and research exist, too, to explain why medical systems operate as they do and how they might be changed to improve outcomes.[86]

The study of criminal justice systems necessarily entails developing theories about systems and the diverse parts of these systems. If we want to understand how a car works, we need to understand both the whole and the parts. Similarly, if we want to understand criminal justice systems, we need accounts that explain the whole and accounts that explain the various parts, as well as how they contribute to the whole. It would be unrealistic to expect one theory to explain the system and all of its parts. Rather, we need multiple theories, including ones that tackle system phenomena and ones that tackle subsystem phenomena.

This point bears emphasis: we cannot reasonably expect a single theory to explain all things. By the same token, we cannot reasonably expect a theory about a particular phenomenon to explain how the phenomenon affects or interacts with diverse other phenomena. Instead, we need theories that are specific to particular tasks. A theory of police officer discretion during traffic stops, for example, of necessity will entail different emphases than a theory of how county punishment practices affect crime. We then need to link such theories to accounts about how systems may operate and the impacts that they may have.

Put differently, narrowly focused work is useful in its own right, but it also can be useful in building theoretical accounts about systems operations and their potential impacts. For example, studies might show that court decision-making greatly weighs legal factors (e.g., offense severity, presence of a gun) more than extra-legal factors (e.g., age, sex, or race or ethnicity). In developing an account of system case processing flows, scholars might use these prior studies to know that the legal characteristics of cases may influence rates at which cases referred to court result in convictions and sentencing to various sanctions. Similarly, studies might show that drug offenders receive more intensive supervision while on probation or after release from prison. These studies would provide grounds for anticipating that rates of drug offender returns to court or prison may be greater than for other groups. (Intensive supervision might deter offenders. Alternatively, and more likely, it may simply result in a greater likelihood of their getting caught.[87]) Research might document that inmates in a particular prison system consistently experience criminogenic influences. In turn, we could anticipate – in seeking to understand system operations and their impacts – that these individuals will be more likely to recidivate. If still other research documented more punitive sentencing and supervision practices in particular counties or a state, we could anticipate that these two forces would interact to produce escalating rates of arrests, detention, conviction, probation, and incarceration.

In short, the strategy advocated here is a theoretically informed approach to understanding systems, one that entails the use of many theories. This strategy might be viewed as somehow too eclectic or open-ended. For example, it would be ideal to have a single theory that could explain virtually any topic of interest. That utopian ideal, however, contradicts the history of scientific development.[88] Science advances in fits and starts, through development of better "micro," "meso," or "macro" theories that explain phenomena at different units of analysis, use more valid measures of constructs and methodologies that allow for estimating effects with greater precision, explore new domains of inquiry, and so on.[89] Criminal justice systems consist of interrelated parts, including subsystems that follow their own internal logic. Accordingly, we need theories that help us to understand the whole and the parts of these systems.

Fortunately, many theoretical accounts exist that provide insights into the whole and parts of criminal justice systems. Peter Kraska, for example, has identified no fewer than eight theoretical orientations, or perspectives, that scholars use to understand criminal justice. These include rationalism-legalism, system, crime control vs. due process, politics, social construction of reality, growth complex, oppression, and late modernity.[90] In addition to these orientations, there exist theories that specifically seek to account for the systems nature of criminal justice.[91]

One of the most prominent is the general systems theory (GST) that Thomas Bernard and his colleagues used to describe, explain, and make predictions about the operations and effects of the criminal justice system.[92] They began by discussing the salience of GST work in other arenas for the study of criminal justice. Prior GST scholarship argued that "open" systems interact with environments; "inputs" enter these systems and the systems then export "outputs" to the environments in which they operate.[93] As a result, "inputs and outputs [create] a natural 'feedback loop' in which the system [adapts] to a changing environment, which [allows] self-regulation."[94] GST maintains that "all systems must maintain equality between inputs and outputs, and any movement away from equality generates corrections to move the system back toward it."[95] Accordingly, system overload results when inputs cannot be adequately processed, and so the system produces "defective" products. A vicious cycle results: "These 'defective' products [return] to the system for further processing, which further [overloads] the system and [increases] the rate of defectiveness in its outputs. System overload therefore [tends] to spiral into a more generalized system breakdown."[96]

These insights have been applied to criminal justice. John Van Gigch, for example, used GST to examine different parts of the criminal justice system (e.g., law enforcement, courts, corrections) as well as agencies.[97] He showed how these parts interact with and affect one another through exchanges of inputs and outputs. His work and that of systems theory scholars established that criminal justice systems not only exist, but cannot be readily understood by somehow "adding up" different parts.

Bernard and colleagues have identified nine ways in which criminal justice operates as a system. Their account warrants discussion because it builds on prior work, succinctly captures how criminal justice is a system, illuminates implications of the systems nature of criminal justice, and identifies predictions about processing and system as well as subsystem impacts. In addition, it highlights the necessity of theories that explain system operations and, separately, theories that explain how each of the different parts of this system operate.

"1. Criminal justice consists in multiple layers of ever more encompassing systems, each of which can be described in terms of input, processing, and output."[98] Indeed, criminal justice not only can be described in this way, it arguably must be to provide an accurate description of its nature. For example, it is a systems view that identifies what most scholars identify to be a critical feature of criminal justice: case processing, whether the "cases" involve offenders, victims, the public, or some other group. The ability to describe the essence of a phenomenon constitutes an important aspect of any theory.[99] GST provides this ability through its emphasis on case processing within and across a system. At the same time, theories provide a basis for making predictions.[100] GST can do so when other dimensions of systems are considered.

"2. Criminal justice processes 'cases,' each of which includes offenders, victims, and the public."[101] Each different part, or subsystem, of the criminal justice system "takes offenders as input, does something to them or for them, and sends them as output to the next subsystem unit or back to the external environment."[102] A core goal, across all parts of the system, is to reduce offending. But "cases" do not include just offenders. They include victims and communities. For example, "victims are processed when police and prosecutors and judges pay attention to their complaints" and seek to leave victims feeling satisfied that justice has occurred or compensated or helped in some way.[103] Dissatisfied victims and communities, in essence, constitute "defective products," while satisfied victims and communities constitute successfully completed "products." Here, again, a systems view is helpful in identifying that multiple subsystems ultimately serve to ensure that "cases" of various types are processed in a timely and appropriate manner that best achieves safety and justice.

"3. When processing terminates prior to completion, products tend to return to the system as 'defective.' That is, products that previously were defined as 'output' return to the system as additional 'input.'"[104] The nature of systems is that "defective" outputs create problems for a given system. For example, if law enforcement and the courts ignore the views of certain groups or communities, then core system goals may not be achieved. These groups or communities may not cooperate with the police, and thus reduce the ability of law enforcement to help them. At the same time, the communities and groups experience less justice. In addition, anger or frustration among these groups or citizens of these communities may rise sufficient to create concerns about the integrity of police or court actions or of the broader criminal justice system. Research on prisoner reentry, for example, has highlighted the disproportionate effect that incarceration may have on minority communities.[105] Prominent incidents involving the death of minority citizens in police encounters have highlighted the possibility that disproportionate effects of policing may exist as well.[106] In these and similar instances, "defective" processing results in feedback loops that influence system operations and, potentially, its impacts.

"4. There is little agreement on how to achieve the goals of criminal justice processing (the production of nonoffenders, satisfied victims, and a satisfied public)."[107] Bernard and colleagues might more accurately have said that variable agreement on how to achieve system goals affects system operations and their impacts. A system is not defined by the extent to which various parts agree on how goals are achieved. It is defined by a design that seeks to achieve goals. Criminal justice is designed to achieve public safety, justice, accountability, and efficiency, among other goals.[108] The design for achieving these goals may be poor, and the implementation of it may be poor as well. Neither limitation, however, contrary to some critiques of systems theories, means that a system does not exist.[109]

Rather, the main implication is a theoretical one: We can anticipate that when different system stakeholder targets or beneficiaries disagree about the best design, which goals should be emphasized more, or how those goals should be realized, the system will operate less efficiently and effectively. In John Hagan's phrasing, such a system is "loosely coupled."[110] That state of affairs characterizes many systems, not just criminal justice. Few if any systems achieve a perfect coupling of all parts to achieve a specific set of goals. Applied policy and program researchers encounter this situation regularly. Many programs, for example, operate with vaguely identified goals and organizational designs for achieving them.[111]

"5. This lack of agreement arises because criminal justice agents lack objective standards for assessing whether processing is 'completed' or 'defective,' so they tend to rely on 'educated guesses.' This means that, at every stage, criminal justice agents have the option to decide that processing is complete. The 'product' then leaves the system and is returned to the external environment as 'output.'"[112] Here, again, a system is not defined, in this instance, by the extent to which objective standards exist for determining success. Rather, the theoretical implication that Bernard and colleagues identify through a systems perspective is that system operations and success can be adversely affected when opportunities exist for system actors to characterize success as they see fit. For example, the police and courts might ignore victim or community wishes and thus leave citizens dissatisfied. Less justice may occur in such situations. Yet, the police and courts might claim success by pointing to high arrest, conviction, or imprisonment rates. What was successful? Perhaps a high level of retribution or public safety resulted. It potentially did so, however, at the expense of justice. In addition, the "outputs" frequently go unevaluated. The police, for example, assert that their actions reduced crime, yet most of the time jurisdictions provide no methodologically rigorous evaluations of the impact of their law enforcement agencies. Likewise, corrections department efforts typically go unevaluated. Whether, for example, they reduce recidivism typically is unknown.[113]

A systems theoretical perspective, in short, highlights the implications of ambiguous operationalizations of success. It also highlights that, where such ambiguity exists, system actors may take advantage of it to advance their own, or their subsystem's, interests and do so in ways that may adversely affect system success. For example, in a weakly integrated system, especially one with little agreement about goals and with few feedback mechanisms to provide objective measures of performance, actors within any given subsystem may take actions that undermine safety and justice. To illustrate, the police might not make arrests in cases where they should, perhaps due to case processing pressures. They may claim that doing so served the interests of safety and justice.[114] In turn, the courts fail to receive "inputs" that they ideally should or otherwise would process. This situation is to some extent unavoidable. For example, no objective standard exists for determining whether an arrest, conviction, or sentence to prison should occur. Ambiguity is part and parcel to such decisions. It can, however, be greater than need be and affect case processing and systems goals.

"6. Declining capacity to process cases generates 'backward pressure' across the system to reduce the flow of cases to the next system stage. Each stage therefore is pressured to output a certain portion of its cases to the external environment."[115] Stated more neutrally, when capacity at one stage of processing or in a subsystem does not match the flow of cases to it, a lack of equilibrium ensues. Then some adjustment occurs. The direction of that adjustment will depend on many factors, including capacity of the next stage of processing or the subsystem that would receive cases. In general, when capacity is limited, a system response is to release cases. For example, the police might counsel and release someone whom they otherwise might arrest, prosecutors might dismiss less-serious cases, and prisons might release inmates earlier. Of course, the direction of release may vary depending on system design. A clear illustration involves mandatory sentencing laws that some states have enacted: these laws stipulate that individuals who go to prison must serve a fixed percentage of their sentence before release.[116] Parole boards in these instances cannot reduce prison population pressure through increased rates of parole. Accordingly, other system responses – such as reduced sentences to prison or increased prison construction (i.e., greater incarceration capacity) – must arise. The more general insight from a systems view is that case processing flows get directed in part by capacity constraints and opportunities throughout the criminal justice system.

"7. This backward pressure supplements the fact that it is quicker and easier to decide that processing is complete than to send the case to the next stage for additional processing."[117] Bernard and colleagues here extended the above insight to show that case processing patterns can be predicted in part by the logic of processing pressures. All else equal, systems will seek the easiest way to ensure smooth and efficient processing of cases. That can include releasing "defective products" rather than allowing them to be forwarded onward for attention that will not likely be forthcoming. This result may be efficient, but of course can result in less safety and justice. Agricultural crime provides a useful illustration. Several colleagues and I once undertook an evaluation of a program that sought to reduce property theft and damage that targeted farmers.[118] A starting point for the program was the fact that the police did not typically actively respond to or investigate farm crime because they did not believe (accurately, it seems) that prosecutors would prioritize processing of such cases.

The program sought to change that situation by promoting greater awareness among the police and prosecutors about the prevalence and harms of agricultural crime. Put differently, it sought to steer the system in a way that resulted in processing of agricultural crime.

"8. Countervailing 'forward' pressure arises because sending cases to the next stage of the system limits the criminal justice agent's exposure to blame for defective processing."[119] Systems orient themselves around and through case processing. In human systems, including criminal justice agencies, accountability constitutes a core goal and a mechanism through which success is supposed to occur. For example, a system in which actors follow rules and procedures would be viewed by society as a goal in itself. In a well-designed system, conformity with rules and procedures should accomplish other goals, such as more safety and justice. Once, again, a GST perspective illuminates system dynamics and the central role of case processing flows. Here, for example, we can see the potential for system processing to be detoured by individuals or subsystems that prioritize their own goals over that of the system. In this instance, an all-too-human desire to protect against blame means that individuals, or the criminal justice systems within which they work, may pass along cases that warrant more attention. They do so rather than process these cases more thoroughly themselves. Calls for greater government accountability in recent decades would contribute to such a problem, especially if it occurred without the resources necessary for full and complete case processing.[120]

"9. These conflicting pressures require that criminal justice agents be able to 'close cases that will stay closed.' As a result of the feedback loop in which cases reopen, incompetent criminal justice workers have difficulty concealing their incompetence."[121] Bernard and colleagues highlighted an implication of system feedback loops in criminal justice. When system actors pass along "defective products," they risk being seen as incompetent. For example, when judges release to the community individuals with a high risk of offending, then, if these individuals recidivate, the judges may not be reelected. When the Massachusetts Governor, Michael Dukakis, lost his bid for the presidency, it was due in part to the claim that he was responsible for the violent recidivism of a furloughed prisoner.[122] Judges know full well the risk of appearing "soft on crime." At the same time, they face real-world constraints. Not all convicted felons can or should be incarcerated. Judges who resist these constraints face a backlash from court personnel and corrections.[123] Although Bernard and colleagues focused on the consequences of these systems-induced tensions for individual actors and subsystems, the broader implication is the existence of tensions that influence case processing and thus system operations and impacts. To understand system actor decisions, one must identify these tensions, what produces them, and their consequences for system success.

Bernard and colleagues identified four theoretical implications that flow from a GST account of criminal justice. The first is the conclusion, arrived at inferentially, that criminal justice in fact is a system, one that is "greater than the sum of its parts."[124] This system creates pressures that provide a context within which activities in one part (e.g., parole board decision-making) can have impacts on other parts (e.g., law enforcement efforts).

The second is that in a systems context the decision-making of actors can be understood more accurately if we understand that they are oriented toward "closing cases."[125] These actors exert little direct control over end outcomes, such as safety and justice. As a result, they focus on following procedures to expeditiously move cases along and simultaneously to avoid being viewed as responsible for adverse incidents. A more general implication is that actor decision-making may be better understood by identifying the extent to which actors (the police, judges, prison officers, etc.) have control over cases. When they have more control (e.g., if they have more time to process cases), they can focus more on efforts that improve system goals. When they have less control (e.g., if they have less time to process cases), they must focus more on efforts to "close cases" to ensure that bottlenecks do not occur and that they are not blamed for them. A medical analogy illustrates the point: Physicians take more time to diagnose patients when they have small caseloads, and they provide perfunctory assessments, typically with more error, when they have heavy caseloads.[126]

The third is a prediction about the conditions under which criminal justice actors or subsystems succeed. Specifically, system actors or subsystems must be sufficiently competent to resist accepting cases sent to them and to discharge cases as soon as they can without appearing negligent, and thus responsible for any adverse incident that may arise (e.g., recidivism, increased crime, miscarriages of justice). Discharging cases too soon can appear (and be) negligent. Holding on to them more than minimally necessary can mean that the actor, or subsystem, assumes more responsibility than they want or than would be fair when assignment of responsibility for adverse events occurs. For actors or subsystems to succeed, then, they must have sufficient competency or management to navigate system pressures.

Notably, standards for what it means to "succeed" may change, depending on system pressures. For example, the greater the increase in caseload pressures, the more normative it may become to "close" higher numbers of cases. By extension, the bar for competency shifts. Competency in closing cases when there is sufficient time to do so differs from competency in closing cases when time is limited. Some physicians may be excellent diagnosticians, for example, but may be terrible emergency room doctors because they may be less competent in making rapid-fire decisions. Similarly, some police officers, prosecutors, judges, prison officers, and so on may be more competent than others when time permits. They may be less competent when time pressures do not permit lengthy, deliberative decision-making. From a systems perspective, this situation leads not only to predictions about which actors will "succeed," but also to the prediction that systems that process large volumes of cases will make worse decisions to the extent that they do not introduce adjustments (e.g., hiring more personnel or changing standards for certain decisions) to accommodate processing pressures.

The fourth is what Bernard and colleagues have referred to as the "paradox of efficiency."[127] In any walk of life, achieving perfection can entail diminishing returns on investment. A certain amount of effort may improve our grade point average (GPA) from a "C" to a "B"; considerably more effort may be required to improve from a "B" to an "A." In our personal lives, a certain degree of imperfection necessarily exists. Effort to stamp it out would be futile and inefficient. No house can be perfectly clean; no wardrobe will cover all occasions; no practicing of a foreign language will lead one to sound exactly like a native speaker; and so on. Effective and cost-efficient systems seek an optimal rate of successfully completed "products," one that necessarily entails a certain rate of defective "products."[128]

What Bernard and his colleagues highlighted is that criminal justice systems are held to an unrealistic and unachievable standard of perfection: no missed arrests, no mistakes in court process, no recidivism, and so on, are supposed to occur. A clear prediction and implication result. In this situation, "intolerance toward defectiveness (e.g., recidivism) becomes exponentially costly while providing smaller and smaller gains in quality (e.g., reductions in the recidivism rate)."[129] Several paradoxes arise because of this intolerance. One is that it obscures the fact that errors are unavoidable. Another is that it can contribute to greater system failure. For example, case processing pressures can lead to increased efforts to follow formulaic decisions for passing along cases quickly while simultaneously circumventing responsibility for outcomes. Examples include sentencing policies that dictate prison sentences and prison sentence length and that remove discretion from the courts; parole board policies that automatically limit the granting of parole; and laws that coerce police officers to arrest or cite youth who engage in minor acts of delinquency in situations where in the past the officers would simply caution the youth.[130] In each instance, greater efficiency in processing may occur. In so doing, however, the rapid processing provides cover for some actors or subsystems to appear to be "doing their job." The end result may be a worsening of safety and justice outcomes.

In short, a systems view of criminal justice provides a foundation for understanding the operations and potential impacts of criminal justice. As detailed here and in Chapter 3, this view anticipates that well-functioning systems – those that are hierarchical and integrated, self-organizing and able to change, and resilient to and able to thrive in the face of changing environments – will be more effective in achieving public safety, justice, accountability, and other goals than those that are not. A systems view does not require a single theory that explains virtually every aspect of relevance (e.g., crime causation, police behavior, court sanctioning practices, prison misconduct and recidivism, victim satisfaction with the courts). Rather, it requires, at the most general level, identifying the structures within and across subsystems that define the criminal justice system and how they interact with and influence one another.

An awareness of system operations and effects creates the opportunity, then, to understand better all aspects of criminal justice. It is not a substitute for non-systems-focused theories. Invariably, we need a range of theories that account for specific activities (arrests, police relationships with community residents, sentencing practices, and so on). These, however, can be informed by understanding systems contexts. For example, officer biases toward minorities might affect decision-making, and the biases might be amplified by case processing pressures. Conversely, "micro-level" theories can inform our understanding of systems. For example, officers might disproportionately arrest minorities and do so in part due to bias; such a possibility is anticipated by a number of theories. This insight creates the foundation, when viewed from a systems perspective, for anticipating disproportionality in minority sentencing and incarceration.

A systems approach requires continuous examination of the complexity inherent to criminal justice. This approach requires simultaneously focusing on system operations and impacts and using a diverse range of theories and empirical research to understand specific subsystems. The goal is to draw on the best available systems and subsystem-specific theories and research to understand the whole and its parts and how both can be improved. The focus on complexity derives from the fact that criminal justice is a complex phenomenon. Criticisms of a systems approach miss this point. They miss, too, that this complexity has not interfered with efforts to use systems analysis successfully in criminal justice and in many scientific studies of social and physical phenomena.[131] The accounts may fail to capture all relevant dimensions or dynamics. But that is not intrinsically problematic, and it does not preclude advances in understanding. Scientific knowledge accumulates through a combination of steady progress for periods of time plus fits and starts of rapid improvements in understanding.[132] If we are to better understand our criminal justice systems – and to make appreciable improvements in them – there is no substitute for embracing efforts to examine the complexity.

4.7 FLAWED RESPONSES TO CRIME AND JUSTICE: INVESTING WITHOUT KNOWLEDGE OF SYSTEMS

Investing in crime and justice policies, programs, or practices without knowledge of systems will not generate appreciable or cost-efficient improvements in safety, justice, accountability, or other goals that society sets for criminal justice. As Robert Sampson and colleagues have argued, "In a causally complex world, ... policy research requires more than the estimation of causal effects, even if precisely and well identified. Rather, it requires system-level knowledge of how policy is expected to work within a larger social context."[133] With systems-level understanding, policy efforts must, by and large, operate in the dark, the equivalent of driving a car along a curving country road with no lights. Stated more strongly: without such understanding, our responses to crime and justice are bound to fail. There will be bright spots here and there – such as a program that reduces recidivism or a policy that increases victim or community satisfaction – but they will not accumulate into large-scale improvements.

The flaws of crime and justice policy nationally, in fact, are numerous, and stand out precisely because they ignore systems. These flaws, anticipated by the discussion in Chapter 2 of systems problems, include but are not limited to, the following.

First, although criminal justice is designed and operates as a system, our local, state, and federal approaches to crime and justice ignore that fact. Reforms by and large occur through piecemeal and one-time efforts to focus on one part of the system or another. Indeed, what perhaps stands out most strikingly about crime and justice policy is the lack of a clear, designated driver. The police, courts, jails, prisons, and community supervision operate as silos. Some cooperation occurs, but no single entity assumes responsibility for ensuring that the entire system operates effectively and efficiently. Consider that a primary way to reduce crime and improve justice would be to target crime-causing factors in communities, to monitor police activity in these areas and how residents perceive and experience local policing, the courts, and sanctions, and then to make adjustments that would enhance safety and justice. No agency exists to do so. That role is not that of the police, the courts, probation or parole, or jails and prisons.

Second, the lack of a designated criminal justice system driver almost necessarily produces harms. Any time a system operates rudderless, its ability to achieve goals declines. As shown in Figure 4.9, many external forces – such as changes in crime, politics, resources, public views, and local, state, or national policy priorities – may affect criminal justice and its subsystems. Responses to crime and justice that do not acknowledge or systematically address these forces simply cannot accumulate into a coherent, effective, or efficient strategy. If anything, it encourages what Edward Latessa and colleagues have termed "quackery."[134] Policymakers and criminal justice administrators adopt laws and interventions that they assume to be effective but that lack any credible theoretical or empirical underpinning. These efforts get pronounced as effective and then proliferate with little to check their adoption or the costs that they create.[135]

Worse than that, though, is the likelihood that our systems of justice create harm – that is, we pay to hurt ourselves. Consider prisoner reentry. Without a clear criminal justice system driver, each part of the system plays a role in institutionalizing reentry failure. Laws get passed that encourage more and lengthier incarceration, courts operate under caseload pressures that inhibit justice and "smart" sanctioning (i.e., punishments and interventions that are evidence-based), prisons provide minimal rehabilitation, communities and states offer little reentry assistance, and community supervision officer caseloads and get-tough philosophies promote revocations and arrests that in turn result in returns to prison.[136] It is a recipe for failure.

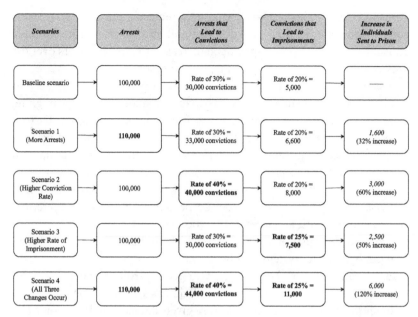

FIGURE 4.10 The Amplifying Effect of Decision Points in Criminal Justice Systems

Inspection of Figure 4.10 illustrates how institutionalized failure can arise.[137] The failure stems from allowing decisions to occur within a systems context but without taking that context into account. The illustration focuses on four scenarios: (1) one in which arrests increase, (2) one in which the rate of conviction (given an arrest) increases, (3) one in which the rate of imprisonment (given a conviction) increases, and (4) one in which all three changes occur. For each scenario, we examine what impact a change in the processing of decisions has on the number of individuals sent to prison in a given year, as compared to the prior year, or "baseline scenario."

In this baseline scenario, we will ignore the "stock" population (i.e., the number of individuals in prison on a given day). Our focus instead is on the number of new admissions. In this scenario, for 100,000 arrests, there are 30,000 convictions; 20 percent of these convictions lead to a prison term. This chain of decisions results in 5,000 new admissions to prison.

Scenario 1 consists of a situation in which arrests in this criminal justice system increase by 10,000, going from 100,000 in the baseline year to 110,000 in the following year. Why would that occur? Perhaps crime is on the rise. Perhaps law enforcement agencies are more aggressively fighting crime. Or perhaps the public is more willing to contact the police when crimes occur. In this scenario, if arrests increase and all else remains equal – for example, the conviction rate and imprisonment rate continue as usual – this system ends up with an increase of 1,600 prisoners over the previous baseline year (going from 5,000 to 6,600).

Scenario 2 consists of a situation in which the percentage of arrests that result in a conviction increases by 10 percent from the previous year, going from 30 percent to 40 percent. Here, for example, perhaps a District Attorney is receiving more prosecutable cases or is more aggressively or successfully securing convictions. In this scenario, the system ends up with an increase, all else equal, of 3,000 prisoners over the previous year.

Scenario 3 consists of a situation in which the imprisonment rate increases by 5 percent, going from 20 percent to 25 percent. Here, the system ends up with an increase of 2,500 prisoners.

Scenario 4 consists of a situation in which all three of the above system changes occur. The system in this instance incarcerates 6,000 more individuals than it did in the previous year (going from 5,000 to 11,000). It more than doubles the number of individuals sent to prison.

In short, processing changes at any given decision-making point can have substantial ripple effects. These effects arise precisely because the changes occur within a systems context. In addition, when multiple changes occur, they can interact to produce even greater ripple effects. For example, an increase in arrests alone produced 1,600 more prisoners annually, an increase in the conviction rate alone produced 3,000 more prisoners, and an increase in the imprisonment rate produced 2,500 more prisoners. By contrast, an increase in all three produced 6,000 more prisoners, or what amounts to a 120 percent increase in imprisonment from the previous year.

Of course, many other changes can occur. Some might counterbalance one another. For example, if police arrests increase, conviction rates might decline. Conversely, other changes may amplify ripple effects. For example, a greater focus on a particular type of crime, such as drug offending, might enhance them.[138] In addition, lengthier prison terms would mean that the "stock" population of prisoners expands, further compounding prison system growth in a context of increased admissions. Notably, systems changes may create further systems changes. For example, when states build more prisons, this capacity remains largely in place. It is politically risky to close prisons.[139] As a result, even if arrests decline, there can be adjustments upward at other decision points that result in higher conviction and imprisonment rates. Then, when crimes occur – any recidivism may be viewed as cause for indicting the criminal justice system – calls arise for tougher sentencing laws. Greater pressure gets exerted on prisons and the only recourse is to build more prisons. Of critical relevance for efforts to improve criminal justice policy is that there is no way of identifying such possibilities without monitoring and evaluating systems.

Against that backdrop exists a startling fact: precious little empirical evidence supports the notion that incarceration, as typically used, reduces recidivism.[140] (Questions exist, too, about whether it has a general deterrent effect and how cost-efficient any such effect may be, relative to other strategies.[141]) That is especially relevant in a context in which prison populations have more than tripled since the early 1980s and time served has increased by up to 30 percent, or more.[142] Recall that the best national estimate suggests that more than three-fourths of released prisoners are rearrested within five years of release.[143] That does not mean that incarceration cannot be effective, only that many conditions necessary for it to improve recidivism and other reentry outcomes must come together. For example, prisons must be rehabilitative, support and supervision after release may be necessary, and opportunities to obtain employment after release likely are needed. Criminal justice is too complex for these conditions to fall into place on their own.[144] Failure to address this complexity results in expensive and ineffective policy and practice. As Kathleen Auerhahn's study of California's sentencing policy reforms showed, for example, "two decades of sentencing policy reforms conceived and implemented with the goal of making California's citizens safer ... resulted in a prison population that is more than four times the size and substantially less dangerous than it was in 1980."[145]

The example here centered on reentry outcomes. However, we could as well illustrate the point through other examples, such as court processing and the quality of decisions that get made, racial and ethnic disparities that exist throughout criminal justice, victim and community perceptions of safety and satisfaction that justice occurs, physical harm to and mental health challenges among those who work throughout the criminal justice system, and so on.[146]

Third, the absence of a "driver" also means that strategies for enhancing system efficiency get missed and that extremes become institutionalized. Crime policy has been criticized by scholars, policymakers, and the public for being politicized. This situation – referred to as the politicization of crime – is enabled by the lack of a designated criminal justice system driver. It allows extreme responses, such as the large-scale commitment to incarceration, to become institutionalized. When political winds shift, new extremes emerge that can change entire systems.[147] Such patterns are inefficient in several ways. Extreme responses alone create inefficiency, as they dictate a one-size-fits-all, "silver bullet" approach to crime and justice. They create inefficiency as well by making it more difficult to right-size or rebalance the portfolio of strategies that can be used to improve safety and justice. Not least, they create inefficiency because one political regime ignores or undoes the efforts that arose under a previous regime and replaces it with a new extreme response. That response then engenders a new push for a swing back. The tough-on-crime vs. rehabilitative approach to crime and justice exemplifies this swing and the inefficiency that it has engendered.[148]

In short, a system without a driver enables subsystems and their parts to be leveraged willy-nilly in ways that can shift the entire system. As Garland has emphasized, "small variations in enacted laws or their enforcement may produce large variations in penal outcomes."[149] The end result may not be more safety and justice; indeed, there may be less. Consider the underfunding of probation.[150] Alongside of "mass incarceration," there was, in recent decades, an equally important phenomenon: "mass probation."[151] It was and is a simple thing to achieve – increase probation officer caseloads. That simple task, though, creates enormous complications, ones that those who work within the criminal justice system readily appreciate.[152] A higher caseload for probation officers translates into less time to assist each probationer. An emphasis, at the same time, on tougher revocation policies means that more probationers get sent to prison for minor infractions. Overlaid on this situation is a more generally hostile environment for felons. They face, for example, housing and employment restrictions that well exceed those faced by felons in previous eras. In such a situation, we can anticipate that probation will do little to reduce recidivism or create a sense among felons or their families or victims that justice has occurred.

Fourth, criminal justice policy and practice does not require that policymakers and crime and justice administrators regularly interact with groups most affected by their efforts. When we make decisions that may greatly affect our own lives, we typically pay attention. Policymakers and criminal justice administrators, however, operate under no similar felt necessity. For example, policymakers may believe that they are responding to the public will, but they usually operate with no systematic, empirical information about public views, the causes or range of solutions to particular crime or justice problems, or the experiences of impacted groups. This situation creates a form of tone-deafness that results in missed opportunities to understand root causes of crime and injustice and how they might best be addressed.[153] The clear alternative, one that would allow for designing more effective responses, is a situation in which policymakers and practitioners operate with credible and up-to-date information about the problems and systems that they wish to change. They would rely, too, on the views of those most likely to implement or to be affected by new policies, programs, or practices.

Fifth, no institutionalized arrangement exists to monitor and empirically evaluate system operations and impacts. Despite frequent calls by policymakers for greater accountability and reliance on "evidence-based" policy, local and state governments by and large provide no support for monitoring and evaluating how their systems and subsystems operate.[154] Some funding and infrastructure exists for targeted evaluations of particular policies or interventions. These, however, provide no foundation for understanding how different parts of a system operate and interact, how particular changes get implemented, what improvements in intended outcomes have occurred, or what impacts have occurred throughout the system. In local and state criminal justice systems, for example, how much have mass-incarceration investments improved public safety; achieved socially desired levels of retribution; improved reentry outcomes (e.g., housing, mental health, drug addiction, and, not least, recidivism); or enhanced public satisfaction with criminal justice processes or with putative gains in safety and justice? It is largely unknown.

This failure to monitor and evaluate systems creates ample room for mistakes to arise and for their harms to go unrecognized. As a result, policymakers and criminal justice officials can claim whatever they like about crime and their systems of justice. They can tout this program or that one or critique past efforts as failures. Such a situation creates the grounds for justifying the diversity of approaches, discussed earlier in the chapter, that local and state governments have taken to fighting crime. What it does not create is the grounds for making empirically based claims about accountability, effectiveness, or efficiency. Put differently, policymakers and criminal justice officials can and do justify all manner of policies and interventions with little credible evidence about the actual operations, impacts, or efficiency of their criminal justice systems. They do so, too, with little insight into how systems affect the implementation or impacts of policies, programs, and practices.

As a society, we spend a great deal of money – scarce taxpayer dollars – on criminal justice, and yet know little about the return on investment. Are our systems of criminal justice successful, resilient, and thriving, as

Chapter 3 suggested would characterize an ideal system? Or are they failing or barely surviving? To answer such questions would require the institutionalization of policy processes and research capacity for systems monitoring, evaluation, and improvement. Fortunately, as Anna Stewart and colleagues have emphasized, "there is increasing awareness of the benefits that could result from policy simulation modeling of the criminal justice system. The development of such models facilitates the simulation of proposed practice, policy, and legislative changes to provide decision-makers with information pertaining to the short-term and long-term consequences of any proposed changes."[155]

4.8 CONCLUSION

During high school and college, I ran cross-country and track. No bravado here: I was not the fastest, strongest, or grittiest. Regardless, to do well and improve, I had to learn to "listen" to my body. That meant monitoring my resting heart rate, how quickly I recovered from runs, how I responded to particular workouts, whether certain aches or pains might warrant attention or could safely be ignored, and so on. Over time, I developed a sense of my body as a "system." Seemingly small changes here or there – such as a shorter stride, stretching more, or including more hill workouts – could make a big difference. The fact is that most of us develop a sense of how we are feeling and what influences us. We may not be fully cognizant of the forces that push and pull us, but we have a sense of them and we make adjustments accordingly.

That sense is completely lacking from criminal justice policy. As this chapter highlighted, we have states and local jurisdictions embarking on ongoing experiments, at great expense, with little to no basis for justifying them on empirical grounds. This lack of awareness, what could be termed a form of "sense-lessness," cannot be cured by undertaking a study here or there, and it cannot be cured by undertaking reforms that target this or that part of the criminal justice system. What is needed is a strategy for continuously collecting information about this system, analyzing it, taking strategic steps to create improvements, and evaluating these efforts.

Instead of this approach, criminal justice operates with little oversight about system activities, processing, or impacts on safety, justice, and other outcomes, such as disparities in the treatment of certain groups. It is akin to steering a boat with no information about currents, tides, impending storms, or the like. The problem is made worse by the fact that most of what occurs within criminal justice goes unevaluated and rests on questionable scientific grounds.[156] From crime prevention efforts through policing to the courts and corrections, we frequently find limited theoretical or empirical evidence that what occurs is needed, rests on strong theoretical grounds, is implemented well, or exerts an appreciable impact on relevant outcomes, or that any putative impacts are generated in a cost-efficient manner.[157]

The limited knowledge about all that occurs within criminal justice is difficult to understate. Consider incarceration: it can vary in length, the conditions of confinement, the amount and intensity of treatment and services, and the amount and quality of supervision upon release. Similarly, consider non-incarcerative sanctions.[158] They can include probation of varying durations and levels of supervision, support, and treatment, halfway houses, boot camps, house arrest, day-reporting centers, electronic monitoring, restitution and fines, drug testing, community service, and more.[159] In every instance, we want information about the credibility of the theory guiding a given effort, the quality of implementation, impacts and how they may vary across groups and context, and cost-efficiency. Yet, despite insight about some specific efforts in specific places at specific times, we know little about the implementation, impacts, or cost-efficiency of these different efforts.[160] The same can be said of efforts in juvenile justice. Diversion, for example, constitutes a mainstay of juvenile justice systems, yet its implementation and impacts remain largely unknown.[161]

This problem is facilitated and made worse by inattention to monitoring and evaluating criminal (and juvenile) justice system operations and impacts. Wayne Welsh and Phillip Harris have written that "because criminal justice officials and agencies often act without consideration of how their decisions might affect those elsewhere in the system, the criminal justice system has often been called a 'nonsystem.'"[162] The system, however, in fact exists. It simply is not well monitored or evaluated. Accordingly, it cannot be well coordinated or "driven." It may seem, then, like a "non-system," but it is more aptly characterized as a poorly functioning system.

Recent decades have been witness to substantial progress in identifying interventions that may be effective in reducing recidivism.[163] That is well and good. However, no amount of investing in particular "best practices" or "evidence-based practices" will fix the problem of a poorly functioning system. Research might show that a particular intervention, such as a drug court, can reduce recidivism more effectively than some other approach. That finding, however, has no relevance for understanding the conditions under which a drug court is needed. Perhaps, for example, recidivism for offenders in a particular area stems primarily from poor supervision. Here, then, the needed approach might well be more and better supervision, not creation of an entirely new way of meting out justice and "fixing" offenders. An evaluation of the Cambridge-Somerville Youth Study intervention illustrates this point. The now-famous intervention proceeded without a credible theoretical foundation and failed to take into account factors, such as family and community context, that an ecological, or systems, perspective would highlight as relevant for reducing offending.[164] Another example: "hot-spots" policing might reduce crime at a particular area and for a particular time. Evidence of such an impact, however, constitutes but one part of an overall decision-making process. There may be competing crime and justice policy priorities, for example, that warrant greater attention. Privatization provides yet another example. It represents a policy that many advocates assume must be effective. Research on privatization, in fact, is minimal and inconclusive.[165] More relevant is that it has largely ignored the systems context in which any public or private criminal justice undertaking occurs and that defines the parameters for assessing effectiveness.[166]

The same problem attends to efforts to promote "alternatives to incarceration."[167] For these alternatives to be effective and cost-efficient, we need information about the goals of incarceration, the populations anticipated to be in it, those who seemingly would do better through some alternative, and the relative impacts and cost-efficiency of these alternatives. We need information, too, about potentially needless expansion. For example, let us assume that in the absence of new alternatives, incarceration levels remain level. If we introduce alternatives, incarceration should decline. However, it may not. Here, then, no "alternative" in fact exists. What we have paid for is "net-widening." The problem is even more complicated. For example, from a systems perspective, we can readily see that incarceration is not the presumptive sanction. It simply constitutes one of a wide range of sanctions available to the courts.[168] Without knowledge of how and for whom these sanctions are employed, we cannot accurately identify how, if at all, any given sanction serves as an "alternative" to another.

We have, then, a remarkable problem: the investment of tremendous expenditures in criminal justice, with little evidence of impact, during an era in which increased calls for accountability and evidence-based practices have occurred.[169] There has been no corresponding investment in creating the infrastructure and processes for this goal to be achieved.

Policymakers and criminal justice officials can call for accountability. They can advocate for evidence-based practices. But without the requisite information for monitoring, understanding, and evaluating system operations – and the forces that shape them – there can be no large-scale, meaningful accountability or effectiveness. The solution? A systems-focused approach to developing, monitoring, evaluating, and improving the criminal justice system.

5

The Systems Improvement Solution for Safety, Justice, Accountability, and Efficiency

Criminal justice is a system that, as many policymakers and scholars have highlighted, has careened out of control. Legislators frequently call for "systems reform." Yet, the changes that they enact typically fall far short of that. A law is passed and the expectation is that somehow an entire system will respond. Similarly, accountability frequently is touted as a priority, yet no investment in the infrastructure necessary for achieving it occurs.

Without that infrastructure, criminal justice will continue to flounder. It will flounder, too, without a process for monitoring and evaluating crime and justice policy and for identifying changes that can be made to achieve the most impact at the least cost. What we need is a solution that addresses this problem and enables criminal justice to be brought under control.

The goal of this chapter is to describe and argue for the Systems Improvement Solution as a way of doing so and, in particular, of reducing crime and increasing justice, accountability, and cost-efficiency. The chapter describes the three core activities, or steps, of the Solution. They include (1) continuous implementation of the evaluation research hierarchy and systems analysis; (2) a multi-stakeholder deliberative process for informing research and developing, evaluating, and improving policy; and (3) adoption of evidence-based policies, programs, practices, and decision-making. The chapter describes, too, the priorities that must guide all of these activities and core principles for ensuring that this systems-focused solution is effective.

If the Systems Solution – or a systems-focused approach similar to it – is adopted, we will have greater public safety, justice, accountability, and

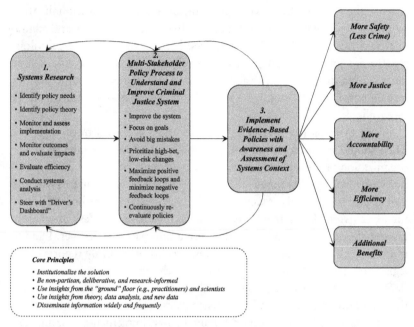

FIGURE 5.1 The Systems Improvement Solution for Producing Less Crime and More Justice, Accountability, and Efficiency

efficiency. These and other benefits are discussed at length in the next chapter. There I discuss as well the pitfalls that may arise and how to avoid them. I discuss, too, examples of promising, systems-focused efforts. The name, "Systems Improvement Solution," does not matter. What does matter is a turn toward systems-focused solutions. I argue that substantial improvements in safety, justice, and other outcomes require that we take control of a criminal justice system that currently is out of control.

5.1 THE SYSTEMS IMPROVEMENT SOLUTION: AN OVERVIEW

The Systems Solution involves three steps, or activities, shown in Figure 5.1. They must occur in conjunction with one another and must occur through a continuous feedback process, as reflected in the series of arrows. No car factory magically produces high-quality cars without someone or some group overseeing the assembly line. Similarly, no policy, program, practice, or decision-making effort successfully achieves diverse goals without continuous attention. For that reason, the Systems Improvement Solution requires institutionalization of a process in which research occurs alongside of policy implementation and change. ("Policy" here is used here as shorthand terminology for formal and informal policies as well as programs, practices, and decision-making among systems actors.) At the same time, policy implementation and change should both shape and be informed by research.

In the Systems Improvement Solution, these activities must co-occur. They should continuously shape one another in constant interplay. The organization of these efforts requires the equivalent of a "captain" agency, one with responsibility for ensuring that the process unfolds in this way and that all steps occur and are well executed. That agency can be housed within the executive or legislative branch of government. Regardless of where it resides, the agency should be operated in a non-partisan manner. In addition, it should be charged with providing weekly or monthly reports to the legislature, agencies, and other relevant stakeholders.

Step 1 consists of systems research. This step includes implementation of the evaluation hierarchy and systems analysis. The evaluation hierarchy – which entails evaluating the need for and theory, implementation, impacts, and cost-efficiency of policy – must be used to examine parts of subsystems and the system as a whole. Systems analysis occurs alongside the evaluation efforts and is informed by them. Specific evaluation research and systems analysis activities should be driven by the multi-stakeholder policy process. The research is not dictated by researchers nor by policymakers or criminal justice officials. Rather, the framing of research questions, determination of which questions most warrant attention, time frames for studies, and so on are decided upon through discussions among stakeholders.

Step 2 consists of a multi-stakeholder policy process. Members deliberate about results of the research and then identify additional analyses that they need to determine better how to proceed. They also identify changes – new or revised policies, programs, practices, or decision-making – that should be implemented based on empirical evidence that aligns with the evaluation hierarchy (e.g., establishment of need, theoretical soundness, the ability to implement the changes, magnitude of impact, cost-efficiency) and systems analyses. The latter seek to identify where the largest gains in effectiveness can be had at least cost and risk of harm. This process, too, should include feedback from those responsible for implementing changes or who will be most affected by it. This feedback enables members to identify research that would help to determine what changes would be most helpful and feasible.

Step 3 entails implementing changes and providing feedback to the multi-stakeholder group about potential implementation challenges and ways to improve system or subsystem operations or policies. These changes should be evidence-based. As envisioned here, "evidence" is based on the evaluation hierarchy and systems analysis. Evidence for any action means that a credible empirical basis exists to believe that a policy *need* exists, that a policy rests on credible *theory*, that a policy can and will be *well implemented*, that it will *improve outcomes* and do so *cost-efficiently*, and that it contributes to, rather than inhibits, the *effectiveness and efficiency of the criminal justice system*. The system's overarching goals include what are described here as the "big four": greater public safety, justice, accountability, and cost-efficiency. Additional goals may be achieved as well, such as increasing responsiveness to victims and communities, reducing racial and ethnic disparity in crime and justice processing and responses, and improving public understanding of crime and the criminal justice system. Evidence goes beyond isolated policy assessments. It includes assessment of the likelihood – based on theory and research – of anticipated benefits occurring within the broader systems context in which existing or proposed changes occur. It includes, too, comparison of the actual or anticipated benefits relative to other potential subsystem or system changes.

Although these steps constitute distinct activities that unfold in a sequence, the process in fact should occur continuously. Improving a system of criminal justice requires constantly undertaking research and "tweaking" policies, programs, practices, and decision-making to achieve maximum gains in safety, justice, accountability, efficiency, and other goals. Accordingly, changes should be considered in light of research about the relative importance, magnitude, and likelihood of improvements as compared to other possible changes.

For these steps to be effective, they must be guided by a commitment to improve the criminal justice system and to maintain a focus on the goals that society expects this system to achieve. It must be guided, too, by a commitment to prioritize avoidance of big mistakes, which alone would be an achievement. And it must be guided by efforts to prioritize high-bet, low-risk changes, to leverage feedback loops, and to continuously monitor and evaluate system activities.

In addition, core principles should guide the Systems Improvement Solution. It must be institutionalized into everyday decision-making and policy discussions. It must be non-partisan and deliberative and must rely on research. It should include insights from those with "boots-on-the-ground" insights into criminal justice, such as citizens and police or prison officers. It should include, too, insights from scientists and other experts who study criminal justice. It should rely on analysis of existing data as well as the creation and analysis of new data about system operations and impacts. And it should disseminate information widely and frequently to all individuals and stakeholder groups, including, not least, the public.

In what follows, I discuss each of these three activities and the policy process priorities and core principles. It is critical to highlight that, as complicated as the proposed Systems Improvement Solution may be, there is no shortcut to creating greater awareness or insight about systems problems and their solution. Substantial improvements in safety and justice, for example, cannot happen if policymakers, criminal justice administrators and officials, and researchers work in isolation from one another. And it cannot happen without credible empirical information about system operations and how they may constrain or facilitate the effectiveness of policies. Proceeding in such a manner is a recipe for enabling systems to operate like runaway freight trains, out of control and causing damage wherever they go.

5.2 STEP 1: CONDUCT SYSTEMS RESEARCH

Policymakers and scholars alike critique criminal justice for suffering from systems problems, yet there has been little sustained attention to researching systems. That creates an odd conundrum. Lawmakers point to a "broken" system. They say it needs to be fixed. Yet, such claims occur without little to no empirical information about how the criminal justice system actually operates or what its impacts may be. An illustration: legislators express dismay at prisoners serving less than their full sentence. Society, and the entire criminal justice system, must be coddling criminals, they may say. How to solve this situation? Require that all inmates serve a certain minimum percentage of their sentence in prison.[1] This response, though, ignores the many different forces that give rise to rates of conviction, the conversion of these convictions into prison terms, time served, and so on, and it does virtually nothing to change "the" system.[2] It simply introduces a small, though potentially important, change to one piece of the much larger machinery of criminal justice. Lengthier terms of confinement may result. Alternatively, inmates may serve shorter terms because the courts issue shorter sentences, with inmates serving a greater percentage of them. Whether society is safer is anyone's guess.

Another illustration: a rise in drug-related offending leads policy-makers to advocate for more drug courts or a specialized treatment program that recently garnered a great deal of media attention. What could be more straightforward? Yet, all too frequently, there is nothing straightforward about such a situation. There may be no actual increase in drug-related offending. Or, even if drug-related offending has increased, the increase may not be appreciable. At the same time, drug courts or the new special program may do little to address the root causes of drug abuse and drug dealing in the community, and so crime continues largely una-bated. And the new widely touted treatment program? It may be too costly for the community to fund, it may not achieve benefits greater than what might be obtained at a lower cost, and it may well not be as effective as proponents claim.[3] Initial studies of treatment effects typically overstate the benefits; as more and more studies accumulate, it becomes clear that, upon closer scrutiny using more rigorous evaluations, the effects either are trivial or non-existent.[4]

These and other problems and inefficiencies arise when no institutio-nalized arrangement exists to monitor, evaluate, and improve systems. Conversely, such problems and inefficiencies can be reduced – and oppor-tunities to create greater efficiency can be increased – by undertaking systems research. Per Figure 5.1, systems research consists of evaluations and systems analyses. Many books, articles, and reports provide informa-tion about them.[5] Accordingly, my focus here centers on the conveying the types of research necessary to create ongoing, systematic, comprehensive insight into criminal justice systems and how to improve them. The discussion then turns to the other steps that collectively constitute the Systems Improvement Solution.

Identify Policy Needs

The first step in emergencies consists of assessing the situation. What has happened? Where exactly is the problem? How large is it? What risks may be present? In surveying the scene of an emergency, we ask such questions for straightforward reasons. We want to be sure to target our efforts toward the actual problem and to avoid missteps that could worsen it.

Much the same logic governs needs evaluations.[6] For an existing or proposed policy (or program, practice, rule, etc.), we want to know what problem warrants our attention. After identifying the problem, we want to know its size and location. We would like to know, too, how important this problem may be relative to others so that we can prioritize effectively.

In assessing need, we would like also to determine what causes the problem and how tractable it may be to different interventions. If we do not know what causes a given problem, it will be difficult to correct it. Even if we do know the cause, it may not be clear that we can much about it. Or it may be that many options exist to address it, in which case we would want to invest in the most cost-efficient option. When making this determination, we will want to take stock of existing strategies for addressing the problem. Perhaps augmenting some of them would be the best way to proceed, or perhaps a new approach is indicated.

This seemingly straightforward logic would seem to serve as the starting point for policy and practice. In reality, however, it often gets skipped entirely. In the example above, policymakers observe that inmates do not serve the entirety of the sentences before release, then enact mandatory sentencing policies that require inmates to serve most or all of their sentence in prison. What, though, exactly was the problem? Was the magnitude of the problem sufficient to warrant attention? What caused it? What options existed to address it? Legislatures bypassed such questions and went straight to crafting new sentencing laws.[7] In the end, such laws appear to have contributed to lengthier prison stays. But in so doing they necessarily reduced the number of individuals who could be incarcerated and they obligated resources that might have been put to better use. Whether such changes were effective remains anyone's guess. Unfortunately, this scenario repeats itself annually. Local and state governments, as well as the federal government, create reforms that rest on minimal evaluation of need for a given policy.

The problem is far worse that that, though. Legislatures and criminal justice administrators simultaneously fail to take stock of crime in communities and its causes, and the needs that exist throughout the criminal justice system. This approach ensures that criminal justice will be ineffective and inefficient. In an era in which lawmakers have called for greater accountability, this policy ensures just the opposite: a lack of accountability. Investing in policies, programs, or practices without clear empirical evidence of need wastes resources. It also diverts attention away from understanding the range, intensity, and causes of problems in criminal justice.

What, then, should be done? The answer is simple, though execution of it is not. Needs evaluations should be conducted throughout the criminal justice system. They should be conducted on existing and proposed policies and programs. They also should be conducted on changes that may affect the operations of any one part of the system or the system as a whole. In essence, needs evaluations should be institutionalized into subsystem operations. And they should be institutionalized in a process that oversees the entire system.

What would that look like? Let us first start with communities and crime. Typically, we use arrest or calls-to-the-police data to estimate crime prevalence and trends. This information provides an inaccurate basis for knowing how to allocate police resources. Why? If agencies allocate more police to certain areas, officers will make more arrests in those areas. It then may appear that more crime occurs in them rather than on other areas. Surveys of residents can offset that problem. They can ask questions about experience with a range of potential criminal victimization events and so provide a more accurate basis for determining crime levels and crime rates. In addition, residents can be asked questions about what they think may be driving crime in their communities and about their experiences with law enforcement. This information can be used to gauge more accurately levels of crime and to become sensitized to potential causes as well as to potential ways that police-citizen encounters might be improved. Citizens, too, can be asked about their level of fear, criminal justice policies that they prefer, their willingness to pay for certain policies over others, and so on. This information then could be used to empirically ground policymaker discussions about what the public wants. Without such types of information, policymakers and law enforcement administrators invariably must make inaccurate statements about crime, its causes and solutions, and the public will.

Similar strategies exist for criminal justice subsystems. For example, law enforcement agencies can support crime and victim surveys. They also can implement surveys of police officers to identify potential issues that may affect officer performance and other efforts to improve public safety and, perhaps as importantly, public satisfaction with law enforcement.[8] They can use other sources of data, too, to assess the need for any of a range of police activities, strategies, programs, or the like. Similarly, the courts and corrections can undertake needs evaluations of critical operational activities and proposed changes. Prisons, for example, can rely on inmate and officer survey data as well as administrative records information to identify the amount, distribution, and causes of misconduct as well as its potential solutions.[9] These examples barely scratch the surface and serve simply to highlight the importance of needs evaluations *and* the feasibility of undertaking them. In an era in which data can be readily collected and analyzed, needs evaluations that incorporate survey data and leverage existing administrative records are entirely feasible.

What, though, about needs evaluations for an entire criminal justice system? As I have argued, one of the central problems that renders criminal justice activities ineffective and inefficient is the lack of a system overseer or captain. Without a group or institution devoted to monitoring and improving this system, the criminal justice system runs amok, out of control. The first step, then, toward greater public safety, justice, accountability, and efficiency rests with taking control of this system. That means that legislatures, or their equivalent in counties and cities, must create a standing group or agency that leads efforts to monitor, evaluate, and identify ways to improve the criminal justice system. As I discuss further below, this agency would be charged with continuously identifying competing needs within and across this system. Information would be distributed to stakeholders who then could deliberate about the relative priority of different needs and do so while considering the larger systems context.

Would such an undertaking be costly and difficult? Yes. But it is important to emphasize that there is no free lunch; there can be no accountability without needs evaluations, and subsystems and systems cannot be managed effectively or efficiently without them.

Identify and Assess Policy Theory

Theory provides an explanation for how one thing is related to another. How, for example, is A related to C? Does A affect B, and then does B in turn affect C? Almost any policy, program, practice, decision, or the like rests on a theory the entails one or more causal sequences. The theory may be correct or it may be incorrect. ("Correct" is not quite the right phrasing, but it aptly captures the basic idea. In science, we typically say that a theory is well-supported, or not, given that we can never truly prove that in all places at all times a given relationship exists.) Theory provides the critical foundation on which we guide our decisions. When we rely on untested theory, we almost invariably make mistakes and fail to achieve goals. When we rely on well-tested theory, we stand a better chance, all else equal, of achieving them.

Reliance on weak or unarticulated theory is, unfortunately, a mainstay of criminal justice. In commenting on prison and community supervision programs, Edward Latessa and his colleagues refer to the problem as "correctional quackery."[10] Prison systems might, for example, use self-esteem programs as a way to reduce recidivism. It seems like common sense: Individuals who feel badly about themselves probably want to lash out at the world, and so may be prone to commit crime. This theory does not exist, *per se*, in the scholarly universe. No matter. A theory does not have to come out of the academy to provide what may be an accurate (or what may become a well-supported) account of the world. Even so, the fact that little theoretical basis exists in the scientific literature for a self-esteem recidivism program should raise a potential red flag. More flags go up when we consider that mainstream criminological theories of offending do not feature self-esteem. And still more flags should go up when we consider that self-esteem programs do not target many of the factors known to contribute to offending.

The solution to this situation is to require recourse to established scientific theory where possible when designing and implementing policies, programs, and the like. Sometimes there may be little clear guidance in the scientific literature. (Quite the opposite holds true, however, when it comes to research on the causes of offending and the types of interventions that can reduce it.[11]) For example, there may be concern that prosecutors are biased against minorities when determining how to proceed with cases. Many theories of bias exist, but which ones apply in a specific court setting may not be clear, and there may be unique forces in that setting that extant theories do not contemplate. Here, theory evaluations can be conducted that entail review of extant literature and interviews with, or observations of, court personnel. Researchers then can create a causal logic diagram that identifies how certain actions may contribute to an end outcome, such as racial disparities in sentencing.[12]

In general, policies and programs that rest on credible theory are more likely to be effective.[13] We want, then, criminal justice systems to comprise policies and programs – and decision-making, more broadly – grounded in such theory. There still can be room for "seat-of-the-pants" decisions. However, any decisions that entail or obligate large amounts of resources warrant careful review and analysis *prior* to implementation. Typical program evaluations do not require consideration of systems. However, the argument here is that major decisions in any part of the criminal justice system should be examined with an eye toward understanding how they may affect other parts.

In addition, there should be a clear articulation of the theoretical, or causal, logic for a system's design and how it is supposed to operate to achieve greater public safety and justice. To illustrate, from a system's perspective, there should be more justice if more criminals are caught and punished. However, apprehension of more criminals will not lead to greater punishment if sufficient resources do not exist for the courts to process larger caseloads. A systems perspective and systems theory highlight such problems and can point to conditions that must be met for overall system performance to improve and generate greater safety and justice at less cost. Without them, the system operates like a driverless car. With them, we have a chance of designing changes that will lead us where we want to go: more safety and justice.

Monitor and Assess Implementation

Implementation evaluations – sometimes referred to as "process evaluations" – examine how well a policy or program operates.[14] If a drug court program dictates that probationers meet with their officers weekly and participate in drug treatment counseling, to what extent do these activities in fact happen? If courts should process youth within 30 days of detention, what percentage of the time does that occur? To what extent does a prison system ensure that certain types of housing or programs serve only inmates appropriate for them. Implementation evaluations not only document how well a given policy or program is implemented, they also examine causes of implementation fidelity. For example, when implementation falls short, what factors contributed to the shortfall? What could have been done, and, going forward, what can be done to improve the delivery of services or to comply with laws, rules, or protocols?

Two main uses of implementation evaluations exist. They can be formative. For example, they can provide insight into challenges in providing services or undertaking particular activities, and what might be done to address these challenges. Alternatively, they can be summative and used to assess performance. Summative evaluations provide the equivalent of a report card; they highlight areas of high-quality implementation and others where shortfalls may have occurred.

Insufficient or low-quality implementation constitutes the Achilles' heel of many policies and programs.[15] The best-laid plans can founder in the real world. Community policing officers interact with local residents in a we-know-better-than-you manner or citizens mistrust the police and so refuse to cooperate. A juvenile court diversion program receives fewer referrals than anticipated and so begins accepting youth who may not be appropriate for it. Prosecutors decide to convict alleged offenders in every domestic violence incident even when victims do not want to cooperate, resulting in a less successful conviction rate, greater delays in processing, and less victim satisfaction with the courts. Political pressures create incentives to adopt prison-based drug treatment programs; then, once federal funding for them ceases, states allow the programs to limp along with minimal staffing or support. Supermax prisons, designed for the so-called "worst of the worst," house nuisance inmates and hold them for extended stays, sometimes for years. A reentry program experiences chronic staff turnover, and, as a result, clients receive little assistance in finding housing or securing employment.

Such issues plague juvenile and criminal justice, yet all too frequently go undocumented.[16] We end up, then, with limited to no accountability and innumerable missed opportunities to improve performance. Here, again, no shortcut exists. Full and quality implementation of policies and programs – and efficient operations of entire criminal justice systems and subsystems – cannot occur without institutionalized monitoring. One-time evaluations cannot compensate for such a situation. Neither can audits. The latter can ensure that appropriate documentation of protocols or the like exist. However, they do not provide ongoing, empirically based assessments of the amount or quality of implementation.[17]

The solution entails requiring criminal justice systems to monitor and assess implementation. That means that subsystems must do the same. A lead agency must ensure that each subsystem operates as intended. And each subsystem must have a corresponding agency or division that serves the same function for examining within-subsystem operations.

This idea is simple, yet its execution requires a considerable investment of resources. There should be little reason to shy away from such an investment. If taxpayers are expected to subsidize billions of dollars in policing, they should have reliable and accurate information about how well the police perform their duties. They should know, too, how well their courts and prisons operate. Put simply, what do we get for the billions that we spend on criminal justice?

Time is on our side. In the past, the generation of new, relevant data on agency or program performance entailed tremendous expense. Merging data within and across agencies presented daunting technical challenges. Computer hard drives lacked the capacity to house large data sets and slow processing speeds impeded the amount of analysis that could occur. The landscape has changed, however. Enhanced computing power alone has created the ability to merge and analyze "big data" and to create new sources of data. Prominent movies illustrate the point. "Moneyball," for example, based on the book by Michael Lewis, depicted the way in which statistical analyses changed the way that baseball teams select players and design their offensive and defensive strategies.[18] These analyses took advantage of the rich repository of information that increasingly existed about player and team performance.[19]

One can readily find many examples in criminal justice of similar transitions toward leveraging existing data to gain insight into system operations. Anne Milgram, for example, as New Jersey's Attorney General, identified a remarkable lack of information about the processing decisions that occurred from arrest through sentencing. She recognized, though, the potential to link different sources of "big data" to create insights into processing flows and what could be done to reduce inefficiency. She termed this approach "moneyballing criminal justice."[20] Similarly, Robert Sampson has highlighted the potential for advances in technology to provide researchers with "increased geographic flexibility and power to measure social characteristics across multiple spatial scales."[21] The ability to collect survey data in real time now exists. It is possible, for example, to survey inmates, officers, and wardens on a daily or weekly basis about prison conditions and experiences, and then to aggregate this information to identify patterns among facilities and over time.[22] Similarly, one could identify the extent to which inmates receive appropriate services and treatment or officers comply with prison system protocols and rules. Something as simple as electronic monitoring can be used to identify when offenders comply with (or fail to comply with) conditions of probation.[23]

Constant monitoring and assessment of implementation should occur for any significant criminal justice policy or program. The focus should be on whether it is implemented well and with fidelity to design and on factors that impede implementation and those that may facilitate it. This undertaking should extend beyond policies and programs, however. It should be focused on monitoring and assessing subsystem implementation. The police, the courts, and corrections – each should institutionalize monitoring efforts. Tying all of these efforts together requires systems monitoring. How well does each part of the overall criminal justice system operate independently and interdependently? As I discuss below, systems analysis can aid in this effort and shed light on precisely the area that needs the most illumination yet remains most shrouded in darkness: how well criminal justice delivers safety and justice.

Monitor Outcomes and Evaluate Impacts

Outcome evaluations identify policy outcome levels.[24] For example, an outcome evaluation of a prisoner reentry program might document the percentage of participants who committed a new crime, found employment, or secured housing. Outcome monitoring entails the ongoing measurement and tracking of these measures of success. This activity can be useful for holding organizations accountable. To illustrate, community surveys can track residents' views of police-citizen interactions. A law enforcement agency might strive to ensure that 90 percent or more of such interactions leave residents satisfied with police responsiveness. Monitoring measures of residents' satisfaction can be useful in gauging progress toward this goal.

Outcomes monitoring can shed some light, too, on whether a policy produces an impact. For example, if citizen surveys show a consistent level of community satisfaction with the police and then this level spikes upward after a new community policing initiative, we could have some confidence that this new initiative caused the increase. The monitoring in this instance would not provide a rigorous assessment of impact, but it would provide empirical evidence of policy effectiveness. Why is that important? The more rigorous approach to estimating impact consists of an experimental or quasi-experimental design. However, many times we cannot undertake such research. Outcome monitoring in these cases provides a corrective against seat-of-the-pants, subjective assessments of effectiveness.

When impact evaluations can be conducted, that is the better approach. With such evaluations, we seek to show that a given policy actually caused an improvement in some outcome. Did participation in a drug treatment program, for example, cause reduced recidivism? Or was recidivism among the treatment group lower because this group was at lower risk of offending than the control group? Experiments provide a strong basis for estimating causal effects. But we frequently can estimate causal effects without experiments. Perhaps a program has an extensive wait list. It accepted all of the individuals on that list but did not have the capacity to serve them all. Here, we might cull individuals from that list and use them as a comparison group. We might, too, introduce statistical controls to adjust for potential differences in the two groups that relate both to participation in treatment and to offending.[25] When done well, this type of quasi-experimental design study and others like it can provide credible estimates of impact.

Unfortunately, impact evaluations can be difficult to do well and so may have limited utility.[26] Data limitations frequently undermine efforts to generate credible impact estimates. In addition, it may not always be clear what to use as a counterfactual. For example, we might want to determine whether a particular diversion program reduces offending among juvenile delinquents. One question that we face, though, is what would happen if no program existed? Would these youth be counseled and released? Alternatively, would they likely be put on probation? Each scenario entails a different counterfactual, or "what would have happened." That matters because the intervention might produce different effects depending on the counterfactual.[27] Still other issues can plague even the most well-executed impact evaluations. For example, a study might have strong internal validity – which is to say that we can trust that a policy produced an impact – but have weak external validity, which is to say that we have little idea how likely this impact would be to produce that result with other groups or in other places.[28]

This issue goes largely unrecognized in policy arenas. Policymakers or criminal justice administrators assume that "evidence-based" equates to a study or two that found a particular program to be effective. As argued here, however, evidence-based can and should include reference to the notion that policies, programs, and practices rest on sound empirical research on need, theory, and implementation, not just impact. In addition, a mere handful of studies provides a highly questionable foundation on which to base policy.[29] The famous Minneapolis Domestic Violence Experiment illustrates the point. Initial results of the evaluation suggested that mandatory arrest in domestic violence cases might reduce recidivism among abusers.[30] Soon after, and despite the researchers' cautions, states created "mandatory arrest" policies. Subsequent research identified much more equivocal results.[31]

Perhaps more concerning is the limited evaluation of policy impact throughout the criminal justice system. A program here or there gets evaluated but the bulk of what occurs in criminal justice goes unevaluated.[32] The situation can be likened to someone shuffling the chairs about on the deck of the Titanic. Perhaps the perfect arrangement of chairs can be achieved in that one small part of the ship; meanwhile, the ship and most of its crew and passengers perish.

The state of impact evaluation in criminal justice is worse than that, though. Evaluations can be more rigorous when they focus on delimited efforts where an intervention consists of one activity and targets a select set of individuals. There is nothing wrong with that, *per se*, unless, as has seemingly occurred in many policymaking arenas, it establishes the bar for "evidence-based."[33] When that occurs, it leaves multifaceted policies, programs, practices, and decision-making unevaluated. Why? Evaluations of such activities cannot be undertaken with as high a degree of rigor as narrowly focused programs, and so they may be viewed as less credible. However, these activities are the ones that affect the largest number of individuals or areas. For example, a sentencing law that increases the number of years that individuals can spend in prison may affect thousands, yet it will be less amenable to a strong-design evaluation. Community policing efforts can affect thousands of residents, but they, too, defy rigorous evaluation, and, certainly, experimental-design studies. Similarly, prosecutorial practices for handling low-risk offenders can result in tens of thousands of arrestees going free, getting plea-bargained to probation or any of a range of intermediate sanctions, or being incarcerated; these, too, cannot be evaluated as easily or with the rigor that is possible with assessments of small-scale programs.

The solution? Require and fund the outcome monitoring of policies, programs, practices, and decision-making throughout the criminal justice system.[34] Mandate the monitoring within each subsystem and for the system as a whole. It is at once that simple and that complicated. The insight is straightforward: without evaluation of these different activities, subsystems, or the system, there can be little clarity about overall effectiveness. Instead, we are left only with pockets of illumination. Would it be complicated and costly to institutionalize impact evaluations into criminal justice system operations? Yes. It is, at the same time, feasible, and the only way on which to create a system that appreciably reduces crime and improves justice.

Evaluate Efficiency

Cost-efficiency – or, simply, "efficiency" – refers to the idea that we are getting the most "bang for the buck" with an investment.[35] Two types of efficiency evaluation exist. Cost-effectiveness analyses (CEAs) tell us how much we must spend to obtain a particular benefit. For example, a cost-effectiveness analysis of a drug court might identify the number of averted crimes achieved for each given amount of cost. When two policies or programs seek to improve the same outcome, cost-effectiveness analyses can be useful in determining which produces the most improvement for each dollar spent. We then can choose the better one.

Cost-benefit analyses (CBAs) provide the better option when we wish to compare policies or programs that may have different goals. For example, one prison program may seek to improve the ability of inmates to obtain employment upon release and another may seek to reduce recidivism. The outcomes differ, so we need some basis for creating a comparison. Cost-benefit analyses do that by monetizing the outcomes. Doing so can involve questionable assumptions or estimates about outcomes. For example, what is the dollar value of a robbery? Researchers can and do generate estimates of crime costs, but they entail considerable error.[36] Regardless, they provide guidance in developing comparisons about the relative cost-efficiency of two dissimilar policies with different goals or outcomes. And, of course, when we invest more in some policies than in others, we make implicit assumptions that the returns will justify the greater investment. These assumptions, however, are untested views that may well be incorrect. To illustrate, when we invest millions of dollars in end-of-life care, we implicitly assume that the benefits outweigh those that would accrue to investing the funds in alternative health care activities, such as disease prevention. That assumption almost assuredly is incorrect.

Policymakers and criminal justice administrators understandably call for cost-efficiency.[37] Indeed, who would *not* call for it? Society unfortunately has many social problems that warrant attention and limited resources with which to do so. We want these resources, therefore, to be expended carefully so that we obtain the most benefit possible.

However, efficiency analyses can be complicated to undertake and to interpret, which can make it difficult for policymakers to use them appropriately. For example, efficiency evaluations typically occur after impact evaluations. We want to know what benefit resulted from a policy and then we want to know what it cost. When no benefit exists, we can readily see that the policy costs constituted a poor investment. Impact evaluations thus are needed. As importantly, the underlying impact evaluations must be credible. Otherwise, efficiency estimates rest on a weak foundation. The complexity goes well beyond that issue. For example, the perspective of analysis can be critical. A policy that reduces crime in one suburban area might be cost-efficient there. If, however, the policy increases crime in a nearby suburb, perhaps through a displacement effect, then it might be viewed as cost-inefficient from the perspective of the larger metropolitan area. Estimation of costs, too, can be extraordinarily challenging. In a study of public vs. private prisons, for example, how exactly do we parse out the cost of a public prison when part of its expense stems from a central administrative office that serves many prisons? It can be done, but only with considerable effort and error.[38]

Tremendous advances in cost-efficiency estimation have occurred in criminal justice.[39] Yet, they still occur rarely, and their limitations and the nuances associated with interpreting them can lead to misunderstanding and misuse. The solution here lies in conducting more efficiency analyses and in creating greater understanding about their uses and limitations. Put differently, we need greater investment in research infrastructure to support cost-efficiency analyses. But we also need investment in educating policymakers and criminal justice administrators about these analyses so that they can be savvier requesters and consumers of them.

Conduct Systems Analysis

Systems analysis is a lynchpin of the Systems Improvement Solution or, I argue, any effort to create substantial improvements in criminal justice. Indeed, without it, we – scholars, policymakers, practitioners, citizens – have little ability to describe, understand, or effectively and efficiently improve public safety or justice. Ascending into prominence in the 1960s, systems analysis has advanced greatly since and is widely used in many fields. Although it initially garnered considerable attention from criminologists in the 1960s and 1970s, it fell into disfavor. A central reason was that systems analyses were difficult to undertake and were limited by data availability and slow computers. These challenges no longer exist. To the contrary, numerous opportunities exist to leverage existing data, combine data sources, and undertake systems monitoring and evaluation efforts that would have been impossible several decades ago. Below, I provide a brief history of its use in criminal justice and describe the contours of systems analysis. I then discuss the central role of systems analysis to the more general set of activities that collectively comprise the Systems Improvement Solution.

Brief History of Systems Analysis in Criminal Justice

Systems analysis grew out of developments in operations research during and immediately after World War II.[40] The RAND Corporation pioneered use of systems analysis to assist the military in decisions, such as what types of equipment to develop to achieve long-range goals.[41] The war constrained the options available to the military and governed assessments about equipment and strategy. After the war, less immediate pressure existed, which led to consideration of a broader range of military goals and options for achieving them. Systems analysis provided a process, including a combination of quantitative and qualitative analyses, aimed at exploring and assessing diverse combinations of decisions and options and the uncertainty associated with each. These decisions and options may be estimated to some extent, but invariably involve assumptions and guesswork. Some uncertainty attends as well to any attempt to build predictions built on how individuals, groups, organizations, and the like will act in the future. The end result, then, was development of an analytic approach that entailed as much art as science; the "art" required incorporation of a process to glean insight into systems.[42]

A central argument for systems analysis, but also perhaps the central tension that has followed its use, is uncertainty. Writing in 1956 for the RAND Corporation, Malcolm Hoag articulated the issue well:

The [individual] who solves complex problems in the span of five minutes on the intuitive basis of "sound" military or business judgment and experience, and that is certainly possible, may then forget about it and sleep easily at night. In contrast, the [individual] who has worked two years on an involved Systems Analysis of the same problem may sleep badly, but only because [he or she] has become acutely aware of all the pitfalls in the problem.[43]

This certainty and uncertainty – they constitute flip sides of the same equation – lies at the heart of systems analysis. Whether applied to military matters, education, medicine, or the criminal justice system, the end goal consists of creating greater awareness, and of ensuring that policymakers, officials, and administrators participate in generating and acquiring this awareness. Indeed, the argument here is that informed awareness about how the criminal justice system works provides an essential foundation for improving this system.

In the 1960s and thereafter, systems analysis penetrated into the academy, government agencies, and businesses. That included criminal justice. As Stanley Vanagunas has written, "Systems thinking entered crime and justice policymaking during the Johnson administration."[44] Specifically, the President's Commission on Law Enforcement and Administration of Justice created the Science and Technology Task Force. Charged in part with identifying how systems analysis might be undertaken to improve the operations and effects of the criminal justice system, the Commission's 1967 report greatly influenced contemporary views about how crime, justice, and various aspects of criminal justice collectively form a "system."[45]

Indeed, the President's Commission on Law Enforcement and Administration of Justice (1967) led to passage of Title I of the Omnibus Crime Control and Safe Streets Act of 1968.[46] Title I "provided for massive federal assistance to states and localities for anticrime purposes and set up the Law Enforcement Assistance Administration (LEAA) to lead the effort and to manage the flow of funds."[47] To help fulfill Congress' goal of encouraging better coordination of justice system efforts, "LEAA ... turned to systems thinking."[48] In so doing, the LEAA obtained guidance from the Institute for Defense Analyses, which provided a description of a comprehensive criminal justice systems model. Alfred Blumstein was intimately involved in these efforts and described them in a series of articles and reports.[49] The most prominent models to emerge were the JUSSIM (Justice Simulation) model and the DOTSIM (Dynamic Offender Tracking Simulation) model.[50] Before this time, state and local criminal justice systems did not generally rely on systems analysis to guide policy and practice.[51]

The JUSSIM model (both the original and JUSSIM 2) examined stocks and flows at different decision points, or transition states, in the criminal justice system. It allowed for inclusion of information about feedback loops that can arise, such as when released prisoners reoffend and are rearrested, reconvicted, or reincarcerated. A similar approach for modeling the Canadian criminal justice system (CANJUS) emerged as well.[52] Both efforts involved attempts to characterize the complexity and nature of each given system and to identify how varying forces – such as rates of arrest and of the application of different types of sanctions – can affect subsystems and, ultimately, the entire system.

Interestingly, the ascendance of systems thinking in the 1970s in criminal justice was paralleled by the dramatic growth in criminology and criminal justice as a field. In the early 1960s, there were 15 baccalaureate and graduate programs, combined, in the United States, but by the late 1970s there were over 410 baccalaureate programs and 220 graduate programs.[53] Vanagunas has argued that "academics were particularly receptive to [a systems] approach because of its clear antecedents both in systems theory and in related academic methodologies and theories known as decision sciences."[54]

Even so, systems analysis ultimately fell out of favor. Why? It remains unclear. One reason assuredly stemmed from the limited capacity of computers to undertake complicated analyses. Another was the equally limited availability, at the time, of computers that were readily available at an affordable cost for researchers. One anecdotal illustration: when I was in graduate school in the mid-1990s, my fellow students and I envied one of the students who had purchased 16 megabytes of random access memory (RAM) for his computer. That memory, as well as the speed of it, pales in comparison to computers that subsequently emerged. At the time, too, I remember seeing, during a meeting with my supervising professor, this strange-looking card that looked to be about 3 inches by 6 inches. He looked at me bemusedly and told me that it was a punch card – a semi-rigid card with holes punched out in various places.[55] When he had been in graduate school in the 1970s, these cards had to be stacked in just precisely the right order and left overnight at the computing center. If even one were out of place, no analysis occurred. This situation meant that researchers had to know exactly what models to run. Simpler models would raise a lower risk of problems. Systems analysis presented, then, a double problem: the models entailed considerable complexity and computing power. Today, of course, researchers can access thousands of data sets, run exploratory models in seconds, and undertake complicated analyses with inexpensive computers. Unfortunately, these advances came after the rapid diminishment of systems analysis on the crime and justice landscape.

Another factor that may have contributed to disenchantment with systems analysis came from systems theory. In sociology, a discipline that substantially shaped criminology, the "grand" theorizing of Talcott Parsons and others during the 1960s and 1970s came to be viewed, whether accurately or not, as too cumbersome and removed from reality.[56] These theories sought to capture the fundamental structure and dynamics of society, systems, organizations, families, and social relationships. That ambitious goal led to theories that critics viewed as vague, unfalsifiable, stultifying, and untethered from empirical reality and testing.

Whatever the causes, the fact remains that systems analysis has begun to garner prominent attention from the researcher and practitioner community.[57] Evidence of the greater embrace of systems analysis can be seen in a 2006 symposium on operations research convened by the National Institute of Justice, the basic and applied research arm of the U.S. Department of Justice for the study of crime and justice.[58] Some states, too, have incorporated variants of systems analysis. The Texas Criminal Justice Policy Council, for example, undertook systems analyses for the Governor and Legislature until it was disbanded by Governor Rick Perry in 2003.[59] The Policy Council stands out because it provides a clear example of an effort to create systems-level analysis and understanding that is institutionalized into executive and legislative deliberations about current and proposed policies and policy changes.

Greater interest in systems analysis may derive from several possible changes. One is the emergence of mass incarceration and, more broadly, the exponential growth in criminal justice size and expenses over the past three decades.[60] States and local jurisdictions have criminal justice systems that obligate an ever-greater portion of available taxpayer funds, and each increase essentially becomes a fixed cost. Why? Most aspects of criminal justice, such as police departments and prisons, never get reduced. States and local jurisdictions need to find ways to operate more cost-efficiently. Systems analyses provide one of the critical tools on which they can rely. Another significant change stems from advances in computing. These advances have led to the availability of more and better data and the analytic and computing capacity to undertake systems analyses that in the 1960s and 1970s simply were not possible.

Systems Analysis Overview

Systems analysis entails the modeling of stocks and flows within and across a system.[61] As discussed in Chapter 3, systems consist of interconnected sets of elements or parts that form a whole and work toward a commonly shared or agreed-upon goal. The interdependence among parts – including stocks and the flow of information, parts, decisions, and the like from one part to another – defines a system. Some systems may be well-defined or discernible and others may not, and some may be more vulnerable to external forces or events than others. Regardless, a central characteristic of systems is that they operate according to their own internal logic. When they operate well, the system amounts to a well-oiled machine; when they do not, it amounts to the chaos of a classroom of over-sugared kindergartners running rampant with no oversight.

As also discussed in Chapter 4, criminal justice operates as a system, though not typically like a well-oiled one. This system has common goals, such as the pursuit of public safety and justice, that society sets out for it. The expectation, too, of this system is that it will operate with accountability, that is, that it will perform well the actions for which it was designed. As a society, we expect this system to operate cost-efficiently. We also expect it to prioritize responsiveness to victims and communities and to operate fairly, such that racial and ethnic or other disparities do not exist or, when they do, that they get addressed quickly. As part of operating with accountability, this system is expected to communicate effectively with the public and policymakers about crime, justice, and the operations, impacts, and cost-efficiency of its efforts.

Alongside these goals stand the many subsystems – law enforcement agencies, courts, probation and parole, and jails and prisons – and their parts. These subsystems have distinct goals. Yet they also interact with one another to achieve broader, systems goals. The criminal justice system and its parts all operate to an internal logic specific to them. At the same time, they can be affected by external forces such as increases in crime, changes in political regimes, or social or economic upheaval. And the system can influence itself. When, for example, courts increase conviction and incarceration rates and, simultaneously, law enforcement departments substantially increase in size, the potential for felons to be rearrested, reconvicted, and reincarcerated goes up in a cyclical process of growth. Throughout each subsystem and the system as a whole, inputs and outputs are central. Recall that inputs constitute resources, such as available machines, tools, staff, programs, or the like. Outputs constitute the products produced by a given part or subsystem, such as the rate of police arrests or court convictions.

Criminal justice systems can be mapped by identifying how each subsystem interacts with the others. Each subsystem in turn can be mapped by identifying constituent parts, the inputs and outputs specific to each part, and the stocks and flows between parts.

The classic example in criminal justice consists of a focus on the flow of offenders across stages of processing, such as the number or rate of offenders who "flow" from one state (e.g., arrest) to another (e.g., conviction). Flows can be viewed as movements of anything (e.g., offenders or cases) from one part or subsystem to another. Stocks represent not a flow, but a relatively static state, such as the amount of individuals in prison on a given day. When the system works well, flows occur unimpeded and stocks do not excessively shrink or balloon. When it does not, then, as Alan Coffey long ago observed, "the criminal justice system is vulnerable to fragmentation and ineffectiveness – perhaps becoming a 'non-system.'"[62]

Standard criminal justice processing flow charts capture the idea that diverse flows occur throughout the system. For example, Coffey's account of systems envisions that law violations serve as inputs (a), these lead to processing by the police, courts, prosecution, and corrections (b), and the resulting output is reduced crime (c).[63] If we focus on a subsystem, such as corrections, the inputs might be adjudicated offenders (a), the process might be investigation, supervision, and treatment (b), and the output might be "corrected" offenders (c).[64] Such an account constitutes an obvious simplification of systems that entail far more complexity. The basic logic, however, remains the same: we seek to depict the interdependent structures and processes that constitute a given system or subsystem.

What many flow charts do not show, but what is essential to systems analysis, is the importance of stocks. These may influence flows and, vice versa, flows may influence stocks. For example, when prisons house more inmates than regulations permit, they may respond by releasing more inmates. That may help the prison system but perhaps not communities. When flows into a prison system decline, the stock population may eventually decline as well. Stocks and flows can and do change, and these changes themselves can derive from many sources. For example, flows into prisons may be steady, but if laws increase the average duration of time served, the stock population in prison will increase. The essence of systems analysis lies in creating greater understanding about the stocks and flows within a system, the factors that influence them, and their effects on system effectiveness.

To improve the accuracy and usefulness of systems analysis, we can aggregate or disaggregate models to varying levels of specificity, depending on interest or policy relevance. In some instances, a highly general systems analysis might be useful. In others, specific nuances may be important to include. For example, as William Rhodes has written, "an aggregate model of the flows and stocks of all felony crimes may not be useful if one is interested in simulating a policy change that applies just to burglars."[65] Conversely, an analysis that focuses only on flows into and out of prisons will not help us to understand the implications of these flows more generally for criminal justice system operations or impacts.

One central challenge with systems analysis hinges on mapping out the parts and the decision points, or branches, that lead to flows from one area to another. For example, if a local jurisdiction increases the availability of drug treatment, then courts may divert more of their caseload to treatment. Here, then, when examining the criminal justice system, we need to disaggregate case flows by type of offense. Whether to disaggregate is guided by the extent to which flows are known to vary or may vary for certain cases, groups, or decisions. JUSSIM, CANJUS, and other systems analysis models provided for varying levels of mapping flows, but they also limited the number of parts, decision points, and disaggregations that could occur, which limited their usefulness.[66] The limitations stemmed precisely from an effort to make the programs more user friendly, but at a cost of restricting the ability to include more detailed systems modeling.[67] Creating more refinements provides a critical avenue through which to improve systems models. But doing so does not necessarily improve matters. For example, an infinite amount of description of parts, flows within and across them – and disaggregation, where these flows are repeated for various groups – creates too much confusion and renders any results all but uninterpretable.[68] However, refinements that incorporate specificity that reflects substantial differences in how, say, burglars are processed relative to drug offenders, result in more accurate accounts of flows and impacts on other parts of systems.

Another challenge – or, more precisely, opportunity – of systems analysis entails inclusion of estimates about external forces that can affect a system. In developing the JUSSIM model, for example, the creators allowed estimates of crime amounts to be included, but not the causes of these amounts or a range of factors that might influence flows into the system. Blumstein has emphasized, however, that "the creation of a richer 'front end'" description in systems modeling is critical.[69] Consider, for example, a situation in which a state pivots toward a more "get-tough" approach to parolees. Perhaps it decides to place more emphasis on supervising parolees and incarcerating them for any violations, even those that, by historical standards, would be considered minor. This situation characterizes what happened in many states during the rise of mass incarceration, as Jeremy Travis and Sarah Lawrence documented.[70] Such information could – and ideally would – be included in a systems analysis as a specific, known contributor to flows into the courts (the "front end" of the system) and prisons.

Crime, or the various sources of flows into the criminal justice system, serves as but one dimension that systems analyses should incorporate. In the above example, the flow of cases from parole violations into the courts might be viewed as "endogenous" to the criminal justice system – that is, one part of the system affects another. Whether or not characterized as such, its influence can extend beyond creating an increase in parole violators coming into the courts. For example, a substantial body of work on prisoner reentry suggests that communities that experience a high rate of withdrawal of residents suffer. This effect may be compounded when communities serve as the repositories of large numbers of residents who have been incarcerated.[71] Children, for example, may lose an able-bodied parent who then, after incarceration, returns less able to provide emotional or financial support.[72] The end result may be that get-tough parole violation policies may not only directly fuel greater court caseloads and incarceration growth, they also may do so indirectly by increasing crime in communities.

It may not always be possible to estimate such potentialities with empirical precision. Yet, it *is* possible to include qualitative accounts from experts in the field, including residents, to generate a range of estimates about potential changes in case-flow that may arise and how they might influence different parts of the criminal justice system.

One illustration of this approach comes from a study of juvenile justice bed-space forecasting efforts in which I participated. The state agency that a colleague and I visited described their statistical model for predicting the bed-space capacity that they would need in coming years, and then emphasized that they relied on a stakeholder meeting to discuss the model results and factors that might shape its accuracy. They emphasized the importance of this meeting. To illustrate its importance, the agency described a meeting at which a prosecutor from a large metropolitan county noted that the assumption about the number of cases their county would send in coming years was overstated. Why? The county had recently invested in a juvenile boot camp, with the intention of trying to use punishments that would keep young offenders in the community. As a result of this information, the analysts then could adjust their forecast using an estimate of how many youth likely would be diverted to the boot camp. The estimate was just that: an estimate that assuredly had some error built into it. But just as assuredly, the overall forecast likely was more accurate because it included information about the county's plans, information that could not have been derived from analysis of extant data.

Systems Analysis as a Part of the Systems Improvement Solution

Criminal justice is designed and operates as a system. To understand its operations and impacts, then, as well as the opportunities to improve it, requires systems research. That includes systems analysis. It also includes, as discussed above, application of the evaluation hierarchy. This hierarchy entails needs, theory, implementation, impact, and cost-efficiency evaluations. They provide critical information for guiding systems analyses. For example, estimates of the impact of a policing initiative on crime rates can guide estimates about the flow of cases into the courts. Conversely, system analyses can be used to undertake or augment evaluations. For example, all "need" – that is, the need for a given program, policy, resource, etc. – is relative to competing priorities. A study of policing might show that a given department operates with fewer officers than other seemingly comparable departments. Here, then, it appears that a given county needs more officers. However, a systems analysis might show that more pressing needs exist. Perhaps, for example, few if any crime prevention programs exist in the county. Or perhaps there is a greater need for jail space or court staff. Perhaps, too, an analysis shows that police activities could be restructured to achieve comparable or better outcomes. Police officers might be diverted from enforcing speed limits – a function that video cameras and other strategies might do better – to other activities.[73]

Systems analysis is critical to the Systems Improvement Solution.[74] Without it, state and local jurisdictions have little ability to understand, monitor, or effectively "drive" their system to improve outcomes. At the same time, it contributes to evaluation efforts and provides guidance about when and where they may be needed. Indeed, one of the central limitations of many evaluations consists of their largely *ad hoc* nature. One prison program out of hundreds might receive a deluxe impact evaluation, while the others go unevaluated. A tragic police shooting leads to calls for examining the need for change. Lawmakers hear about an amazing new specialized court approach to sanctioning drug offenders and then fund evaluations of it. In these and other cases, the evaluations may yield important insights. Yet, they occur alongside of near-complete inattention to a wide range of other issues that warrant attention.

In the law, it is said that "bad cases make for bad law." With any system, focusing only on extreme or isolated cases makes for an ineffective system. The Systems Improvement Solution thus calls for institutionalizing systems analysis and the evaluation hierarchy into all aspects of understanding, monitoring, evaluating, and improving criminal justice.

Systems, Subsystems, and Relevant Outcomes

The criminal justice system itself consists of subsystems, as discussed in Chapter 4 and as depicted in Figure 4.9. These include the police, courts, probation and parole, and jails and prisons. Put differently, every part of the "[criminal justice system] process is a subsystem – a system-within-a-system."[75]

Without active management of the overall system, these subsystems can and do steer taxpayer investments in ways that ultimately may do little to achieve the ultimate goals of public safety, justice, accountability, and efficiency. At the same time, the effectiveness of this system depends on each subsystem's effectiveness. The implication, then, is clear – the Systems Improvement Solution must be implemented both for the system as a whole and for each subsystem. In the ideal scenario, the Systems Solution is undertaken by one central agency or organization and coordinates its efforts with "branch" offices in each of those subsystems.

It is often said that "all politics is local." Much the same can be said for each subsystem. Law enforcement agencies may have different cultures those that hold in courts or corrections. Their immediate goals can and do differ. Accordingly, among subsystems, evaluation research and systems analyses must be driven by the "local" emphasis. The Systems Improvement Solution must be institutionalized in each subsystem. For example, law enforcement agencies, the courts, probation and parole, and jails and prisons all should have their own systems research and multi-stakeholder process, per Figure 5.1. Their efforts, in turn, should be coordinated by and inform the centralized Systems Improvement Solution.

Across all systems-focused analyses, there must be clarity about relevant goals and attendant outcomes.[76] A lack of clarity about them plagues many policy and program evaluations.[77] Researchers may be asked to assess the effectiveness of a program. To do so, however, requires identification of relevant goals, associated outcomes, how much to weight each one, and measures that can be gauged using existing or new data. This process seems straightforward. Yet, programs and organizations frequently are vague about their goals or how best to measure them. The situation can be likened to a homeowner who wants an architecture firm to make a house feel more "comfortable." What does he or she mean by "comfortable"? What exactly is the homeowner trying to achieve? After questioning the homeowner at length, the architects may discover that the owner wants more sunlight to infuse the interior, a more open kitchen, and maple-colored wood flooring throughout the home. During the discussion, the spouse arrives home and says that a spiral staircase must be part of the new home design. The architects scratch their heads and try to push the owners gently to clarify what should be the top priority. Eventually, it becomes clear that the owners have a budget that will only allow one, possibly, two of the desired changes. That information leads to further discussion about the relative importance of certain changes. In this example, the homeowners perhaps come to the realization that what they most want is to paint the interior a bright color that both lightens the interior and makes it feel warmer. All of this work, of course, serves to ensure that the owners end up with changes that best achieve their goals within a budget that they can afford.

A similar process can and does unfold with evaluations. When researchers cut corners, they do the equivalent of emphasizing one goal or outcome over others, even though these may not be the most important or relevant ones. If the architects in the above example cut corners, they might end up installing a spiral staircase even though the owners ultimately determined that this change lay at the bottom of their list of desired changes. Similarly, if researchers cut corners, they assess impacts on goals and outcomes that may be largely irrelevant.

Consider policing. Public safety and satisfaction are among the most important goals for law enforcement agencies. Few agencies, however, collect data on actual crime rates or how the public views police professionalism or responsiveness.[78] Or consider prosecutors. The courts might track information about the percentage of all prosecutions that result in a conviction. Yet, this measure tells us virtually nothing about how well prosecutors select cases; perhaps there are many cases that they should have pursued but did not do so, opting instead for "safe" cases that would result in a high conviction rate. It tells us nothing, too, about, say, their professionalism in handling cases. To what extent did they adhere to rules and procedures? How just were the imposed sanctions? How well were prosecutorial efforts targeted toward different types of crimes? How well did prosecutors work with the police and communities to enhance crime prevention through a variety of efforts, not just convictions?[79] Consider, not least, corrections. Typical evaluations center on recidivism as a measure of success. Yet, we need far more than that to assess correctional system performance. For example, to what extent do prison systems adhere to various rules and procedures, offer appropriate or needed programming and services, or train and monitor staff? And to what extent do their efforts improve not only recidivism but also housing and employment outcomes after inmates return to society?[80]

It is, in short, critical that the Systems Improvement Solution focus on the system as a whole as well as each subsystem, and that relevant goals and outcomes are identified. These steps then create the foundation for undertaking useful evaluations. They help us, for example, to know what measures to collect and what outcomes to monitor.

The Driver's Dashboard: Tying the Different Types of Research All Together

The first component of the Systems Improvement Solution entails conducting systems research. That entails identifying policy needs, monitoring and assessing implementation of various parts of the criminal justice system (including policies, programs, and practices), monitoring outcomes, evaluating impacts and cost-efficiency, and conducting systems analysis. It seems like a lot. And it is. But, as with many complicated endeavors, it is possible to distill a great deal of information and present it in an accessible manner. In the past, doing so was difficult because of the amount of information involved and limits in computing power and graphics. The computing landscape has changed dramatically in the last two decades. As but one illustration, smartphone "apps" emerged in 2008, and in but a few years software developers created thousands of apps, many of which were available for free. With advances in computing power, including programs designed for conducting statistical analyses and producing results graphically, it now is possible to organize "big data" and to present it in myriad ways.

One problem with many analyses lies in the presentation of the results. Researchers tend to provide information in formats that confuse others needlessly.[81] To be sure, some analyses entail considerable complexity and some may not be readily distilled down to a few simple charts. That situation is atypical. A simple example: regression analysis constitutes the "workhorse" methodology for many studies. A "dependent variable," or outcome, is "regressed" on an "independent variable," such as participation in a program, and many "control variables" are included as well. The latter serve to help the researcher approximate what we might get with an experimental design. After developing the model specification that seems most likely to generate a credible estimate of the independent variable's effect on the outcome – for example, the effect of program participation on recidivism – we end up with a page or so of "output," which consists of many numbers. These numbers are coefficients that quantify how much the independent variable affects the outcome. Researchers will tend to present all the different numbers and to point to a coefficient. For most people, though, that coefficient is not intrinsically meaningful. Better is to translate the results into percentages. For example, "The program reduced recidivism by 20 percent."

When there are many more results to present, it is all the more necessary that they be presented graphically using charts, diagrams, tables, or the like. An illustration of the approach recommended here is what might be termed the "driver's dashboard." Drivers use a dashboard to know when to buy gas, how much to adjust our speed, and whether to get an oil change or have the engine checked. Airplanes and many other vehicles typically operate in a similar manner; the dashboards simply are bigger. In a similar manner, information about different aspects of a system or any given subsystem can be distilled down to the equivalent of dashboard meters and gauges, presented and arrayed in any easy-to-understand and easy-to-use manner.

One benefit of a "dashboard" approach to understanding the criminal justice system, or any subsystem (e.g., a prison system), is the ability to use the equivalent of "control knobs."[82] These knobs represent opportunities to adjust this or that part of a system and identify *a priori* potential ripple effects. For example, systems analyses can be undertaken to determine what the likely impacts would be of a particular change to one part of the system. Adjusting the sentence length knob, for example, might seem like a good idea. Add a few months or years on to prison sentences and then wait for deterrence to kick into gear. Such a logic in fact undergirded much of the "get-tough" movement in the 1980s, 1990s, and 2000s.[83] A potential problem with this approach would be readily apparent from a systems analysis perspective. Adjust the knob upward, for example, and it instantly would become clear that other dynamics – such as an increase in rates of arrests for lower-severity crimes, an increase in rates of converting these arrests to convictions and in turn to terms of incarceration, or an increase in rates of parolee revocation for technical violations – could result in much greater demands for prison space than would otherwise be apparent. This possibility would become apparent by simultaneously turning the number-of-arrests *and* sentence length knobs.[84]

To illustrate the utility of a dashboard-driven approach to monitoring and understanding system operations and the potential impacts of various changes, consider a scenario where one serves as the director of an entire prison system. At present, few states provide valid, up-to-the-minute information about different activities and outcomes at each prison.[85] Imagine, though, a dashboard that consists of a map with every prison in the state on it. As the director, we might want to know about the level of prison infractions at each facility. We could press a button and see which facilities have the highest infraction rates. Perhaps we want to isolate our focus just to maximum-security facilities; a separate button allows the map to regenerate using only these facilities.

A variant: perhaps we want to know which facilities have experienced the largest increases in misconduct or violence in the last month. The dashboard could include a button, or slide, that allows us to identify such facilities. Any number of additional variants exist. For example, we could repeat this exercise but do so with different outcomes, which we might select from a pull-down menu of possibilities, each of which is supported by different sources of data. One concern in prison systems, for example, is riots.[86] Accordingly, we might select a map that identifies those facilities where the reported level of inmate satisfaction with their treatment has worsened by more than 10 percent or where officer morale has greatly declined. This information might provide insight about those facilities where inmate and officer morale has appreciably declined and where, by extension, the risk of a riot may be greatest.

In each instance, the generation of maps allows us then to take action. We may not know what produced the changes, but at least we know that a problem may exist. In turn, we can investigate. For example, we could select an option that allows us to view a profile of changes in the facilities that experienced a substantial decrease in inmate or officer morale. It may be that a clear pattern surfaces, such as evidence of a large increase in officer turnover or new inmates. At the least, knowledge about substantial changes in these facilities would enable the director to call wardens to discuss the changes and what may have produced them.

Is such a dashboard possible? Absolutely. In an era of "big data," one in which surveys can be administered readily through phones, tablets, laptops, kiosks, and more, prison systems can frequently poll inmates, officers, staff, and wardens about their own or others' behaviors, attitudes, performance, and more. This information can be instantly compiled into a database, analyzed, and transferred into graphical displays. In addition, it can be combined with administrative records data or other sources of data. Doing so would allow for the creation of comprehensive portraits of inmates, officers, facilities, and systems operations, as well as for conducting evaluations of policy or program need, implementation, impact, and cost-efficiency.

In short, the dashboard approach would allow for accessible presentation of the results of systems research, including simulation modeling and forecasting efforts and evaluations of need, implementation, impact, and cost-efficiency.[87] And it would enable exploration of ways that different parts of a system may influence one another and what might happen if one or another part were changed.[88] Multi-stakeholder policy groups, as well as agency directors, could use a dashboard approach to examine how inputs and outputs within and across parts of the system do or may affect the system as a whole and its parts. This approach could incorporate, too, information about monetary dimensions associated with decisions. For example, information about expenditures and estimated monetary costs or benefits of certain outcomes could be included to identify the potential net gains or losses associated with particular changes. Not least, the dashboard could include the option to depict the uncertainty associated with different modeling scenarios. Uncertainty attends to all decisions and estimates, especially those that involve changes within a systems context. It is critical that this uncertainty be acknowledged and, to the extent possible, quantified. That way, stakeholders can evaluate the merits of particular changes with a clear understanding about the potential benefits – and risks – involved.

The dashboard approach accords well with calls in recent decades to use "big data" to understand how systems work and what policy options exist.[89] One of the central barriers to effective use of "big data" – that is, the large amounts of electronically accessible information increasingly collected by various local and state agencies and other organizations – is a clear roadmap for how to organize and analyze this information.[90] That is precisely what systems research and a "dashboard" mode of presenting results provides.

However, as discussed below, systems research needs someone or some group to steer it. There is no understanding or solution that the availability of data or systems research alone can provide. Data and research ultimately are tools. These tools must be designed and used by knowledgeable individuals and groups. Only then will the resulting information and analysis provide credible insights and guidance for policy and practice and allow these individuals and groups to make better decisions for achieving criminal justice system goals.[91]

5.3 STEP 2: USE A MULTI-STAKEHOLDER POLICY PROCESS TO UNDERSTAND AND IMPROVE CRIMINAL JUSTICE

Analysis is but one part of the Systems Improvement Solution. The incorporation of diverse stakeholders, per Figure 5.1, in a research-based policy review and design process is another critical part of the solution. This process should guide and improve analyses. It also should enable appropriate use of them to identify areas where improvements can and should be made. Here, I describe the contours of "good" process and critical priorities to guide it.

The Critical Role of "Good" Process

The decisions that policymakers and criminal justice administrators and practitioners make frequently occur without sufficient, if any, awareness of the broader contexts in which these decisions occur. They also can and do occur with insufficient information. Legislative activity that entails *ad hoc* policy creation every two to four years illustrates the problem. Congressional elections change the composition of criminal justice committees, most members have little long-standing involvement with or understanding of the criminal justice system, and they meet for an all-too-brief period of time to deliberate quickly, with little information about system operations or impacts, and pass new legislation. Criminal justice administrators enjoy the advantage of focusing full-time on their work, but typically their purview extends only to one narrow part of the criminal justice system. If they run an agency, they may have done so only for a year or so. Those who have served longer are better positioned to understand the system that they oversee. However, they almost invariably operate with little relevant systems information. In large part, that stems from the fact that research divisions with criminal justice system agencies undertake their work with minimal staffing. Available research personnel then perforce must focus on descriptive reports that reveal little about the operations or effectiveness of the system and its parts. Compounding this situation is the fact that research divisions typically have little systematic information about offenders, victims, communities, and the like.

A better way is needed. In particular, state and local governments need "good" process – that is, an effective way of understanding the criminal justice system, identifying how to improve it, adopting and evaluating improvements, "tweaking" the system, and then engaging in review and evaluation of these changes. What, then, are the contours of such a process?

First, there must be a lead, or "captain" agency to conduct the process and ensure that it stays on track. As Vanagunas has observed, "the critical flaw in the criminal justice systems [analysis] concept is the lack of a central system controller."[92] That flaw applies to systems analysis and any type of research. Without someone to oversee the research process – and to ensure that it responds to diverse stakeholders – decisions invariably must rest on poor to non-existent or irrelevant studies or "facts."[93] We then fail to see important patterns, which is precisely what contributed in part to the 9/11 terrorist attack. That is, too many silos existed. Each had bits and pieces of insights, but little ability to put all of them together. The 9/11 Commission Report emphasized, for example, that the different agencies that focus on intelligence and terrorism needed the equivalent of an "attending physician who makes sure they work as a team."[94] They did not have one. Any successful effort to process and analyze information and to collect the views and perspectives of multiple stakeholders requires the functional equivalent of an attending physician, that is, a lead agency or organization responsible for effectively coordinating the efforts of all parties. This work should be focused on the entire system as well as subsystems to ensure that it works effectively and efficiently.

Second, this agency must be institutionalized into criminal justice system decision-making and must involve members of the executive and legislative branch and include diverse stakeholders. For example, senate and house legislators or staff members, as well as executives from law enforcement, the courts, and corrections should participate. Such an approach accords with call by the US Office of Justice Programs for involvement of the executive, legislative, and judicial branches in non-partisan efforts to guide justice investments.[95] It accords, too, with the call that Blumstein made 50 years ago in advocating that independent research organizations exist that collaborate with other research institutions and with criminal justice agencies to undertake systems research.[96] It accords, not least, with examples, discussed further below, of agencies in Texas and Washington that have undertaken independent criminal justice research on behalf of the legislative and executive branches of government and criminal justice agencies.

At the local level, a similar process can and should be institutionalized. Other critical stakeholder groups who should participate include those who work in the system (e.g., police officers, prosecutors, defense counsel, judges, prison staff) and those who are affected by it (e.g., offenders, victims, community representatives). These individuals can provide critical insight into problems and opportunities as well as into systems dynamics that may influence the success of current or proposed initiatives.[97] A process that includes such diverse groups requires sustained attention to coordinating meetings and ensuring that deliberations result in decisions. Accordingly, state or local jurisdictions must commit the necessary resources to support the agency and the process. These resources should include funding for the collection, compilation, and analysis of criminal justice data, and creating and distributing reports to the multi-stakeholder group and to the broader community.

Involvement of multi-stakeholder groups is critical for many reasons. One is that research too-frequently is left to researchers; the end results are analyses of questionable accuracy or usefulness. By contrast, inclusion of stakeholders can increase the accuracy and usefulness of research. For many policymakers and criminal justice administrators and practitioners, research can seem like some far-removed undertaking, one that only researchers can do and understand. That belief is wrong and dangerous. Research can entail complicated analyses. However, that does not mean that understanding the motivating questions, assumptions, implications, or limitations of analyses requires special knowledge. As importantly, much research requires judgment calls. Asking researchers to make these calls is akin to homeowners letting an architect decide what type of features they want in a house.

Consider the following examples. If we want to estimate the impacts of supermax housing, we need to identify the counterfactual. That is, what would a prison system have done if it did not build a supermax facility? A researcher might assume that the alternative would have been to rely on maximum-security housing. However, policymakers or prison officials might have invested in other policies, such as the hiring and training of a specialized officer workforce, if they had not pursued supermax housing. Here, then, we should compare the effects of supermax housing to what likely would have arisen if the prison system had pursued this other alternative. Inclusion of policymakers and corrections officials would help us to identify this research design.

Another example centers on the individuals most affected by the criminal justice system. They can and frequently do hold special insight into the relationships between certain dynamics within or across a system. This insight then can be included in systems analyses to provide more realistic estimates of system operations and their impacts. To illustrate, recall that in Chapters 3 and 4, many different forms of causation were identified. For example, there may be tipping points involved in a particular undertaking. Below the tipping point we may see little evidence of an impact, but past it we may witness a tremendous one. Community policing, for example, may be especially difficult to implement in areas of concentrated disadvantage or where relations between a minority community and law enforcement have been contentious. In such a context, policing efforts may produce little appreciable change in public views toward law enforcement or in public safety. However, sustained efforts to work with the community may eventually result in greater cooperation with and support from residents. That eventually may lead to lowered rates of crime and higher levels of citizen satisfaction with the justice system.[98] Evaluators might fail to recognize this possibility, however. By contrast, citizens and law enforcement officers alike might well highlight it. Researchers then would know to include tipping points into their assessments of community policing impacts.

Yet another example involves interactions that involve the police, courts, jails, prisons, probation, and parole. Researchers tend to ignore these interactions. Why? Interactions can be difficult to identify, theories rarely anticipate them, and analyses to detect them can be complicated to undertake and interpret. Policymakers, too, tend to ignore interactions. They enact laws or fund new programs as if these efforts can be implemented and "work" in isolation, with no interference from or effects on diverse parts of the justice system. By contrast, those who work in or are directly affected by this system may see numerous interactions that bear directly on the likely implementation or impacts of a particular policy or program. Prosecutors, for example, may be able to discern readily that a mandatory domestic violence arrest law may not translate into more convictions and may well slow down court processing times.[99]

In these and many other instances, improved systems research can only result from including diverse stakeholders. These individuals can guide identification of the types of scenarios that may unfold and that should be included in systems analyses or evaluations. A multi-stakeholder process is necessary for providing information to policymakers and criminal justice administrators on a timely basis and for helping them to understand the system that they seek to improve. The importance of stakeholder understanding cannot be overstated. Creating change without awareness of the broader systems context is a recipe for failure and reinforces failure. By contrast, inclusion in the research process, especially in systems-focused analyses, can increase stakeholder awareness of systems dynamics and provide information necessary for creating targeted change that has the greatest likelihood of achieving the goals that society sets for the criminal justice system. As Blumstein has emphasized, systems modeling "plays the important role of forcing planners to consider the entire system and the interdependency of its parts in their planning."[100] Indeed, "one basic tenet of the systems approach is that important but seemingly narrow questions be viewed in a sufficiently broad system context."[101]

John Gibson and colleagues, in their account of systems analysis, have expanded on this point. They have highlighted, for example, the usefulness of systems analyses in helping stakeholders to gain clarity about policy goals and systems contexts and interdependencies. Such analyses are helpful, too, in documenting the following: what is known or not known about specific aspects of this system or particular issues; uncertainties in assumptions and estimates about a policy's or system's likely implementation and effectiveness; and the potential for optimization through diverse strategies rather than committing to one seemingly commonsensical policy option that in fact may not have a high probability of success.[102]

Not least, inclusion of diverse stakeholders serves to address the conflicts that arise when different parts of a system pursue their own interests and ignore those of the other parts. As Donella Meadows has emphasized, "resistance to change arises when goals of subsystems are different from and inconsistent with each other."[103] In such cases, "the most effective way to deal with policy resistance is to find a way of aligning the various goals of the subsystems, usually by providing an overarching goal that allows all actors to break out of their bounded rationality."[104] Criminal justice systems and subsystems in fact share many goals. Continuous discussions among stakeholders can help to ensure that this fact is recognized and that efforts to improve subsystem operations should further these goals.

Third, the group must meet monthly or quarterly. Considerable changes can and do occur "on the ground." Meeting regularly enables the group to respond quickly when needed. More importantly, it enables the group to participate in the research design process, identifying issues that bear scrutiny and requesting new analyses that evaluate a particular policy or program or that explore the feasibility and likely benefits of particular changes. Frequent meetings allow, too, for creation of greater institutional knowledge about the design and operations of the system and greater appreciation among diverse stakeholders about the views that each holds. Consider, as one example, efforts to forecast law enforcement or prison populations. Any forecasts beyond a year carry with them substantial uncertainty. Assumptions that previously were justified may no longer be so, unanticipated events can occur, and so on. Frequent reviews of projections help to reinforce that such uncertainty exists and simultaneously forces participants to understand better the nature of the projections, including their assumptions and limitations.

Fourth, meetings should center on discussion of systems analyses and as-needed (e.g., need, theory, implementation, impact, and efficiency) evaluations. Stakeholders should be presented with up-to-the-minute systems and subsystem analyses as well as results from any critical policy and program evaluation activities. Any such effort must be guided by the equivalent of an executive summary of analyses and evaluation results that are disseminated in written format prior to meetings so that attendees can be prepared to discuss them. The results should include clearly identified feedback both from those responsible for implementing policies, programs, practices, and decisions and from those affected by them.

Fifth, the meetings should focus on identifying problems that need to be addressed and, based on systems research, changes that may be warranted. This discussion should entail review of the uncertainty associated with any changes. The discussions should focus first on how best to improve the effectiveness and efficiency of the entire criminal justice system and second on how to ensure that each subsystem can achieve its goals. As part of this discussion, uncertainty should of course be discussed. Stakeholders should understand the assumptions made in systems research and the potential for errors or random events to affect the implementation or effectiveness of policies.[105] Researchers should not be left to understand these problems alone. Stakeholders should understand them as well so that they have realistic expectations. They should understand them as well so that the successes or failures of policies do not become politicized. Discussion of uncertainty also helps members to be aware that systems analyses "are not designed to *predict* what will happen. Rather, they're designed to explore *what would happen*, if a number of driving factors unfold in a range of different ways."[106]

Sixth, attention then should turn to identifying and securing funding for agreed-upon changes. Inclusion of diverse stakeholders from across the system should help to avoid situations where "squeaky wheels" garner more attention than they should, at the expense of reduced overall system effectiveness and efficiency. Reliance on research helps to avoid this problem as well by creating greater understanding about empirical reality and by reducing the ability or willingness of participants to make grandiose and unfounded claims about the need for particular policies or why they merit so much more attention than some other issue or policy.

Priorities to Guide the Policy Process

Ultimately, other processes for guiding research and policy could be followed.[107] What matters here, however, is that the policy process include diverse stakeholders and that it be informed by systems research. In addition, the process should be guided by *core priorities*. These ensure that analyses and decision-making consistently stayed focused on improving the criminal justice system or any given subsystem. The systems focus bears emphasizing: policymaker and scholarly critiques of criminal justice policy and practice consistently point to "systems" problems that undermine efforts to create a safe and just society. Without sustained commitment to a research-informed policy process aimed at improving the *system*, criminal justice will continue to be out of control.

Improve the System

Systems can be ineffective and inefficient or, if designed and implemented well, highly effective and efficient. The multi-stakeholder policy process serves to push the criminal justice system and subsystems in the latter direction. It will not happen of its own accord. Instead, the different subsystems will do what they always do (e.g., pursue their own interests) and legislatures will do the same (e.g., introduce *ad hoc*, spur-of-the-moment changes that alter the shape the entire system). No simple design exists for improving a system. Rather, the changes that would most strengthen a given state or local justice system may vary enormously.[108] The paramount focus thus needs to be on the changes that, based on systems research and multi-stakeholder deliberations, would help the *system* to become more effective and efficient.

Alvin Drake and his colleagues long ago identified the pitfalls of not having an over-arching systems focus and of not having a lead agency or "captain" in charge of maintaining a focus on the system:

> A danger arises of which every analyst and every manager must be wary, the danger of excessive *suboptimization*. It may often occur that "optimizing" one part of the system is detrimental to the effectiveness of the system as a whole... It follows that analysts must learn how each part of a system behaves and they must refrain from advocating the suboptimization of one part before they learn what this will do to the system as a whole.[109]

Drake and colleagues emphasized the analyst's role. However, the responsibility for maintaining a systems focus lies with the lead agency responsible for implementing the Systems Improvement Solution and with the participating stakeholder groups.

Focus on Goals

A system that is not focused clearly and always on its goals will veer off course. In criminal justice, the central problem lies in the fact that traditionally no single agency controls or oversees the criminal justice system. The parts instead operate like fiefdoms, ones that in turn get buffeted about by legislatures through enactment of new laws or changes in funding decisions.

Precisely for that reason, the Systems Improvement Solution policy process should be continuously focused on public safety, justice, accountability, efficiency, and other goals that society expects the criminal justice system to achieve. These goals may vary by jurisdiction. At a minimum, though, they include prioritizing responsiveness to victims and communities, reducing racial, ethnic, and other forms of disparity, and enhancing public understanding of crime and the criminal justice system. A system that lets any of these goals fall off the radar screen – by not targeting efforts to improve them – deprioritizes them. When, for example, a system neglects to measure victim satisfaction or the perceptions or experiences of minorities who come in contact with the police, it essentially states that victims' needs or minority experiences do not matter. Worse, it signals that victimization and racial or ethnic disparities will be tolerated.

Accordingly, the System Solution's policy process should, in checklist fashion, always be focused on reviewing how well the *system* achieves all goals. In addition, the process should be continuously focused on identifying how the system can be improved to achieve these goals and how to measure progress. Without measures, we cannot document whether the system is effective. Fortunately, many examples exist. As but one illustration: a 1993 compendium published by the US Bureau of Justice Statistics highlighted numerous ways in which different parts of the criminal justice system – including the police, courts, and prisons – could be evaluated using many different performance measures.[110] James Wilson, one of the participants, provided a simple account of ways to prioritize policing and to measure policing effectiveness.[111] Policing should, for example, be focused on creating safe, orderly neighborhoods. The police can achieve this goal by examining community conditions, identifying levels of crime and their causes, implementing strategies that target these causes, and gauging success through measurement of how well the strategies were undertaken, citizen satisfaction with police responses, and levels of crime.[112] The common denominator is a focus on reorienting subsystems – and the system as a whole – to achieve their goals.

Avoid Big Mistakes

In the rush to treat a patient, physicians may worsen the very illness they seek to cure. The medical dictum, "first, do no harm" (from the Latin phrase, *primum non nocere*), taught to medical students, derives from that concern. As a moral guide, it may be lacking; avoiding mistakes hardly provides a clear roadmap for policy. Even so, it provides an important check against roadmaps that may fail or create more harm than good. Consider the systems problems discussed in Chapter 1. All manner of ineffectiveness and potential harm arises when systems or subsystems operate with no one clearly taking charge of systems effectiveness or efficiency. The squeaky-wheel problem alone can result in substantial misallocations of funds. For example, one aggressive policymaker who can convince others of the wisdom of a new law may eventually generate legislation that obligates large sums of taxpayer money to little gain.

Small mistakes provide little basis for concern, though, of course, they can accumulate into large-scale systems inefficiencies. They are, however, more difficult to identify *a priori*. By contrast, big mistakes can be more readily identified in advance. Building prisons that may not be needed illustrates the point. Supermax prisons, in particular, are illustrative. The growth in supermax prisons in recent decades has been built in no small part on the idea that individuals, by themselves, cause prison disorder. This view runs counter to the vast bulk of prison scholarship, which points to the prison environment and administration as sociological forces that exert a much greater influence on disorder.[113] Do inmate histories and propensity for violence matter? Absolutely. But a system built on the notion that only the individual-level factors matter runs counter to the bulk of research to date. In addition, it not only creates a reliance on potentially ineffective strategies to promote order but also creates missed opportunities to structure and operate prisons in ways that are more conducive to order and safety.

The criminal justice landscape is littered with examples where "insiders" – those who work within the system – identified problems with new policies or programs but whose concerns went unheeded. It is littered, too, with situations where insiders held views that ran counter to research. The lived experience of prison officers, for example, may indicate to them that locking up "bad apples" in solitary will improve prison order. Research does not bear out that view. These countervailing possibilities underscore the importance of a policy process that includes the views of diverse stakeholders, especially those with a boots-on-the-ground perspective, and that simultaneously draws on empirical research to ground or test claims.

Prioritize High-Bet, Low-Risk Changes

Policymakers seem drawn to high-profile sweeping changes, perhaps so they can leave their "mark" on an agency or system. So, too, executives seem to embrace a multitude of reforms, as if to show their effectiveness as "change agents." Change for change's sake is, however, a poor basis for improving social policy. When policymakers or executives seek to create "big" change that rests on flimsy theoretical or empirical grounds, the basis is hardly better. The problem is straightforward: betting the farm on a high-risk venture almost always leaves us with empty pockets. Worse, it leaves us in debt and with little to show for it. Mass incarceration illustrates the point: despite large-scale growth in prisons for several decades running, we have little evidence that this investment made society safer or more just or that it improved accountability.[114] We did not have to pursue so single-mindedly that option. Prison was not and is not the only strategy for punishing offenders.[115]

An alternative approach to betting the farm on one expensive policy can be far more effective: target potentially high-bet investments that entail little risk.[116] In the world of stock investing, for example, we might allocate funds not to the one company that we hope will be the next Microsoft or Google but rather to many different companies that have a record of success and show signs of expanding. This strategy amounts to investing in a diversified portfolio of well-researched, high-quality bonds and stocks rather than in a single company. Following a similar strategy would enable policymakers and criminal justice administrators to avoid the potential dangers of high-risk investing and increase the probability that their diversified investments will pay off.

The possibilities for high-bet, low-risk changes are constrained primarily by the imagination of lawmakers and agency leaders and personnel. Consider, again, the use of imprisonment. Local courts and communities typically do not bear the brunt of relying on state prisons. Put differently, they can use this resource and do not have to worry about the costs.[117] This "tragedy of the commons" can waste taxpayer funds. It also can divert attention away from efforts that would improve the long-term success of convicted felons. For example, when felons are sent to prison, their ties to communities weaken, continuity of care for medical conditions declines, and families and communities may suffer.[118] Punishing offenders locally can avoid this problem while still providing "real" consequences; a host of community-based sanctions in fact exists that entail significant punishment.[119] Indeed, some individuals prefer prison over such sanctions![120] A relatively low-risk change with the potential for a high return – that is, lower costs and less recidivism and crime – is, then, to incentivize the use of community corrections.[121]

Another example is problem solving or community-based policing. When done well, there is little likelihood of harm, the costs are not great, and the returns may be considerable.[122] Traditionally, the police have been assessed based on the number of arrests that occur, not on averted crime. They have not, by and large, been assessed based on how citizens view them. The end result? Police may fail to take steps that reduce crime and they may act in ways that engender hostility among citizens. Problem solving and community-based policing entail efforts to work with communities to reduce crime. Such efforts, if combined with research that gauges citizens' views of and experiences with the police, might do more to reduce crime than would police-driven efforts that focus on arrests and ignore citizens.

Many such possibilities exist. Some may not work; others may surprise us with their effectiveness. In each instance, the emphasis on low-risk bets insulates us from costly investments that preclude a more diversified approach and leave us spending more for nothing, or, sometimes, for more of the problems – crime and injustice – that we wanted to reduce.

Maximize Positive Feedback Loops and Minimize Negative Feedback Loops

A feedback loop – which is formed "when changes in a stock affect the flows into or out of that same stock" – can be helpful or harmful.[123] If the police increase arrests and some of these arrests involve questionable judgment calls, prosecutors will not take action in these cases. Police then indirectly receive feedback that only arrests that meet certain standards will garner prosecutorial attention, and they adjust their actions accordingly. That may reduce the number of arrests. Alternatively, prosecutors may call for greater attention to certain types of cases that they previously have neglected. The police may respond by increasing arrests in such cases. Prosecutors pursue these cases; police officers take notice and continue or increase their emphasis on them. For example, crime that occurs on farms typically has not received much attention from law enforcement or prosecutors because farmers may be reluctant to report crime and because the evidence needed to successfully prosecute may be lacking. One decade ago, in Tulare County, California, prosecutors took note of this problem. They worked closely with law enforcement to train them on the types of evidence needed. At the same time, the police reached out to farmers to emphasize that they would wanted to help reduce the amount of theft and damage on their farms. The end result? Police made more arrests of farm-related crime and prosecutors increased their successful prosecution of individuals who engaged in such crime.[124]

Maximizing positive feedback loops or minimizing negative feedback loops requires information. A central pillar of the Systems Improvement Solution involves creating systems research that provides such information and ensures that it lands in front of the individuals capable of acting on it. An illustration: when prison officials in states that worked with the Vera Institute learned that some wardens frequently used segregated housing (i.e., isolation cells) for nuisance inmates rather than for the most serious or violent inmates, they took action to correct the situation.[125] Similarly, spatial analysis of crime or its potential causes (e.g., "broken windows") increasingly provides critical information to law enforcement agencies about where to target their attention.[126] Of course, system actors may not always use information to good effect. The information is, however, essential for making informed decisions about changes to improve system and subsystem operations and impacts. When, moreover, diverse stakeholders discuss the information, the chances increase that knee-jerk responses are avoided and that changes occur that have the greatest likelihood of success.

The importance of focusing on, controlling, and leveraging feedback loops can be seen in the emergence of mass incarceration. During a span of over three decades, beginning roughly in the 1980s, the number of inmates in prison systems nationally increased by almost 400 percent, rising, for example, from approximately 320,000 in 1980 to 1.6 million in 2014 (see Figure 4.2).[127] The correctional system increased exponentially as well, rising from 1.8 million to almost 7 million individuals in prison or on probation or parole during the same time span.[128] As discussed earlier, many factors may have contributed to the increase, but one prominent and likely influential dynamic involved out-of-control feedback loops. For example, states funded more police, courts, and prisons. They enacted laws that enhanced penalties for various crimes. And, most notably, they lengthened prison terms, increased parole officer caseloads, and simultaneously emphasized a "law and order" approach to parole violations (e.g., violations were more likely to be caught and to result in a prison term). Prison populations increased, which fueled increases in parole populations. Aggressive enforcement of parole supervision then led to greater returns of parolees to prison. At the same time, tougher responses to crime led to greater use of probation. New, punitive approaches meant that individuals who violated the conditions of probation were more likely to be sent to prison and less likely to receive support or services.[129]

It appears unlikely that policymakers, the police, courts, and correctional system sought sustained and dramatic growth in the criminal justice system. However, the different decisions that unfolded – such as increased numbers of officers, tougher sentencing, lengthier prison terms, use of prison as a consequence for violating conditions of probation and parole, and so on – occurred within a systems context and constituted the equivalent of levers. Each one alone could leverage a system into growth. Combined, though, they launched a period of growth that went unchecked and led to states being now, and likely for decades to come, obligated to spend billions more on punishment than was intended or necessary. This system will continue to operate out of control if left alone. Indeed, precisely for that reason, William Kelly has argued that criminal justice stands at a crossroads.[130] Either take control of a system designed to provide safety and justice or let it run amok, providing neither and doing so at great expense.

How can state and local jurisdictions maximize positive feedback loops and minimize negative ones? Rely on a process that enables diverse stakeholders and knowledgeables, such as those who work within or study the criminal justice system or are affected by it, to identify potential problems and solutions. Complement this effort with systems analysis. Then zero in on those changes that hold the greatest potential to serve as leverage points for maximizing effectiveness and efficiency. Nonlinear relationships are a key place to start.[131] At certain thresholds, a change may produce dramatically greater negative or positive effects. We want, then, to rely on stakeholders and systems research to identify where non-linear effects may be at play and then target the tipping points for change.[132] For example, the simple act of the police communicating more effectively with community residents may garner a substantial increase in calls to law enforcement for assistance or a willingness to implement crime prevention strategies.

Continuously Reevaluate Policies

As part of the System Improvement Solution – or any effort aimed at improving systems – there must be continuous evaluation and re-evaluation of policies, programs, and systems operations. All too frequently, policymakers or agency administrators become enamored of a particular policy, a new program or intervention, or the like. In such cases, their advocacy for a given policy, program, or intervention may not be based on credible empirical evidence that it is needed, grounded in established theory, well-implemented, effective, or cost-efficient However, let us assume in this case that it is. For example, let us assume that a study occurs and finds that X policy was needed, that it built on established theories, was implemented well, improved outcomes, and achieved benefits that well exceeded costs. That is well and fine, but it tells us little about whether a year later, two years later, three years later, and so on, it continues to be needed or implemented well or to achieve benefits in a cost-efficient manner. Perhaps, for example, a drug court initially proved to be highly successful. In subsequent years, however, funding for it may have declined and markedly reduced the quality of implementation. The likelihood of producing beneficial outcomes then declines. Indeed, precisely such a dynamic has been observed with many drug courts. During the 1990s, they were popular and promoted by the federal government. Then, as federal funding dried up, so, too, did the quality of implementation, since many local jurisdictions could not afford to continue operating their drug courts with all the "bells and whistles" (services, treatment, supervision, etc.).[133]

Performance measurement efforts, it bears emphasizing, do little to address this situation. They typically entail the monitoring of certain agency activities. That provides some accountability, but little insight into policy need, theory, implementation, impacts, or cost-efficiency, and it tells us next to nothing about systems operations, impacts, or efficiency.

What is needed is continuous re-evaluation of existing policies, programs, and practices, as well as a continuous revisiting of changes that should be considered, to them and to the system. This focus is critical for ensuring that the system operates as effectively and as efficiently as possible, and it is precisely the approach taken in efforts to improve forecasting efforts.[134] No one forecast is viewed as set in granite and somehow "best." Rather, forecasts must be continuously updated to reflect changes in science and in the conditions that affect the outcome of interest.

5.4 STEP 3: IMPLEMENT EVIDENCE-BASED POLICIES, PROGRAMS, PRACTICES, AND DECISION-MAKING

The Systems Improvement Solution entails three steps. After undertaking research (step 1) and a deliberative, multi-stakeholder policy process, one aimed at understanding system operations and impacts and changes that might be needed or would create the greatest improvements (step 2), the final step is to implement these changes (step 3). Many policy changes and organizational changes center on relatively *ad hoc* assessments of what is needed. They entail little to no comprehensive assessment of system or subsystem needs and how the criminal justice system or its subsystems can be improved. This approach results in piecemeal legislation and adoption of this or that program that seems popular but may not have been evaluated at all or may have had only a few, select evaluations. By contrast, the Systems Improvement Solution approach consists of adopting evidence-based changes and doing so with an eye toward improving the criminal justice system and its parts.

Per Figure 5.1, implementation of evidence-based changes is the final step in creating the types of systems and subsystems changes that can best promote public safety and increase justice, accountability, and efficiency, and achieve other benefits as well. It is not, however, truly the "final" step, because the Systems Improvement Solution calls for continuous research and policy revision. Systems operations continue to be monitored and special attention is given to evaluating the implementation and effectiveness of changes. Simultaneously, the multi-stakeholder policy process continues to examine empirically the need for current or proposed changes that would improve the criminal justice system and its constituent subsystems. What, though, is meant by "evidence-based," and how are changes to be initiated and implemented?

"Evidence-Based" as Credible Empirical Research on Systems and Their Parts

As emphasized in Chapter 1, there has been a paradigm shift in recent decades, with policymakers increasingly calling for policies, programs, practices, and decision-making that rest on sound science.[135] At its best, this shift has led to greater attention to relying on credible scientific research to guide efforts across many social policy arenas, not least criminal justice. It has promoted, for example, less reliance on "correctional quackery."[136] At its worst, it has led to superficial changes, such as adoption of "soup-of-the-day" programs that may have a few studies that support them. In these situations, a program may be evaluated in a study or two, sometimes by the individuals or organizations that implement them. The studies show significant positive effects. Media accounts point to the new, seemingly novel intervention to reducing crime or recidivism. Lawmakers respond by touting their efforts to adopt such "evidence-based" programs in their hometowns or states.

This all-too-common approach to criminal justice "reform" is not and cannot be effective. First, it proceeds from a vague articulation of what counts as "evidence-based." Is it one study? Two studies? How about ten? What number of highly rigorous studies must be conducted? How do we deal with a situation where an evaluation's external validity is unknown or is likely to be highly limited? For example, an experimental-design study might show that a drug court reduces recidivism as compared to "business as usual" practices in a jurisdiction. However, "business as usual" may be terrible, in which case it would not be difficult to implement an intervention that could improve outcomes. The problem here is that any identified beneficial effect will be unlikely to arise in areas where "business as usual" sanctioning is relatively effective. Put differently, a similar study undertaken in this second context might identify that a drug court has no effect on recidivism. Why? The bar is much higher: the jurisdiction already effectively intervenes with offenders, and the new intervention may not be likely to do much better.

External validity captures this idea. Studies with high external validity are those that identify effects that can be expected to arise in other contexts or with other populations. Those with low external validity will not have such effects or the effects simply are unknown.[137] There are, of course, many programs that have been repeatedly evaluated and consistently shown to reduce recidivism or improve other outcomes; the rigor of these studies means that they have high "internal validity."[138] Yet, at the same time, we have many registries of effective programs that disagree with one another and that provide limited information on the external validity of programs.[139] Against that backdrop, then, it is questionable to refer to policy efforts as "evidence-based" when they involve adoption of this or that "evidence-based" program, where the latter is so designated based on a few studies or a published list of "effective" programs.

There is a much larger problem. In seeking to promote evidence-based policy and practice, lawmakers and criminal justice administrators frequently equate "evidence-based" with the notion that we know that a given policy, program, practice, or the like improves some outcome. "Evidence-based" in this sense is equated with the existence of studies that seemingly show that an intervention is effective. This definition, in my view, is too limited to be useful. For example, what is a "credible" study? It cannot be tantamount to experimental studies, given that the vast bulk of crime and justice policies, programs, practices, and decisions will never be subject to such studies or simply cannot be. For example, no study is likely to emerge in which inmates are randomly assigned the death penalty. More generally, experiments are too expensive to undertake except in relatively rare instances.

In addition, a focus on effectiveness ignores many dimensions of relevance for policy, dimensions that can be subject to empirical scrutiny. For example, an empirical study might show that a policymaker assumption about the existence of a social problem, such as rising prison violence, is incorrect. In such a situation, policymakers might proceed to enact new and costly laws aimed at reducing prison violence, whereas violence might in fact have been decreasing rapidly for several years. Here, a needs evaluation can provide empirical evidence that an assumed social problem does not exist and so does not necessarily require a new policy. Such an evaluation could and, I argue, should be viewed as contributing to evidence-based policy. How? When undertaken using credible data and methodologies, it provides empirical information that can guide policy-making. In this case, for example, it would lead policymakers not to invest scarce resources in interventions that may not be needed.

The same can be said of other evaluations. For example, studies that examine the theoretical underpinnings of existing or proposed policies may show that these policies are unlikely to be effective. Why? They may rest on unarticulated or untested theories or entail activities that run directly counter to what theory indicates would be most likely to improve an outcome. Similarly, we can undertake evaluations that assess policy implementation. Or we can assess the extent to which a policy's benefits exceed its costs and whether they do so more than for other investments. In each instance, we can rely on empirical research to guide decision-making. When we do so, we are undertaking "evidence-based" policy efforts, and doing so in ways that go well beyond adopting a program here or there that has been found to be effective in a few select settings.

Evidence-based policy, then, as viewed here, entails efforts that are grounded in credible empirical research about their *need, theory, imple-mentation, impacts*, and *cost-efficiency*.[140] What are these "efforts"? They include laws, policies, programs, practices, rules, decisions, and, not least, systems changes. As emphasized throughout this book, law-makers and criminal justice system officials rarely rely on information about systems operations or impacts. They focus on isolated parts of systems or they enact piecemeal changes, each addressing one narrow issue. Evidence-based efforts thus also entail empirical monitoring and evaluation of criminal justice system operations and their impacts on the system's goals.

What Implementation Entails

The implication of the above observations is that an evidence-based approach policymaking and decision-making involves reliance on empiri-cal research about systems, their parts, and the many policies, programs, and practices that collectively seek to improve safety and justice. This view of evidence-based policy grounds the Systems Improvement Solution as well as selection of the changes that should be made. For example, it leads to a focus on systems operations. It leads, too, to a focus on establishing the need for (besides theory) the implementation, impact, and cost-efficiency of any given change. It leads, not least, to a focus on credible empirical research – such as studies that rely on established theory and rigorous designs and methodologies – to guide assessments about past and proposed changes.[141] In turn, it leads us away from a reliance on one-time studies. No evidence-based policy can or does exist in a vacuum. An intervention might be effective one year and ineffective the next, depending on its implementation and on changes in a community or society. Accordingly, evidence-based policy requires continuous empirical evaluation of systems.

Implementing "evidence-based" policies necessarily means attending to all aspects of the evaluation hierarchy and applying it to policies and systems. It means, for example, that one can document solid theoretical grounds for the design of a policy and can point to credible empirical research to ground assumptions about the policy. It means that one undertakes ongoing monitoring of each policy and collects information that could inform deliberations about how to introduce changes that might improve implementation. It means evaluating the impact of policies or, at the least, documenting improved outcomes. Even if a strong causal claim cannot be made about impact, outcome monitoring can help to ensure that the policy may be effective. It means evaluating the cost-efficiency of policies. And it means undertaking these efforts for isolated policies, programs, and practices as well as for the system as whole.

Who, though, weighs and balances the evidence from systems research and determines what next to do? One approach is for legislatures to receive a voluminous amount of information annually or bi-annually, when they convene, sift through all of the findings, and then enact a plethora of changes. Similarly, criminal justice agency officials might review such findings once or twice a year and then decide which changes to implement. Such an approach will not and cannot be effective. In both scenarios, lawmakers and officials have too little time to review and understand the analyses. They also will have missed innumerable opportunities to introduce changes that could and should have been made on a more timely basis. It is an approach that can be likened to driving a car along an incredibly complicated route through a major urban city to arrive at a destination, and doing so by first skimming through one hundred different street maps and then, after several hours and getting lost, doing so again for five minutes. The driver will drive, gas will be consumed, but no destination other than frustration will be reached.

The Systems Improvement Solution, as envisioned here, does not serve as alternative to the typical legislative or administrative process. Rather, as discussed under step 2, it constitutes an ongoing, institutionalized undertaking that regularly – daily, weekly, monthly, and annually – provides information to the legislature or other government officials and to criminal justice agencies. The organization that helms this effort would be paralleled by smaller units within legislative, governmental, and criminal justice agency offices, populated with staff who participate in and understand the multi-stakeholder policy process. This process provides real-time information to all parties so that they can make decisions that fall within their purview.[142] Heads of corrections, for example, can determine changes that would be sensible for their part of the criminal justice system and would make sense within the broader systems context. Similarly, legislative staff can apprise legislators about evolving changes and opportunities in systems operations that may bear attention. Legislators then can take actions in the short-term and then, when they are "in session," can focus on deliberating about larger-scale decisions, such as the warrant for legal reforms or substantial changes in the allocation of resources across the criminal justice system.

Continuously Link Implementation to Steps 1 and 2

The Systems Improvement Solution is a process. This process serves to illuminate how the criminal justice system is just that, a system. It serves to illuminate the importance of understanding the interactions among parts of the system. It serves, too, to illuminate the necessity of credible empirical research about the system and its parts. It serves, not least, to illuminate the need for buy-in from diverse stakeholders. Without such buy-in, each part of the criminal justice system can and will go its own way, and willy-nilly adoption of flavor-of-the-month policies and programs occurs. The "end" of the process, step 3, is not the end. Rather, it constitutes but one part of a continuous undertaking. That is why the arrows in Figure 5.1 lead back from step 3 to the prior steps. Any effective, long-term solution to improving safety and justice must – as accounts of successful criminal justice systems analysis and policymaking highlight – entail continuous research, discussion of the research and systems changes that are needed or that could yield the most beneficial impacts, adoption of evidence-based policies, and then further research and discussion.[143]

5.5 THE SYSTEMS IMPROVEMENT SOLUTION: CORE PRINCIPLES

The proposed strategy for taking control of criminal justice runs completely counter to the *ad hoc* piecemeal approach that local, state, and federal governments all-too-frequently employ. Under the latter approach, legislators or agencies adopt a new policy and then move on. Sometimes there may be large-scale "reforms." These typically only address a relatively small set of problems. In addition, after initial excitement about the reforms passes, systems revert back to business as usual. Little attention is given to ensuring full and high-quality implementation of the changes. Then another round of "reforms" emerge, and the cycle repeats itself, again and again. A new approach is needed, one grounded in good information and an effective process. The Systems Improvement Solution provides the contours of one such approach. It cannot be effective or helpful, however, unless it is implemented well. Here, then, I identify several core principles that should be used to ground the Systems Improvement Solution. They constitute conditions that must be met if it – or any similar, systems-focused strategy – is to be effective.

Institutionalize the Solution

As noted at the outset of the chapter, there must be a lead, or "captain," agency responsible for implementing the Systems Improvement Solution (or, again, a similar undertaking). More generally, though, the process must be institutionalized not only through a lead agency but also through legal requirements that policymakers and administrators participate in the process and ground their decisions in research-based discussions with other stakeholders. Funding to support the process must be a core part of local, state, and federal budgets as well. The saying, "No free lunch," applies here. Without sufficient investment in research and a multi-stakeholder policy process, criminal justice systems will continue to operate in a dysfunctional and ineffective manner. At the least, systems rather than people will drive criminal justice, and the outcome almost assuredly will not be as effective or efficient as it would be with us at the wheel.

A central benefit of institutionalizing the solution, or a similar process, is that it educates policymakers and administrators. In particular, it helps to ensure that policymakers and administrators understand the broader, systems context of the decisions that they make and the interdependence of the various parts of the criminal justice system.[144] Information is not a cure-all, but without it, policymakers and administrators literally cannot know how best to proceed.

Failure to institutionalize the solution will result in precisely the same outcome as occurs with failure to evaluate large-scale reforms: we learn nothing, we fail to know when to change course to create improvements, and we waste a lot of money. As but one example, consider the California

Public Safety Realignment Law, enacted in 2011. This law was created in response to the US Supreme Court decision, *Brown v. Plata*, which required the state to reduce its prison population. To this end, the law required counties to assume responsibility for managing offenders. Over $1 billion annually was given to counties to do so. The state did not, however, as Joan Petersilia has observed, "fund a statewide evaluation, so there is no single organization responsible for assessing the costs and benefits of Realignment statewide."[145] That situation is typical. States invest tremendous amounts of money and resources into policies, but provide little to no funding of or support for research. In California, did the policy shift and funding reduce crime, improve justice, and do so more efficiently than other reforms? Did it lead law enforcement, courts, jails, probation, prisons, or parole to work more effectively and efficiently? Insights about these questions exist, but little systematic research on them has been done because of the lack of institutionalized research for examining them.[146]

The institutionalization of any undertaking can be challenging, and that is no less true for a systems-focused, research-guided policy process. Ultimately, no specific set of steps will suffice. There must be a commitment to taking control of criminal justice. There are several examples, discussed in the next chapter, of efforts that illuminate this commitment and the possibility of institutionalizing research into policy and practice. There can be a better melding of research with policy and practice, but it will require sustained commitment and resources.

Be Non-Partisan, Deliberative, and Research-Informed

A productive discussion about how to improve criminal justice will not occur if partisanship dictates the process and the information generated from it. Policymakers and criminal justice officials and administrators are a savvy lot; they know that research can be twisted like a pretzel to fit particular political agendas. They understandably resist information that stems from a partisan viewpoint. That, though, leaves them selecting only the research that conforms to what they believe must be true or, in much the same vein, from organizations whose political "leanings" veer in their direction. Although understandable, this approach leaves credible research in the lurch. A two-pronged problem results: partisan research, which may be biased, rules the day, and credible research gets ignored.

Partisan views, of course, are not problematic in and of themselves. To the contrary, they form the bedrock of democracy. They become problematic when each side gets to identify the "facts" and when neither side gets the facts "right." Some organizations exist that seek to provide non-partisan insight into policy. It can be done, but it is challenging. Congress charges the US Government Accountability Office (GAO), for example, with providing credible research to it – not to one party or the other, but rather to the institution. Even so, the GAO struggles – less with conducting objective research than with ensuring that the processes it relies on for designing studies and communicating findings can be trusted.[147] In so doing, however, the GAO provides an illustration of how to proceed. Specifically, the Systems Solution must conduct rigorous, scientific research. Yet, it also must ensure that the research reflects the priorities and insights of different political groups and it must ensure that processes exist to establish the actual and perceived integrity of the results. A multi-stakeholder policy process thus is not just necessary for conducting relevant, helpful research, it is necessary for establishing the credibility of research results.

The process must be deliberative. As emphasized above, regular and frequent discussions among diverse stakeholders must occur. Systems analyses in particular can be difficult to understand.[148] Meeting frequently can overcome that problem. In addition, it ensures that researchers do not veer off into an alternative universe, one untethered from reality. Much of the scholarly literature on systems analysis, for example, "assumes away nearly all of the most important constraints on government agencies."[149] Who better than policymakers and criminal justice agency officials and administrators to know these constraints? Researchers then can work to ensure that analyses reflect more accurately the conditions, such as changes in anticipated budgets or in policy priorities, that may affect systems. A deliberative process creates trust as well. Participants come to appreciate different viewpoints and the many factors that can influence systems, ways in which one subsystem may affect another, and so on.

Not least, the process must center on the design, review, interpretation, and use of research to guide policy discussions. Letting discussions founder on opinion will lead nowhere, or not to a productive plan of action. Instead, it simply fosters greater partisanship. For that reason, any systems-focused solution should entail regularly scheduled meetings of all key stakeholders. These meetings should include updates on past, current, and proposed systems research, such as evaluations of particular policies or areas of need and results from systems and subsystems analyses. To facilitate productive discussions, reports would be distributed prior to the meetings and would be available online. They would include analyses of "standing" issues, such as systems analyses, but also would include one-time evaluations and research on time-sensitive issues, such as concerns about a sudden rise in certain types of crime.

A central benefit of systems analysis lies in the ability to identify decisions that, while potentially beneficial for a subsystem, may be harmful for a system as a whole. Research is essential for helping stakeholders to understand that all decisions they make may affect the whole system and do not exist in isolation. At the same time, policymakers, criminal justice officials and administrators, community residents, and other stakeholders develop a better understanding of research. In turn, they become savvier requesters and consumers of it. They also develop a better understanding of the criminal justice system. That includes how it works and how proposed policy shifts may "work" or not in the context of that system. Indirectly, they learn that systems problems cannot magically be solved by tinkering with this problem or that.

Use Insights from the "Ground Floor" and Scientists

A common shortfall of many efforts to understand organizations and systems is that they fail to take into account the lived experiences and insights of those with "boots on the ground." Within the social sciences, this problem can be seen in debates about the relative advantages and disadvantages of quantitative "versus" qualitative methods.[150] Quantitative data and analyses sometimes provide a more credible foundation for trusting that observed patterns reflect reality. They obscure reality, however, when they focus on narrow slices of it. By contrast, qualitative data and analyses can provide more insight into potential patterns that exist; they allow, too, for understanding complicated interactions among causal forces as well as the nuances that characterize so much of human life, organizations, and society. Analyses without theory amount to the equivalent of groping about the dark without a flashlight, and analyses that center on only one type of data amount to much the same. Excessive reliance on quantitative analyses leads to significant blindness and inattention to important features of systems; excessive reliance on qualitative analyses leads to undue emphasis to issues that occur rarely or in fact do not exist.

Juxtaposed against such considerations is the fact that, despite calls for "evidence-based" policy and practice, there remains a disconnect between scientific research and the actions that criminal justice lawmakers and agencies take.[151] The rise of mass incarceration, for example, largely ignored insights from criminology about the causes of crime and the effectiveness of various types of punishments and interventions.[152] Mass incarceration constitutes but one example of many criminal justice "reforms" that illustrate this disconnect.

We have, in short, a situation in which policy and practice proceeds without consistent recourse to two critical sources of insight: (1) the boots-on-the-ground perspective of those on the "ground level" of every-day criminal justice decision-making, and (2) the scientific perspective of those who study and research criminal justice. This problem is not specific to crime and justice policy. We can find it many walks of life, including various efforts aimed at predicting such diverse phenomena as which baseball players and teams will perform best and which businesses or sectors of the economy will be most successful.[153]

The solution is simple: practitioners on the front line and researchers alike must be included as core stakeholders in the Systems Improvement Solution multi-stakeholder policy process.[154] Together, they can provide insights about actual patterns or relationships or those that may exist that warrant careful attention. Inclusion of parole officers, for example, in discussions about reentry policy might well lead to greater awareness among policy-makers that excessive offender caseloads all but preclude effective super-vision of or assistance to ex-prisoners.[155] Aarti Bhaté-Felsheim and colleagues, for example, have described the use of simulation analyses under-taken in Minnesota to describe and understand correctional system perfor-mance. The analyses pointed to potential changes that could be made to parolee caseloads that might improve efficiency and help to meet new standards. Inclusion of parole officers in discussion of the analyses, however, highlighted that assumptions about the per-appointment time estimates of 45 minutes significantly understated the time needed to address crises, unplanned court appearances, and travel to and from various worksites.[156] This insight was unanticipated by the researchers. As Bhaté-Felsheim and her colleagues emphasized, "the difficulty in scheduling appointments with officers ... was unknown prior to the simulation."[157]

Similarly, inclusion of researchers in policy discussions, as evidenced in the above example, is critical.[158] For example, their involvement in dis-cussions about punishment policy could highlight that prison is not necessarily the most effective way to reduce recidivism and it is not always the toughest punishment.[159] Front-line practitioners and researchers, too, can help illuminate potential nonlinearities that influence systems and subsystems. For example, certain thresholds in caseload processing in criminal court might exist; beyond these thresholds, prosecutors may resort to more perfunctory assessments that might well implicitly weight race or ethnicity in determining the potential risk of future offending.[160] In a related vein, prosecutors might highlight that police efforts to target particular types of crimes are not useful unless they meet certain evidentiary bars. Conversely, police might highlight ways in which they prioritize their efforts based on anticipating the types of crimes that prosecutors will prioritize.[161]

Use Insights from Theory, Data Analysis, and New Data

As emphasized above, it is important to draw on the insights of practitioners and researchers. Just as important, however, is the need to draw on theory, data analysis, and new data. These, too, form a critical foundation for ensuring that systems research, stakeholder deliberations, and implementation and evaluation of evidence-based policies achieve system goals.

Theory

As discussed in Chapter 4, we have an abundance of theory about different aspects of crime and justice and about the criminal justice system. Too little of it, however, guides the design of criminal justice policy. The problem is not solved by more data. As Robert Sampson has argued, "one can have big data and small ideas."[162] A simple illustration: many prediction instruments that seek to identify the risk of recidivism among those on probation or in prison fail to draw on mainstream criminological theories about the causes of offending; many correctional interventions do the same.[163] Quite rightly, theory can be critiqued for being esoteric, far removed from reality, difficult to understand, and frequently untestable. Such criticisms do not change the fact, though, that seeking to understand recidivism risk without scientific guidance means that we generate error-filled predictions. The same can be said for virtually any aspect of the criminal justice system. Accordingly, theories relevant to policing, court decision-making, punishment, prison operations, community corrections, and so on – and for the system as a whole – should be central to deliberations about the design and implementation of policy.

Data Analysis

The advent of computers and automated data collection and databases has ushered in the era of "big data." There have been, at the same time, remarkable advances in methodologies for examining these data to uncover patterns that traditional modeling techniques typically would miss. Machine learning techniques, for example, have been developed to mine data to identify those individuals with the greatest likelihood of offending.[164] Traditional analyses apply an additive modeling approach. More of X and Y and Z sum up to create a score; individuals with higher scores are anticipated to be at greater risk of offending. Machine learning techniques allow for interactive relationships and other types of nonlinearities to be estimated. For example, X and Y or Y and Z may interact; the modeling considers this approach. If an interaction exists, the model incorporates it and potentially provides a more accurate assessment of the risk of recidivism. Systems and data mining analyses, too, have advanced greatly in recent decades and offer powerful approaches for gleaning insight into systems and subsystems operations and impacts.[165] Alone, they suffer from providing insights that may not always make sense.[166] However, if coupled with efforts to apply and develop theory – that is, to focus on providing coherent explanations for patterns – these new advances in analysis create tremendous opportunities to illuminate criminal justice and guide efforts to improve it.

The advent of "big data" has yet to be fully recognized or leveraged. Consider the experience of Anne Milgram, the former New Jersey Attorney General. Upon becoming the Attorney General in 2007, she "discovered a few startling facts: not only did her team not really know who they were putting in jail, but they had no way of understanding if their decisions were actually making the public safer."[167] That discovery led her to call for and use "big data" and statistical analysis to better understand criminal justice system operations and impacts. Her account is at once depressing and inspiring. It is depressing because we invest a great deal of resources in supporting prosecutors' offices around the country and yet have little information about whether their decisions improve safety or justice. It is inspiring because it illustrates the potential for leveraging existing data to make better decisions. Similarly depressing accounts and inspiring possibilities can be found in accounts of large-scale investments in prison programming, prisoner reentry efforts, community policing, and more.[168]

Advances in analysis and the widespread availability of administrative records data, in fact, have created innumerable opportunities for combining sources of data to understand better the dynamics that underlie and affect criminal justice systems. A simple illustration: across the country, criminal justice agencies can, but rarely do, create information about county-level variation in recidivism rates of released offenders. This information could be examined and then linked to other sources of data. We might learn, for example, that counties with the highest recidivism rates have higher ratios of probationers or ex-prisoners to supervising officers. In turn, we could investigate whether reducing these ratios might improve recidivism outcomes. Such possibilities barely scratch the surface, but they highlight how we can and should improve criminal justice systems monitoring, evaluation, and improvement efforts.[169]

New Data

When concluding a study or contemplating a new one, researchers often glumly observe, "If only we had better data." Indeed, one can easily critique many studies for lacking even passably valid measures of core constructs. For my master's thesis in graduate school, I relied on a widely known and used data set, the National Youth Survey, that was nationally representative.[170] It did not, however, have a rich array of measures to test one of the most examined theories of delinquency: differential association theory. My colleagues and I used a measure that asked respondents how frequently they associated with others who engaged in crime. The measure is commonly used in research, yet it serves as a weak indicator of core parts of differential association theory. Much the same can be said about many studies – they rely on the best measures available, but all too often these measures barely suffice.

Fortunately, technological changes in recent years enable researchers to go well beyond the measures available in administrative (e.g., courts, prison) records data. The public, policymakers, criminal justice administrators and personnel, victims, community residents, offenders – they all can be easily and cost-effectively polled about their views and experiences. With the advent of smartphones, tablets, laptops, and other portable devices and the widespread availability of wireless internet access, we now can quickly administer short or long questionnaires to gauge myriad dimensions. Residents, for example, can be asked about crime in the community, their satisfaction with policing, changes in their community that might indicate a need for greater law enforcement assistance, and so on. Similarly, prisoners and officers can be polled about prison conditions to determine where action might need to be taken to prevent problems, such as riots, from occurring. These approaches exist in the medical arena; patients supply ongoing feedback to physicians through brief surveys.[171] Indeed, the advent of smartphone and tablet "apps" has allowed us to collect all manner of information, and do so not just once a year or month but also daily, hourly, or even by the minute.

With guidance from researchers, practitioners, and theory and empirical studies that rely on both quantitative and qualitative analysis, we can devise ways to increase the amount and the quality, or relevance, of information.[172] We then can improve systems research, the deliberations of stakeholders in crafting or adjusting policy, and the everyday decision-making of criminal justice system actors. We also can ensure that policymakers have an accurate understanding of public views and concerns. For example, policymakers wrongly assume that public opinion is straightforward and that, for example, the public wants nothing but "get-tough" responses to crime. Nothing could be further from the truth. In fact, even in strongly conservative states, the public supports rehabilitation and a spectrum of sanctions to reduce crime and to punish criminals.[173]

In creating new data, we must be careful not to emphasize quantitative research over qualitative research. Systems entail dynamics that may not be readily reducible to simple measures or to the collection of representative or valid data. Consider efforts in the intelligence community to combat terrorism. Some types of quantitative analyses are possible, but one cannot, for example, obtain a random sample of terrorists and ask them to complete a survey.[174] In such contexts, qualitative data collection and analysis is critical.[175]

Theory, advanced techniques in data analysis, and new data collectively provide the foundation for greatly advancing our understanding of criminal justice systems and their parts. This potential can inform scholarship as well as policy and practice. The ability to collect new and different types of measures on a regular basis, and to do so for an entire criminal justice system, creates innumerable opportunities for scholars to test and develop theories about different aspects of the system and the operations and effects of the system as a whole. At the same time, it gives criminal justice officials and administrators in any given part of the system the ability to understand better the "pulse" of their organization and to investigate potential problems and their causes and solutions. There has never been a time in US history when the stars have aligned so well for making dramatic improvements in our understanding of crime and justice.

Disseminate Information Widely and Frequently

The entire process underlying the Systems Improvement Solution depends on generating and sharing information through a central website and through various social media outlets. This information should be conveyed to all individuals involved in the multi-stakeholder process. At the same time, citizens should be provided with the research that informs the deliberations of this stakeholder group. Although all citizens cannot be actively involved in all parts of the deliberations, they can be apprised of information resulting from it. Doing so can increase understanding, avoid misunderstanding, and, potentially, reduce the ability of lawmakers and other officials to politicize crime and justice policy through selective cherry-picking of facts or the presentation of distorted or incorrect "facts."

5.6 CONCLUSION

Meadows has argued that we should build systems that are "meta-resilient" and Nassim Taleb has argued likewise that we should strive for "antifragility."[176] In both cases, the idea boils down to the notion that if we build systems that can take challenges, bend a little, and then grow stronger, we have a situation that goes beyond mere resilience. The concept of resilience brings to mind a tree bending back into shape; for people, it means the ability to bounce back and not be broken by events. But we should aspire for more. We should, for example, seek not only to bounce back but to return stronger and better, able to tackle bigger challenges. The ideal is not stability; rather, it is to confront change and become the stronger for it.

That means devising systems that can respond to challenges. Any such effort, however, requires an understanding of how systems operate. It requires strengthening the various parts, or subsystems, that make up these systems. To this end, we need more and better information about criminal justice systems throughout America. For example, we need to understand the need for changes, the theory that underlies existing or proposed changes, the implementation of the changes, their impacts, and, not least, their benefits and costs and how these compare to alternative strategies. Not least, we need systems analyses that can identify how well the system operates as a system and what can be done to ensure that it achieves the lofty goals – safety and justice, in particular – that we as a society set for it.

But information alone will not do. Diverse groups have a stake in criminal justice. Lawmakers, the individuals who work in criminal justice, suspects, offenders, victims, the communities where they reside, and citizens in general – they all want and expect criminal justice to be helpful, not harmful, and to be responsive, not intransigent. These groups have a great deal to offer in guiding our understanding of what criminal justice can and should be. They understand many of the aspirations and the constraints that affect criminal justice. They know, too, many of the intricacies of the criminal justice system. Accordingly, we need their insights in understanding and improving criminal justice.

Information and stakeholder deliberations alone will not do, either. We need policies, programs, practices, and decision-making that actually improve public safety and justice. These efforts should be evidence-based, but evidence-based along many different dimensions. We should have evidence about the scope and nature of particular crime and justice problems, for example, and we should have evidence that particular investments warrant greater attention than others. Piecemeal change will not work, and so the lynchpin of smarter, more efficient investments lies in understanding the systems nature of criminal justice and which changes can be leveraged to create the greatest amount of improvement. One-time evaluations will not work either. We need systems that frequently and systematically evaluate particular policies, programs, and various interventions, and that evaluate systems operations and impacts.

These different steps – research that provides more and better information about criminal justice system operations, a multi-stakeholder policy process, and reliance on evidence-based efforts – collectively constitute the Systems Improvement Solution. This "solution" is not the only way to proceed. I argue, though, that the contours it identifies are those that form the foundation of any viable effort to create large-scale, sustained improvements in criminal justice. When combined, they force us to improve the system of criminal justice, to stay focused on the goals we set for it, to avoid big mistakes, and to seek those changes that hold the greatest chance of improving safety, justice, accountability, and efficiency.

Implementing a systems-focused solution will not be easy. It will require the institutionalization of efforts to improve criminal justice. A lead, or "captain," agency must be funded and supported, and the funding must be provided for supporting research and the inclusion of diverse stakeholders. The process must be non-partisan, deliberative, and research-informed. It must draw on the insights of diverse groups and the results of analyses and deliberations must be disseminated widely and frequently. If done well, the benefits – described in the next chapter – would, I submit, more than justify the costs.

6

Benefits of the Systems Improvement Solution and Pitfalls to Avoid in Implementing It

The goal of this chapter is to discuss the anticipated benefits of the Systems Improvement Solution. These include more safety, justice, accountability, and efficiency. They also include other potential benefits, such as greater responsiveness to victims and communities, less racial and ethnic disparity throughout the criminal justice system, greater public understanding of crime and justice policy, greater understanding of the causes of crime and the nature of justice, improvements in subsystem operations and impacts, and reductions in the number of big mistakes that plague criminal justice systems. The chapter also discusses the potential pitfalls that may face those who seek to implement the Systems Solution. Any efforts that might appreciably improve criminal justice require a high degree of cooperation and support among diverse groups. That situation opens the door to problems that may undermine the integrity and effectiveness of such efforts. However, as the chapter discusses, they can be avoided or over-come. That possibility is reflected in the existence of efforts, which I discuss, that rely on systems analyses or systems-focused approaches to improving criminal justice.

6.1 BENEFITS OF THE SYSTEMS IMPROVEMENT SOLUTION

The earlier chapters and Figure 5.1 have highlighted many potential benefits that can arise from implementing the Systems Improvement Solution or a similar systems-focused approach to improving criminal justice. This view might seem to be Pollyannaish, given that such efforts require considerable investments in research and policy processes. In addition, they necessarily entail complicated analyses and challenging discussions. For example, how much weight should be placed on competing system and subsystem goals? How credible is the empirical evidence in support of a particular policy or program relative to another? How much uncertainty are we willing to entertain when implementing specific changes?

Juxtaposed against these considerations, however, is the fact that criminal justice is an expensive and complicated enterprise. States and the federal government have seen fit, since the 1980s, to double, triple, or even quadruple their correctional systems, and then to support the new expanded size of these systems, all with little to no empirical basis for the investments. They have enacted innumerable new policies and variations on extant ones. In such a context, and during an era in which calls for "evidence-based" practice and "government accountability" have become ubiquitous, investing substantially to improve research and the process of devising, implementing, and revising policy seems far from Pollyannaish. It is exactly what would allow policymakers and officials to fulfill calls for greater accountability, safety, and justice.

A complicated solution, in short, is needed for a complicated problem. Implementing such a solution will not be easy. It will require active and sustained support from society, policymakers, and diverse sectors of the criminal justice system. It will require, too, commitment to a new way of guiding and evaluating the criminal justice system and of holding policymakers and justice system officials accountable. In the end, the "Solution" is not magical. It consists of taking to scale the notion of evidence-based policy and accountability. It consists of committing to more and better research, to a policy creation and review process that involves multiple stakeholders, to continuous monitoring and evaluation of the criminal justice system, and to instituting changes based on this process. There is nothing radical in that idea. Indeed, as will be discussed further below, there are examples of efforts that align with it. "In life," the saying goes, "you get what you pay for." We pay a great deal for our criminal justice system, yet we spend little on research and helpful processes to guide this system. The Systems Improvement Solution points to an alternative approach that can provide the critical insights and science necessary for creating greater safety, justice, accountability, and cost-efficiency.

More Safety (Less Crime)

Crime results from myriad factors. Any appreciable, large-scale reduction in crime, then, requires a strategy that addresses these factors in a deliberate, calibrated manner. A lynchpin of the Systems Solution is the focus on just such an approach. It calls for careful, empirical assessments of all parts of the criminal justice system and of the system as a whole. It calls as well for stakeholders to participate in designing and interpreting research. Not least, it calls for them to participate collectively in identifying changes that appear to enjoy the most theoretical and empirical support. It is the systems focus, involvement of multiple stakeholders in seeking to understand and improve the criminal justice system, and the simultaneous reliance on empirical research, that holds promise, I argue, for the greatest reductions in crime.

How? First, the Systems Solution draws attention to systems operations and impacts, and thus to the potential for changes within systems to generate large-scale harms or improvements. It leads to a focus on aggregate outcomes – public safety writ large, not just in one place or at one time. In so doing, it highlights the idea that investing in a program here or there will not appreciably affect, among other things, recidivism rates among the millions of individuals released from prison each year. It highlights, too, that minor improvements in systems management – such as the supervision and treatment of all prisoners – can lead to large increases in safety.

Consider two policy scenarios. Option 1: obtain a reduction of 10 fewer crimes by investing in a program that serves 100 inmates and reduces the percentage who recidivate from 60 percent to 50 percent. It is, admittedly, an impressive showing – a 10 percent absolute reduction in recidivism and a 17 percent relative reduction in recidivism (10 / 60 = 17 percent). Option 2: obtain a reduction of 1,000 fewer crimes by investing in a policy (e.g., improving facility conditions, training officers) that targets the entire prison population, which we will assume consists of 100,000 inmates, and that reduces the percentage who recidivate from 60 percent to 59 percent. The reduction seems absurdly small – a measly 1 percent absolute reduction in recidivism – but when applied across 100,000 inmates, it creates a substantial impact.

So, choose option 1 and obtain 10 fewer crimes or choose option 2 and obtain 1,000 fewer crimes? The choice would seem obvious: option 2 wins, hands down. Yet, criminal justice policymaking and practice by and large adopts the former approach. It ignores the systems context of criminal justice and prioritizes small-scale programs. The latter have one significant advantage over systems-focused efforts: they can more readily be evaluated with stronger researcher designs, such as experiments or any of a range of quasi-experimental approaches. But this approach to policymaking is akin to driving without a map and looking only 10 feet in front of the car. We lose sight of where we are supposed to go and fail to anticipate turns that we should take to reach our destination more quickly. Criminal justice policy tends to be designed in this way. One crisis piles on another, each one dictating an extreme response. All the while no one takes stock of the system and how it might influence the effectiveness of each response or how it might be changed to produce better outcomes at less cost. In the end, a systems-based approach to understanding and designing policy cannot be evaluated using quasi-experimental designs. Yet many of the changes that can be implemented with guidance from a systems-focused approach can be evaluated in that way. There is, then, no loss in the credibility of research.

Second, the Systems Solution requires that policies, programs, practices, and decisions build on empirical research and on the insights of individuals who are most likely to use or be affected by them. The potential for reducing crime stems from a greater reliance on research about what may be needed, effective, and cost-efficient, and from the avoidance of knee-jerk or short-term efforts that may be ineffective and may create harms. Numerous critiques of criminal justice policy and practice indict policymakers, criminal justice officials, and the public for a failure to understand crime and justice. They can be indicted, too, for their adherence to "gut instincts" or to politicized accounts of what somehow "must" be needed or work.[1] The Systems Solution addresses these issues directly by creating greater understanding and by requiring diverse stakeholders to appreciate and take into account the systems nature of crime and justice. This reliance on research and a multi-stakeholder process serves as a check against extreme responses and it promotes a more balanced, empirically based approach to reducing crime.

Third, the Systems Solution process requires that the system be "driven" by a focus on public safety, and not simply on capturing and punishing "criminals." Local, state, and federal criminal justice efforts typically lack the equivalent of a "captain" who can ensure that all parts of the system work in tandem to produce maximum amounts of safety. By contrast, the proposed systems approach inverts this approach. It focuses the system on better ways to integrate efforts within and across subsystems to reduce crime. An illustration: probation officers may expend considerable time supervising individuals who present a small risk to the community, and they may have little time to expend on high-risk individuals.

This situation can and does unfold daily throughout the United States. It persists because probation officers' views do not percolate up to policymakers. If they did, a recalibration likely would occur that would enable probation officers to better supervise and assist high-risk individuals. The typical response, however, ignores the broader, systems context and instead focuses on hiring more officers. That strategy might help somewhat, but it does not address the possibility that the courts place too many low-risk individuals on probation.[2] If that practice changed, there would be less of a need to hire more officers. Another example: incarcerating individuals without providing rehabilitation or supervision or assistance upon release will do little to reduce recidivism. Still another: law enforcement, court, and correctional system efforts, whatever their level of effectiveness, will do little to reduce crime if there are not community-focused efforts to address the root causes of offending. Catching and punishing criminals can improve safety, but larger gains in crime reduction require that we address community conditions. Punishment-oriented policies miss that simple, yet no less important, insight. The Systems Solution avoids these types of problems by requiring the continuous involvement of multiple stakeholders in understanding, evaluating, and improving criminal justice.

Fourth, the Systems Solution requires not only a systems focus but also an emphasis on research that describes and evaluates the system and its parts. This approach includes systems analysis and incorporation of the evaluation hierarchy into examining and understanding criminal justice. It entails not just impact evaluations of particular policies or programs, but also systems analysis and evaluations of policy need, theory, implementation, and cost-efficiency. The benefit for crime reduction stems from several reinforcing mechanisms. For example, the proposed approach requires that policymakers and criminal justice administrators undertake needs evaluations of changes that they wish to make, especially those that may require substantial resources. For any given crime problem, there may be different causes. A needs evaluation helps to ensure that the scope and causes of the problem are identified as a prelude to devising an effective response. No amount of implementing "evidence-based" programs can offset the ineffectiveness and inefficiency that comes with slighting the assessment of need.

All types of evaluations – needs, theory, implementation, impact, and efficiency – must feature prominently in any effort to create sustainable, large-scale improvements in public safety. These research efforts must, as Brandon Welsh and colleagues have advocated, involve policymakers and criminal justice administrators.[3] Moral and pragmatic considerations bear on all criminal justice matters. Policymakers and administrators are uniquely positioned to understand some of these considerations, especially the resources and policy options that are most viable. Accordingly, their involvement and insight are critical to devising research-based responses to crime that collectively may generate the greatest gains in public safety. At the same time, the requirement that attention center squarely on systems analysis and on needs, theory, implementation, impact, and efficiency evaluations serves to enjoin policymakers and administrators to focus on creating a coherent and balanced response to crime.

There is, admittedly, a substantial element of faith required here: short of forcing a set of similar jurisdictions or states to participate in a large-scale experiment over many years, it will not be possible to demonstrate empirically that investing in the Systems Improvement Solution will create greater public safety. However, there is the following inescapable logic: public safety cannot magically arise when diverse criminal justice efforts occur with little oversight or coordination; or when the bulk of such efforts lack much, if any, empirical support; or when policymakers and criminal justice officials and practitioners have little understanding about the research that would be needed to monitor, evaluate, and improve the criminal justice system. Indeed, it is precisely these observations that have led to the numerous critiques of criminal justice and to calls for greater evidence-based policy and accountability.

Without a mechanism for requiring the use of research in policy, for diverse stakeholder participation in the research and policy-development-and-review enterprise, and for attention to the entire system, there can be, I submit, little appreciable advance in public safety beyond what may occur at random. There will be, as there always have been, examples of isolated improvements. At one place and time, crime may have gone down because of a particular policy effort. Recidivism may be lowered by a particular program. Such examples typically serve as bases for steering policy. They should not do so, at least not if we want appreciable, large-scale improvements in public safety. Instead, these successes should be celebrated for what they are: examples of how perhaps one might proceed when considering an overall constellation of changes within a systems context. That context, however, should be first and foremost in our consideration if we are to reduce crime appreciably and to sustain reductions over time.

More Justice

Studies of policy impacts on crime or recidivism frequently give short shrift to how policies affect retribution, victims and communities, and, more generally, justice. Perhaps because we call our system of justice a "criminal justice" system, we allow this slight to occur. The phrasing suggests that our focus should be on "criminals." We could rename the system so that it more accurately reflected the different targets and goals it serves. A more accurate name would be the "criminal and victim justice system that seeks to achieve public safety, retribution, victim and community satisfaction or compensation, and, more generally, justice." No advertising executive would let that name be used; it is too long and clunky. That is too bad, because all parts of that name fall under the purview of the criminal justice system.

The fact that "justice" appears as part of "criminal justice" captures the notion that justice should be on our radar screen when evaluating the processes and outcomes of the criminal justice system. We want to address crime and criminals, but we also want justice. Somehow, though, even "justice" gets distal billing compared to a focus on criminals. Even then, safety gets distal billing as well, at least insofar as the appellation "criminal justice" leads to a focus on catching and punishing criminals rather than on investing in a portfolio of approaches to reducing crime.

The Systems Solution mechanisms for promoting more public safety provide, at the same time, a conduit for promoting more justice. The Solution calls for a process that prioritizes public safety *and* justice. In writing about prisoner reentry, Jeremy Travis underscored the significance of priorities, saying that without them, our efforts amount to so much tilting at windmills.[4] Even if prioritized, more is needed. Neither safety nor justice can be substantially improved unless a *process* exists for prioritizing them. The Systems Solution places both goals at center stage and calls for research and decision-making that keeps these goals continuously in focus. In addition, it calls for research on all aspects of the criminal justice system and how the parts and whole contribute to these goals, and it requires the involvement of victims, communities, and groups affected by crime and the decisions and policies of the criminal justice system.

Justice is an ephemeral concept. Numerous philosophical accounts of it exist. By contrast, credible empirical research that documents the types and amounts of justice that occur are few and far between.[5] The Systems Improvement Solution addresses this issue directly by promoting data collection and analysis efforts that monitor and evaluate the experiences of offenders, victims, communities, and other groups, and the ways that criminal justice system actions influence these experiences. Twenty or thirty years ago, such an undertaking would not have been technically or financially feasible. That no longer is the case. Data from these different stakeholders can be collected cost-effectively through a diverse set of approaches, including focus group discussions that can be conducted via the internet, merging data from multiple sources, and surveying individuals through the internet, phones, and kiosks.

The processing power of computers and the ability to collect and analyze data in near-real time means that justice can be examined and not relegated to the back burner. Consider policing. For decades, the primary outcomes used to evaluate police agency performance centered on crime rates. Citizen satisfaction with police responses, demeanor, and support, however, constitutes a central outcome in its own right.[6] "Compstat" (from "Compare Statistics") management information systems used by the police can be augmented to include information from citizen surveys about their experiences.[7] Such an approach can be used to monitor offender, victim, and community member experiences with the courts and corrections as well. In each instance, information can be examined to improve subsystem operations and effectiveness, but it also can be used to identify how well the different subsystems interact to produce justice. For example, a study might reveal that domestic violence victims feel doubly victimized by the way in which prosecutors proceed with cases.[8] That might reflect poorly on how the prosecutor's office or the courts operate. However, it also might reflect a need by the prosecutor's office or courts to streamline the handling of such cases in the face of dramatically increased domestic violence arrests. Efforts aimed at monitoring law enforcement and court processing pressures as well as the views of the police, prosecutors, and victims would highlight such possibilities and lead to insights about how best to advance the interests of justice.

More Accountability

Accountability is a term frequently used by lawmakers and agency officials. Its precise meaning is, however, unclear. One approach is to define accountability as policies, programs, practices, and decisions that accord with what was expected. For example, if the law and accreditation standards dictate that criminal court cases get processed in a certain amount of time, then we might document the percentage of cases in a given court or jurisdiction that fall within the required time frame. This view of accountability is too narrow for our purposes.

A more useful approach consists of defining accountability as evidence that a policy, program, or practice is needed, well-grounded theoretically, implemented well and fully, produces expected impacts while minimizing harms, and is cost-efficient.[9] From this perspective, policymakers, criminal justice officials, and agencies act accountably when they implement policies or the like that accord with these five dimensions, which collectively constitute the evaluation hierarchy. Conversely, they do not act accountably when they implement policies that do not accord with these dimensions.

Much of what occurs throughout the criminal justice system occurs within the equivalent of a "black box."[10] Research studies occur here and there, but they typically focus on one narrow topic at one place in time. Similarly, annual reports may document overarching patterns in an agency, but they shed little light on what occurs within a subsystem or throughout the larger criminal justice system. That leaves us in the dark about the extent to which the criminal justice system operates as it should, is effective, or takes steps to correct problems or capitalize on opportunities to improve the system or its subsystems. The end result is a litany of problems, such as police abuse; insufficient staffing levels that compromise police, court, and correctional system services; inappropriate placement of individuals into diversion programs, jails, and prisons; racial and ethnic disparities in criminal justice system policies and practices; poor defense representation; lack of preparation for ex-prisoners as they reenter society; unprofessional or incomplete provision of services to victims of crimes; and so on.

The Systems Improvement Solution addresses this "black box" problem – and the attendant lack of accountability that it engenders – by requiring systems analysis and application of the evaluation hierarchy to the system and subsystems and by requiring continuous monitoring, evaluation, and improvement efforts. Here, again, inclusion of stakeholders in this process is essential. By enabling them to guide and to interpret research, system and subsystems are held accountable. In this way, the Systems Solution accords with and supports efforts to promote accountability through performance benchmarking efforts.[11]

When little to no information about criminal justice system operations exists, we can do little to address problems and inefficiencies. Even when information exists, little action will result from it unless individuals have it and feel compelled to act. The Systems Solution therefore puts a premium on putting these two "ingredients" together so that information about system and subsystem operations is generated and diverse stakeholders meet to review the information. The charge – to the lead organization responsible for implementing the Systems Solution and to the members who participate in its implementation – is to identify how well the system and subsystems operate, what factors influence operations, and what can be done to improve them.

More Efficiency

A great deal of crime prevention and criminal justice policy occurs with little – or, typically, no – empirical guidance about cost-efficiency.[12] Prison growth over the past several decades illustrates the problem.[13] This growth proceeded with little evidence about the magnitude of benefits (e.g., reduced crime rates and recidivism, improved justice) that would accrue relative to alternative approaches. Fortunately, an increase in attention to cost-efficiency in criminal justice is occurring.[14] This work primarily focuses on evaluations of particular programs, however, and sheds little light on the efficiency of agencies, particular practices, or the system as a whole.

The point can be illustrated through drug courts. Studies might show that drug courts can cost-effectively reduce recidivism relative to traditional court sanctioning processes.[15] What they typically do not show is how the estimates vary, depending on how the overall system adjusts. Many jurisdictions adopted drug courts because of financial support from the federal government. When this support declined, jurisdictions found themselves needing to eliminate their drug courts (an inefficiency in its own right) or to divert funds from other uses in order to continue using them.[16] The latter change alters the "counterfactual" – that is, what would have happened without the drug courts: no longer is the comparison to traditional sanctioning processes, but instead, it is a comparison to whatever way the system adjusts. That might include diverting funds from one program or from many interventions, probation, administrative services, and so on.

We need, therefore, more cost-efficiency evaluations, but we need them conducted in ways that consider the broader, systems context in which any given policy, program, or practice occurs. The Systems Solution adopts that approach. It begins with a focus on system goals, empirical research, and collaborative discussion and decision-making. Policy change then flows from that process. This process promotes greater efficiency in several ways.

First, the mandate to achieve four critical goals – public safety, justice, accountability, and efficiency – helps to ensure that policymakers and criminal justice administrators stayed focused on the "big picture" and avoid becoming mired in subsystem shortfalls and "fixes." It avoids, for example, a situation in which too much emphasis might get placed on adopting a program that has been documented in the literature to be "cost-efficient." Cost-efficiency is not absolute. Whether a given effort would be cost-efficient in a particular systems context depends entirely on that system. More relevant, however, is the fact that no one program can compensate for an inefficiently operating criminal justice system.

Second, this mandate occurs alongside a process that includes diverse stakeholders and research aimed at illuminating system operations, impacts, and opportunities to create improvements. This process would create greater awareness among policymakers and criminal justice administrators and practitioners about how the criminal justice system operates and how a change to one part may or may not work as planned. In so doing, it would reduce the inefficiency that arises when parts of the system, or parts of subsystems, operate with no regard for or understanding of how their actions may create harmful ripple effects.

Steven Levitt and Stephen Dubner have argued for policy efforts that involve "pre-mortems."[17] In the medical arena, post-mortems entail an after-the-fact assessment of what went wrong and what could be done better next time. A pre-mortem amounts to an *a priori* assessment of what likely will happen. That approach is precisely what the Systems Improvement Solution seeks to achieve. A multi-stakeholder process, informed by research, serves to identify where changes may be most needed and how any particular change likely would play out in reality. Many good ideas fall short when applied in the real world. That is especially true when they occur within a complicated systems context. Cancer treatments, for example, exist that may not penetrate into daily medical practice because they do not advance the bottom-line profit margins of pharmaceutical companies.[18] The Systems Solution seeks to reduce the occurrence of this type of problem in criminal justice through a continuous process of "pre-mortems" and "post-mortems" that occur as part of the review of system operations and changes. For example, a pre-mortem assessment could easily identify that if probation caseloads increase and officers shift their emphasis primarily to supervision rather than support, increased revocations will be likely, which will place greater pressure on jails and prisons.[19] It could identify as well that it might be cost-inefficient to respond by building more jails and prisons and that it would be cost-efficient to consider alternative strategies. Perhaps, for example, counties could be incentivized to provide more community interventions and to rely less on prisons.[20]

Third, the Systems Solution builds on the insights of those with "boots on the ground," who may have unique insights into policy challenges and limitations. A system without any institutionalized arrangement for tapping such insights almost invariably will adopt strategies that "pre-mortems" would have flagged as problematic. In addition, it will consistently miss opportunities to tweak system operations in ways that could garner greater benefits at less cost.

Fourth, the Solution creates the flexibility to anticipate and adapt to change. The ability to adapt can be viewed as the mark of a system that is not only resilient but also can grow stronger through change, a characteristic that Nassim Taleb has referred to as "antifragile."[21] The continuous evaluation, monitoring, and improving feature of the Systems Solution underscores that adjustments are a necessity and that tinkering without relevant information will cause problems. Focusing continuously on opportunities to improve means that the system has the ability not only to identify such opportunities but also to act on and evaluate them. In so doing, it can help steer policy shifts away from extreme responses. It can steer them instead toward more nuanced efforts that leverage the criminal justice system effectively and efficiently.

Finally, the process required of the Systems Improvement Solution highlights the contours of what can and cannot be known. Almost all policy changes involve uncertainty. When, as is frequently the case, data do not exist that would enable quantitative estimation of specific aspects of a system, we must make assumptions about these aspects. A discussion centered on how a system works and what assumed values are reasonable can be highly instructive; it constitutes a form of sensitivity analysis, which is central to efficiency evaluations.[22] It serves, too, to restrain a tendency to assume that best-case scenarios necessarily will occur. That restraint is important, given that policymakers and program advocates frequently assume benefits that could, in reality, only arise under the most fortuitous, or outright implausible, circumstances.[23]

The Systems Solution process underscores for all stakeholders that opportunities to improve system operations and impacts always entails uncertainty. For example, many policymakers and others equate "evidence-based" with experimental-design program evaluations. Yet, such evaluations entail considerable uncertainty. For example, we frequently cannot be sure of their internal validity or external validity.[24] The process at the same time highlights that many changes to systems can occur that may never be susceptible to evaluations using experiments (though experiments are ideal[25]), and yet may be evaluated with a high degree of credibility through a range of rigorous research methodologies.

Additional Potential Benefits

The central argument of this book is that the Systems Improvement Solution can contribute to the "big four" goals discussed above: more safety, justice, accountability, and efficiency. There are, however, additional goals that may be achieved. As discussed in Chapter 5, these include responsiveness to victims and communities, less racial and ethnic disparity, and greater public understanding of crime and justice. Other benefits may arise as well from the Systems Solution. For example, the process it envisions could help to advance research aimed at understanding the causes of crime and of criminal justice system operations and impacts. That constitutes a goal of central relevance to scholars, but it also would contribute to efforts to improve policy. The proposed Systems Solution also is an approach that could be used by subsystems to help them achieve subsystem-specific goals. Not least, it can be used to avoid big mistakes. This goal aligns with the medical dictum, "Do no harm." Avoiding mistakes does not *per se* constitute an ultimate "destination" goal. It is not, for example, in the same category as reducing threats to public safety or improving justice. Yet it constitutes an unequivocal positive when viewed as an alternative to a situation in which policy efforts cause harm or entail considerable expenditure without producing appreciable benefits. Avoiding big mistakes serves, then, as a priority that guides the policy process described in Chapter 5 under step 2; it also, when achieved, can be viewed as a mark of a successful system. Better systems make fewer big mistakes.

Greater Responsiveness to Victims and Communities
One of the central limitations of criminal justice consists of its inattention to victims and communities.[26] That situation results from a lack of an institutionalized basis for advocating for these groups. Yes, law enforcement agencies, courts, and correctional systems implement strategies that seek to help victims and communities, but that is not their primary mandate. Assistance is a nicety, an extra, something to be undertaken when the "real" nuts-and-bolts business of criminal justice – arresting and punishing criminals – has been completed. Time and resources permitting, a victim assistance or community crime prevention program might be

initiated, but otherwise it is a secondary concern. The closest exception, one that entails an institutionalized strategy for listening and responding to victims and communities, is community policing.[27] Such efforts have much to recommend them, but they still are deprioritized relative to the focus on identifying and punishing criminals. This situation is reflected in the fact that local and state governments invariably have no "victim justice" or "community justice" system.

The Systems Improvement Solution seeks to redress this situation by ensuring that victim and community representatives participate in the research-and-policy process. It seeks to do so, too, by placing "justice" center stage in all criminal justice system activities. The system as a whole, as well as the subsystems, is called on to ensure that "just" responses occur for offenders (who frequently are victims and almost always are members of the communities where they committed their crimes), victims, and communities. What those responses should and can be may vary from community to community, which is precisely why multiple stakeholder groups must participate in the process and why analyses must be localized. Alongside of this process must be a reliance on research that includes information from victims and community residents about their experiences with law enforcement and the courts. It should include, too, their experiences with the reentry of individuals from jails and prisons. In short, the "voices" of victims and communities should be reflected in ongoing data collection efforts and analyses. Their voices should be part of a process, too, of examining, evaluating, and modifying the criminal justice system. When included in this way, victims and communities become central, rather than ancillary, to criminal justice system priorities and efforts. In turn, that can ensure that crime prevention efforts have larger and more sustainable impacts.[28]

Less Racial, Ethnic, and Other Disparity

Racial and ethnic disparity has plagued the US criminal justice system since the founding of the United States. It arises in a variety of guises. There is, for example, the history of racism in America and the insufficient attention to the challenges, including higher rates of crime and poverty, faced in many minority communities.[29] There are many laws that have deliberately or unwittingly created a greater burden for or have a greater effect on minorities. Tougher sentencing laws, for example, have resulted in greater concentrations of prisoners leaving and returning to minority communities.[30] Individual police officers as well as entire police agencies may discriminate against minorities.[31] Correctional systems, too, may discriminate against minorities and, for example, subject them to both more punishment and less rehabilitation.[32]

Numerous efforts to address racial and ethnic disproportionalities in criminal justice exist. However, they have primarily served to highlight that there is a problem. What causes it remains open to speculation and isolated case studies. For example, exactly how much disproportionality exists by jurisdiction or state or how much of it reflects discriminatory processes is largely unknown. Even when documented disparities exist, we typically have little empirical information about the causes.[33] Consider racial differences in rates of highway police stops. Here, identifying disproportionality is difficult. Among other things, we need information on racial differences in stop-worthy driving or vehicles.[34] Even when a difference in the probability of a stop has been identified and determined to be greater than what we would expect by chance, we are left needing to know what contributed to it. Without such information, we cannot effectively reduce the disproportionality. Consider another example: prison systems might incarcerate disproportionately more minorities in supermax housing. However, any such disproportionately may reflect a greater involvement of minorities in the types of behavior that lead to such placements.[35] Even so, that would not eliminate the possibility of disparate treatment. For example, minorities might receive less rehabilitative programming or be subject to more hostile treatment from officers. We might well anticipate that minorities in that instance would be more likely to act out and wind up in higher-security prison facilities. Yet, this result would stem fundamentally from unfair, or disparate, treatment by the correctional system.

Disparities that affect minorities and other groups – such as the very young or the elderly, women, pregnant women, and the mentally ill – can only be reduced if they, and their causes, are identified. The Systems Improvement Solution calls expressly for monitoring the extent and causes of group disparities. It calls, too, for adopting strategies for addressing them and then evaluating and revising those strategies based on research and a multi-stakeholder policy review process. Can such monitoring occur? Absolutely – numerous sources of data, or for generating data, exist for identifying where and how disparities arise throughout the criminal justice system.[36]

Greater Public Understanding of Crime and Justice Policy
Democracy can be a wonderful thing. But, when the populace does not understand certain issues, democracy can be abused. Lawmakers, for

example, can claim "mandates" that do not exist. "The public demands tougher punishment," a lawmaker might say. The claim might be true. However, it begs not one but many questions. What percentage of citizens want tougher punishment? What drives their views? Correct or incorrect assessments about crime trends in their communities? Just how much more punishment do they want? To what extent do they also support rehabilitation and crime prevention programs? How much are they willing to pay in the short term and longer term for more punishment or for any other crime-related policies? Answers to myriad such questions are essential to creating a criminal justice system that responds to the public. Indeed, without credible answers to them, the system cannot be highly responsive. It instead will be responsive to how well policymakers, or criminal justice officials, convince others about *their* views of what, somehow, "the" public thinks.

The problem? Citizens do not possess an accurate understanding of crime or the criminal justice system.[37] Nature abhors a vacuum, and that holds as well for public opinion. When individuals lack credible information, they latch onto whatever information is available or fits their worldview. Indeed, a large constellation of factors influence how individuals perceive the world about them when they lack relevant information for making sense of it.[38]

One approach to improving public understanding entails providing citizens with regular and accurate information about crime, criminal justice systems, and practitioner and citizen views. Indeed, absent provision of such information there can be no informed populace. The Systems Improvement Solution, if implemented, would address this situation. It would do so by creating a process that requires dissemination of information not only to stakeholders involved in the process but also to citizens. This dissemination could occur through an agency website and diverse news and media outlets, and be undertaken on a regular (e.g., monthly or quarterly) basis.

The effectiveness of any information dissemination depends heavily on how well the information is conveyed. Accordingly, results must be disseminated in a timely, easily accessible manner. At the same time, the effectiveness of dissemination efforts depends, too, on the perceived credibility of the process used to generate the information. That is why the Systems Solution requires not only rigorous research but also the active engagement of diverse stakeholders with a commitment to non-partisan analysis of system operations and effects.

Greater Scholarly Understanding of the Causes of Crime and Justice System Activities

The generation of knowledge for knowledge's sake constitutes a time-honored justification for any scientific undertaking.[39] The Systems Improvement Solution provides a platform for advancing scientific efforts to understand and reduce crime and improve justice. One barrier to scientific progress in criminological and criminal justice research is what Peter Kraska has called a lack of a "recognized and readily accessible theoretical infrastructure about the criminal justice system and crime control."[40] Some of this situation stems from debates about "criminological" theory as against "criminal justice" theory.[41] More of it, I argue, stems from the lack of systematic attention to the links between crime and criminal justice system activities and policy and to the limited availability of data for examining these links. The Systems Solution addresses this situation through the ongoing generation of data about crime and criminal justice and the inclusion of researchers into the data construction and analysis process. Some examples of how improvements in scientific insight into crime and justice follow.

One example is the opportunity to develop, extend, and test theories of crime. The criminal justice system includes many low-risk to high-risk individuals. If we include the juvenile justice system, it includes even more low-risk individuals. (The vast bulk of youth referred to juvenile courts are low-risk.[42]) These individuals provide an easy-to-tap population to use for studies about a wide range of individual-, family-, school-, and community-level factors that may contribute to offending. By and large, criminological theories of offending have relied on random samples of the general population. This approach has the advantage of being more representative of society. Yet, it ignores the fact that many individuals who enter the criminal justice system do so only once, and so may not differ appreciably from individuals who never offended or did so once and were not caught. It misses, at the same time, an opportunity to examine a wide range of factors – especially community-level contextual forces – that may affect criminal behavior. In recent decades, it has become increasingly easier to merge information about community conditions into other data sources. Doing so with data about criminal justice populations affords numerous opportunities to examine how crime may drive offending or amplify the effects of individual-level or other crime-causing factors.

Another example is the ability to merge criminological and criminal justice explanations of crime. To illustrate, a systems view of mass incarceration points to issues that might cause increased recidivism and do so through mechanisms that crime theories anticipate. For example, unless commensurate resources are allocated to rehabilitation, a dramatic increase in the prison population would result in fewer inmates receiving rehabilitative services while incarcerated and after release. Accordingly, a prison stint and parole end up providing little or no attention to reducing the risk factors of inmates.[43] There is, though, no free lunch. Less investment in targeting the broad spectrum of factors that contribute to offending necessarily means that the odds are stacked in the direction of the correctional system failing to reduce recidivism as much as it could if these factors were addressed.[44] Coupled with research that finds little clear and consistent evidence of strong recidivism benefits of prison – and that finds that prison terms may as likely increase recidivism – this consideration indicates that mass incarceration should worsen offending and do so on a large-scale basis sufficient to worsen crime in communities.[45]

A wealth of systems theory and research exists to highlight these and other possibilities.[46] This work also identifies ways that system operations may be influenced by aspects of the system, such as court culture. The Systems Solution is grounded in collection of data about all aspects of system operations, and so creates the foundation for going well beyond current studies of processing and sentencing by including information that, to date, either does not exist or is collected only in one-time snapshot studies in particular locales. An example: "court culture" has been identified as a factor that greatly influences case processing outcomes.[47] However, few studies include measures created to directly measure court culture. The Systems Solution relies not only on administrative records data but also on survey-created data from criminal justice personnel that could be used to create this type of measure and many others.

The Systems Solution also prioritizes valuing the insights of stakeholders and system actors at all levels – from the "ground up," to administrators and legislators. Their views can be especially important to advancing understanding in situations that involve difficult-to-quantify considerations, such as the potential for several co-occurring factors to drive policymaker decisions. Difficult-to-quantify dimensions at least can be identified and sensitivity analyses can be undertaken to estimate the potential impacts of these dimensions. An illustration: a District Attorney in a large metropolitan area may plan on using a soon-to-open boot camp as a sanction for juvenile offenders. Almost any statistical forecasting methodology would work from past data to identify past patterns that appear likely to persist into the future. It would be unable to take into account future actions, because no data on these actions exist. However, if a state used a forecasting process that included such information – which could arise if multiple stakeholders met regularly to discuss systems operations and changes – a forecast could be undertaken that likely would predict better a state-level need for juvenile correctional facilities.[48]

Finally, and not least, the Systems Solution – through inclusion of multiple stakeholders and the analysis of existing and newly created data – provides the equivalent of a "think tank" that can generate ideas and then test them. In many fields, the separation of "basic research" from "applied research" slows progress on both fronts. Siddhartha Mukherjee, for example, has written eloquently about ways in which a near-exclusive emphasis on treatment-focused research during much of the twentieth century prevented advances in understanding cancer.[49] "Basic" research – that is, studies of the causes of a given phenomenon – can proceed along many avenues, many of which may wind up as dead-ends, at least from the standpoint of intervention.[50] Yet now and again, it generates insights that lead to breakthroughs in treatment and prevention. "Applied" research – that is, studies of which treatments improve patient health – can generate such insights as well. Yet it also can lead to a myopic view of the treatment or prevention possibilities. In the case of criminal justice, as with cancer, "applied" research can dictate what gets studied. Alfred Blumstein observed this phenomenon in the 1970s and 1980s. Policymakers passed get-tough legislation, and as a result many researchers studied the effects of get-tough policies.[51] This myopic approach indirectly created the impression that somehow deterrence-focused approaches to crime control constituted the main avenue through which to enhance public safety. A more balanced approach to research – one that systematically examined "basic" and "applied" questions – might well have led to more rapid accumulation of knowledge about how best to improve safety and to more balanced policies.[52]

Placing research at the center of decision-making and coupling it systematically with insights from diverse arenas – lawmaking, front-line practice, the "academy" – provides a unique opportunity to achieve this balance. One illustration of this possibility in the corrections context can be found through reference to the functional equivalent of a "mission control center." This center might include a display where, in real time, the head of corrections receives updated information from multiple sources, such as surveys of wardens, officers, and inmates, as well as analysis of administrative records reports. The advent of smartphones, tablets, and other devices that can be used to collect data makes it increasingly inexpensive to collect information from these groups. Based on analysis of these data, the display might show which facilities have experienced sudden decreases or increases in inmate assaults. The director then could hold a conference call with the warden and several officers and inmates to identify explanations. Some of the explanations might appear far-fetched, others less so. A revision to the officer and inmate surveys could be undertaken to test which ones appear to be empirically warranted. This process would allow for directly relevant policy insights about whether the director needs to take action and, if so, what type of action to take. It also would allow researchers to apply or develop and then test theoretical accounts of inmate behavior. Importantly, it would include views from diverse perspectives, not just those of, say, wardens.

Much the same interactive and iterative process could happen for the criminal justice system or any subsystem. Science progresses in many different ways, including development of better theories, measures, methodologies, descriptions, empirical tests, and so on.[53] It includes evaluations of policies and programs. But it includes as well the testing of theories whose policy relevance may not be immediately apparent. The Systems Solution emphasis on a multi-stakeholder process, and the leveraging and creation of diverse sources of data, provides a foundation for advancing science through these different avenues.

Achievement of Subsystem Goals
The Systems Solution can be used by local and state government, as well as the federal government, and by subsystems. The discussion throughout this book has centered primarily on the argument that the greatest benefits to public safety and justice come from ensuring that the entire criminal justice system operates in a more well-coordinated manner and that policymakers and administrators steer the system in ways that leverage the system into improving safety and justice. A well-run system should enable subsystems to run more effectively and efficiently.

However, law enforcement agencies, the courts, and correctional systems can – and, I argue, should – use a process such as the Systems Improvement Solution to ensure that subsystem activities best achieve subsystem goals. The correctional system example above illustrates this idea. A corrections director, for example, has every interest in understanding how exactly the prison system operates and what changes might be made to steer the system in directions that best advance inmate, officer, and public safety. Similarly, police chiefs ideally would have information about how their agency efforts combine to affect crime, public views about law enforcement, and opportunities to improve. They then could target internal changes that would better achieve goals and advocate for external efforts to address forces, such as poverty or limited employment opportunities, that the police cannot readily address but that may affect crime or amplify potential adverse effects of criminal justice system involvement.[54]

Fewer Big Mistakes

The Systems Solution entails a process that prioritizes avoiding big mistakes. From that perspective, a successful process should reduce big mistakes and contribute to the "big four" outcomes (more safety, justice, accountability, and efficiency). Even so, I emphasize the avoidance of big mistakes here to stress that a significant approach to policy can center on it alone. Why? Many if not most criminal justice policies constitute what many policymakers and scholars would view largely as significantly misguided efforts.[55] "Mass incarceration" constitutes the most glaring example. Although many defenders of mass incarceration exist, the overarching trend across states nationally has been to call for "smarter" policies that more cost-efficiently reduce crime and promote justice.

The Systems Solution can help governments, and the people that government is supposed to represent, avoid big mistakes. From this perspective, the Solution does not have to entail incredibly accurate assessments. Rather, it simply has to help sensitize us to the assumptions that are being made. That can help to avoid making decisions based on clearly unreasonable assumptions that may lead to substantial long-term costs.[56] This benefit is especially important given a criminal justice system in which diverse types of decision-making errors prevail.[57] Consider, as but one example, privatization.[58] To conservatives and liberals alike, it can seem like a good idea. However, without insight into the conditions under which it results in greater efficiencies, states can easily lock themselves into contracts that entail more, not less, cost. For example, errors in prison population forecasts can lead states to pay private vendors even when the need for prison bed space declines and public prison cells remain empty.[59] Avoiding even one such expensive mistake would cover the costs of investing substantially more in research.

6.2 PITFALLS AND HOW TO AVOID THEM

The Systems Improvement Solution has the virtue that it can be scaled up or down to available resources at state and local levels. It has the virtue, too, of according directly with policymaker and scholarly calls for systems-aware understanding and policies and for evidence-based approaches to improving public safety and justice. But there is no free lunch. Implementation of the solution will require sustained investment of financial resources and political and system agency support. Some of the more likely challenges, or pitfalls, that are likely to arise – and how to avoid them – are discussed below.

Failure to Institutionalize the Systems Solution

The Systems Solution, by design, requires institutionalizing a research-and-policy process. There must be continuous monitoring, evaluating, and stakeholder discussions. Institutionalizing the Solution requires charging an agency to lead the effort, funding the effort, and mandating, preferably in statute, that it be followed. Without a "captain" agency, the Solution cannot and will not be effective. The most obvious strategy is to locate responsibility for leading the effort in a local or state criminal justice agency and to charge it with spearheading implementation of the Solution. Policymakers and criminal justice officials would not lead the effort, but would be required to participate and to ground their decision-making in information that resulted from it. A variant of this approach is to create an independent agency that leads the effort. One example is the Texas Criminal Justice Council, which consisted of approximately 20 staff. For many years, until it was eliminated by Governor Rick Perry, it provided independent research on the juvenile and criminal justice system in Texas. The Governor and Legislature were the primary conduits through which requests for research occurred. Analyses it undertook focused on the system and its parts and were provided to the Governor, the Legislature, and the general public.[60]

What is critical, in the end, is that the effort be required and that an agency lead the effort. Without such a lead, the Systems Solution cannot be undertaken. It is too complicated. That complexity requires that there be the equivalent of a "central system controller."[61] More, though, is required to institutionalize the Solution. The stakeholder groups – policymakers and representatives from law enforcement, the courts, corrections, and communities – must be involved. These groups can provide critical insight into system operations and contexts that might influence the implementation or effectiveness of proposed policy shifts. They also can learn from the process about factors that influence sub-system operations. Systems analysis has been criticized as providing information that is "remote from the realities of criminal justice administration."[62] That problem is addressed in the Systems Solution by incorporating stakeholder views from throughout the criminal justice system. Their inclusion, too, helps to ensure that widespread advocacy for research occurs. Members of the systems improvement efforts, for example, can more readily identify, through participation in the process, the resources necessary to ensure that they receive credible, helpful information in a timely manner.

One problem to be avoided that would undermine the effectiveness and long-term viability of the Systems Improvement Solution is engagement in poor process. Multiple stakeholder groups hold critical insights into crime and the operations and potential impacts of criminal justice system operations. Prioritizing the views of select groups, such as prosecutors, would distort understanding of these operations and impacts. Similarly, prioritizing select "facts" without their being discussed by diverse stakeholder groups would contribute to excessive emphasis on certain changes rather than thoughtful consideration of changes that might be more needed or effective. In trainings on emergency first-aid response, individuals typically are told to first survey the scene to identify any dangers that may need to be considered – "Don't 'dive in' head-first." The Systems Solution design seeks to avoid this problem. However, as with any human endeavor, some individuals or groups can subvert good process – or politicize it – to achieve their own ends. If, however, good process gets bypassed, analyses and findings will lack credibility. Accordingly, active and sustained involvement of diverse stakeholders is paramount.

Insufficient Funding for the Systems Solution

Investment in the Systems Solution will cost money and require substantial effort. That is inescapable. But without such an investment, system-wide criminal justice policy and practice will continue to occur with little credible empirical basis to guide it. This point bears emphasis: current criminal justice investments in crime prevention, policing, the courts, jails, prisons, probation and various intermediate sanctions, parole, the death penalty, and more occur with little information about their need, operations, or effects on one another or the end goals of safety, justice, accountability, and efficiency.[63] Better information systems and monitoring efforts can help to avoid needless investments. Doing so is consistent with the arguments of those who promote a more business-minded approach to government. Multi-billion-dollar businesses invest millions of dollars on research – not just for development but also for monitoring their activities – and yet most criminal justice systems spend little on it.[64]

One way to ensure funding is to mandate it. Legislatures could require that 5 percent or more of criminal justice spending support research. For example, if a state spent $1 billion on criminal justice, it would be required to spend $50 million on research. Would that be justified? There are different ways to answer the question. One response: we should know whether the expenditures are necessary and invested in evidence-based efforts and whether the system operates effectively and efficiently. Consider that one well-done experimental design evaluation of a program might alone cost several million dollars. From this perspective, then, the $50 million funding is indicated. The example illustrates an important point: $50 million would purchase only a relatively small number of experimental design studies. If used for systems analysis, it would provide for illumination of how an entire criminal justice system operates and what impacts the system as a whole, and in its parts, may have. Here, then, consider that investment in one unnecessary prison would offset the research investment.

There is, ultimately, no correct percentage or figure. That situation parallels what exists in the performance monitoring literature. Many calls for such monitoring exist, but there is no set guideline for what amount, say, a town, city, or state should set aside for it.[65] Rather, the focus centers on more of a logical requirement: If local or state government is to undertake certain activities, then monitoring efforts should be sufficient to ensure that performance meets expectations. The problem lies in the fact that, in general, local and state governments spend little on performance monitoring. For that reason, the recommendation here is to mandate that a percentage amount of criminal justice expenditures go to research and, ideally, to implementing the Systems Improvement Solution or research-based processes similar to it.

Local vs. State Systems Solution Efforts

States typically will have more resources to devote to systems analyses, implementing the evaluation strategically, and undertaking an institutionalized process for discussing, guiding, undertaking, reviewing, and acting on research findings. Cities, towns, and counties generally – some large cities and counties notwithstanding – operate with far fewer resources. Clearly, any implementation of the Systems Solution must be scaled down to what is possible locally. One guiding consideration, however, is that the failure to implement systems monitoring and analysis invariably opens the door to inefficiency. It is, for example, one thing for a state to build a prison it does not need, and entirely another for a city of 200,000 to build additional jail space that may not be needed. The state can absorb such inefficiencies more so than a city can. An aphorism attributed to Voltaire states that "the perfect is the enemy of the good."[66] Local jurisdictions can implement the Systems Improvement Solution – not perfectly, but to the extent that local resources permit. The benefits of the solution do not rest alone on better quantitative data. They rest on better information and a deliberative process that educates the involved stakeholders about how their criminal justice operates and how it might be improved. Small companies can, should, and do monitor their operations and what can be done to improve quality and profit. Indeed, businesses of all sizes seek to do so. Limited resources for research and process do not have to mean that no research and no systems improvement efforts occur.

This issue highlights a related one. A central source of inefficiency for states and local jurisdictions comes from state efforts and local efforts, respectively, operating in the equivalent of silos. Local jurisdictions, for example, can waste state resources by overusing state prisons.[67] Similarly, states can and do create policies that place excessive resource demands on cities, towns, and counties. Use of the Systems Improvement Solution at state and local levels provides an important avenue through which such inefficiencies can be avoided. For example, as noted, local jurisdictions may seek to offload punishment costs by sending greater numbers of convicted felons to state prison facilities. That step not only creates more cost for the state, it ultimately can harm local public safety, if the individuals return to local communities and commit more crime than they otherwise would have, had they served their sentence through probation.[68] Public safety declines, too, if certain communities experience high rates of the withdrawal and return of individuals who, notwithstanding their criminal background, may have provided support for families.[69] Similarly, when states incarcerate but do so with little emphasis on or support for reentry assistance, they place a burden on local communities that may well not be met, and thus increase the likelihood that ex-prisoners will recidivate.[70] Such problems can be reduced by parallel efforts at the state and local levels to implement the Systems Solution. These efforts ideally would include reciprocal memberships. For example, state stakeholders would serve on select local Systems Solution committees or boards and, conversely, local stakeholders would serve on a given state's Systems Solution committee or board.

Bureaucracy and Resistance to Implementing the Systems Solution

Bureaucracy and resistance to change – along with a scarcity of resources – may impede implementation of the Systems Solution. These very problems, in fact, testify to the need for systems-focused efforts. Without them, bureaucracy and resistance to change are more likely, and resources will not easily be shifted to where they are most needed. Consider the "silo" problem, in which each part of a system advocates for itself alone. The police argue for more officers, courts argue for more personnel, corrections argues for more jails, prisons, and staff, and so on. Allocation of resources on a "squeaky wheel" basis provides a poor foundation for policy.

As argued above, the paramount way to reduce resistance lies with an inclusive process that provides actionable information for guiding the criminal justice system, writ large, and for guiding subsystem efforts. An illustration: counties typically get to use a state resource (prisons), with little to no financial impact on the counties. One solution lies with ensuring that counties have "skin in the game." If they use state prisons, they must contribute to subsidizing them; conversely, if they use less of this resource, they could receive funds that they could use to reduce local crime.[71] The success of such a plan depends not only on creating such incentives; it also depends on state and local stakeholders collectively examining how prisons are being used and how the incentives process might be improved to ensure appropriate and effective reductions in incarceration.

Some criticisms of the systems analysis approach highlight that it can entail such a high level of generality that it may not be useful to subsystem actors.[72] Systems analyses necessarily operate at a high level of generality for the entire system. That does not vitiate, however, the relevance of insights from those analyses for subsystems, and it does not constitute a substitute for subsystem analyses. In addition, advances in computing power, the internet, and data availability mean that system and subsystem analyses today can be far more detailed and can be customized to address questions and concerns of system actors.

Complicated, Incomplete, or Inaccurate Rendering of Systems

Evaluation research and systems analysis are central to the proposed solution. Without them, criminal justice systems and subsystems will continue to lack systematic, empirical guidance on their operations or impacts. One criticism of the proposed solution is that any systems account of criminal justice may be too complicated to understand or may be incomplete or inaccurate.

The world is complicated, so by extension we should expect that accounts of how it works may be complicated as well. That does not justify needlessly complicated accounts, nor does it mean that "simpler" accounts are irrelevant;[73] rather, it simply means that if systems exist, then they invariably will entail complicated sets of structures, activities, relationships within and between parts of the system, and so on. In the end, if the Systems Improvement Solution is followed, then a series of checks and balances exists to ensure that analyses reflect as well as possible the complexity of a given system and also to ensure that it can be explained in a way that is sufficiently simple for stakeholders to understand. Continuous inclusion and participation of diverse stakeholders helps to ensure that any systems account will be accessible to these groups. At the same time, it helps to ensure that important nuances that they observe are featured in the account.

Incomplete rendering of systems is inevitable. All of the details of a given criminal justice system simply cannot be included.[74] Here, again, inclusion of diverse stakeholders and reliance on continuous involvement of researchers serve to provide a check against a failure to consider important system parts, activities, and outcomes. Whatever level of incompleteness remains necessarily will be less than what occurs in the absence of any systems analysis.

Inaccuracy, too, is inevitable. More precisely, a scientific account of a system, subsystem, or, indeed, any social phenomenon, involves levels of accuracy and inaccuracy. A highly accurate recidivism prediction instrument, for example, still entails error.[75] One strength of the Systems Improvement Solution lies with the focus on *continuous* research, discussion of it, and changes in response to the research and discussions. This process will not eliminate inaccuracy, but it should serve to limit egregious errors and to guide efforts to improve accuracy. For example, the boundaries of any system may not always be clear. A systems account thus might fail to consider that some structure or activity should be included in the description of a particular system. It also might make incorrect assumptions about the extent to which science justifies inclusion of certain parameters in models.[76] Inclusion of diverse stakeholders, including, not least, those who work in and study criminal justice, can help to avoid such problems. The criterion ultimately is whether revised system descriptions provide greater insight into how a system operates, its effects, and how it might be changed to improve outcomes.[77]

Failure to Include Boots-on-the-Ground Insights

Thirty years ago, Stanley Vanagunas observed that systems analyses frequently failed to "adequately take into account the more informal and discretionary aspects of the administration of justice, that is, those aspects of criminal procedure which make law enforcement tolerable, just and administratively feasible."[78] This problem pervades criminal justice and is more generalizable: efforts to improve any type of system that do not incorporate in a meaningful way the insights of those with "boots on the ground" almost assuredly will fail.[79] It amounts to creating a strategy for driving a race car without consulting the drivers or the teams who support the drivers during races. Inaccurate assumptions and predictions result. Impractical strategies arise. We lose the race. Or, in the context of public policy, we end up spending money to achieve worse outcomes than if we had spent nothing.[80]

A simple example – inmate visitation – illustrates the point. All prison systems have rules about the conditions under which visits may occur. However, what actually happens typically occurs unmeasured and thus out of sight and mind. One warden may work to ensure that visits happen as frequently as possible, while another may impede visits through impractical visitation hours, inhospitable visitor screenings, limited or no games, books, or the like to facilitate positive family visits, and the like.[81] Notably, visitation has gone largely unexamined.[82] Potential impacts on misconduct or recidivism, as well as potential benefits and harms for staff, have gone largely unexamined as well.[83] Inmates report that severance of ties to family, friends, and community constitutes one of their primary fears.[84] Some studies suggest that visitation may be helpful in reducing inmate misconduct and recidivism.[85] Thus, the inattention to monitoring visitation and taking steps to increase visitation and the quality of the visitation experience represents a significant oversight. It is, however, one that easily could be addressed through periodic surveys of inmates, staff, and visitors. The resulting data could be analyzed to identify what can be done to improve visitation and to limit potential problems or harms for staff and prison operations. It might identify, for example, that some groups (e.g., women or minorities) are less likely to be visited and that certain factors, such as travel or economic barriers, contribute to this difference.[86] It might identify, too, facility-level differences, where the administrative culture in one prison may be conducive to visitation, and less so in another.

Such examples can be found throughout the prison system, police departments, and courts, and in the communities most affected by crime. What is needed is a mechanism for tapping into the insights of those who work in or are influenced by these subsystems and by criminal justice policies more generally. The Systems Improvement Solution responds directly to this need by requiring the active engagement of stakeholders from throughout the criminal justice system. These individuals serve to help shape research questions and to identify critical considerations when implementing or evaluating policies and practices. Concerns about law enforcement officer abuse of minorities, for example, could be expressed by victims, and could help to drive the focus of studies of police behavior. At the same time, concerns about risks to police officers could be identified and examined through inclusion as well in the research and policy improvement process.

Scholars and Researchers May Not Be Willing or Able to Collaborate with Practitioners

It can be difficult to engage scholars in policy-relevant research or in assisting with policy development or implementation.[87] The reasons vary. One of the most significant, perhaps, is that tenure and promotion decisions typically place a premium on scholarship. A decision to evaluate a program rather than publish several articles in top peer-review journals can jeopardize an academic career. It need not necessarily do so, but it can. The situation creates a negative feedback loop: faculty teach students that "scholarly" research, not policy research, matters. Students then do not learn how to undertake policy or program evaluations. If they become faculty, they then teach students what they were taught.

A related problem is that university researchers sometimes may feel that evaluations should entail critiques. Scientific articles, for example, frequently are written with a slant toward identifying limitations in prior research and important gaps in knowledge. Researchers may extend that approach to evaluations. They then write scathing accounts about the many problems with a policy or program. Such an approach understandably does not engender trust in researchers or a willingness to collaborate. That willingness may be further undermined if researchers adopt a smug, know-it-all attitude or make unreasonable demands.

Many other barriers interfere with academic researchers' playing a role in policy or practice. For example, they have no formal role in the legislative progress. Also, they may not have the time to learn how to work with complicated databases used by criminal justice agencies. Non-academic researchers face similar constraints. Although numerous research centers and institutes exist, staff members do not typically have a role in local, state, or national policy development. If they do, it tends to involve a one-time invitation to present on a specific issue.

Exceptions assuredly exist. Many researchers within and outside of academic settings have made tremendous strides in helping to inform policy and practice through research.[88] For example, some universities have centers or institutes whose focus directly centers on such work. By and large, however, there is no widespread institutionalized basis for "applied" research.[89] There has been progress in forging stronger ties between researchers and practitioners, in part due to the increased emphasis on evidence-based policy.[90]

The Systems Improvement Solution takes heed of the lessons from this progress by relying on researchers, practitioners, policymakers, and key stakeholder groups to participate in the process of developing, undertaking, and interpreting research. This collective undertaking is critical for ensuring that researchers are included in the improvement of policy and practice. It helps to ensure that they understand the types of questions that policymakers and practitioners need answered and the constraints within which they operate. At the same time, it helps to ensure that policymakers and practitioners understand the possibilities and limits of research.

Institutionalizing the proposed solution, or one like it, provides a strategic mechanism for addressing some of the barriers to university researchers' involvement in applied research. One is that no pre-arranged pathway or structure exists for their involvement. Another barrier is that agencies may not want to share data, and the data may be difficult to understand and use. Still another is researchers' lack of understanding about the priorities that guide policymakers and criminal justice officials and the constraints under which they operate. Such barriers become largely irrelevant when university researchers are invited to collaborate. There still would remain the need for universities to "credit" faculty involvement in such undertakings. For example, tenure ideally could be achieved by undertaking both "basic" and "applied" research.[91] The fact that many top criminology and criminal justice programs hire and have tenured scholars who undertake both types of research suggests cause for optimism. And their approach certainly accords with how scientific progress occurs: some advances come from purely theoretical undertakings and some come from tackling specific, "real-world" challenges.[92]

Data Limitations that Limit the Usefulness of Research

Credible analyses rest on credible data. The dictum "garbage in, garbage out" applies well to empirical research. No methodologies exist to compensate for data that do not exist or are of poor quality. Consider concerns about minority disproportionalities in the criminal justice system. A study might show that blacks are more likely to be sent to supermax incarceration as compared to whites.[93] What, though, creates this difference? Do blacks commit more supermax-warranted infractions than whites? If they do, what contributes to that difference? Perhaps prison staff act more hostile toward blacks? If so, that likely would increase the probability of misconduct and, in turn, placement in supermax housing. In short, the fact of disproportionality tells us little. We need information about behavioral differences and how staff treat whites and minorities, respectively. Without such information, we are left in the dark.

Data limitations are pervasive in criminal justice, and they undermine our ability to undertake credible policy and program evaluations or systems analyses.[94] How to avoid this problem? The solution here is the same as for research in general – that is, greater resources must be expended to improve the amount and quality of data. Resources alone do not suffice, however. A diverse set of perspectives is needed. Left to their own devices, researchers may answer questions that they think warrant attention, but these questions may not be the most important ones for policy or practice. Similarly, policymakers and criminal justice officials may need guidance in thinking through the research questions most relevant to them and in determining what types of studies they most need. Research costs money and, in the end, a triage process must be used to identify the studies that policymakers and practitioners most need and can afford.

The process envisioned for the Systems Improvement Solution is one that requires the active involvement of diverse stakeholders across the criminal justice system, including communities and policymakers. It also includes the analysis of data from different sources, including each subsystem, to identify how the entire system or a given subsystem operates and what its impacts may be. A limitation that confronts any such effort is what might be characterized as "calcified data systems." Databases are designed and implemented. The costs of changing them preclude making changes to them for many years. At some point, a call arises for whole-cloth adoption of a new database. In this all-too-common scenario, a system of increasingly limited usefulness continues to be used, and increasingly it becomes more costly to convert to a new database system.

The Systems Solution calls for designing flexible systems that can be modified to enable measurement of dimensions that matter. When that cannot occur, augmentation of database systems is, at a minimum, possible. For example, relevant stakeholder groups (e.g., prison officers and inmates, police and citizens) can be surveyed and asked questions about their activities, experiences, and potential outcomes. Focus groups and observations can be undertaken as well. These data may be "soft," yet may be no less relevant for assessing system effectiveness and efficiency. Importantly, they increasingly can be generated at little cost, and yet shed light on diverse aspects of the criminal justice system.

Analyses May Be Misused

One concern with the Systems Improvement Solution is the risk that evaluation and systems analysis research may be misused. Brian Forst has described the kinds of instances where systems analyses in particular might be misused.[95] For example, they might lead to a recommendation that judges reduce jail sentences to alleviate overcrowding. Such a recommendation, however, would encroach on the jurisdiction of the courts. This concern has merit. As Forst has emphasized, "One legitimate objective threatened by an increased reliance on the systems approach is judicial independence... In searching for a more coordinated, planned, and effective criminal justice system, system analysis planners may tend to ignore the importance of preserving what is most basic to our constitution; often they seem willing to modify the character of the criminal justice system in the name of more efficient government."[96]

That risk is more likely if analyses occur outside of a decision-making process that involves diverse stakeholders. The proposed solution reduces this risk by making sure that a wide range of stakeholders participate in guiding and reviewing research and the potential impacts of policy or practice changes on subsystems and the system as a whole.

Also, without analyses, policy changes can and do occur that impinge on one or another group or part of the criminal justice system. Sentencing reforms in the 1980s and 1990s, for example, greatly empowered prosecutors and reduced the authority of judges.[97] Many of these behind-the-scenes impacts went undocumented, save for select studies of particular jurisdictions over delimited observation periods. By contrast, a systems analysis approach can highlight patterns and trends in criminal justice.

It can be used, for example, to identify when jail overcrowding occurs and what drives it. Policymakers and criminal justice system officials and personnel then can deliberate over the information and determine how best to proceed.

A related harm that can arise is when analyses – as with any type of performance monitoring – serve as a bludgeon for blaming or harming others. Any monitoring efforts, for example, hold the potential to highlight poor performance in a given area or by a given person or group. Inappropriate targeting of them then may occur. Recall here a central theme of this book: efficiencies can arise naturally if we rely on ground-level insights to avoid "big" problems, as Nassim Taleb has argued.[98] Accordingly, appropriate use of systems monitoring and evaluation does not include using it to punish. It should be used instead to identify steps than can be taken to prevent big problems, to address the inefficiencies that arise from myriad small problems and mistakes, and to increase efficiency by capitalizing on opportunities for improvement that otherwise would go unnoticed. Reliance on a multi-stakeholder process provides a crucial check against egregious misuse of research or policy priorities.

The view taken here is that virtually any approach to improving government can be abused or poorly implemented. The same holds true for systems analysis. If the analysis is harnessed to good process – one that involves all aspects of government, that informs all parties about the consequences of specific decisions, and that is widely publicized or made available to the public – there should be little cause for concern. The courts, for example, could maintain their focus on "justice," but they would do so in a context where policymakers understand the implications of how state or federal law affects court operations and criminal justice system dynamics. A simple illustration: policymakers can pass laws that triple the length of incarceration sentences. That is their prerogative. But any such change ultimately will mean that more prisons must be built or that prosecutors, and by extension, the courts, must refine and narrow down the population to whom they give prison sentences. Something has to give. A systems analysis approach creates the ability to identify, *a priori*, when such problems will arise.

Some Policies or Approaches May Be Misprioritized over Others

The Systems Solution may lead to some policies being prioritized over others. That, in fact, is a good thing. We want prioritization that is informed by research and by deliberative processes. However, as Todd Clear has noted, some critics of systems analysis "have raised questions about the patterns of strategies it tends to promote."[99] For example, if not channeled appropriately, systems analysis may lead to a primary focus on risk reduction among sanctioned offenders and may limit attention to policies that might reduce offending on a larger scale. It may lead, too, to a greater emphasis on government agencies rather than on communities as a way of reducing crime. However, these risks exist with or without systems analyses. Virtually any analysis can be misused. That is precisely why the Systems Improvement Solution places diverse stakeholders front and center in guiding and discussing the results of research.

Excessive Trust in and Reliance on Numbers

Even the best analyses typically suffer from a wealth of methodological limitations. Non-representative samples, invalid measures of key constructs, missing data, incorrect specification of the relationship between two or more forces, inappropriate statistical modeling, mistaking correlation for causation, inferring change effects without directly assessing them, biased estimates of effects, and so on.[100] Not least among such limitations is the fact that studies undertaken under ideal, laboratory-like conditions (what are referred to as "efficacy" studies) can and frequently do produce results that differ markedly from those of research undertaken under real-world conditions (what are referred to as "effectiveness" studies).[101] Many other limitations exist, including a large number that apply even to gold-standard, experimental-design studies.[102]

Accordingly, skepticism and careful review should attend to interpretation of any results.[103] That is one central reason for a process that includes multiple stakeholders. Doing so helps to educate all parties about the results of analyses. As importantly, it creates the opportunity for all members of the process to identify potential problems with or limitations of the analyses. It also highlights that some, perhaps many, critical parts and goals of systems cannot be readily quantified. Policy changes might well still be pursued, but they could be undertaken with clarity about the uncertainty, or partial knowledge, involved.[104]

An example of the need for a research-based policy process that understands the limits of available data can be seen in criticisms of mass incarceration. This policy can be critiqued for not reducing crime and perhaps even increasing it relative to what might have occurred through other policies. However, public safety constitutes but one goal of punishment. Retribution constitutes an important goal, too. It is not, however, readily measured, and so evaluations of policy impact in criminal justice tend to ignore it. That is a mistake. At best, public safety studies speak to only part – an important part, no doubt – of a balanced evaluation of any criminal justice system. Justice, too, also typically goes unevaluated. But justice is central to democracy and what we expect of law enforcement, the courts, and our correctional system. Ideally, we could and would quantify how well criminal justice improves public safety, accomplishes retribution, and attains justice. When we cannot quantify these dimensions, then that limitation should be named and included in discussions – as the Systems Improvement Solution requires – about the merits of proposed changes to the system.

6.3 SYSTEMS-FOCUSED SOLUTIONS AND TOOLS EXIST AND ARE POSSIBLE

Systems problems plague almost all social policy arenas. Consider health care. Martin Makary and Michael Daniel conducted an analysis that identified health care system problems that resulted in more than 250,000 deaths from medical errors. That made medical errors the third leading cause of death in the United States. The authors concluded,

Human error is inevitable. Although we cannot eliminate human error, we can better measure the problem to design safer systems mitigating its frequency, visibility, and consequences. Strategies to reduce death from medical care should include three steps: making errors more visible when they occur so their effects can be intercepted; having remedies at hand to rescue patients; and making errors less frequent by following principles that take human limitations into account. This multi-tier approach necessitates guidance from reliable data.[105]

A central starting point for improving criminal justice, or health care or other policy arenas, stems from understanding that unmonitored systems produce a great deal of error. Because these errors affect large swaths of individuals, their existence creates harms – or missed opportunities to help – that overwhelm the benefits that accrue from investing in small-scale programs. Should we invest in "best" or "evidence-based" programs? Yes, when they are needed, appropriate, and more effective and efficient than some other alternative. When these conditions are met, many options exist for implementing interventions with a high likelihood of success.[106]

However, the contention here is that such efforts should be undertaken secondary to a careful assessment of the criminal or juvenile system and to a multi-stakeholder process to review the findings. Only then is it possible to know which areas of need most warrant attention, and what systems considerations may influence the benefits of a given program or change. The point bears emphasis: small-scale programs may be effective on a case-by-case basis when needed and when used with appropriate individuals or in appropriate areas. Identification of the need for them relative to other options or to other systems needs, however, is a critical first step. When jurisdictions implement these programs, there is, too, the need to evaluate not only their implementation and impacts but also how they may affect other parts of the system. A gain in one part of a system that is offset by inefficiencies or harms in others constitutes a net loss. In short, a systems-focused approach to improving criminal justice should be pursued as the platform on which evidence-based programs build or are used. It need not "compete" with such programs, but instead provides the foundation on which to make rational assessments about which investments will lead to the greatest gains in public safety and justice.

Are systems-focused approaches such as the proposed solution possible? Absolutely. One sign of the viability of such an approach is that policymakers and scholars have recognized the need for systems, or systematic, improvements rather than piecemeal change.[107] Jeremy Travis, in writing about ways to improve prisoner reentry, emphasized the critical importance that policy priorities play in creating large-scale returns.[108] It is well and fine to support a reentry program here or there. To improve reentry outcomes appreciably, however, we must commit to making reentry a systems priority. Otherwise, the small-scale efforts, which may make news headlines and get touted as success stories, add up to little gain in public safety or justice.

Recognition of the importance of attending to systems can be seen in many areas of criminal justice. For example, despite decades of contentious debate about restrictive housing – sometimes referred to as segregation, isolation, or "supermax" incarceration – careful attention to identifying the need for such housing and how to implement it appropriately and effectively has been largely bypassed. Recently, however, policymakers and many state correctional systems have called for revisiting this approach to managing inmates and prisons using a systems approach. It includes a focus on outcomes among inmates placed in the housing as well as the safety and operations throughout the prison system, monitoring closely the process that leads to inmate placements in restrictive housing, and examining what happens during and after placement in the housing and what influences success.[109] In writing about this systems approach, Dan Pacholke and Sandy Mullins have underscored the importance of examining inflows and outflows into restrictive housing cells and facilities. This approach ensures that corrections officials recognize that inmate behavior can be affected by the prison contexts into which they transition. As Pacholke and Mullins emphasized, "to ensure successful reintegration back into the general prison population (as well as to redirect inmates who otherwise would have been placed in segregation), inmates need to be placed in a facility or unit in which their needs can be met, where they feel safe, and where there are opportunities and programs that motivate them to engage in prosocial behaviors."[110] The insight is straightforward, yet few correctional systems in the past have acted on it. Instead, they proceeded from the assumption that inmates would be deterred into prosocial conduct and that rehabilitation or prison context would be irrelevant.[111]

Systems-focused approaches exist in criminal justice, and they illustrate that the foundation exists for implementing the Systems Improvement Solution. However, it bears emphasizing that, as discussed in Chapter 2, such approaches have been adopted in many policy arenas outside of criminal justice, such as health care and environmental protection. They, too, illustrate that systems-focused solutions are possible. For example, in the field of infectious diseases, "systems science methods have been critical in moving theories of disease transmission from simplistic temporal models that assume random mixing to sophisticated models which recognize the importance of geography, social connections, travel patterns, and nonrational behavior."[112] The Models of Infectious Disease Agent Study (MIDAS), funded by the National Institutes of Health, is a case in point. This network of researchers collaborates in creating models of disease outbreaks. These models incorporate multiple levels of analysis and test the potential effects of different combinations of interventions. In undertaking such work, researchers include public health officials both in generating insights about potential outbreaks and in identifying effective and viable strategies for preventing them or reducing their effects.[113] At a much broader scale, there exist systems of universal health care in all other developed countries except the United States.[114] These systems provide templates for how to provide health care that could serve to invert the current situation, one in which the United States leads the world in health care expenditures but lags far behind in the health of its citizens. They are, to be sure, far from perfect and could not be whole-cloth adopted. They exist, though, and, with sufficient political will and financing, could be adopted in modified form. Even then, there would remain the need to invest in continuous research on the operations and impacts of the health care system.

In the field of environmental protection, we can find other examples of the use of systems approaches to improve decision-making. In 1998, the House Committee on Science advocated for the use of scientific tools to "[help] society make good decisions," which contributed in part to the EPA and other federal agencies' creating such tools and repositories of information about similar efforts.[115] One example is the Planning Land and Communities to be Environmentally Sustainable (PLACES) tool, which "encourages and enables local jurisdictions to direct their land-development strategies to sustain the ecosystem services necessary to protect the environment and human health."[116] Another is the National Stormwater Calculator.[117] This software allows for analysis of storm-water runoff that takes into account local soil conditions, drainage systems, historical rainfall, and the like to support identification of the most effective strategies for reducing flooding and its attendant risks, such as sewer overflow and the spread of disease.[118] In both examples, users can model different system configurations, input known parameters, estimate others, identify areas of uncertainty, and draw on insights from local residents, businesses, and government agencies and officials to improve model accuracy. These approaches reflect that an understanding the regulations and policies alone cannot improve the environment or, in turn, society. Analysis of environmental and social context, along with buy-in and understanding of citizens and key stakeholders, must co-occur to identify and sustain effective policies, programs, and practices.

If we turn directly to criminal justice, several examples exist that high-light not only that a systems-focused approach to improving criminal justice can occur but also that some states and countries implement aspects of the Systems Improvement Solution. To illustrate, almost all states already have Statistical Analysis Centers (SACs). Their origin stems indirectly from the 1968 Omnibus Crime Control and Safe Streets Act, which created the Law Enforcement Assistance Administration (LEAA), an agency that served to fund state efforts to improve criminal justice.[119] LEAA efforts led to the creation of SACs. Currently, the Justice Research and Statistics Association (JRSA) coordinates SACs efforts. However, the SACs operate as independent entities "that use operational, management, and research information from all components of the criminal justice system to conduct objective analyses of statewide and systemwide policy issues."[120] SACs are housed within a wide variety of agencies. They typically do not operate with many staff or sufficient funding to undertake systems monitoring or evaluation or to oversee a multi-stakeholder research and policy review process. Even so, they provide a foundation on which such efforts could proceed. Their very existence highlights that policymakers support research-based approaches to improving criminal justice. At the same time, their underfunding highlights a lack of awareness of the significant increase in funding needed to achieve that goal. Viewed more cynically, the underfunding could be viewed as an effort on the part of lawmakers to appear to support research-based policy without actually doing so. Regardless, the presence of SACs illuminates that states can institutionalize research into the design, implementation, evaluation, and improvement of the criminal justice system.

Two prominent examples of state-specific efforts to institutionalize criminal justice systems research are Texas and Washington. From 1983 until 2003, when then-Governor Rick Perry defunded it through a line-item veto, the Texas Criminal Justice Policy Council (CJPC) served to provide the Legislature and Governor with objective, non-partisan research analyses on criminal justice system operations and impacts as well as current and proposed policies and programs.[121] It had a budget of approximately $2.5 million annually and operated with approximately 20 staff.[122] Although Texas dramatically grew its prison population during the 1990s, it adopted what is arguably a more restrained approach because of the CJPC's forecasting efforts, which identified for the Legislature the fiscal consequences of additional growth.[123] After it was disbanded, Texas faced a prison overcrowding crisis, which led to renewed interest in creating the institutional capacity to undertake forecasting and other systems-focused research. As State Senator John Whitmire, a Democrat, emphasized in 2007 during the crisis, "We've been handicapped for good information... We wouldn't be in this crisis about capacity if we had had good information. We've been hurt tremendously [by the lack of information]."[124] Republicans expressed the same view. For example, House Corrections Committee Chairman Jerry Madden, a Republican, noted, "There's a lot of information we don't have now that we used to have when the Policy Council was around... We need a study group that will help us better project future growth."[125]

The Texas example is of interest for several reasons. First, in a state that expends over $3 billion annually on the Texas Department of Criminal Justice (TDCJ) – and much more if we include the costs of law enforcement and the courts – the expenditure of $2.5 million on an agency for monitoring and evaluating criminal justice constitutes less than 1 percent of expenditures. More precisely, it represents less than one-tenth of

1 percent.[126] (Just 1 percent of TDCJ's annual budget would provide over $30 million to support research.) In absolute and relative terms, the expenditure provides nominal funding for research. TDCJ and the Texas Legislative Budget Board undertake additional analyses, but they do so with far fewer staff than CJPC had and with different responsibilities.[127] In short, even were the CJPC to still exist, its funding would not be sufficient to undertake systematic monitoring and assessment of the criminal justice system. A single experimental-design study, for example, can easily cost $1 to $2 million. Forecasting efforts alone require dedicated staff for creating databases, undertaking analyses, and including diverse stakeholders in developing credible estimates.[128]

Second, despite its limited funding, CJPC reportedly improved decision-making processes in the state.[129] Consider a single potential improvement: by reducing admission of probationers and parolees to prison for technical violations, a state can reduce the need to build one or more prisons.[130] Similarly, avoiding construction of supermax housing when it is not needed can result in hundreds of millions of dollars in savings through reduced construction and operational costs.[131] Put differently, the bar in many respects is quite low; a single decision, such as either of these, holds the potential to create savings that would fund a much larger research infrastructure than the CJPC for decades. Improving systems can create savings that go well beyond the break-even costs of supporting research.[132]

Third, the ultimate demise of the CJPC appeared to result from "politics." The Governor's office promoted prison privatization, and analyses indicated that it was unclear that doing so was needed or would result in cost-savings.[133] Whether accurate or not, this explanation highlights the need for a research-based process that is not insulated from political discussions and process but that nonetheless operates in a non-partisan manner. For example, it must be, and must be perceived as, a provider of credible information.[134] Any appearance to the contrary risks the potential for the process to be undermined and, as with CJPC, terminated.

Fourth, CJPC existed through Democratic-led and Republican-led administrations, and since its demise legislators have called for its resuscitation.[135] Its longevity stemmed from its responsiveness to the legislative and executive branches in providing empirical research on criminal and juvenile justice system operations and impacts and on existing and proposed policies. In so doing, the Policy Council's existence highlights the potential for research to guide policy. It highlights, too, the need for processes that include the two branches of government and that ensure that a number of conditions are met. For example, research needs to be undertaken in a timely manner so that decision-makers can act on it. The research should incorporate insights from legislators, governors, and agency officials, among others. It should educate these groups about research results, including relevant assumptions and limitations.[136] And it needs to be – and be perceived as – a credible source of non-partisan and objective information.

A second state, Washington, also illustrates the viability and potential benefits of institutionalizing a research effort aimed at improving criminal justice. As discussed in Chapter 2, the Washington State Institute for Public Policy, or WSIPP, exists to "carry out practical, non-partisan research at the direction of the legislature or Board of Directors."[137] Its mission parallels that of the former CJPC and, like CJPC, it was created in 1983. The Institute, too, relies on approximately 20 staff and a process that includes diverse stakeholders in the formation of research questions: "WSIPP works closely with legislators, legislative and state agency staff, and experts in the field to ensure that studies answer relevant policy questions."[138] Notably, however, the Institute's purview greatly exceeds that of the Policy Council. Whereas the Policy Council focused only on criminal and juvenile justice, the Institute focuses on all social policy areas, including education, mental health, public health, and welfare. Even so, the Institute produces many analyses, reports, and cost-benefit analyses that have contributed to state-level decision-making about criminal justice. They also feature prominently in scholarly reviews of "what works."[139] Their credibility as a source of non-partisan, objective research has led to interest among other states in adopting a similar effort or some of the methodological tools, including meta-analysis and cost-benefit analysis, that WSIPP uses in its research.[140]

WSIPP illustrates the potential benefits of investing in research. As David Farrington has written, "As a result of research undertaken by WSIPP, the Washington State legislature abandoned plans to build two new state prisons and in their place approved a sizable spending package on evidence-based intervention programs."[141] Similarly, Gary Vanlandingham observed that, in 2007, the Washington State Legislature "invested $48 million in a portfolio of prevention, juvenile justice, and adult corrections programs that the model determined to be evidence-based and economically sound, thereby enabling the legislature to remove a $250 million prison from the state's long-term forecast."[142] The ultimate impact of such decisions cannot be assessed through experimental designs. For example, the State of Washington cannot go back in time and invest $250 million in a prison rather than $48 million in a portfolio of alternative investments. Such decisions can be assessed, however, on how well they comport with needs evaluations for specific policies or interventions, including prisons, and with research on policies, programs, and practices that rest on credible theoretical and empirical grounds.[143] A central limitation of the WSIPP model is that it does not include systems analysis. Even so, its efforts to guide decision-making about a range of criminal justice and juvenile justice policy decisions likely contributes to greater overall system effectiveness and efficiency. In addition, the WSIPP model illustrates that states are interested in and can create the infrastructure for supporting research on criminal justice and juvenile justice systems. They are interested, too, and can create the infrastructure for multi-stakeholder processes that guide research and its uses.

Similar examples outside of the United States exist as well. For example, in Australia, the Queensland criminal justice system developed a Juvenile Justice Simulation Model (JJSM), based on efforts in the United States, such as JUSSIM and JUSSIM 2, and agent-based simulation modeling in the United Kingdom.[144] These models have tended to be used for predicting flows of individuals through the criminal justice system and for forecasting prison populations. In Queensland, the JJSM has been used for this purpose and to estimate potential impacts of policy changes on crime and the justice system. For example, given a baseline description of case flows, the model allows users to estimate how a change in key leverage points – such as crime prevention programs that reduce admissions into the system, pre-court diversion efforts, and post-court interventions – would affect all case flow processing and the system as a whole. Sensitivity analyses allow users and, by extension, policymakers to identify how likely a given outcome may be. The motivation to undertake the modeling and simulations derives from the insight that "planning and management of [the criminal justice] system (e.g., estimating prison requirements, measuring the impact of policing changes, examining alternative sentencing options, etc.) is necessary to ensure that the limited resources available are put to the best possible use."[145] JJSM was developed with an eye toward usability. This approach stems from the recognition that, in the past, systems analyses could be so complicated that policymakers and criminal justice officials would not understand or use them.[146]

Alongside of these different state and county efforts is the emergence of tools that decision-makers can use as part of efforts to create an effective and cost-efficient criminal justice system. These tools build on advances in crime prevention, criminological, and criminal justice science and in technology. Many of them incorporate "process" into systems analyses.

For example, the Urban Institute, a non-profit, non-partisan research organization in Washington, DC, has developed a Prison Population Forecaster (http://webapp.urban.org/reducing-mass-incarceration) that states can use, and modify, to estimate how changes in admissions or sentence length would affect projected prison populations. The Urban Institute created a similar tool for estimating the amount of future juvenile justice system bed space capacity need.[147] In both instances, the tools highlight that, while no one can know what will happen in the future, it nonetheless is possible to identify the potential and likely impacts of changing parts of the system. For example, merely increasing or decreasing average time served in prison, per inmate, by one or two months can greatly increase prison populations unless offsetting systems changes, such as reduced admissions, occur. A multi-stakeholder process can be critical to identifying whether such changes are likely. They can be critical, too, for determining whether other changes might yield greater and more certain beneficial impacts at less cost.

Another tool that local and state governments can use to improve criminal justice systems outcomes is the Risk-Need-Responsivity (RNR) Simulation Tool.[148] Building on a large body of research on the causes of recidivism, this tool can be used to identify the criminogenic risks and needs of offenders and the types of programs that would best address them. The emphasis is on systems. As the Center for Advancing Correctional Excellence has emphasized, effective programs can reduce recidivism on a small scale, but when implemented as needed throughout a criminal justice system, large-scale gains accrue: "While effective programs can reduce recidivism for individual offenders, *effective systems can reduce recidivism for populations of offenders.*"[149] This approach may seem like common sense, yet criminal justice systems to date have not operated in this way. A total stock-taking of the risks and needs of offenders and of the available vs. needed interventions typically has not happened. For example, "few studies or government reports identify the degree to which correctional programming is available, and the limited studies that are available are not routinely updated."[150] By contrast, "the RNR framework reinforces the need for jurisdictions to have a range of effective, well-implemented programs that target the varying needs of the justice-involved population. It is important to address gaps in services to develop responsive programs and ultimately, a responsive *system.*"[151] Greater understanding of the causes of recidivism and the greater availability of computerized databases and automated analytic methods has created the ability and opportunity to implement efforts like the RNR Simulation Tool.

This tool does not allow for modeling, monitoring, or evaluating criminal justice system case flows or the operations and impacts of subsystems, but it illustrates that tools exist to aid in such efforts.

A more process-oriented approach can be seen in the Reclaiming Futures (RF) project (http://reclaimingfutures.org).[152] Funded by the Robert Wood Johnson Foundation, the project, which began in 2001, seeks to work with communities to reduce drug problems and crime among young people. Impetus for the project derived in part from the observation that the juvenile justice system frequently does not provide sufficient accountability, assistance, services, or treatment for teenagers with drug or alcohol problems. Justice system responses, too, tend to be short-lived and more punitive in nature, with little emphasis on youths' strengths. Reclaiming Futures relies on a team-based approach – one that involves judges, probation officers, substance abuse treatment professionals, and community citizens – to identify how to provide more and better treatment for youth and to help the youth to become enmeshed in prosocial networks and activities. To this end, the teams help youth to navigate the juvenile justice system, social service agencies and treatment, and the community, all with an eye toward ensuring that the efforts of the youth and different stakeholders result in a beneficial outcome.

Reclaiming Futures was implemented in ten sites, and the focus was for each site to develop models of systems change that would be appropriate and possible to implement. The focus was on systems, not any one program or effort. As Jeffrey Butts and John Roman, who evaluated Reclaiming Futures, have written,

> Reclaiming Futures was founded on the assumption that positive outcomes for youth are best achieved when service delivery systems are well managed and coordinated, and when they provide young people with comprehensive, evidence-based substance abuse treatments along with other interventions and supports. Unlike many initiatives in the substance abuse field, RF was not designed to test the behavioral impact of any particular intervention or treatment technique. It was an effort to design and implement a model of organizational change and *system reform* that could improve the juvenile justice response to youth with drug and alcohol problems.[153]

Each site operated with specific populations, types of resources, constraints, and so on. Any viable or effective systems change needed to reflect these considerations. However, all sites were unified by several emphases:

> The ten projects focused on their own unique goals and strategies, but all projects relied on judicial leadership, court/community collaborations, interorganizational performance management, enhanced treatment quality, and multiagency

partnerships to improve their systems of care for youthful offenders with substance abuse problems.[154]

Across all sites, members of the RF teams worked to improve inter-agency networks that would create more effective responses to drug-involved juvenile offenders. The RF evaluation found that respondents across the sites perceived that the system worked more effectively in providing appropriate, needed, and better treatment.[155] Perhaps more notable, however, was the development of a survey-based strategy for monitoring and evaluating systems change. This approach was needed because there were ten sites, each in a unique community and undertaking different reforms with different relevant outcomes. Much the same can be said for local and state criminal justice systems. RF, then, illustrates how surveys can be used to augment administrative records data and other sources of information to provide insight into systems operations and impacts, and how they can be improved.

One final, related example that warrants discussion is the Criminal Justice System Project (CJSP).[156] Implemented in 1997 by the National Institute of Corrections (NIC), "its primary goal was to assist criminal justice policymakers in selected jurisdictions in their effort to develop a more coordinated, rational, and cost-effective system of criminal justice sanctions."[157] One result was creation of a guide – *Getting It Right: Collaborative Problem Solving for Criminal Justice* – to aid jurisdictions in such an effort.[158] This initiative was systems-focused and proceeded from the premise that better information is essential for building a more effective criminal justice system and that, so, too, is collaboration among key stakeholders.

The CJSP initiative built on the insights of key criminal justice system stakeholders. It identified that a central starting point for effective systems change entails a collaborative approach: "All of the parts of the system sitting down together to address their common responsibilities is a vital part of doing the people's business more responsibly and effectively."[159] It also identified that a systems approach must be adopted. As Peggy McGarry and Becky Ney, who were involved in the initiative, emphasized, "Public safety has little chance of being furthered if we wait for crime to happen and then assign each part of the system one piece of 'handling' its aftermath."[160] CJSP recognized that information and collaboration are essential. It recognized, too, that any process that requires better informa-tion and effective collaboration entails considerable effort and complex-ity. As McGarry and Ney cautioned,

Gaining a true picture of this process and the features of this approach is not simple, primarily because the tasks involved are so different from one another. Some tasks relate to improving interpersonal communication and trust as the basis for building interagency communication and cooperation. Others are straightforward parts of traditional strategic planning, for example, system mapping and data gathering.[161]

The tasks that CJSP advocated all build on collaboration, but focus on different goals. Some tasks, for example, involve creating a common and shared understanding about the system's goals. Others involve empirical assessment of how the system operates. Still others focus on creating plans for change and strategies for effectively implementing them.

In contrast to calls to improve criminal justice through specific tools, the CJSP calls for improvement through better process and systems information. As with the Reclaiming Futures project, it emphasizes reliance on collaboration. And, as with the RNR Simulation Model, it calls for generating information about current system operations, the risk-and-needs profile of the offender population, and a mapping of available resources.

If the CJSP guide to collaborative problem solving were created by scholars far removed from the nuts and bolts of criminal justice legislation and operations, it might correctly be viewed as a pie-in-the-sky approach to improving criminal justice. However, it was built through the insights of policymakers and criminal justice stakeholders. Accordingly, it highlights that systems-focused efforts to improve criminal justice are possible and, indeed, desired by those who understand it best. Precisely for that reason, the Systems Improvement Solution contemplates a similar approach. It calls for the use of better data, systems analysis, targeted evaluation efforts, and continuous involvement of stakeholders in guiding, interpreting, and using research, all with the aim of creating a criminal justice system that truly improves safety and justice, provides accountability, and does so in a cost-efficient manner.

6.4 CONCLUSION

The stakes for criminal justice are always high. When the criminal justice system performs poorly, society experiences more crime and less justice, accountability, and efficiency. We literally pay to be harmed. When this system works well, society is, conversely, safer, and there is more justice, accountability, and efficiency. For decades, policymakers have called for a more systematic approach to improving criminal justice. Scholars have echoed this call based on extensive research on the adverse effects of politicized and piecemeal change.

A systematic approach to improving criminal justice has not emerged, however. States and local jurisdictions continue to rely on piecemeal changes. Even when they introduce large-scale reforms, the changes typically target only a few select parts of the criminal justice system. Somewhat promisingly, governments have increasingly emphasized "evidence-based" programs. However, although such programs can be effective under certain conditions, they are not a panacea. They cannot offset the harms and inefficiencies that come from an out-of-control system of justice. They cannot substitute for a lack of research on the operations and impacts of this system. And they cannot substitute for a policymaking or administrative process that fails to include the insights of diverse stakeholder groups from across the criminal justice system and from the communities most affected by it. Better information and a better process are needed if we are to substantially improve criminal justice.

The Systems Improvement Solution, as presented in Chapter 5, is offered as an approach to improving criminal justice. It responds to calls by policymakers and scholars for a more systematic and research-based strategy for increased safety, justice, accountability, and efficiency. It focuses on the system, generation of better information about the operations and impacts of the system and its parts, and inclusion of key stakeholder groups in devising research and interpreting and acting on it. The argument for the Systems Solution goes beyond responding to calls for a more systematic approach to improving criminal justice. It reflects a logical necessity: there simply cannot be effective or efficient decision-making without useful information in the hands of individuals who shape or implement policy. When decisions occur within a systems context, there cannot be an effective or efficient system without someone, or some group, monitoring and steering the system.

This chapter has argued that many benefits could and would flow from implementing the Systems Improvement Solution or a similar systems-focused effort. The "big four" benefits include less crime and more justice, greater government accountability, and increased cost-efficiency. Other benefits can accrue, too, from efforts to use systems monitoring and evaluation to guide policies, programs, practices, and the day-to-day decision-making of those who work in or directly affect the system. Local or state criminal justice systems can be more responsive to victims' and communities' needs. They also can better detect when disparities – whether by race, ethnicity, sex, age, or other dimensions – exist, what causes the disparities, and what might be done to reduce them. The Systems Solution, too, has the potential to increase public understanding of crime and justice. Information from the deliberative process would be disseminated widely and freely to the public. At the same time, the solution entails creating a rich repository of information that scholars could use to understand better the causes of crime and of criminal justice system operations and impacts. The solution also holds the potential for enhancing the ability of subsystems (e.g., the police, courts, and corrections) to achieve their goals. Not least, it could help jurisdictions to make fewer big mistakes.

As with any policy effort – what really might more aptly be termed a research-and-policy or policy-and-research strategy – poor implementation can and invariably will undermine the effectiveness of the Systems Improvement Solution. This chapter identified different barriers to effective implementation of the proposed solution. These included such factors as a failure to institutionalize or fund it, bureaucracy and resistance to change, incomplete or inaccurate depictions of the system, and failure to include the insights and views of individuals who work in or are most affected by the criminal justice system or of scholars. They included as well the fact that many scholars and researchers may not be willing or able to collaborate with practitioners in undertaking policy studies. Data limitations may limit our ability to undertake systems analyses. Results from the analyses may be misused. Some policies might be emphasized over others when perhaps they should not be. And participations in the research-and-policy process may place excessive trust in "hard," empirical numbers and dismiss "fuzzy" qualitative accounts that may provide greater insight into complicated system dynamics. These and other pitfalls may beset efforts to implement the Systems Improvement Solution or to do so well. In each instance, however, steps can be taken to reduce their likelihood or impacts.

Can a strategy like the Systems Improvement Solution be adopted, and is it feasible? Absolutely. This chapter identified examples of efforts used in different places and policy arenas, such as health care and environmental protection, to implement systems analyses and systems-focused approaches to understanding, evaluating, and guiding policy and practice. Examples include the Washington State Institute for Public Policy, juvenile justice systems simulation modeling efforts in Australia, incorporation of risk-need-responsivity analyses into justice system decision-making, Reclaiming Futures, the Criminal Justice System Project, and others. SACs in particular offer an illustration of how states might begin to implement the Systems Improvement Solution. They serve to collect data on criminal justice and to coordinate efforts to share, merge, and analyze the data to identify policy issues and solutions. They typically do not have the resources to undertake the amount and kinds of analyses necessary for the Systems Solution, and they also do not partake in the research-and-policy process that would be central to the strategy. Even so, their very existence underscores that states understand, at least in part, the critical importance of research to improving policy.

In the end, the different examples vary considerably but are unified by accounts that indicate that improvements in criminal justice system operations and impacts can occur through research-based efforts that target systems. They are unified, too, by an emphasis on understanding what changes may be needed and may be possible. The latter consideration is critical, as Taxman and her colleagues have highlighted in examining efforts to incorporate the RNR model into the decision-making of system actors. Not all systems have the same needs or resources. Solutions to improving criminal justice thus must consider the problems that exist in specific jurisdictions *and* the solutions that realistically, given available resources in these jurisdictions, can be implemented. Effective solutions also must, I argue, be harnessed to an institutionalized process that brings together different stakeholder groups to guide, review, and act on research. That is the Systems Improvement Solution. It is an effort to use research to improve the operations and effectiveness of the entire criminal justice system. It is, too, an effort to rely on a process that requires continuous involvement of policymakers, criminal justice administrators and practitioners, and the citizens and communities most affected by crime and the justice system.

7

Conclusion: Criminal Justice under Control

Policymakers frequently advocate for whole-cloth change to crime and justice policy. This approach can be seen in federal laws. Every decade, presidents and legislators enact seemingly comprehensive policy reform.[1] I say "seemingly" because, while the various reforms introduce a bewildering array of changes, they do not target all aspects of crime and justice, nor are they informed by comprehensive empirical study of the system of criminal justice in America or among states. In one fell swoop, then, "big" changes occur, yet they miss the mark.

Indeed, the changes leave almost entirely untouched the root causes of crime, injustice, the lack of accountability, and inefficiency. They necessarily do so because they do not build on empirical assessment of the system of crime and justice. A comprehensive plan for improving financial investments, marriages, military operations, health care, and so on can hardly be expected to work if it proceeds with empirically based insights about delimited aspects of each. So, too, with crime and justice. There is no free lunch: either policymakers build reforms based on empirically based assessments of the criminal justice system or they build them based on hunches, ideology, presumed benefits, and insights about this or that part of the system.

The latter route is the one well traveled. It has created an out-of-control criminal justice system that over several decades has burgeoned into a costly mess. Could it have been the "right" – most effective and efficient – avenue to take? Sure. But there is little empirical evidence to support that claim. Indeed, the research infrastructure for supporting it does not, by and large, exist, so we must accept any such claim on faith. Consider, as but one illustration, the finding of a National Academy of

Sciences review: "Scientifically strong impact evaluations of [crime prevention and crime control] programs, while improving, are still uncommon in the context of the overall number of programs that have received funding."[2]

What, then, if we had "merely" doubled or tripled correctional expenditures since 1980? No one knows. That is, in a word, stunning. As a nation, America grew its prison system by historically unprecedented levels and opted to do so with little to no empirical guidance about the broader system of crime and justice, the diverse factors that contribute to it, how it works, and what the likely effects would be or were. It chose to do so not only in the 1980s but again in subsequent decades. Democrats and Republicans drove this change. Certainly, political conservatives bear more of the "credit" for promulgating tough-on-crime policies, but political liberals have promoted them, too. Presidents Ronald Reagan and George H. W. Bush promoted such policy, but so, too, did Presidents Clinton and Obama.

Alongside of such growth was a seemingly positive event: calls for "evidence-based" policy and for "government accountability" reached a crescendo. One illustration of the pervasiveness of this shift was the renaming of the US General Accounting Office to the US Government Accountability Office in 2004. Scholarship helped to fuel this shift. An increasingly large body of research emerged that documented the diverse strategies that exist to address crime and to promote more and better justice. Meta-analyses became common and consistently pointed to the benefits of a wide range of rehabilitative programs and practices, especially those built on principles of effective correctional intervention.[3]

Yet, there emerged no systematic, empirically informed assessment, whether at federal, state, or local levels, of crime and justice or of the criminal justice system. In addition, it was and remains unclear what "evidence-based" meant. Did it mean the results from one or two studies? A handful of experimental evaluations of a particular program? Replication of a given intervention across a diverse range of settings? Use of a program in one state that appeared, based on a descriptive study, to have been effective in another? Concerns about the potentially delimited contexts in which a program might be effective were largely bypassed. Some interventions may be effective in some contexts or for certain populations, but not in others.[4] In addition, investment in an expensive but not needed "evidence-based" intervention can divert resources from other effective and more-needed investments, and so create more harm than good.

That is an out-of-control situation. It is one where scarce resources get expended willy-nilly, with little to no empirical guidance. The criminal justice system gets continuously modified with no basis for evaluating the need for the changes or what their impacts have been or will be. The end result, not surprisingly, leaves everyone unhappy.

Whether crime goes up or down, policymakers face unreasonable demands to "fix" crime and justice, or they perceive a need to do so. Many members of the public have little understanding about the actual operations or effects of criminal justice, but nonetheless express grave concern about crime and profound disappointment with the police, courts, and corrections. All too often, victims and others touched by the criminal justice system end up feeling doubly victimized. All too often, too, offenders receive little in the way of effective punishment and instead are frequently are the beneficiaries of sanctions and restrictions that contribute to more crime rather than less. Communities then bear the brunt of these and other changes. The many barriers to reentry that ex-prisoners face, for example, create potential hardships not only for them but also for their families and neighborhoods.[5] At the same time, overburdened police departments, public defenders, courts, jails, prisons, and probation and parole departments work to process large numbers of cases; some get handled well and many do not. At its worst, the situation creates disparities in punishment that more adversely affect low-income and minority communities and engender ill will toward the police and the justice system.

This problem should not exist and it does not have to exist. Policymakers and the public want better, more efficient government. And, importantly, scholars have amassed a body of knowledge about effective programs and practices. Simultaneously, technological advances have created the possibility of undertaking dramatically more and better "real-time" research on the day-to-day operations of the criminal justice system. This research can focus, too, on the causes of the very problems that this system is designed to address and on the factors that impede or facilitate its effectiveness and efficiency. It can do so by leveraging existing data and by creating new information through surveying the public, criminal justice officials and staff, practitioners, offenders, victims, and community residents.

All of the ingredients can be combined to institutionalize research in ways that enable policymakers and practitioners to understand and improve the criminal justice system. We can bring it "under control." "Institutionalizing" is the operative word. The research cannot consist of a one-time study here and there. It cannot consist of testimony from this or that scholar. It cannot occur with no funding. Rather, it requires ongoing involvement of diverse groups – policymakers, practitioners, citizens, victims, offenders, and researchers – in requesting and interpreting research and discussing its implications. It requires investment in databases and data collection systems as well as in analytic capacity to undertake analyses and present the information in an understandable, useful way. Not least, it requires a focus on the *entire* criminal justice system, not just one aspect or another. In so doing, a commitment to process and research is necessary. Without them, piecemeal research, piecemeal change, and ideology run the day. There may be small pockets of improvement that result, but not large-scale improvements in public safety, justice, accountability, or cost-efficiency.

That, in a nutshell, is the argument underlying the proposed Systems Improvement Solution. A system of justice that exists both to reduce crime and to promote justice can hardly do so well if it proceeds with little to no empirical information about system operations and their effectiveness. It also cannot introduce sustainable, beneficial, large-scale change if undertaken in a piecemeal manner with little guidance or involvement from diverse parties affected by or responsible for the administration of justice. Accordingly, the Systems Solution consists of a three-part focus.

The first part is research that seeks to identify policy needs and to monitor and assess policy implementations, impacts, and cost-efficiency. It seeks, too, to analyze systems operations and impacts and provides the resulting information in the equivalent of a "driver's dashboard." The second is a multi-stakeholder policy process aimed at understanding and improving criminal justice and guided by an emphasis on several priorities: focusing on goals; avoiding big mistakes; prioritizing high-bet, low-risk changes; minimizing negative feedback loops; leveraging positive feedback loops; and continuously undertaking policy evaluation and reevaluation. And the third is implementation of evidence-based policies, programs, and practices, as determined by the systems research and the multi-stakeholder policy process. Implementation occurs with awareness and assessment of the broader systems context and a commitment to improving systems outcomes. Each of these three parts contributes to the others and provides a self-reinforcing mechanism for ensuring adherence to research-based change that targets the areas of greatest need with policies that are the most cost-efficient.

Core principles guide the process. They amount to conditions that must be met for the process to be effective. An agency must be charged with implementing the process and provided with the support and funding to do so well. The process must be non-partisan, include frequent deliberations among stakeholders, and emphasize the use of research to guide decisions. Insights about research and policy should consistently draw on the knowledge that those on the "ground floor" – the practitioners, for example, who work in police departments or prisons, or the citizens most affected by crime – have about criminal justice. Scholars who have expertise in crime and justice constitute another critical group to include in the process. There is little need to reinvent the wheel in criminal justice. A large body of theory and research on criminal justice exists that can and should guide development of new and better data. New technologies and analytic methods exist to identify patterns in and insights about criminal justice. These, too, should be used to understand how the criminal justice system operates and what can be done to improve it. And information from analyses should be shared widely and frequently with diverse stakeholder groups and the public. Doing so provides accountability, a shared understanding about crime and justice, and an evidence-based foundation for creating systems change.

Federal, state, and local governments can implement this approach. Indeed, examples exist of efforts that accord with the spirit of the Systems Improvement Solution. The name of course does not matter. What does matter is investment in *systems-focused strategies* to improve safety and justice. But to implement the proposed solution or a comparable effort at a scale commensurate with criminal justice and correctional system costs will require a substantial increase in research funding and infrastructure. Here, no apology is needed. Businesses recognize the need for information that can guide them toward greater efficiency and profits. By extension, if we are going to spend billions of dollars on criminal justice, then we need to invest in generating the kinds of information that can enable policymakers, administrators, and practitioners to make solid, empirically based decisions to promote safety and justice. Much the same holds for other policy arenas, such as health care and education. Without relevant information and without a process for acting on that information, systems take over and leave us with worse outcomes. We literally pay to be harmed. There is a better way, one that requires no magical "silver bullet" solution, but instead requires simply a commitment to research and to a multi-stakeholder policy process.

Of necessity, then, researchers should be at the policy-and-practice "table." Their involvement is critical on many fronts. They obviously can and should undertake research. But they also can help to guide it, to understand better what questions policymakers and practitioners need answered, and to inform these groups about the possibilities and limits of particular research undertakings. Of necessity, any institutionalized research arrangement requires permanent staff who take responsibility for all core research efforts. They should, however, be complemented by the involvement of researchers from other settings, such as think tanks and colleges and universities. Such individuals have competing responsibilities, yet can offer valuable insight into relevant theory, methodology, or substantive issues. Their involvement in policy and practice typically is *ad hoc*, driven more by circumstance, personal preference, or luck than by anything else. For this reason, institutionalizing the Systems Improvement Solution requires careful planning to ensure the active involvement of the broader research community and, no less important, criminal justice staff, victims, offenders, and members of the public.

The active involvement of these different groups holds great promise for improving criminal justice policy and practice and, at the same time, our understanding of crime and justice. Scholars have a penchant for creating theories that rarely can or do get tested. They have a penchant as well for conducting narrowly focused research because the data at their disposal only permit such an approach. Not least, they have a penchant for residing in a so-called "ivory tower," one removed from the "real world." A critical benefit of the proposed solution is the active engagement of multiple groups in research. In a very real sense, researchers are brought down to earth. Simultaneously, they have the opportunity to help design, collect, and analyze a much more rich set of data about crime, justice, and the criminal justice system. As but one example, an effort to understand the effects of a new sentencing law might entail surveying prosecutors throughout a state about their views concerning the conditions under which they might use the law. In one fell swoop, then, researchers would have access to information about sentencing decisions that typically remains in a "black box." Such a possibility barely scratches the surface. Real-time collection of information from practitioners, victims, offenders, residents, and more would provide endless opportunities to develop and test theories of crime, justice, formal and informal social control, and more.

It may seem Pollyannaish to think that the proposed Systems Improvement Solution – or any systems-focused strategy for improving safety and justice – could greatly improve policy and knowledge. Perhaps it is. Yet, I would submit that it is more Pollyannaish to think that large-scale improvements in policy or knowledge can come from approaches that are divorced from empirical reality. That includes passing laws that ignore the context in which they occur, or implementing "evidence-based" programs while ignoring systemic problems. To ignore this reality and focus exclusively on small, bite-size problems and "solutions" dooms society to harmful and expensive failure. Smaller-scale solutions have their place. To tackle a big problem sometimes requires breaking it down into bite-size pieces. Politically, that may be the only way to proceed in some instances. At the end of the day, though, when literally billions of lives and dollars are at stake, it is the height of folly to invest so little in understanding the criminal justice systems in which we have spent, and of which we expect, so much. If we are to obligate societal resources for a safe and just society, we should benefit from it. It is time to bring criminal justice under control and make it work for us and for future generations.

Notes

I INTRODUCTION: OUT-OF-CONTROL CRIMINAL JUSTICE

1. Blumstein (1997); Nagin et al. (2009); Mears (2010); Garland (2013); Kelly (2015, 2016).
2. Rossi et al. (2004); Mears (2010).
3. Mears (2010); Welsh, Braga, and Bruinsma (2013); Welsh and Pfeffer (2013); Kelly (2015, 2016).
4. Welsh, Braga, and Bruinsma (2013:3).
5. Details about the Commission can be found on its website (www.cep.gov). As described there, the Commission's mission is "to develop a strategy for increasing the availability and use of data in order to build evidence about government programs, while protecting privacy and confidentiality. Through the course of the Commission's work, members will study how data, research, and evaluation are currently used to build evidence, and how to strengthen the government's evidence-building efforts."
6. Tonry (2004, 2009); Spelman (2006, 2009); Garland (2013); Travis et al. (2014); Kelly (2015, 2016).
7. Latessa et al. (2014).
8. Lipsey and Cullen (2007); Cullen, Jonson, and Stohr (2014); Mears and Cochran (2015).
9. Mears (2013).
10. Travis et al. (2014); Mears and Cochran (2015); Phelps and Pager (2016).
11. Clear (2007); Cochran, Mears, and Bales (2014); Latessa et al. (2014).
12. See, for example, Spelman (2006, 2008, 2009).
13. Nagin et al. (2009); Cochran, Mears, and Bales (2014); Mears and Cochran (2015); Mears, Cochran, and Cullen (2015); Mears et al. (2016).
14. See, for example, Tonry (2004); Travis (2005); Clear (2007); Mears (2010), Cullen, Jonson, and Nagin (2011); Garland (2013); Mears and Cochran (2015); Mears and Siennick (2016); Phelps and Pager (2016); and Cullen, Jonson, and Mears (2017).

15. Durose et al. (2014); see, generally, Nagin et al. (2009), Cullen, Jonson, and Nagin (2011), and Cochran, Mears, and Bales (2014).
16. Skogan and Frydl (2004); Unnever and Gabbidon (2011); Baumer (2013); Spohn (2013); Mears, Cochran, and Lindsey (2016).
17. Nagin et al. (2009); Nagin (2013); Cullen, Jonson, and Stohr (2014); Latessa et al. (2014); Mears and Cochran (2015).
18. Forer (1994); Nadelmann (2004); Travis (2005); Sevigny et al. (2013).
19. Travis (2005); Clear (2007); Mears and Cochran (2015).
20. Feld (1999); Feld and Bishop (2012); Howell et al. (2012).
21. Ebbesen and Konečni (1985); Forst (2004); Mears and Bacon (2009).
22. Roberts (1992); Roberts and Stalans (1998); Cullen, Fisher, and Applegate (2000); Roberts, Stalans, Indermaur, and Hough (2003); Roberts and Hough (2005a, 2005b).
23. Mears (2010).
24. See Freilich and Newman (2016) for an illustration of this problem, and one avenue for addressing it.
25. Mears (2012).
26. Mears (2012).
27. Mears, Kuch, Lindsey, Siennick, Pesta, Greenwald, and Blomberg (2016).
28. Mears and Butts (2008); Howell et al. (2012).
29. Humes (1996).
30. Mears, Cochran, and Cullen (2015); Mears, Cochran, Bales, and Bhati (2016).
31. Mears (2010).
32. Durose et al. (2014).
33. Cullen, Jonson, and Nagin (2011).
34. Donnelly (2017).
35. Herman (2010).
36. Lum and Nagin (2017).
37. Mears (2012).
38. Blomberg (1980); Phelps and Pager (2016).
39. Mears, Kuch, Lindsey, Siennick, Pesta, Greenwald, and Blomberg (2016).
40. See, generally, Ebbesen and Konečni (1985); Mears (2008a); Mears and Butts (2008); Mears and Bacon (2009); Mears, Shollenberger, Willison, Owens, and Butts (2010); Mears, Cochran, Greenman, Bhati, and Greenwald (2011); Mears, Cochran, and Lindsey (2016); and Mears and Lindsey (2016).
41. Nagin et al. (2009); Cochran, Mears, and Bales (2014); Mears and Cochran (2015).
42. Lawrence and Mears (2004).
43. See, generally, Mears (2010); Kelly (2015, 2016); and Freilich and Newman (2016).
44. Charles Colson Task Force (2016).
45. Charles Colson Task Force (2016:57).
46. Kahneman (2011).
47. Auerhahn (2002:380); see also Auerhahn (2004).
48. Silver (2012).

49. Mears (2010). See also Mears (2007, 2008a, 2008b); Mears and Butts (2008); and Mears and Barnes (2010).
50. Mears and Cochran (2015).

2 SYSTEMS PROBLEMS ARE NOT SPECIFIC TO CRIME AND JUSTICE

1. Hellander (2015).
2. Peterson Foundation (2016), analyzing data from the Organization for Economic Cooperation and Development (www.oecd.org), for 2014.
3. Hellander (2015:707).
4. Hellander (2015).
5. Hellander (2015:708).
6. Gawande (2007:14).
7. Makary and Daniel (2016).
8. Gawande (2007:15).
9. Gawande (2007:22).
10. Makary and Daniel (2016).
11. Reid (2009:2).
12. Groopman (2007); Mears and Bacon (2009).
13. Groopman (2007:35).
14. Groopman (2007:36).
15. Groopman (2007:65); see, generally, Mears and Bacon (2009).
16. Sanders (2009:97).
17. Groopman (2007:17).
18. Groopman (2007:86); see also Sanders (2009).
19. Groopman (2007:181).
20. For example, citing Millenson's (1997) discussion of a 1983 US Office of Technology Assessment study, Sherman (2003:7) noted that "85 percent of everyday medical treatments had never been scientifically tested." See, generally, Gawande (2007); Groopman (2007); Mears and Bacon (2009); Reid (2009).
21. Groopman (2007:242).
22. Groopman and Hartzband (2011).
23. Gawande (2007, 2009); Groopman (2007); Salamon (2008); Mears and Bacon (2009); Reid (2009); Sanders (2009).
24. Groopman (2007:31).
25. Groopman (2007:46).
26. Gawande (2007); Mears and Bacon (2009); Reid (2009); Sanders (2009); Banja (2010).
27. Gawande (2007:64).
28. Banja (2010:10).
29. Drake et al. (1972); Roberts, Hsiao, Berman and Reich (2008); Reid (2009); Luke and Stamatakis (2012).
30. Kelleghan et al. (2012).
31. Reese (2013:6).

32. Kelleghan et al. (2012).
33. Kelleghan et al. (2012).
34. Bettinger (2005).
35. Bettinger (2005).
36. Bettinger (2005); Hanushek et al. (2007); Imberman (2011); Berends (2015).
37. Katz (1976:403); see also Platt (1977); Tanenhaus (2004); Bernard and Kurlychek (2010).
38. Nelson et al. (2015).
39. Darling-Hammond (2010:3).
40. Darling-Hammond (2010:3).
41. Darling-Hammond (2010); Kelleghan et al. (2012); Croft et al. (2016).
42. Darling-Hammond (2010:2).
43. Darling-Hammond (2010:2).
44. Raudenbush and Willms (1991).
45. Raudenbush and Willms (1991:xi).
46. Darling-Hammond (2010:277).
47. Hecht and Fiksel (2015:75).
48. Hecht and Fiksel (2015:75).
49. Kolbert (2006, 2014).
50. Hecht and Fiksel (2015:77).
51. Hecht and Fiksel (2015:78).
52. Hecht and Fiksel (2015:79).
53. Hecht and Fiksel (2015:82).
54. See, for example, Siff and Mears's (1999) account of efforts to clean up the Mississippi River, Kolbert's (2006) account of climate change, Hernan's (2010) discussion of various high-profile environmental disasters, and McKinney et al.'s (2013) introduction to environmental science and systems views of how to understand and address environmental problems.
55. Fagin (2013).
56. Fagin (2013:137).
57. Fagin (2013:143).
58. Fagin (2013:144).
59. Fagin (2013:175).
60. Freilich and Newman (2016).
61. Hecht and Fiksel (2015).
62. Kean and Hamilton (2004).
63. Silver (2012:425); see, generally, Rumsfeld (2011).
64. Silver (2012).
65. Rumsfeld (2011).
66. Kean and Hamilton (2004:339).
67. Silver (2012:420).
68. Silver (2012:421).
69. Kean and Hamilton (2004:358).
70. Kean and Hamilton (2004:353, emphasis added).
71. General Accounting Office (1997:3).
72. Kean and Hamilton (2004:353).
73. Kean and Hamilton (2004:255).

74. Weiner (2012:428).
75. Silver (2012:444).
76. Kean and Hamilton (2004).
77. Mears (2008a, 2010).
78. Pratt and Maahs (1999); Gaes et al. (2004); Thomas (2005); Mears (2008a, 2010).
79. Reisig and Pratt (2000).
80. Altiok (1997).
81. Altiok (1997).
82. Meadows (2008:58).
83. Reich (1998:75).
84. Darling-Hammond (2010); Kelleghan et al. (2012); Davidson et al. (2015); Croft et al. (2016).
85. Mears and Cochran (2015).
86. See, for example, Tocci et al. (2007); Emery et al. (2009); Mathias et al. (2012).
87. Agnew (2005).
88. See, for example, Messner et al. (1989); Agnew (2005); Akers and Sellers (2012).
89. Blumstein (1997); Cullen and Gendreau (2000); Cullen and Jonson (2011).
90. Blumstein (1997); Cullen and Gendreau (2000); Lipsey and Cullen (2007); Cullen, Jonson, and Mears (2017).
91. Mears and Bacon (2009).
92. Mears (2010).
93. Berk and Rossi (1997); Mears (2010).
94. Mears and Cochran (2015); Cullen, Jonson, and Mears (2017).
95. This account is described in Malcolm (1958). I have used the radius illustration from Mears and Stafford (2002:10) and Mears (2010:170).
96. Kahneman (2011).
97. Mears (2010).
98. Latessa et al. (2014).
99. Farabee (2005); Mears and Cochran (2015); Cullen, Pratt, and Turanovic (2016).
100. Meadows (2008:175–176) has eloquently described, for example, the tendency to focus our efforts on quantifiable dimensions and to ignore those that are difficult to quantify but that may be critically important to the operations of a system.
101. See, for example, Levitt and Dubner (2014:199).
102. Meadows (2008:181).
103. Mears (2013).
104. Mears and Watson (2006).
105. Mears and Reisig (2006).
106. Bottoms (1999); Mears (2008a).
107. Meadows (2008:91).
108. Mears, Cochran, Bales, and Bhati (2016).
109. In a related vein, see Brame (2017) concerning risk prediction and the use of algorithms that anticipate curvilinear and interactive (i.e., nonlinear)

relationships between various factors and recidivism; see also Berk and Bleich (2013) and Ridgeway (2013).

110. Mears (2012).
111. Texas Criminal Justice Policy Council (1997:17).
112. Heilbroner (1990).
113. Forst (2004); Mears and Bacon (2009).
114. See, for example, Bridges and Steen (1998); see, more generally, Mears and Bacon (2009); Mears, Cochran, and Lindsey (2016).
115. Forst (2004); Mears and Bacon (2009).
116. Milgram (2012).
117. Washington State Institute for Public Policy (www.wsipp.wa.gov).
118. Perry (2003).
119. Washington State Institute for Public Policy (www.wsipp.wa.gov/About).
120. Kaminsky (2013).

3 WHAT IS A SYSTEM?

1. Meadows (2008:11).
2. Rapoport (1986:xvi).
3. Bernard et al. (2005:204).
4. Silver (2012).
5. Parsons (1951, 1977); Abbott (1988).
6. Lieberson (1985).
7. Kahneman (2011).
8. Soled (2001).
9. Sober and Wilson (1994).
10. See, generally, Lieberson (1985:107–108).
11. Hatry (2006); Mears (2010).
12. Hatry (2006); Mears (2010).
13. Gould (1987).
14. Mears and Barnes (2010).
15. Mears and Cochran (2015).
16. Reich (1998).
17. Meadows (2008:12).
18. Meadows (2008).
19. Mears (1998a, 1998b, 2000).
20. Rhodes (1990); Hanneman (1995); Auerhahn (2008a, 2008b).
21. Meadows (2008:17).
22. Meadows (2008:187).
23. Meadows (2008:22).
24. Sabol (1999); Mears (2002a).
25. Hatry (2006:15).
26. Different types of causal relationships have been described in a variety of sources (see, e.g., Marini and Singer 1988; Lieberson 1985; Meadows 1998; Agnew 2005; Stafford and Mears 2015).
27. Mears, Cochran, and Beaver (2013).

28. Meadows (2008:91); see also Agnew (2005); Mears and Cochran (2013); and Mears, Cochran, and Beaver (2013).
29. Meadows (2008:91); see also Abbott (1988); Agnew (2005); Mears and Cochran (2013); and Mears, Cochran, and Beaver (2013).
30. Agnew (2005:87).
31. Meadows (2008:25, 30).
32. Bernard et al. (2005); Mears and Bacon (2009).
33. Mears and Cochran (2015).
34. Stafford and Mears (2015:6).
35. Meadows (2008:25); see, generally, Taleb (2012).
36. Lewin (1952:169).
37. See, for example, Blalock (1964); Merton (1968, 1973); Gibbs (1972); Cole (1975); Dubin (1978); Marini and Singer (1988); Hage (1994); Mears and Stafford (2002); Reynolds (2006); Jaccard and Jacoby (2010); and Swanson and Chermack (2013).
38. Reynolds (2006).
39. Geertz (1973:7).
40. Mears and Stafford (2002); Reynolds (2006).
41. Cole (1975); Gibbs (1995, 1997); Mears and Stafford (2002).
42. Meadows (2008:75).
43. Meadows (2008:82).
44. Meadows (2008:76).
45. Taleb (2012).
46. Meadows (2008:85).
47. Meadows (2008).
48. Rossi et al. (2004); Taleb (2012).
49. See, for example, Marini and Singer (1988); see, generally, Mears and Stafford (2002).
50. Abbott (1988).
51. Bottoms (1999).
52. Weber (1949).
53. Meadows (2008:28).
54. Homans (1964).
55. Mears (2010).
56. Lewin (1952); Merton (1973); Cole (1975); Mears and Stafford (2002); Weinberg (2015).

4 THE CRIMINAL JUSTICE SYSTEM

1. See, however, Messinger's (1969) masterly analysis of the emergence and operations of the California prison system.
2. See, for example, Blalock (1964); Blumstein (1967, 1972); and Blumstein and Larson (1972); see, generally, Cassidy and Turner (1978); Vanagunas (1987); Rhodes (1990); and Auerhahn (2008a).
3. Auerhahn (2008a:295).
4. Downes (1988); Garland (2013).

5. Mears (2007, 2010).
6. Messinger (1969).
7. Kleck, Tark, and Bellows (2006).
8. Blumstein (1997).
9. See Rand and Catalano (2007) and Truman and Morgan (2016).
10. Mears (2010); Mears and Cochran (2015); Cullen, Jonson, and Mears (2017).
11. DiIulio (1995); Fox (1996).
12. Lynch and Addington (2007); Fay and Diallo (2015).
13. Regoeczi and Banks (2014).
14. Mears (2010); Mears and Cochran (2015).
15. Bureau of Justice Statistics (2016).
16. Blumstein and Beck (1999); Blumstein and Wallman (2006).
17. Zawitz (1996); Kleck and Kates (2001).
18. See the Bureau of Justice Statistics (2009) for the 1980–1999 statistics, Glaze and Kaeble (2014) for the 2000–2013 statistics, and Kaeble et al. (2015:2) for the 2014 statistic.
19. Kaeble et al. (2015:2).
20. Petersilia (2003); Travis (2005); Travis et al. (2014); Mears and Cochran (2015).
21. Kaeble et al. (2015).
22. Mears (2010); Mears and Cochran (2015).
23. Garland (2013:478); see also Corbett (2015).
24. See Kyckelhahn (2011) regarding justice system expenditures from 1982–2007; see also Kyckelhahn (2013, 2015) regarding local government corrections spending.
25. Mears (2010); Mears and Cochran (2015).
26. Mears and Cochran (2015).
27. Forst (2004); Mears and Barnes (2010).
28. See, for example, Rawls (1971); Baird and Rosenbaum (1988); Von Hirsch and Ashworth (1992); and Rossi and Berk (1997).
29. Baird and Rosenbaum (1988); Von Hirsch and Ashworth (1992).
30. Ekland-Olson et al. (1983).
31. Mears, Cochran, and Lindsey (2016).
32. Rossi and Berk (1997); Roberts, Stalans, Indermaur, and Hough (2003).
33. Cullen, Jonson, and Mears (2017) have identified a diverse range of strategies that exist for achieving criminal justice system goals.
34. Herman (2010); Mears and Cochran (2015).
35. Roberts (1992); Flanagan and Longmire (1996); Cullen, Fisher, and Applegate (2000); Roberts, Stalans, Indermaur, and Hough (2003); Roberts and Hough (2005a, 2005b); see also Mears (2010) and Mears and Cochran (2015).
36. Mears (2010); Welsh and Harris (2016).
37. Rossi et al. (2004); Mears (2010).
38. Mears (2010); Roman, Dunworth, and Walsh (2010); Welsh, Farrington, and Raffan-Gowar (2015).
39. Lum and Nagin (2017).
40. Mears and Barnes (2010); Langton and Truman (2014).
41. Mears, Cochran, and Lindsey (2016).

42. Lum and Nagin (2017).
43. Mears and Bacon (2009).
44. Heilbroner (1990); Humes (1996); Petersilia and Reitz (2012).
45. Kelly (2015, 2016).
46. Mears (2010); Corbett (2015).
47. Piehl and LoBuglio (2005).
48. May and Wood (2010); Corbett (2015).
49. Corbett (2015:1699); the precise estimate, for 2013, was, as Corbett noted, 57 percent.
50. Pew Charitable Trusts (2009:13).
51. Corbett (2015); Phelps and Pager (2016).
52. Cochran, Mears, and Bales (2014); Mears, Cochran, and Cullen (2015).
53. Mears (1998a, 1998b, 2000); see also Corbett's (2015:1709) discussion of judicial variation in the reasons for administering probation as a sanction.
54. See Durkheim (1985), which includes essays that he wrote in the late 1800s and early 1900s.
55. Durkheim (1985:100).
56. Cullen, Fisher, and Applegate (2000); Roberts, Stalans, Indermaur, and Hough (2003); Roberts and Hough (2005b).
57. Mears and Cochran (2015).
58. Mears and Cochran (2015).
59. Butts and Mears (2001); Mears (2002b); Bernard and Kurlychek (2010).
60. Mears (1998); Petersilia and Reitz (2012); Ulmer (2012); Baumer (2013).
61. Davis et al. (2003).
62. See, for example, Nagin et al. (2006); see, generally, Cullen, Fisher, and Applegate (2000); Roberts, Stalans, Indermaur, and Hough (2003); and Roberts and Hough (2005a, 2005b).
63. Mears (2010); Mears and Cochran (2015).
64. See, for example, Roberts and Stalans (1998); Cullen, Fisher, and Applegate (2000); Mears (2001); Roberts, Stalans, Indermaur, and Hough (2003); Roberts and Hough (2005a, 2005b); Mears, Hay, Geertz, and Mancini (2007); Mears, Mancini, Geertz, and Bratton (2008); Unnever (2014); and Mears, Pickett, and Mancini (2015).
65. Stolz (2002); Burstein (2003); Bardach (2006); Mancini and Mears (2013).
66. Burstein (2003).
67. Luke and Stamatakis (2012:2).
68. Heilbroner (1990).
69. Mears, Cochran, and Lindsey (2016).
70. A small sampling of examples includes the following: Sykes (1958); Sudnow (1964); Skolnick (1966); Blumstein (1972); Blomberg (1980); Cassidy (1985); Ebbesen and Konečni (1985); DiIulio (1987); Sutton (1988); Heilbroner (1990); Spelman (1995); Humes (1996); Feld (1999); Sabol (1999); Beckett and Sasson (2000); Stolz (2002); Davis et al. (2003); Forst (2004); Tonry (2004); Gottschalk (2006); Manza and Uggen (2006); Western (2006); Leo (2008); Sampson (2009, 2012, 2013); Bernard and Kurlychek (2010); Reisig (2010); Garland (2013); Mears (2013); Sevigny et al. (2013); Ridgeway and MacDonald (2014); Mears and Cochran (2015).

71. Ekland-Olson and Kelly (1993); Mears and Bacon (2009).
72. Mears, Cochran, and Lindsey (2016).
73. Reisig (2010); Lum and Nagin (2017).
74. Reisig (2010); Lum and Nagin (2017).
75. See, for example, Heilbroner (1990).
76. Lynch and Sabol (2001); Mears and Cochran (2015).
77. Mears and Cochran (2015).
78. See, generally, Lum and Nagin (2017).
79. Mears, Mancini, and Stewart (2009); Mears and Stewart (2010); Mancini et al. (2015); Mears, Cochran, and Lindsey (2016).
80. Mears and Cochran (2015).
81. See, for example, Adams (1992); Sparks et al. (1996); Bottoms (1999); Mears and Cochran (2015); and Cullen, Jonson, and Mears (2017).
82. Travis and Visher (2005); Mears and Cochran (2015).
83. Blumstein and Kadane (1983); Austin (2016); Cullen, Jonson, and Mears (2017).
84. Bernard et al. (2005:204).
85. See, generally, Hagan (1989); Bernard and Engel (2001); Bernard et al. (2005); Kraska (2006); Crank and Bowman (2008); Cooper and Worrall (2012); Dooley and Rydberg (2014); and Duffee (2015).
86. Mears and Bacon (2009).
87. Piehl and LoBuglio (2005); Mears and Cochran (2015).
88. Kuhn (1962); Merton (1968, 1973); Mears and Stafford (2002); Weinberg (2015).
89. Mears and Stafford (2002).
90. Kraska (2006:178).
91. See, generally, Blumstein (1967, 1972); Van Gigch (1978); Hagan (1989); Walker (1992); Maguire et al. (1998); Kraska (2004); Bernard et al. (2005); Auerhahn (2008a, 2008b); cf. Skoler (1977); Duffee (1990); and Bernard and Engel (2001).
92. Bernard et al. (2005).
93. Bernard et al. (2005:204).
94. Bernard et al. (2005:204).
95. Bernard et al. (2005:205).
96. Bernard et al. (2005:204).
97. Van Gigch (1978).
98. Bernard et al. (2005:205).
99. Weber (1949, 1978); Merton (1968, 1973); Geertz (1973); Gould (1987); Mears and Stafford (2002).
100. Gibbs (1997).
101. Bernard et al. (2005:205).
102. Bernard et al. (2005:205).
103. Bernard et al. (2005:205).
104. Bernard et al. (2005:206).
105. Mears and Cochran (2015).
106. Mears, Cochran, and Lindsey (2016).
107. Bernard et al. (2005:206).

108. For a related observation, see Maguire et al. (1998).
109. See, for example, Skoler's (1977) critique and Duffee (1990).
110. Hagan (1989).
111. Rossi et al. (2004); Mears (2010).
112. Bernard et al. (2005:206).
113. Mears and Cochran (2015); Mears, Cochran, and Cullen (2015).
114. Bernard et al. (2005:207).
115. Bernard et al. (2005:207).
116. Petersilia (2003); Travis (2005); Travis et al. (2014).
117. Bernard et al. (2005:207).
118. Mears, Scott, and Bhati (2007a, 2007b, 2007c).
119. Bernard et al. (2005:207).
120. Mears (2010).
121. Bernard et al. (2005:208).
122. Mears (2010).
123. See illustrations of these responses in Heilbroner (1990) and Humes (1996).
124. Bernard et al. (2005:208).
125. Bernard et al. (2005:208–209).
126. Mears and Bacon (2009).
127. Bernard et al. (2009:209).
128. Bernard et al. (2005:209).
129. Bernard et al. (2005:209).
130. Bernard et al. (2005:209); see also Mears and Cochran (2015) and Mears, Kuch, Lindsey, Siennick, Pesta, Greenwald, and Blomberg (2016).
131. As noted earlier, a small sampling of illustrative works includes Parsons (1951, 1977); Blumstein (1967, 1972); Navarro and Taylor (1967); Kelleher (1970); Chartrand (1971); Blumstein and Larson (1972); Drake et al. (1972); Coffey (1974); Bertalanffy (1975); Bohigian (1977); Forst (1977); Hoos (1972); Cassidy and Turner (1978); Cassidy (1985);Vanagunas (1987); Rhodes (1990); Hanneman (1995); Burke et al. (1996); Maltz (1996); Auerhahn (2002, 2003, 2004, 2007, 2008a, 2008b); Bhaté-Felsheim et al. (2002); Bernard et al. (2005); Bardach (2006); Livingston et al. (2006); Meadows (2008); Stewart et al. (2008); Foster et al. (2012); Luke and Stamatakis (2012); Dabbaghian et al. (2014); Dennis et al. (2014); and Gibson et al. (2016).
132. Kuhn (1962); Merton (1968, 1973).
133. Sampson et al. (2013:587–588).
134. Latessa et al. (2014); Welsh and Rocque (2014).
135. Project HOPE provides a recent illustration (Cullen, Pratt, and Turanovic 2016).
136. Mears and Cochran (2015).
137. A similar example was used in Mears and Cochran (2015:66–67).
138. For examples of how systems forces may interact with one another, see Zimring (2005, 2007), Simon (2007, 2012), and Mears and Cochran (2015).
139. Mears (2010).
140. Cullen, Jonson, and Nagin (2011); Mears, Cochran, and Cullen (2015).
141. Mears and Cochran (2015).

142. See Mears and Cochran (2015), who, drawing on Bonczar (2011), estimated average time served among state prisoners from 1986–2009; see also Pew Charitable Trusts (2012).
143. Durose et al. (2014).
144. Mears (2010); Freilich and Newman (2016).
145. Auerhahn (2008b:262).
146. Mears (2010); Mears and Barnes (2010); Mears and Cochran (2015).
147. Bernard and Kurlychek (2010).
148. Cullen and Jonson (2011); Welsh and Farrington (2012); Garland (2013); Cullen, Jonson, and Stohr (2014); Kelly (2015, 2016); Cullen, Jonson, and Mears (2017).
149. Garland (2013:484).
150. Corbett (2015:1704).
151. Corbett (2015); Mears and Cochran (2015); Cullen, Jonson, and Mears (2017).
152. See, generally, Corbett (2015).
153. For a similar view in arenas outside of criminal justice, see Taleb (2012).
154. Mears (2010).
155. Stewart et al. (2008:365).
156. Mears (2007, 2010).
157. Mears (2007, 2010).
158. Mears, Cochran, and Cullen (2015).
159. Mears and Cochran (2015).
160. Nagin et al. (2009); Piehl and LoBuglio (2005); Mears (2010); Mears and Barnes (2010); Mears et al. (2011); Cochran, Mears, and Bales (2014); Mears and Cochran (2015); Mears, Cochran, Bales, and Bhati (2016); Mears, Kuch, Lindsey, et al. (2016); Mendel (2016).
161. Mears, Kuch, Lindsey, Siennick, Pesta, Greenwald, and Blomberg (2016); see also Mears and Butts (2008) and Mears (2012).
162. Welsh and Harris (2016:52).
163. See, for example, Sherman et al. (2002); MacKenzie (2006); Lipsey and Cullen (2007); Mears (2010); Welsh and Farrington (2012); Welsh, Braga, and Bruinsma (2013); Welsh, Rocque, and Greenwood (2014); Mears and Cochran (2015); cf. Mears and Barnes (2010); Mears, Cochran, Greenman, Bhati, and Greenwald (2011); Welsh and Rocque (2014); and Mears, Cochran, and Cullen (2015).
164. Zane et al. (2016).
165. Lindsey et al. (2016).
166. Lindsey et al. (2016).
167. Austin and Krisberg (1982); see, generally, Cullen, Jonson, and Mears (2017).
168. Tonry (1997, 2004, 2009); Mears and Barnes (2010); Mears, Cochran, Greenman, et al. (2011).
169. Mears (2010); Welsh and Farrington (2012); Welsh, Braga, and Bruinsma (2013).

5 THE SYSTEMS IMPROVEMENT SOLUTION FOR SAFETY, JUSTICE, ACCOUNTABILITY, AND EFFICIENCY

1. Mears and Cochran (2015).
2. Blumstein and Beck (1999); Pfaff (2011).
3. See, for example, Littell (2005) and Duriez et al. (2014).
4. Ioannidis (2005a, 2005b); Lehrer (2010); Mears (2010); Latessa et al. (2014); Cullen, Pratt, and Turanovic (2016).
5. See, for example, discussions of the evaluation hierarchy in Rossi et al. (2004) and Mears (2010). A listing of but some of the works that discuss systems analysis (and related endeavors, such as general systems theory, operations research, and systems simulation modeling) in general or as applied to criminal justice includes: Parsons (1951, 1977); Blumstein (1967, 1972); Navarro and Taylor (1967); Kelleher (1970); Chartrand (1971); Blumstein and Larson (1972); Drake et al. (1972); Coffey (1974); Bertalanffy (1975); Bohigian (1977); Forst (1977); Hoos (1972); Cassidy and Turner (1978); Cassidy (1985); Vanagunas (1987); Rhodes (1990); Hanneman (1995); Burke et al. (1996); Maltz (1996); Auerhahn (2002, 2003, 2004, 2007, 2008a, 2008b); Bhaté-Felsheim et al. (2002); Bernard et al. (2005); Bardach (2006); Livingston et al. (2006); Meadows (2008); Stewart et al. (2008); Luke and Stamatakis (2012); Dabbaghian et al. (2014); Dennis et al. (2014); and Gibson et al. (2016).
6. For discussion of needs evaluation and other types of evaluations, see Rossi et al. (2004) and, for a discussion of such evaluations in a criminal justice context, see Mears (2010).
7. Mears and Cochran (2015).
8. Lum and Nagin (2017).
9. Mears (2008a).
10. Latessa et al. (2014).
11. See, for example, Cullen and Jonson (2011) and Latessa et al. (2014).
12. Sampson et al. (2013); Mears, Cochran, and Lindsey (2016).
13. Mears (2010).
14. Rossi et al. (2004); Mears (2010).
15. Rossi et al. (2004); Wholey et al. (2004); Chen (2005); Mears (2010).
16. Mears (1998a, 1998b, 2007, 2008a, 2010); Mears and Butts (2008); Mears and Bacon (2009); Mears and Barnes (2010); Mears and Cochran (2015); see also Blumstein (1997), Lipsey et al. (2005), Kraska (2006), Welsh et al. (2013), Latessa et al. (2014), and Blomberg et al. (2016).
17. See Chelimsky (1985) and Mears (2010).
18. Lewis (2003).
19. See, generally, Silver (2012).
20. Milgram (2012, 2013).
21. Sampson (2013:9).
22. Cullen, Jonson, and Mears (2017).
23. Gable and Gable (2005).
24. Rossi et al. (2004); Mears (2010).
25. See, generally, Rossi et al. (2004).

26. Sampson et al. (2013).
27. Mears, Cochran, Greenman, Bhati, and Greenwald (2011); Mears, Cochran, and Cullen (2015); Mears, Kuch, Lindsey, Siennick, Pesta, Greenwald, and Blomberg (2016).
28. Mears (2010); Fagan and Buchanan (2016).
29. Ioannidis (2005a, 2005b).
30. Sherman and Berk (1984).
31. Maxwell et al. (2002); Hines (2009); see Cullen, Pratt, and Turanovic (2016) for a similar example involving Project HOPE.
32. Mears (2007).
33. Mears (2010, 2016).
34. Mears and Butts (2008); Mears and Bacon (2009); Mears and Barnes (2010).
35. See, generally, Rossi et al. (2004); Mears (2010); Roman, Dunworth, and Marsh (2010); and Welsh, Farrington, and Raffan-Gowar (2015).
36. See, for example, Cohen (2000, 2005).
37. Mears (2010); Mears and Cochran (2015).
38. Gaes et al. (2004); Gaes (2008); Mears (2010); Lindsey, Mears, and Cochran (2016).
39. See, for example, Roman, Dunworth, and Marsh (2010) and Welsh, Farrington, and Raffan-Gowar (2015).
40. Hoag (1956:1); see also Kelleher (1970) and Gibson et al. (2016).
41. Gibson et al. (2016).
42. Hoag (1956:18).
43. Hoag (1956:19).
44. Vanagunas (1987:260).
45. President's Commission on Law Enforcement and Administration of Justice (1967:261–271); see also Burke et al. (1996) and Welsh and Harris (2016).
46. Vanagunas (1987:260).
47. Vanagunas (1987:260).
48. Vanagunas (1987:260).
49. See, for example, Blumstein (1967, 1972) and Blumstein and Larson (1972).
50. Vanagunas (1987:261); see also Chaiken et al. (1975) and Auerhahn (2008a).
51. Vanagunas (1987:260).
52. Cassidy (1985).
53. Vanagunas (1987:261).
54. Vanagunas (1987:261).
55. White and Downs (2014).
56. Parsons (1951, 1977); Gould (1987); Bernard et al. (2005); the critique emerged even earlier (see, e.g., Mills 1959; Black 1961) and crescendoed in the 1970s (see, e.g., Hoos 1972).
57. Examples include Auerhahn (2002, 2003, 2004, 2007, 2008a, 2008b); Bhaté-Felsheim et al. (2002); Livingston et al. (2006); Stewart et al. (2008); and Dabbaghian et al. (2014).
58. See, for example, Butler and Johnson (1997), who used a variant of systems analysis to evaluate the efficiency of prisons. Many other examples exist (see, generally, Cassidy and Turner 1978; Cassidy 1985; Vanagunas 1987; Rhodes

1990; Auerhahn 2008a, 2008b; Livingston et al. 2006; Stewart et al. 2008; Dabbaghian et al. 2014). The symposium is discussed in Samuelson (2006).

59. Rhodes (1990); Perry (2003).
60. Mears and Cochran (2015).
61. The nuts-and-bolts of undertaking systems analysis – what sometimes is termed "systems research" or "operations research" (Blumstein 1967:93) – has been discussed extensively in many places (see, e.g., Meadows 2008; Dennis et al. 2014; Gibson et al. 2016), including accounts that describe how to undertake it in criminal justice system applications (see, e.g., Blumstein 1967, 1972; Blumstein and Larson 1972; Vanagunas 1987; Auerhahn 2002, 2003, 2004, 2008a, 2008b; Dabbaghian et al. 2014). Accordingly, and given the book's argument for systems analysis as part of a more general set of activities aimed at improving criminal justice, the discussion here serves to provide an overview of the logic and uses of systems analysis.
62. Coffey (1974:6).
63. Coffey (1974:12).
64. Coffey (1974:12).
65. Rhodes (1990:7).
66. Rhodes (1990:49); see, generally, Auerhahn (2008a, 2008b).
67. Rhodes (1990:52).
68. Blumstein (1980:252).
69. Blumstein (1980:253).
70. Travis and Lawrence (2002).
71. Travis (2005); Clear (2007).
72. Mears and Siennick (2016).
73. Mears and Lindsey (2016).
74. The argument for the Systems Improvement Solution overlaps partially with the argument made by the President's Commission on Crime and the Administration of Justice (1967) for systems analysis. In the Commission's report, systems analyses were asserted to provide three benefits: "[1] They develop an explicit description of the criminal justice system and its operating modes so that the system's underlying assumptions are revealed. [2] They provide a vehicle for simulated experimentation in those instances in which 'live' experimentation is unfeasible. [3] They identify the data that must be obtained if essential calculations are to be made of the consequences of proposed changes" (p. 262). Systems analyses may have other benefits, however. For example, they may be used to create greater understanding about the systems nature of criminal justice and identify factors that may moderate the effectiveness of specific policies or programs. The Systems Improvement Solution calls for systems analysis and, at the same time, for institutionalized use of the evaluation hierarchy and a multi-stakeholder policy process that guides the creation and use of research to guide decision-making.
75. Coffey (1974:13).
76. See, for example, Burt (1981); DiIulio et al. (1993); and Logan (1993), for diverse examples in criminal justice.
77. Mears (2010).
78. Lum and Nagin (2017).

79. Heilbroner (1990) has provided one of the most illuminating accounts of all that goes into prosecutorial activities, the discretion that prosecutors exercise, and the range of outcomes that may be relevant to assessing their performance and outcomes.
80. Mears and Barnes (2010).
81. Petersilia (1991).
82. Luke and Stamatakis (2012).
83. Mears and Cochran (2015).
84. The notion of "control knobs" is discussed in Roberts, Hsiao, Berman, and Reich (2008:6–7) account of systems analysis and health reform. In their analysis, five health care system "control knobs" (payment, financing, organization, regulation, and behavior) can be "turned" (i.e., changed) for improving health care system performance.
85. Mears (2008a).
86. Mears (2008a).
87. Hanneman (1995).
88. Systems research, as viewed here, encompasses a wide variety of analyses, including simulation and forecasting models. Pure simulation models tend to focus on discrete events or policies and rely on limited data or test hypothetical events. Similarly, forecasting efforts frequently are atheoretical and rely on few empirical measures of systems dynamics. Even so, they can incorporate considerable information and generate estimates that draw on or complement statistical analyses (see, e.g., Sabol 1999; Auerhahn 2003, 2004, 2007, 2008a, 2008b; Eck and Liu 2008; Greasley 2013; and Sullivan 2013). The emphasis with the systems research approach advocated here is that there may be *ongoing*, empirically based systems monitoring, testing and probing of the impacts of extant policies and programs as well as the potential impacts of proposed interventions. In addition, there is an emphasis on the implementation of the evaluation hierarchy in a targeted manner to assess the need for and implementation, impacts, and cost-efficiency of specific policies, programs, or activities. These evaluations can be informed by systems analyses.
89. Milgram (2012, 2013).
90. Silver (2012).
91. Edward Kaplan (2011:32) has emphasized the idea that systems research should be focused on helping organizations to make "better decisions":

    The rationale for studying operations is not only to understand them (which is the usual goal of scientific investigation), but also to use such understanding to make better operational decisions. "Better" refers to improving matters in terms of the organization's fundamental objectives: What decisions lead to higher (if not maximal) profits, lower (if not minimal) costs, increased numbers of infections averted, or reduced numbers of successful terror attacks? Thus, perhaps, a more complete definition of OR [operations research] is the scientific study of operations to make better decisions.

92. Vanagunas (1987:262); see also Welsh and Harris (2016).

93. Fabelo (1994).
94. Kean and Hamilton (2004:353).
95. Office of Justice Programs (2010); see also National Institute of Justice (2004) and Clear (2011).
96. In particular, Blumstein (1967:100) wrote: "In the future, it would be reasonable to expect that [systems] analyses would be conducted first at research institutions closely coupled to, but independent of, operating criminal justice agencies. Their work would involve explorations into fundamental questions underlying crime in society and the operation of the criminal justice system."
97. See, generally, Hastie (2011), regarding the value of group processes in arriving at better decisions than individuals alone may make.
98. See, generally, Reisig (2010) and Lum and Nagin (2017).
99. See, generally, Mears (2010) as well as Heilbroner (1990) and Davis et al. (2003).
100. Blumstein (1980:250); Wright and Cesar (2013) have provided an illuminating account of the systems nature of prisoner reentry and the salience of multiple contexts in influencing recidivism (see also Chaiken et al. 1975; Cassidy 1985; Travis and Visher 2005; and Mears and Cochran 2015).
101. Blumstein (1967:95).
102. Gibson et al. (2016); see also the discussion in Blumstein (1980:238) on the role systems analysis can play in helping stakeholders to understand the uncertainty in various estimates.
103. Meadows (2008:113).
104. Meadows (2008:115).
105. Meadows (2008:45–46; emphases in original).
106. Meadows (2008:45–46; emphases in original).
107. See, for example, Welsh and Harris (2016).
108. Meadows (2008).
109. Drake et al. (1972:2–3; emphasis in original).
110. See, generally, DiIulio et al. (1993); see, especially, Logan (1993) and J. Wilson (1993).
111. J. Wilson (1993).
112. See also Lum and Nagin (2017).
113. Bottoms (1999); Mears (2013).
114. Mears and Cochran (2015).
115. Cullen, Jonson, and Mears (2017).
116. Taleb (2012).
117. Cullen, Jonson, and Mears (2017).
118. Clear (2007); Mears and Cochran (2015).
119. Corbett (2015); Mears and Cochran (2015); Cullen, Jonson, and Mears (2017).
120. May and Wood (2010).
121. Austin (2016); Cullen, Jonson, and Mears (2017).
122. Reisig (2010); Lum and Nagin (2017).
123. Meadows (2008:25).
124. Mears, Scott, and Bhati (2007a, 2007b, 2007c).

125. See, generally, Browne, Cambier, and Agha (2011); Browne, Hastings, Kall, and diZerega (2015); Browne (2015); and Cloud et al. (2015).
126. Braga, Weisburd, Warring, et al. (1999); Weisburd and Eck (2004); Wortley and Mazerolle (2008); Braga, Welsh, and Schnell (2015).
127. Snell (1993) and Kaeble et al. (2015).
128. Snell (1993) and Kaeble et al. (2015).
129. Mears and Cochran (2015).
130. Kelly (2015, 2016).
131. Taleb (2012).
132. Gladwell (2000).
133. Goldkamp (2003); Mears (2010).
134. Silver (2012).
135. See, generally, Sherman, Gottfredson, MacKenzie, Eck, Reuter, and Bushway (1997); Sherman, Farrington, Welsh, and MacKenzie (2002); Lipsey et al. (2005); MacKenzie (2006); Mears (2010); Welsh and Farrington (2012); Welsh, Braga, and Bruinsma (2013); Welsh, Rocque, and Greenwood (2014); and Mears and Cochran (2015).
136. Latessa et al. (2014).
137. Mears, Cochran, Greenman, Bhati, and Greenwald (2011); Mears, Cochran, and Cullen (2015).
138. Butts and Mears (2001); Sherman, Farrington, Welsh, and MacKenzie (2002); Taxman et al. (2014); Welsh, Rocque, and Greenwood (2014); MacKenzie and Farrington (2015); Welsh and Greenwood (2015); Welsh (2016).
139. Mears, Cochran, Greenman, Bhati, and Greenwald (2011); Welsh and Rocque (2014); Fagan and Buchanan (2016).
140. See, generally, Mears (2010).
141. What is "credible" research? Legislators and media accounts, and even many scholarly accounts, treat experiments as the "gold standard" for credible research. However, experiments can and frequently do suffer from many problems, such as weak external validity (e.g., the policy only works on ideal, laboratory-like conditions but does not likely work under "real world" conditions). They also only apply to assessments of impact. In the end, "credibility" depends on consensus among scientists about validity claims concerning how the world works. They may be incorrect in their views. However, there is no other clear basis for adjudicating when a given type of empirical research can be viewed as defensible and resting on strong scientific grounds.
142. Mears (2014).
143. See, generally, Blumstein (1967, 1972); Vanagunas (1987); Burke et al. (1996); Bhaté-Felsheim et al. (2002); Mears (2002a, 2010); McGarry and Ney (2006); Dennis et al. (2014); Gibson et al. (2016); and Welsh and Harris (2016).
144. Blumstein (1980:250).
145. Petersilia (2016:11).
146. See especially Bird and Grattet (2016) and Lofstrom and Raphael (2016). See, generally, the special issue of *The Annals of the American Academy of Political and Social Science*, volume 664, March 2016, "The Great Experiment: Realigning Criminal Justice in California and Beyond."

147. Basu et al. (1999); in a related vein, see Fabelo (1994).
148. Zegart (2011).
149. Zegart (2011:324).
150. Feagin et al. (1991).
151. Blomberg et al. (2016).
152. Lipsey and Cullen (2007); Cullen, Jonson, and Mears (2017).
153. Silver (2012); Taleb (2012).
154. Fabelo (1994); McGarry and Ney (2006); Mears (2010); Still (2016).
155. See, generally, Schaefer et al. (2016).
156. Bhaté-Felsheim et al. (2002).
157. Bhaté-Felsheim et al. (2002:153).
158. Ebbesen and Konečni (1985); see also the National Institute of Justice (2004); McGarry and Ney (2006); and Mears and Bacon (2009).
159. May and Wood (2010); Cullen, Jonson, and Mears (2017).
160. Forst (2004); Mears and Bacon (2009); Mears, Cochran, and Lindsey (2016); Brame (2017).
161. See, for example, Mears, Scott, and Bhati (2007a, 2007b, 2007c).
162. Sampson (2013:10).
163. Latessa et al. (2014); Mears and Cochran (2015).
164. Berk and Bleich (2013); Brame (2017); Taxman (2017).
165. See, for example, Berk (2008); the Center for Excellence in Corrections (2013); and Taxman and Pattavina (2013).
166. Kaplan (2011); Mears and Cochran (2015).
167. Milgram (2013); see also Milgram (2012).
168. Visher and Travis (2003); Lattimore et al. (2010); Mears (2010); Reisig (2010); Taxman et al. (2014); Mears and Cochran (2015).
169. Cullen, Jonson, and Mears (2017).
170. Mears, Ploeger, and Warr (1998).
171. Cullen, Jonson, and Mears (2017).
172. For example, Burt (1982) and Logan (1993) have provided comprehensive lists of dimensions that should be monitored in prison systems and accompanying measures and data sources that can be used. Many such sources exist.
173. Thielo et al. (2016); see, generally, Roberts (1992); Roberts and Stalans (1998); Cullen, Fisher, and Applegate (2000); Roberts, Stalans, Indermaur, and Hough (2003); Roberts and Hough (2005a, 2005b); and Mears, Pickett, and Mancini (2015).
174. Silver (2012).
175. Skinner (2011).
176. Meadows (2008); Taleb (2012).

6 BENEFITS OF THE SYSTEMS IMPROVEMENT SOLUTION AND PITFALLS TO AVOID IN IMPLEMENTING IT

1. See, for example, the following illustrative discussions: Berk and Rossi (1997); Blumstein (1997); Roberts and Stalans (1998); Beckett and Sasson (2000); Cullen, Fisher, and Applegate (2000); Roberts, Stalans, Indermaur, and

Hough (2003); Gaes et al. (2004); Tonry (2004); Gottschalk (2006); Clear (2007); Mears and Bacon (2009); Bernard and Kurlychek (2010); May and Wood (2010); Mears (2010); Simon (2012); Welsh and Farrington (2012); Sampson et al. (2013); Welsh and Pfeffer (2013); Cullen, Jonson, and Stohr (2014); Kelly (2015, 2016); Welsh, Farrington, and Raffan-Gowar (2015); Blomberg et al. (2016); Mears (2016); Zane et al. (2016); Cullen, Jonson, and Mears (2017).

2. Petersilia (2003); Piehl and LoBuglio (2005); Travis (2005); Corbett (2015); Mears and Cochran (2015); Taxman (2017).

3. Welsh, Farrington, and Raffan-Gowar (2015:492).

4. Travis (2005).

5. A small sampling of illustrative discussions about a variety of dimensions, beyond crime, relevant for evaluating the effectiveness of criminal justice systems: Skolnick (1966); Von Hirsch and Ashworth (1992); Logan (1993); Berk and Rossi (1997); Feld (1999); Cullen, Fisher, and Applegate (2000); Roberts, Stalans, Indermaur, and Hough (2003); Forst (2004); Leo (2008); Mears and Butts (2008); Mears and Bacon (2009); Herman (2010); Mears (2010); Mears and Barnes (2010); Corbett (2015); Mears and Cochran (2015); Cullen, Mears, Jonson, and Thielo (2016); Mears and Lindsey (2016); Roberts and Ashworth (2016); Tonry (2016); Cullen, Jonson, and Mears (2017); Lum and Nagin (2017).

6. Lum and Nagin (2017).

7. Lum and Nagin (2017).

8. Davis et al. (2003).

9. Mears (2010).

10. Mears (2007, 2008a, 2010).

11. Ridgeway and MacDonald (2014).

12. Mears (2010); Roman, Dunworth, and Walsh (2010); Welsh, Farrington, and Raffan-Gowar (2015).

13. Pfaff (2011); Mears and Cochran (2015).

14. Roman, Dunworth, and Walsh (2010); Welsh, Farrington, and Raffan-Gowar (2015).

15. See, for example, Roman and Harrell (2001).

16. Mears (2010).

17. Levitt and Dubner (2014:199).

18. Mukherjee (2010).

19. Mears and Cochran (2015); Phelps and Pager (2016).

20. Blumstein and Kadane (1983); see, more generally, Cullen, Jonson, and Mears (2017).

21. Taleb (2012).

22. Mears (2010).

23. Mears (2010).

24. Mears (2010).

25. Welsh, Braga, and Bruinsma (2003); Welsh, Farrington, and Raffan-Gowar (2015).

26. Fattah (1986).

27. Reisig (2010); Lum and Nagin (2017).

28. See Welsh, Sullivan, and Olds (2010) concerning the challenge of achieving large and sustainable impacts when crime prevention policies or programs are scaled up.
29. Western (2006); Unnever and Gabbidon (2011); Alexander (2012).
30. Petersilia (2003); Travis (2005); Ulmer (2012); Baumer (2013); Spohn (2013); Mears and Cochran (2015).
31. Mears, Cochran, and Lindsey (2016).
32. Cochran and Mears (2015); Cochran, Mears, Bales, and Stewart (2016).
33. Mears, Cochran, and Lindsey (2016).
34. Tillyer et al. (2008).
35. Mears and Bales (2010).
36. See, generally, Mears (2010); Ulmer (2012); Baumer (2013); Spohn (2013); Mears and Cochran (2015); and Mears, Cochran, and Lindsey (2016).
37. See, for example, Roberts (1992); Roberts and Stalans (1998); Cullen, Fisher, and Applegate (2000); Roberts, Stalans, Indermaur, and Hough (2003); Kleck, Sever, Li, and Gertz (2005); Roberts and Hough (2005a, 2005b); Nagin et al. (2006); Unnever and Cullen (2010); Kleck and Barnes (2013); Mancini and Mears (2013); Ramirez (2013); Unnever (2014); and Thielo et al. (2016).
38. Kahneman (2011).
39. Mukherjee (2010); Weinberg (2015).
40. Kraska (2006:168).
41. Mears and Cochran (2015).
42. Mears (2012).
43. Kelly (2015, 2016).
44. Latessa et al. (2014); Taxman et al. (2014); Taxman (2017).
45. Nagin et al. (2009); Mears, Cochran, and Cullen (2015); Mears, Cochran, Bales, and Bhati (2016).
46. Blumstein (1967); Hagan (1989); Bernard and Engel (2001); Bernard et al. (2005); Kraska (2006); Mears (2007); Crank and Bowman (2008); Eck and Liu (2008); Cooper and Worrall (2012); Dooley and Rydberg (2014); Steinmetz et al. (2014).
47. Mears (1998a, 1998b); Mears and Cochran (2017).
48. Mears (2002a).
49. Mukherjee (2010).
50. DeVita and DeVita-Raeburn (2015).
51. Blumstein (1997).
52. Cullen and Gendreau (2000).
53. Mears and Stafford (2002).
54. Mears, Cochran, and Lindsey (2016).
55. See Kelly's (2015, 2016) accounts, for example, as well as others (e.g., Tonry 2004; Travis 2005; Mears and Cochran 2015; Cullen, Jonson, and Mears 2017).
56. See, generally, Taleb (2012) for how this approach applies to a wide range of police arenas.
57. Forst (2004); Mears and Bacon (2009).
58. Lindsey, Mears, and Cochran (2016).

59. Imse (2013); see, generally, In the Public Interest (2013) and Lindsey et al. (2016).
60. Mears (2010).
61. Vanagunas (1987:262).
62. Vanagunas (1987:262).
63. Mears (2010).
64. Blumstein (1997, 2008).
65. Hatry (2006).
66. In French, "Le mieux est l'ennemi du bien," from Voltaire's poem, "La Bégueule" (1772).
67. Cullen, Jonson, and Mears (2017).
68. Cullen, Jonson, and Mears (2017).
69. Travis (2005).
70. Mears and Cochran (2015).
71. Cullen, Jonson, and Mears (2017).
72. See, for, example, Vanagunas (1987:266) and Bernard et al. (2005:10); see, generally, Hoos (1972) and Keeney and Raiffa (1972).
73. Levitt and Dubner (2014).
74. Meadows (2008).
75. Mears and Cochran (2015).
76. Smith (2014).
77. Meadows (2008:95).
78. Vanagunas (1987:263).
79. Kelly (2015, 2016).
80. Taleb (2012).
81. Bales and Mears (2008); Cochran (2012); Mears, Cochran, Siennick, and Bales (2012).
82. Bales and Mears (2008); Mears, Cochran, Siennick, and Bales (2012); Cochran and Mears (2013).
83. Siennick et al. (2013).
84. Adams (1992).
85. See, generally, Bales and Mears (2008); Cochran (2012); Mears, Cochran, Siennick, and Bales (2012); and Cochran, Mears, Bales, and Stewart (2016); cf. Siennick et al. (2013).
86. Lindsey, Mears, Cochran, Bales, and Stults (2016); Cochran, Mears, Bales, and Stewart (2016).
87. Petersilia (1991); Mears (2010); Kelly (2015).
88. See, for example, Petersilia (1991); Cullen (2005); and Kelly (2015); see, generally, Blomberg et al. (2016).
89. Mears (2010).
90. Blomberg et al. (2016).
91. Petersilia (1991).
92. Rossi (1980).
93. Mears and Bales (2010).
94. President's Commission on Crime and the Administration of Justice (1967:266); DiIulio et al. (1993); Livingston et al. (2006); Mears (2010).
95. Forst (1977:410).

96. Forst (1977:412).
97. Forer (1994); Mears (1998b).
98. Taleb (2012).
99. Clear (2011:590).
100. Hoos (1972:xvii).
101. Mrazek and Haggerty (1994:372); Rossi et al. (2004:260).
102. Mears (2010).
103. Manski (2013).
104. See, generally, Manski (2013).
105. Makary and Daniel (2016:i2139).
106. Travis (2005); MacKenzie (2006); Cullen, Jonson, and Stohr (2014); Latessa et al. (2014); Welsh, Braga, and Bruinsma (2013); Welsh and Pfeffer (2013); Welsh, Rocque, and Greenwood (2014); Kelly (2015, 2016); Mears and Cochran (2015); Cullen, Mears, Jonson, and Thielo (2016); Cullen, Jonson, and Mears (2017).
107. See, for example, Blumstein and Larson (1972); Forst (2004); Tonry (2004); Travis (2005); Milgram (2012, 2013); Cullen, Jonson, and Stohr (2014); Kelly (2015, 2016); Mears and Cochran (2015); Blomberg et al. (2016); and Petersilia (2016).
108. Travis (2005).
109. For a specific example, Pacholke and Mullins (2015); see, generally, the presentations and papers from the October 2015 meeting of the National Institute of Justice's Topical Working Group on the Use of Administrative Segregation in the United States (www.nij.gov/topics/corrections/institutional/Pages/restrictive-housing.aspx#twg).
110. Pacholke and Mullins (2015:8).
111. Mears and Reisig (2006); Mears and Watson (2006); Mears (2013).
112. Luke and Stamatakis (2012:7).
113. Luke and Stamatakis (2012); see, specifically, the MIDAS website (www.nigms.nih.gov/Research/specificareas/MIDAS/Pages/default.aspx).
114. Reid (2009).
115. Hecht and Fiksel (2015:86).
116. Hecht and Fiksel (2015:86).
117. Hecht and Fiksel (2015:86); see the EPA's website (www.epa.gov/water-research/national-stormwater-calculator).
118. Hecht and Fiksel (2015:86).
119. Sedgwick (2016).
120. Sedgwick (2016:8).
121. Fabelo (1994); Burka (2007); Mears (2010).
122. Fabelo (1994); Burka (2007); Mears (2010).
123. See, for example, Fabelo (1994); Texas Criminal Justice Policy Council (1997); and Mears (2002a).
124. Burka (2007).
125. Ward (2006).
126. Texas Department of Criminal Justice (2015:4).
127. Ward (2006).
128. Sabol (1999); Butts and Adams (2001); Mears (2002, 2010).

129. Fabelo (1994); Mears (2002); Burka (2007).
130. Travis (2005); Mears (2010).
131. Lawrence and Mears (2004); Mears and Watson (2006).
132. R. Wilson (2014).
133. Burka (2007).
134. Fabelo (1994); Basu et al. (1999); Mears (2010).
135. Burka (2007).
136. Fabelo (1994); Mears (2010).
137. Washington State Institute for Public Policy (www.wsipp.wa.gov/About).
138. Washington State Institute for Public Policy (www.wsipp.wa.gov/About).
139. See, for example, Loeber and Farrington (2012), Crowley (2013), Greenwood (2013), and Farrington (2016).
140. Vanlandingham and Drake (2012).
141. Farrington (2016:69); see, generally, Vanlandingham and Drake (2012).
142. Vanlandingham and Drake (2012:558).
143. Mears (2010).
144. Blumstein (1980); Livingston et al. (2006); Stewart et al. (2008); see Malleson et al. (2010) for an example of how agent-based simulation can be adapted to specific locales.
145. Livingston et al. (2006:1).
146. Livingston et al. (2006:6); see also Stewart et al. (2008).
147. Butts and Adams (2001); Mears (2002a); Butts and Mears (2004).
148. Taxman and Pattavina (2013); Taxman et al. (2014); Taxman (2017).
149. Center for Advancing Correctional Excellence (2013:1; emphasis added).
150. Taxman et al. (2015:56); see also Mears (2004) and Kelly et al. (2005).
151. Center for Advancing Correctional Excellence (2013:1; emphasis added).
152. Roman, Butts, and Roman (2011).
153. Butts and Roman (2007:2; emphasis added).
154. Butts and Roman (2007:2).
155. Butts and Roman (2007:1).
156. McGarry and Ney (2006).
157. McGarry and Ney (2006:xiii).
158. McGarry and Ney (2006).
159. McGarry and Ney (2006:xiv).
160. McGarry and Ney (2006:xiv).
161. McGarry and Ney (2006:xvi).

7 CONCLUSION: CRIMINAL JUSTICE UNDER CONTROL

1. Stolz (2002).
2. Lipsey et al. (2005:vii); see also Sherman et al. (1997), Sherman et al. (2002), Blumstein (2008); Mears (2010).
3. Cullen and Gendreau (2000); MacKenzie (2006); Lipsey and Cullen (2007); Welsh, Braga, and Bruinsma (2013); Welsh and Pfeffer (2013); Latessa et al. (2014); Welsh, Rocque, and Greenwood (2014).
4. Mears, Cochran, Greenman, Bhati, and Greenwald (2011).
5. Mears and Cochran (2015).

References

Abbott, Andrew. 1988. "Transcending General Linear Reality." *Sociological Theory* 6:169–186.

Adams, Kenneth. 1992. "Adjusting to Prison Life." Pp. 275–359 in *Crime and Justice*, edited by Michael H. Tonry. Chicago: University of Chicago Press.

Agnew, Robert. 2005. *Why Do Criminals Offend? A General Theory of Crime and Delinquency.* Los Angeles: Roxbury.

Akers, Ronald L., and Christine S. Sellers. 2012. *Criminological Theories: Introduction, Evaluation, and Application.* 6th edition. New York: Oxford University Press.

Alexander, Michelle. 2012. *The New Jim Crow: Mass Incarceration in the Age of Colorblindedness.* New York: The New Press.

Altiok, Tayfur. 1997. *Performance Analysis of Manufacturing Systems.* New York: Springer-Verlag.

Auerhahn, Kathleen. 2008a. "Dynamic Systems Simulation Analysis: a Planning Tool for the New Century." *Journal of Criminal Justice* 36:293–300.

————. 2008b. "Using Simulation Modeling to Evaluate Sentencing Reform in California: Choosing the Future." *Journal of Experimental Criminology* 4:241–266.

————. 2007. "Do You Know Who Your Probationers Are? Using Simulation Modeling to Estimate the Composition of California's Felony Probation Population, 1980–2000." *Justice Quarterly* 24:28–47.

————. 2004. "California's Incarcerated Drug Offender Population, Yesterday, Today, and Tomorrow: Evaluating the War on Drugs and Proposition 36." *Journal of Drug Issues* 34:95–120.

————. 2003. *Selective Incapacitation and Public Policy: Evaluating California's Imprisonment Crisis.* Albany, NY: State University of New York Press.

————. 2002. "Selective Incapacitation, Three Strikes, and the Problem of Aging Prison Populations: Using Simulation Modeling to See the Future." *Criminology and Public Policy* 1:353–388.

Austin, James. 2016. "Regulating California's Prison Population: the Use of Sticks and Carrots." *The Annals of the American Academy of Political and Social Science* 664:84–107.

Austin, James, and Barry Krisberg. 1982. "The Unmet Promise of Alternatives to Incarceration." *Crime and Delinquency* 28:374–409.

Baird, Robert M., and Stuart E. Rosenbaum, eds. 1988. *Philosophy of Punishment*. Buffalo, NY: Prometheus Books.

Bales, William D., and Daniel P. Mears. 2008. "Inmate Social Ties and the Transition to Society: Does Visitation Reduce Recidivism?" *Journal of Research in Crime and Delinquency* 45:287–321.

Banja, John. 2010. "The Normalization of Deviance in Healthcare Delivery." *Business Horizons* 53:139–148.

Bardach, Eugene. 2006. "Policy Dynamics." Pp. 336–366 in *The Oxford Handbook of Public Policy*, edited by Michael Moran, Martin Rein, and Robert E. Goodin. New York: Oxford University Press.

Basu, Onker N., Mark W. Dirsmith, and Parveen P. Gupta. 1999. "The Coupling of the Symbolic and the Technical in an Institutionalized Context: the Negotiated Order of the GAO's Audit Reporting Process." *American Sociological Review* 64:506–526.

Baumer, Eric P. 2013. "Reassessing and Redirecting Research on Race and Sentencing." *Justice Quarterly* 30:231–261.

Beckett, Katherine, and Theodore Sasson. 2000. *The Politics of Injustice: Crime and Punishment in America*. Thousand Oaks, CA: Pine Forge Press.

Berends, Mark. 2015. "Sociology and School Choice: What We Know after Two Decades of Charter Schools." *Annual Review of Sociology* 41:159–180.

Berk, Richard A. 2008. "How Can You Tell if the Simulations in Computational Criminology Are Any Good." *Journal of Experimental Criminology* 4:289–308.

Berk, Richard A., and Justin Bleich. 2013. "Statistical Procedures for Forecasting Criminal Behavior: a Comparative Assessment." *Criminology and Public Policy* 12:513–544.

Berk, Richard A., and Peter H. Rossi. 1997. *Just Punishment: Federal Guidelines and Public Views Compared*. New York: Aldine de Gruyter.

Bernard, Thomas J., and Robin S. Engel. 2001. "Conceptualizing Criminal Justice Theory." *Justice Quarterly* 18:1–30.

Bernard, Thomas J., and Megan C. Kurlychek. 2010. *The Cycle of Juvenile Justice*. 2nd edition. New York: Oxford University Press.

Bernard, Thomas J., Eugene A. Paoline III, and Paul-Philippe Pare. 2005. "General Systems Theory and Criminal Justice." *Journal of Criminal Justice* 33:203–211.

Bertalanffy, Ludwig V. 1975. *Perspectives on General System Theory: Scientific-Philosophical Studies*. New York: George Braziller, Inc.

Bettinger, Eric P. 2005. "The Effect of Charter Schools on Charter Students and Public Schools." *Economics of Education Review* 24:133–147.

Bhaté-Felsheim, Aarti S., Rebecca D. Ericson, W. David Kelton, Marcy C. Podkopacz, Dinesh H. Wadhwani, and Sarah G. Welter. 2002. "Simulation of a Probation/Parole System." *Socio-Economic Planning Sciences* 36:139–154.

Bird, Mia, and Ryken Grattet. 2016. "Realignment and Recidivism." *The Annals of the American Academy of Political and Social Science* 664:176–195.

Black, Max, ed. 1961. *The Social Theories of Talcott Parsons.* Englewood Cliffs, NJ: Prentice-Hall.

Blalock, Hubert M., Jr. 1964. *Causal Inferences in Nonexperimental Research.* New York: Norton.

Blomberg, Thomas G. 1980. "Widening the Net: an Anomaly in the Evaluation of Diversion Programs." Pp. 572–592 in *Handbook of Criminal Justice Evaluation*, edited by Malcolm W. Klein and Katherine S. Teilmann. Beverly Hills, CA: Sage Publications.

Blomberg, Thomas G., Julie M. Brancale, Kevin M. Beaver, and William D. Bales, eds. 2016. *Advancing Criminology and Criminal Justice Policy.* New York: Routledge.

Blumstein, Alfred. 2008. "Federal Support of Local Criminal Justice." *Criminology and Public Policy* 7:351–358.

    1997. "Interaction of Criminological Research and Public Policy." *Journal of Quantitative Criminology* 12:349–362.

    1980. "Planning Models for Analytical Evaluation." Pp. 237–258 in *Handbook of Criminal Justice Evaluation*, edited by Malcolm W. Klein and Katherine S. Teilmann. Beverly Hills, CA: Sage Publications.

    1972. "Systems Analysis and Planning for the Criminal Justice System." *Long Range Planning* 5:61–66.

    1967. "Systems Analysis and the Criminal Justice System." *The Annals of the American Academy of Political and Social Science* 374:92–100.

Blumstein, Alfred, and Allen J. Beck. 1999. "Population Growth in U.S. Prisons, 1980–1996." Pp. 17–61 in *Prisons*, edited by Michael H. Tonry and Joan Petersilia. Chicago: University of Chicago Press.

Blumstein, Alfred, and Joseph B. Kadane. 1983. "An Approach to the Allocation of Scarce Imprisonment Resources." *Crime and Delinquency* 29:546–560.

Blumstein, Alfred, and Richard C. Larson. 1972. "Analysis of a Total Criminal Justice System." Pp. 317–355 in *Analysis of Public Systems*, edited by Alvin W. Drake, Ralph L. Keeney, and Philip M. Morse. Cambridge, MA: MIT Press.

Blumstein, Alfred, and Joel Wallman. 2006. *The Crime Drop in America.* 2nd edition. New York: Cambridge University Press.

Bohigian, Haig E. 1977. "Simulation of the Criminal Justice System and Process." *Proceedings of the 9th Winter Simulation Conference* 1:246–256.

Bonczar, Thomas P. 2011. *National Corrections Reporting Program: Time Served in State Prison, by Offense, Release Type, Sex, and Race.* Washington, DC: U.S. Department of Justice. Available online (www.bjs.gov/index.cfm?ty=pbdetail&iid=2045).

Bottoms, Anthony E. 1999. "Interpersonal Violence and Social Order in Prisons." Pp. 205–282 in *Prisons*, edited by Michael H. Tonry and Joan Petersilia. Chicago: University of Chicago Press.

Braga, Anthony A., David L. Weisburd, Elin J. Waring, Lorraine G. Mazerolle, William Spelman, and Francis Gajewski. 1999. "Problem-Oriented Policing in Violent Crime Places: a Randomized Controlled Experiment." *Criminology* 37:541–580.

Braga, Anthony A., Brandon C. Welsh, and Cory Schnell. 2015. "Can Policing Disorder Reduce Crime? A Systematic Review and Meta-Analysis." *Crime and Delinquency* 52:567–588.

Brame, Robert. 2017. "Static Risk Factors and Criminal Recidivism." Pp. 67–92 in *Handbook on Risk and Need Assessment: Theory and Practice*, edited by Faye S. Taxman. New York: Routledge.

Bridges, George S., and Sara Steen. 1998. "Racial Disparities in Official Assessments of Juvenile Offenders: Attributional Stereotypes as Mediating Mechanisms." *American Sociological Review* 63:554–570.

Browne, Angela. 2015. "*A Systems Approach to Reducing the Use of Segregation in Confinement.*" Washington, DC: American Society of Criminology Annual Meeting.

Browne, Angela, Alissa Cambier, and Susanne Agha. 2011. "Prisons within Prisons: the Use of Segregation in the United States." *Federal Sentencing Reporter* 24:46–49.

Browne, Angela, Allison Hastings, Kaitlin Kall, and Margaret diZerega. 2015. *Keeping Vulnerable Populations Safe under PREA: Alternative Strategies to the Use of Segregation in Prisons and Jails.* New York: National PREA Resource Center.

Bureau of Justice Statistics. 2016. *Drugs and Crime Facts.* Washington, DC: Bureau of Justice Statistics. Available online (www.bjs.gov/content/dcf/duc.cfm#drug-related).

———. 2009. *Correctional Populations in the United States.* Washington, DC: Bureau of Justice Statistics. Available online (https://www.bjs.gov/index.cfm?ty=pb se&sid=5; accessed 10/1/2009).

Burka, Paul. 2007. "No Justice." *Texas Monthly*, February 7. Available online (www.texasmonthly.com/burka-blog/no-justice/).

Burke, Peggy, Robert Cushman, and Becki Ney. 1996. *Guide to a Criminal Justice System Assessment: a Work in Progress.* Washington, DC: National Institute of Justice.

Burstein, Paul. 2003. "The Impact of Public Opinion on Public Policy: a Review and an Agenda." *Political Research Quarterly* 56:29–40.

Burt, Martha R. 1981. *Measuring Prison Results: Ways to Monitor and Evaluate Corrections Performance.* Washington, DC: National Institute of Justice.

Butler, Timothy W., and W. Wesley Johnson. 1997. "Efficiency Evaluation of Michigan Prisons Using Data Envelopment Analysis." *Criminal Justice Review* 22:1–15.

Butts, Jeffrey A., and William Adams. 2001. *Anticipating Space Needs in Juvenile Detention and Correctional Facilities.* Washington, DC: Office of Juvenile Justice and Delinquency Prevention.

Butts, Jeffrey A., and Daniel P. Mears. 2004. *Results of an Effort to Develop a Policy-Sensitive Forecasting Process to Anticipate Future Needs for Juvenile Confinement Space in Washington, D.C.* Washington, DC: The Urban Institute.

———. 2001. "Reviving Juvenile Justice in a Get-Tough Era." *Youth and Society* 33:169–198.

Butts, Jeffrey A., and John Roman. 2007. *Changing Systems: Outcomes from the RWJF Reclaiming Futures Initiative on Juvenile Justice and Substance Abuse.* Portland, OR: Reclaiming Futures National Program Office, Portland State University.

Cassidy, R. Gordon. 1985. "Modeling a Criminal Justice System." Pp. 193–207 in *Prediction in Criminology*, edited by David P. Farrington and Roger Tarling. New York: Oxford University Press.

Cassidy, R. Gordon, and Ronald E. Turner. 1978. "Criminal Justice System Behavior." *Behavioral Science* 23:99–108.

Center for Advancing Correctional Excellence. 2013. *The Risk-Need-Responsivity Simulation Tool.* Fairfax, VA: George Mason University.

Chaiken, Jan M., Thomas B. Crabhill, L. P. Holliday, David L. Jaquette, M. Lawless, and E. S. Quade. 1975. *Criminal Justice Models: an Overview.* Washington, DC: National Institute of Law Enforcement and Criminal Justice, Law Enforcement Assistance Administration.

Charles Colson Task Force. 2016. *Transforming Prisons, Restoring Lives.* Washington, DC: Charles Colson Task Force on Federal Corrections.

Chartrand, Robert L. 1971. *Systems Technology Applied to Social and Community Problems.* New York: Spartan Books.

Chelimsky, Eleanor. 1985. "Comparing and Contrasting Auditing and Evaluation: Some Notes on Their Relationship." *Evaluation Review* 9:483–503.

Chen, Huey Tsyh. 2005. *Practical Program Evaluation: Assessing and Improving Planning, Implementation, and Effectiveness.* Thousand Oaks, CA: Sage Publications.

Clear, Todd R. 2011. "A Private-Sector, Incentives-Based Model for Justice Reinvestment." *Criminology and Public Policy* 10:585–608.

———. 2007. *Imprisoning Communities: How Mass Incarceration Makes Disadvantaged Neighborhoods Worse.* New York: Oxford University Press.

Cloud, David H., Ernest Drucker, Angela Browne, and Jim Parsons. 2015. "Public Health and Solitary Confinement in the United States." *American Journal of Public Health* 105:18–26.

Cochran, Joshua C. 2012. "The Ties that Bind or the Ties that Break: Examining the Relationship between Visitation and Prisoner Misconduct." *Journal of Criminal Justice* 40:433–440.

Cochran, Joshua C., and Daniel P. Mears. 2015. "Race, Ethnic, and Gender Divides in Juvenile Court Sanctioning and Rehabilitative Intervention." *Journal of Research in Crime and Delinquency* 52:181–212.

———. 2013. "Social Isolation and Inmate Behavior: a Conceptual Framework for Theorizing Prison Visitation and Guiding and Assessing Research." *Journal of Criminal Justice* 41:252–261.

Cochran, Joshua C., Daniel P. Mears, and William D. Bales. 2014. "Assessing the Effectiveness of Correctional Sanctions." *Journal of Quantitative Criminology* 30:317–347.

Cochran, Joshua C., Daniel P. Mears, William D. Bales, and Eric A. Stewart. 2016. "Spatial Distance, Community Disadvantage, and Racial and Ethnic Variation in Prison Inmate Access to Social Ties." *Journal of Research in Crime and Delinquency* 53:220–254.

Coffey, Alan R. 1974. *Administration of Criminal Justice: a Management Systems Approach*. Englewood Cliffs, NJ: Prentice-Hall.

Cohen, Mark A. 2005. *The Costs of Crime and Justice*. New York: Routledge.

——— 2000. "Measuring the Costs and Benefits of Crime and Justice." Pp. 263–315 in *Measurement and Analysis of Crime and Justice*, edited by David Duffee. Washington, DC: National Institute of Justice.

Cole, Stephen. 1975. "The Growth of Scientific Knowledge: Theories of Deviance as a Case Study." Pp. 175–220 in *The Idea of Social Structure: Papers in Honor of Robert K. Merton*, edited by Lewis A. Coser. New York: Harcourt.

Cooper, Jonathon, and John L. Worrall. 2012. "Theorizing Criminal Justice Evaluation and Research." *Criminal Justice Review* 37:384–397.

Corbett, Ronald P., Jr. 2015. "The Burdens of Leniency: the Changing Face of Probation." *Minnesota Law Review* 99:1697–1733.

Crank, John P., and Blythe M. Bowman. 2008. "What Is Good Criminal Justice Theory?" *Journal of Criminal Justice* 36:563–572.

Croft, Sheryl J., Mari Ann Roberts, and Vera L. Stenhouse. 2016. "The Perfect Storm of Education Reform: High-Stakes Testing and Teacher Evaluation." *Social Justice* 42:70–92.

Crowley, D. Max. 2013. "Building Efficient Crime Prevention Strategies: Considering the Economics of Investing in Human Development." *Criminology and Public Policy* 12:353–366.

Cullen, Francis T. 2005. "The Twelve People Who Saved Rehabilitation: How the Science of Criminology Made a Difference – The American Society of Criminology 2004 Presidential Address." *Criminology* 43:1–42.

Cullen, Francis T., Bonnie S. Fisher, and Brandon K. Applegate. 2000. "Public Opinion about Punishment and Corrections." *Crime and Justice* 27:1–79.

Cullen, Francis T., and Paul Gendreau. 2000. "Assessing Correctional Rehabilitation: Policy, Practice, and Prospects." Pp. 109–175 in *Policies, Processes, and Decisions of the Criminal Justice System*, edited by Julie Horney. Washington, DC: National Institute of Justice.

Cullen, Francis T., and Cheryl L. Jonson. 2011. "Rehabilitation and Treatment Programs." Pp. 293–344 in *Crime and Public Policy*, edited by James Q. Wilson and Joan Petersilia. New York: Oxford University Press.

Cullen, Francis T., Cheryl L. Jonson, and Daniel P. Mears. 2017. "Reinventing Community Corrections: Ten Recommendations." *Crime and Justice* 46:27–93.

Cullen, Francis T., Cheryl L. Jonson, and Daniel S. Nagin. 2011. "Prisons Do Not Reduce Recidivism: the High Cost of Ignoring Science." *The Prison Journal* 91:48S–65S.

Cullen, Francis T., Cheryl L. Jonson, and Mary K. Stohr. 2014. *The American Prison: Imagining a Different Future*. Thousand Oaks, CA: Sage Publications.

Cullen, Francis T., Daniel P. Mears, Cheryl L. Jonson, and Angela J. Thielo. 2016. "Seven Ways to Make Prisons Work." Pp. 159–196 in *What Is to Be Done about Crime and Punishment? Towards a Public Criminology*, edited by Roger Matthews. London: Palgrave Macmillan.

Cullen, Francis T., Travis C. Pratt, and Jillian J. Turanovic. 2016. "It's Hopeless: Beyond Zero-Tolerance Supervision." *Criminology and Public Policy* 15:1–13.

Dabbaghian, Vahid, Jula Payman, Peter B. Borwein, E. Fowler, Christopher Giles, N. Richardson, Alexander R. Rutherford, and Alexa van der Waall. 2014. "High-Level Simulation Model of a Criminal Justice System." *Theories and Simulations of Complex Social Systems* 52:61–78.

Darling-Hammond, Linda. 2010. *The Flat World and Education: How America's Commitment to Equity Will Determine Our Future*. New York: Teacher's College Press.

Davidson, Elizabeth, Randall Reback, Jonah Rockoff, and Heather L. Schwartz. 2015. "Fifty Ways to Leave a Child Behind: Idiosyncrasies and Discrepancies in States' Implementation of NCLB." *Educational Researcher* 44:347–358.

Davis, Robert C., Barbara E. Smith, and Bruce Taylor. 2003. "Increasing the Proportion of Domestic Violence Arrests that Are Prosecuted: a Natural Experiment in Milwaukee." *Criminology and Public Policy* 2:263–282.

Dennis, Alan, Barbara H. Wixom, and Roberta M. Roth. 2014. *Systems Analysis and Design*. 6th edition. Hoboken, NJ: Wiley.

DeVita, Vincent T., Jr., and Elizabeth DeVita-Raeburn. 2015. *The Death of Cancer*. New York: Farrar, Straus, and Giroux.

DiIulio, John J., Jr. 1995. "Moral Poverty." *Chicago Tribune*, December 15, A31. 1987. *Governing Prisons*. New York: Free Press.

DiIulio, John J., Jr. Geoffrey P. Alpert, Mark H. Moore, George F. Cole, Joan Petersilia, Charles H. Logan, and James Q. Wilson. 1993. *Performance Measures for the Criminal Justice System*. Washington, DC: Bureau of Justice Statistics.

Donnelly, Ellen A. 2017. "The Disproportionate Minority Contact Mandate: an Examination of Its Impacts on Juvenile Justice Processing Outcomes (1997–2011)." *Criminal Justice Policy Review* 28:347-369.

Dooley, Brendan D., and Jason Rydberg. 2014. "Irreconcilable Differences? Examining Divergences in the Orientations of Criminology and Criminal Justice Scholarship, 1951–2008." *Journal of Criminal Justice Education* 25:84–105.

Downes, David M. 1988. *Contrasts in Tolerance: Post-War Penal Policy in the Netherlands and England and Wales*. Oxford: Clarendon Press.

Drake, Alvin W., Ralph L. Keeney, and Philip M. Morse, eds. 1972. *Analysis of Public Systems*. Cambridge, MA: MIT Press.

Dubin, Robert. 1978. *Theory Building*. 2nd edition. New York: Free Press.

Duffee, David E. 2015. "Why Is Criminal Justice Theory Important?" Pp. 5–26 in *Criminal Justice Theory: Explaining the Nature and Behavior of Criminal Justice*, edited by Edward R. Maguire and David E. Duffee. New York: Routledge.

1990. *Explaining Criminal Justice*. 2nd edition. Prospect Heights, IL: Waveland.

Duriez, Stephanie A., Francis T. Cullen, and Sarah M. Manchak. 2014. "Project HOPE Creating a False Sense of Hope? A Case Study of Correctional Popularity." *Federal Probation* 78:57–70.

Durkheim, Emile. 1985. *The Rules of Sociological Method*. Translated by Steven Lukes. New York: The Free Press.

Durose, Matthew R., Alexia D. Cooper, and Howard N. Snyder. 2014. *Recidivism of Prisoners Released in 30 States in 2005: Patterns from 2005 to 2010*. Washington, DC: Bureau of Justice Statistics.

Ebbesen, Ebbe B., and Vladamir J. Konečni. 1985. "Criticisms of the Criminal Justice System: a Decision Making Analysis." *Behavioral Sciences and the Law* 3:177–194.

Eck, John E., and Lin Liu. 2008. "Contrasting Simulated and Empirical Experiments in Crime Prevention." *Journal of Experimental Criminology* 4:195–213.

Ekland-Olson, Sheldon, and William R. Kelly. 1993. *Justice Under Pressure: a Comparison of Recidivism Patterns among Four Successive Parolee Cohorts*. New York: Springer-Verlag.

Ekland-Olson, Sheldon, William R. Kelly, and Michael Supancic. 1983. "Sanction Severity, Feedback, and Deterrence." Pp. 129–165 in *Evaluating Performance of Criminal Justice Agencies*, edited by Gordon P. Whitaker and Charles D. Phillips. Thousand Oaks, CA: Sage Publications.

Emery, Derek J., Alan J. Forster, Kaveh G. Shojania, Stephanie Magnan, Michelle Tubman, and Thomas E. Feasby. 2009. "Management of MRI Wait Lists in Canada." *Healthcare Policy* 4:76–86.

Fabelo, Tony. 1994. "Sentencing Reform in Texas: Can Criminal Justice Research Inform Public Policy?" *Crime and Delinquency* 40:282–294.

Fagan, Abigail A., and Molly Buchanan. 2016. "What Works in Crime Prevention: Comparison and Critical Review of Three Crime Prevention Registries." *Criminology and Public Policy* 15:617–649.

Fagin, Dan. 2013. *Toms River: a Story of Science and Salvation*. New York: Random House.

Farabee, David. 2005. *Rethinking Rehabilitation: Why Can't We Reform Our Criminals?* Washington, DC: The AEI Press.

Farrington, David P. 2016. "Juvenile Delinquency Prevention Programs." Pp. 69–81 in *Advancing Criminology and Criminal Justice Policy*, edited by Thomas G. Blomberg, Julie M. Brancale, Kevin M. Beaver, and William D. Bales. New York: Routledge.

Fattah, Ezzat A., ed. 1986. *From Crime Policy to Victim Policy: Reorienting the Justice System*. London: Macmillan.

Fay, Robert E., and Mamadou Diallo. 2015. *Developmental Estimates of Subnational Crime Rates Based on the National Crime Victimization Survey*. Rockville, MD: Westat.

Feagin, Joe R., Anthony M. Orum, and Gideon Sjoberg, eds. 1991. *A Case for the Case Study*. Chapel Hill: University of North Carolina Press.

Feld, Barry C. 1999. *Bad Kids: Race and the Transformation of the Juvenile Court*. New York: Oxford University Press.

Feld, Barry C., and Donna M. Bishop, eds. 2012. *The Oxford Handbook of Juvenile Crime and Juvenile Justice*. New York: Oxford University Press.

Flanagan, Timothy J., and Dennis R. Longmire, eds. 1996. *Americans View Crime and Justice: a National Public Opinion Survey*. Thousand Oaks, CA: Sage Publications.

Forer, Lois G. 1994. *A Rage to Punish: the Unintended Consequences of Mandatory Sentencing*. New York: Norton.

Forst, Brian. 2004. *Errors of Justice: Nature, Sources, and Remedies*. New York: Cambridge University Press.

Forst, Martin L. 1977. "To What Extent Should the Criminal Justice System Be a 'System'?" *Crime and Delinquency* 23:403–416.

Foster, E. M., Serhan Ziya, Nomesh Bolia, and Michael Hosking. 2012. "Rehabilitation and Juvenile Justice Policy: a Mathematical Modeling Approach." *Mathematical Modeling and Applied Computing* 3:71–91.

Fox, James A. 1996. *Trends in Juvenile Violence: a Report to the United States Attorney General on Current and Future Rates of Juvenile Offending*. Washington, DC: Bureau of Justice Statistics.

Freilich, Joshua D., and Graeme R. Newman. 2016. "Transforming Piecemeal Social Engineering into 'Grand' Crime Prevention Policy: Toward a New Criminology of Social Control." *Journal of Criminal Law and Criminology* 105:203–232.

Gable, Ralph Kirkland, and Robert S. Gable. 2005. "Electronic Monitoring: Positive Intervention Strategies." *Federal Probation* 69:21–25.

Gaes, Gerald G. 2008. "Cost, Performance Studies Look at Prison Privatization." *National Institute of Justice Journal* 259:32–36.

Gaes, Gerald G., Scott D. Camp, Julianne B. Nelson, and William G. Saylor. 2004. *Measuring Prison Performance: Government Privatization and Accountability*. New York: AtlaMira Press.

Garland, David. 2013. "The 2012 Sutherland Address: Penality and the Penal State." *Criminology* 51:475–517.

Gawande, Atul. 2009. *The Checklist Manifesto: How to Get Things Right*. New York: Henry Holt.

2007. *Better: a Surgeon's Notes on Performance*. New York: Metropolitan Books.

Geertz, Clifford. 1973. *The Interpretation of Cultures*. New York: Basic Books.

General Accounting Office, United States. 1997. *Combatting Terrorism: Federal Agencies' Efforts to Implement National Policy and Strategy*. Washington, DC: US General Accounting Office.

Gibbs, Jack P. 1997. "Seven Dimensions of the Predictive Power of Sociological Theories." *National Journal of Sociology* 11:1–28.

1995. "The Notion of Control and Criminology's Policy Implications." Pp. 71–90 in *Crime and Public Policy: Putting Theory to Work*, edited by Hugh D. Barlow. Boulder, CO: Westview Press.

1972. *Sociological Theory Construction*. Hinsdale, IL: Dryden Press.

Gibson, John E., William T. Scherer, William F. Gibson, and Michael C. Smith. 2016. *How to Do a Systems Analysis*. 2nd edition. Hoboken, NJ: Wiley.

Gladwell, Malcolm. 2000. *The Tipping Point: How Little Things Can Make a Big Difference*. Boston: Little, Brown and Company.

Glaze, Lauren E., and Danielle Kaeble. 2014. *Correctional Populations in the United States, 2013*. Washington, DC: Bureau of Justice Statistics.

Goldkamp, John S. 2003. "The Impact of Drug Courts." *Criminology and Public Policy* 2:197–206.

Gottschalk, Marie. 2006. *The Prison and the Gallows: the Politics of Mass Incarceration in America*. New York: Cambridge University Press.

Gould, Mark. 1987. *Revolution in the Development of Capitalism*. Beverly Hills, CA: University of California Press.

Greasley, Andrew. 2013. "*The Simulation Modeling Process*." Pp. 41–72 in *Simulation Strategies to Reduce Recidivism: Risk Need Responsivity (RNR) Modeling for the Criminal Justice System*, edited by Faye S. Taxman and April Pattavina. New York: Springer.

Greenwood, Peter. 2013. *Evidence-Based Practice in Juvenile Justice: Progress, Challenges, and Opportunities*. New York: Springer.

Groopman, Jerome. 2007. *How Doctors Think*. New York: Houghton Mifflin.

Groopman, Jerome, and Pamela Hartzband. 2011. *Your Medical Mind: How to Decide What Is Right for You*. New York: Penguin Press.

Hagan, John. 1989. "Why Is There So Little Criminal Justice Theory? Neglected Macro- and Micro-Level Links between Organization and Power." *Journal of Research in Crime and Delinquency* 26:116–135.

Hage, Jerald, ed. 1994. *Formal Theory in Sociology*. Albany, NY: State University of New York Press.

Hanneman, Robert A. 1995. "Simulation Modeling and Theoretical Analysis in Sociology." *Sociological Perspectives* 38:457–462.

Hanushek, Eric A., John F. Kain, Steven B. Rivkin, and Gregory F. Branch. 2007. "Charter School Quality and Parental Decisionmaking with School Choice." *Journal of Public Economics* 91:823–848.

Hastie, Reid. 2011. "Group Processes in Intelligence Analysis." Pp. 169–196 in *Intelligence Analysis: Behavioral and Social Scientific Foundations*, edited by Baruch Fischhoff and Cherie Chauvin. National Research Council's Committee on Behavioral and Social Science Research to Improve Intelligence Analysis for National Security. Washington, DC: The National Academies Press.

Hatry, Harry P. 2006. *Performance Measurement: Getting Results*. 2nd edition. Washington, DC: The Urban Institute.

Hecht, Alan D., and Joseph Fiksel. 2015. "Solving the Problems We Face: the United States Environmental Protection Agency, Sustainability, and the Challenges of the Twenty-First Century." *Sustainability: Science, Practice, and Policy* 11:75–89.

Heilbroner, David. 1990. *Rough Justice: Days and Nights of a Young D.A.* New York: Pantheon.

Hellander, Ida. 2015. "The US Health Care Crisis Five Years after Passage of the Affordable Care Act: a Data Snapshot." *International Journal of Health Services* 45:706–728.

Herman, Susan. 2010. *Parallel Justice for Victims of Crime*. Washington, DC: National Center for Victims of Crime.

Hernan, Robert E. 2010. *This Borrowed Earth: Lessons from the Fifteen Worst Environmental Disasters*. New York: St. Martin's Press.

Hines, Denise A. 2009. "Domestic Violence." Pp. 115–139 in *The Oxford Handbook of Crime and Public Policy*, edited by Michael H. Tonry. New York: Oxford University Press.

Hoag, Malcolm W. 1956. *An Introduction to Systems Analysis.* Santa Monica, CA: RAND.

Homans, George. 1964. "Contemporary Theory in Sociology." Pp. 951–77 in *Handbook of Modern Sociology,* edited by Robert E. L. Faris. Chicago: Rand McNally.

Hoos, Ida R. 1972. *Systems Analysis in Public Policy: a Critique.* Berkeley: University of California Press.

Howell, James C., Barry C. Feld, and Daniel P. Mears. 2012. "Young Offenders and an Effective Justice System Response: What Happens, What Should Happen, and What We Need to Know." Pp. 200–244 in *From Juvenile Delinquency to Adult Crime: Criminal Careers, Justice Policy, and Prevention,* edited by Rolf Loeber and David P. Farrington. New York: Oxford University Press.

Humes, Edward. 1996. *No Matter How Loud I Shout: a Year in the Life of Juvenile Court.* New York: Simon and Schuster.

Imberman, Scott A. 2011. "The Effect of Charter Schools on Achievement and Behavior of Public School Students." *Journal of Public Economics* 95:850–863.

Imse, Ann. 2013. "State Pays Millions as Prison Populations Sink." *The Gazette,* March 9. Available online (http://gazette.com/state-pays-millions-as-prison -populations-sink/article/152065).

In the Public Interest. 2013. *Criminal: How Lockup Quotas and 'Low-Crime Taxes' Guarantee Profits for Private Prison Corporations.* Washington, DC: In the Public Interest.

Ioannidis, John P. A. 2005a. "Contradicted and Initially Stronger Effects in Highly Cited Clinical Research." *Journal of the American Medical Association* 294:218–228.

———. 2005b. "Why Most Published Research Findings Are False." *PLoS Medicine* 2:0696–0701.

Jaccard, James, and Jacob Jacoby. 2010. *Theory Construction and Model-Building Skills: a Practical Guide for Social Scientists.* New York: Guildford Press.

Kaeble, Danielle, Lauren Glaze, Anastasios Tsoutis, and Todd Minton. 2015. *Correctional Populations in the United States, 2014.* Washington, DC: Bureau of Justice Statistics.

Kahneman, Daniel. 2011. *Thinking, Fast and Slow.* New York: Farrar, Straus and Giroux.

Kaminsky, Jonathan. 2013. "The Great Evaluator." *State Legislatures Magazine,* July/August, 39(7):52–55. Available online (www.ncsl.org/research/fiscal -policy/the-great-evaluator_sl-magazine-july-2013.aspx).

Kaplan, Edward H. 2011. "Operations Research and Intelligence Analysis." Pp. 31–56 in *Intelligence Analysis: Behavioral and Social Scientific Foundations,* edited by Baruch Fischhoff and Cherie Chauvin. National Research Council's Committee on Behavioral and Social Science Research to Improve Intelligence Analysis for National Security. Washington, DC: The National Academies Press.

Katz, Michael B. 1976. "The Origins of Public Education: a Reassessment." *History of Education Quarterly* 16:381–407.

Kean, Thomas H., and Lee Hamilton. 2004. *The 9/11 Commission Report: Final Report of the National Commission on Terrorist Attacks upon the United States.* Washington, DC: National Commission on Terrorist Attacks upon the United States.

Keeney, Ralph L., and Howard Raiffa. 1972. "A Critique of Formal Analysis in Public Decisionmaking." Pp. 64–74 in *Analysis of Public Systems*, edited by Alvin W. Drake, Ralph L. Keeney, and Philip M. Morse. Cambridge, MA: MIT Press.

Kelleghan, Thomas, George F. Madaus, and Peter W. Airasian. 2012. *The Effects of Standardized Testing.* Boston: Kluwer.

Kelleher, Grace J., ed. 1970. *The Challenge to Systems Analysis: Public Policy and Social Change.* New York: John Wiley.

Kelly, William R. 2016. *The Future of Crime and Punishment: Smart Policies for Reducing Crime and Saving Money.* Lanham, MD: Rowman and Littlefield.
    2015. *Criminal Justice at the Crossroads.* New York: Columbia University Press.

Kelly, William R., Tammy S. Macy, and Daniel P. Mears. 2005. "Juvenile Court Referrals in Texas: an Assessment of Criminogenic Needs and the Gap between Needs and Services." *The Prison Journal* 85:467–489.

Kleck, Gary, and J. C. Barnes. 2013. "Deterrence and Macro-Level Perceptions of Punishment Risks: Is There a 'Collective Wisdom'?" *Crime and Delinquency* 59:1006–1035.

Kleck, Gary, and Don B. Kates. 2001. *Armed: New Perspectives on Gun Control.* New York: Prometheus.

Kleck, Gary, Brion Sever, Spencer Li, and Marc Gertz. 2005. "The Missing Link in General Deterrence Research." *Criminology* 43:623–660.

Kleck, Gary, Jongyeon Tark, and Jon J. Bellows. 2006. "What Methods Are Most Frequently Used in Research in Criminology and Criminal Justice?" *Journal of Criminal Justice* 34:147–152.

Kolbert, Elizabeth. 2014. *The Sixth Extinction: an Unnatural History.* New York: Henry Holt and Company.
    2006. *Field Notes from a Catastrophe: Man, Nature, and Climate Change.* New York: Bloomsbury.

Kraska, Peter B. 2006. "Criminal Justice Theory: Toward Legitimacy and an Infrastructure." *Justice Quarterly* 23:167–185.
    2004. *Theorizing Criminal Justice.* Long Grove, IL: Waveland.

Kuhn, Thomas S. 1962. *The Structure of Scientific Revolutions.* Chicago: University of Chicago Press.

Kyckelhahn, Tracey. 2015. *Justice Expenditure and Employment Extracts, 2012 – Preliminary.* Washington, DC: Bureau of Justice Statistics. Available online (www.bjs.gov/index.cfm?ty=pbdetail&iid=5239).
    2013. *Local Government Corrections Expenditures, FY 2005–2011.* Washington, DC: Bureau of Justice Statistics.
    2011. *Justice Expenditures and Employment, FY 1982–2007 – Statistical Tables.* Washington, DC: Bureau of Justice Statistics.

Langton, Lynn, and Jennifer Truman. 2014. *Socio-Emotional Impact of Violent Crime.* Washington, DC: Bureau of Justice Statistics.

Latessa, Edward J., Shelley J. Listwan, and Deborah Koetzle. 2014. *What Works (and Doesn't) in Reducing Recidivism*. Waltham, MA: Anderson Publishing.

Lattimore, Pamela K., Christy A. Visher, and Danielle M. Steffey. 2010. "Prisoner Reentry in the First Decade of the 21st Century." *Journal of Victims and Offenders* 5:253–267.

Lawrence, Sarah, and Daniel P. Mears. 2004. *Benefit-Cost Analysis of Supermax Prisons: Critical Steps and Considerations*. Washington, DC: The Urban Institute.

Lehrer, Jonah. 2010. "The Truth Wears Off." *The New Yorker* LXXXVI (40):52–57.

Leo, Richard A. 2008. *Police Interrogation and American Justice*. Cambridge, MA: Harvard University Press.

Levitt, Steven D., and Stephen J. Dubner. 2014. *Think Like a Freak*. United Kingdom: Penguin Random House.

Lewin, Kurt. 1952. *Field Theory in Social Science: Selected Theoretical Papers*. London: Tavistock.

Lewis, Michael. 2003. *Moneyball: the Art of Winning an Unfair Game*. New York: Norton.

Lieberson, Stanley. 1985. *Making It Count*. Berkeley: University of California Press.

Lindsey, Andrea M., Daniel P. Mears, and Joshua C. Cochran. 2016. "The Privatization Debate: a Conceptual Framework for Improving (Public and Private) Corrections." *Journal of Contemporary Criminal Justice* 32:308–327.

Lindsey, Andrea M., Daniel P. Mears, Joshua C. Cochran, William D. Bales, and Brian J. Stults. 2017. "In Prison and Far From Home: Spatial Distance Effects on Inmate Misconduct." *Crime and Delinquency* (forthcoming).

Lipsey, Mark W., John L. Adams, Denise C. Gottfredson, John V. Pepper, David Weisburd, eds. 2005. *Improving Evaluation of Anticrime Programs*. Washington, DC: The National Academies Press.

Lipsey, Mark W., and Francis T. Cullen. 2007. "The Effectiveness of Correctional Rehabilitation: a Review of Systematic Reviews." *Annual Review of Law and Social Science* 3:297–320.

Littell, Julia H. 2005. "Lesson from a Systematic Review of Effects of Multisystemic Therapy." *Children and Youth Services Review* 27:445–463.

Livingston, Michael, Anna Stewart, and Gerard Palk. 2006. *A Micro-Simulation Model of the Juvenile Justice System in Queensland*. Canberra: Australian Institute of Criminology.

Loeber, Rolf, and David P. Farrington, eds. 2012. *From Juvenile Delinquency to Adult Crime: Criminal Careers, Justice Policy, and Prevention*. New York: Oxford University Press.

Lofstrom, Magnus, and Steven Raphael. 2016. "Incarceration and Crime: Evidence from California's Public Safety Realignment Reform." *The Annals of the American Academy of Political and Social Science* 664:196–220.

Logan, Charles. 1993. "Criminal Justice Performance Measures for Prisons." Pp. 15–59 in *Performance Measures for the Criminal Justice System*. Washington DC: Bureau of Justice Statistics.

Luke, Douglas A., and Katherine A. Stamatakis. 2012. "Systems Science Methods in Public Health: Dynamics, Networks, and Agents." *Annual Review of Public Health* 33:357–376.

Lum, Cynthia, and Daniel Nagin. 2017. "Reinventing American Policing: a Seven-Point Blueprint for the 21st Century." *Crime and Justice* 47:339–393.

Lynch, James P., and Lynn A. Addington, eds. 2007. *Understanding Crime Statistics: Revisiting the Divergence of the NCVS and UCR*. New York: Cambridge University Press.

Lynch, James P., and William J. Sabol. 2001. *Prisoner Reentry in Perspective*. Washington, DC: The Urban Institute.

MacKenzie, Doris L. 2006. *What Works in Corrections: Reducing the Criminal Activities of Offenders and Delinquents*. New York: Cambridge University Press.

MacKenzie, Doris L., and David P. Farrington. 2015. "Preventing Future Offending of Delinquents and Offenders: What Have We Learned from Experiments and Meta-Analyses?" *Journal of Experimental Criminology* 11:565–595.

Maguire, Edward R., Gregory J. Howard, and Graeme Newman. 1998. "Measuring the Performance of National Criminal Justice Systems." *International Journal of Comparative and Applied Criminal Justice* 22:31–59.

Makary, Martin A., and Michael Daniel. 2016. "Medical Error – the Third Leading Cause of Death in the US." *BMJ* 353:i2139. Available online (www.bmj.com/content/353/bmj.i2139).

Malcolm, Norman. 1958. *Ludwig Wittgenstein: a Memoir*. New York: Oxford University Press.

Malleson, Nick, Alison Heppenstall, and Linda See. 2010. "Crime Reduction through Simulation: an Agent-Based Model of Burglary." *Computers, Environment, and Urban Systems* 34:236–250.

Maltz, Michael D. 1996. "From Poisson to the Present: Applying Operations Research to Problems of Crime and Justice." *Journal of Quantitative Criminology* 12:3–61.

Mancini, Christina, and Daniel P. Mears. 2013. "The Effect of Agency Scandal on Public Views toward the Correctional System." *Criminal Justice Review* 38:5–28.

Mancini, Christina, Daniel P. Mears, Eric A. Stewart, Kevin M. Beaver, and Justin T. Pickett. 2015. "Whites' Perceptions about Black Criminality: a Closer Look at the Contact Hypothesis." *Crime and Delinquency* 61:996–1022.

Manski, Charles F. 2013. *Public Policy in an Uncertain World: Analysis and Decisions*. Cambridge, MA: Harvard University Press.

Manza, Jeff, and Christopher Uggen. 2006. *Locked Out: Felon Disenfranchisement and American Democracy*. New York: Oxford University Press.

Marini, Margaret M., and Burton Singer. 1988. "Causality in the Social Sciences." Pp. 347–409 in *Sociological Methodology*, edited by Clifford C. Clogg. Washington, DC: American Sociological Association.

Mathias, Jason S., Joe Feinglass, and David W. Baker. 2012. "Variations in US Hospital Performance on Imaging-Use Measures." *Medical Care* 50:808–814.

Maxwell, Christopher D., Joel H. Garner, and Jeffrey A. Fagan. 2002. "The Preventative Effects of Arrest on Intimate Partner Violence: Research, Policy, and Theory." *Criminology and Public Policy* 2:51–80.

May, David C., and Peter B. Wood. 2010. *Ranking Correctional Punishments: Views from Offenders, Practitioners, and the Public.* Durham, NC: Carolina Academic Press.

McGarry, Peggy, and Becky Ney. 2006. *Getting It Right: Collaborative Problem Solving for Criminal Justice.* Silver Spring, MD: Center for Effective Public Policy.

McKinney, Michael L., Robert Schoch, and Logan Yonavjak. 2013. *Environmental Science: Systems and Solutions.* 5th edition. Burlington, MA: Jones and Bartlett.

Meadows, Donella H. 2008. *Thinking in Systems: a Primer.* White River Junction, VT: Chelsea Green Publishing.

Mears, Daniel P. 2016. "Policy Evaluation and Assessment." Pp. 26–39 in *Advancing Criminology and Criminal Justice Policy,* edited by Thomas G. Blomberg, Julie M. Brancale, Kevin M. Beaver, and William D. Bales. New York: Routledge.

2014. "The Role of Information in Changing Offender Behavior, Criminal Justice System Actions, and Policy Maker Decisions." *Criminology and Public Policy* 13:441–449.

2013. "Supermax Prisons: the Policy and the Evidence." *Criminology and Public Policy* 12:681–719.

2012. "The Front End of the Juvenile Court: Intake and Informal vs. Formal Processing." Pp. 573–605 in *The Oxford Handbook of Juvenile Crime and Juvenile Justice,* edited by Barry C. Feld and Donna M. Bishop. New York: Oxford University Press.

2010. *American Criminal Justice Policy: an Evaluation Approach to Increasing Accountability and Effectiveness.* New York: Cambridge University Press.

2008a. "Accountability, Efficiency, and Effectiveness in Corrections: Shining a Light on the Black Box of Prison Systems." *Criminology and Public Policy* 7:143–152.

2008b. "An Assessment of Supermax Prisons Using an Evaluation Research Framework." *The Prison Journal* 88:43–68.

2007. "Towards Rational and Evidence-Based Crime Policy." *Journal of Criminal Justice* 35:667–682.

2004. "Mental Health Needs and Services in the Criminal Justice System." *Houston Journal of Health Law and Policy* 4:255–284.

2002a. *The Role of Statistical Models in Planning Juvenile Corrections Capacity.* Washington, DC: The Urban Institute.

2002b. "Sentencing Guidelines and the Transformation of Juvenile Justice in the Twenty-First Century." *Journal of Contemporary Criminal Justice* 18:6–19.

2001. "Getting Tough with Juvenile Offenders: Explaining Support for Sanctioning Youths as Adults." *Criminal Justice and Behavior* 28:206–226.

2000. "Assessing the Effectiveness of Juvenile Justice Reforms: a Closer Look at the Criteria and the Impacts on Diverse Stakeholders." *Law and Policy* 22:175–202.

1998a. "Evaluation Issues Confronting Juvenile Justice Sentencing Reforms: a Case Study of Texas." *Crime and Delinquency* 44:443–463.

1998b. "The Sociology of Sentencing: Reconceptualizing Decisionmaking Processes and Outcomes." *Law and Society Review* 32:667–724.

Mears, Daniel P., and Sarah Bacon. 2009. "Improving Criminal Justice through Better Decisionmaking: Lessons from the Medical System." *Journal of Criminal Justice* 37:142–154.

Mears, Daniel P., and William D. Bales. 2010. "Supermax Housing: Placement, Duration, and Time to Reentry." *Journal of Criminal Justice* 38:545–554.

Mears, Daniel P., and James C. Barnes. 2010. "Toward a Systematic Foundation for Identifying Evidence-Based Criminal Justice Sanctions and their Relative Effectiveness." *Journal of Criminal Justice* 38:702–810.

Mears, Daniel P., and Jeffrey A. Butts. 2008. "Using Performance Monitoring to Improve the Accountability, Operations, and Effectiveness of Juvenile Justice." *Criminal Justice Policy Review* 19:264–284.

Mears, Daniel P., and Joshua C. Cochran. 2017. "Who Goes to Prison?" In the *Oxford Handbook on Prisons and Imprisonment*, edited by John D. Wooldredge and Paula Smith. New York: Oxford University Press. (Forthcoming.)

2015. *Prisoner Reentry in the Era of Mass Incarceration*. Thousand Oaks, CA: Sage Publications.

2013. "What Is the Effect of IQ on Offending?" *Criminal Justice and Behavior* 40:1280–1300.

Mears, Daniel P., Joshua C. Cochran, William D. Bales, and Avinash S. Bhati. 2016. "Recidivism and Time Served in Prison." *Journal of Criminal Law and Criminology* 106:83–124.

Mears, Daniel P., Joshua C. Cochran, and Kevin M. Beaver. 2013. "Self-Control Theory and Nonlinear Effects on Offending." *Journal of Quantitative Criminology* 29:447–476.

Mears, Daniel P., Joshua C. Cochran, and Francis T. Cullen. 2015. "Incarceration Heterogeneity and Its Implications for Assessing the Effectiveness of Imprisonment on Recidivism." *Criminal Justice Policy Review* 26:691–712.

Mears, Daniel P., Joshua C. Cochran, Sarah J. Greenman, Avinash S. Bhati, and Mark A. Greenwald. 2011. "Evidence on the Effectiveness of Juvenile Court Sanctions." *Journal of Criminal Justice* 39:509–520.

Mears, Daniel P., Joshua C. Cochran, and Andrea M. Lindsey. 2016. "Offending and Racial and Ethnic Disparities in Criminal Justice: a Conceptual Framework for Guiding Theory and Research and Informing Policy." *Journal of Contemporary Criminal Justice* 32:78–103.

Mears, Daniel P., Joshua C. Cochran, Sonja E. Siennick, and William D. Bales. 2012. "Prison Visitation and Recidivism." *Justice Quarterly* 29:888–918.

Mears, Daniel P., Carter Hay, Marc Gertz, and Christina Mancini. 2007. "Public Opinion and the Foundation of the Juvenile Court." *Criminology* 45:223–258.

Mears, Daniel P., Joshua J. Kuch, Andrea M. Lindsey, Sonja E. Siennick, George B. Pesta, Mark A. Greenwald, and Thomas G. Blomberg. 2016. "Juvenile

Court and Contemporary Diversion: Helpful, Harmful, or Both?" *Criminology and Public Policy* 15:953–981.

Mears, Daniel P., and Andrea M. Lindsey. 2016. "Speeding in America: a Critique of, and Alternatives to, Officer-Initiated Enforcement." *Criminal Justice Review* 41:55–74.

Mears, Daniel P., Christina Mancini, Marc Gertz, and Jake Bratton. 2008. "Sex Crimes, Children, and Pornography: Public Views and Public Policy." *Crime and Delinquency* 54:532–559.

Mears, Daniel P., Christina Mancini, and Eric A. Stewart. 2009. "Whites' Concern about Crime: the Effects of Interracial Contact." *Journal of Research in Crime and Delinquency* 46:524–552.

Mears, Daniel P., Justin T. Pickett, and Christina Mancini. 2015. "Support for Balanced Juvenile Justice: Assessing Views about Youth, Rehabilitation, and Punishment." *Journal of Quantitative Criminology* 31:459–479.

Mears, Daniel P., Matthew Ploeger, and Mark Warr. 1998. "Explaining the Gender Gap in Delinquency: Peer Influence and Moral Evaluations of Behavior." *Journal of Research in Crime and Delinquency* 35:251–266.

Mears, Daniel P., and Michael D. Reisig. 2006. "The Theory and Practice of Supermax Prisons." *Punishment and Society* 8:33–57.

Mears, Daniel P., Michelle L. Scott, and Avinash S. Bhati. 2007a. "A Process and Outcome Evaluation of an Agricultural Crime Prevention Initiative." *Criminal Justice Policy Review* 18:51–80.

2007b. "Opportunity Theory and Agricultural Crime Victimization." *Rural Sociology* 72:151–184.

2007c. *Policy, Theory, and Research Lessons from an Evaluation of an Agricultural Crime Prevention Program*. Washington, DC: The Urban Institute.

Mears, Daniel P., Tracey L. Shollenberger, Janeen B. Willison, Colleen E. Owens, and Jeffrey A. Butts. 2010. "Practitioner Views of Priorities, Policies, and Practices in Juvenile Justice." *Crime and Delinquency* 56:535–563.

Mears, Daniel P., and Sonja E. Siennick. 2016. "Young Adult Outcomes and the Life-Course Penalties of Parental Incarceration." *Journal of Research in Crime and Delinquency* 53:3–35.

Mears, Daniel P., and Mark C. Stafford. 2002. "Central Analytical Issues in the Generation of Cumulative Sociological Knowledge." *Sociological Focus* 35:5–24.

Mears, Daniel P., and Eric A. Stewart. 2010. "Interracial Contact and Fear of Crime." *Journal of Criminal Justice* 38:34–41.

Mears, Daniel P., and Jamie Watson. 2006. "Towards a Fair and Balanced Assessment of Supermax Prisons." *Justice Quarterly* 23:232–270.

Mendel, Dick. 2016. "Case Now Strong for Ending Probation's Place as Default Disposition in Juvenile Justice." *Juvenile Justice Information Exchange*, April 14. Available online (http://jjie.org/case-now-strong-for-ending -probations-place-as-default-disposition-in-juvenile-justice/227322/).

Merton, Robert K. 1973. *The Sociology of Science: Theoretical and Empirical Investigations*. Chicago: University of Chicago Press.

1968. *Social Theory and Social Structure*. New York: Free Press.

Messinger, Sheldon L. 1969. *Strategies of Control.* Doctoral dissertation. Los Angeles: University of California (available through Quid Pro Books, New Orleans, LA, in a revised 2016 edition with a foreword by Howard S. Becker: http://quidprolaw.com/?p=6953).

Messner, Steven F., Marvin D. Krohn, and Allen E. Liska, eds. 1989. *Theoretical Integration in the Study of Deviance and Crime: Problems and Prospects.* Albany: State University of New York Press.

Milgram, Anne. 2013. *Why Smart Statistics Are the Key to Fighting Crime.* San Francisco, CA: TED Talks. Available online (www.ted.com/talks/anne_milgram_why_smart_statistics_are_the_key_to_fighting_crime).

——— 2012. "Moneyballing Criminal Justice." *The Atlantic Monthly*, June 20. Available online (www.theatlantic.com/national/archive/2012/06/moneyballing-criminal-justice/258703/).

Millenson, Michael. 1997. *Demanding Medical Excellence: Doctors and Accountability in the Information Age.* Chicago: University of Chicago Press.

Mills, C. Wright. 1959. *The Sociological Imagination.* New York: Oxford University Press.

Mrazek, Patricia J., and Robert J. Haggerty, eds. 1994. *Reducing Risks for Mental Disorders: Frontiers for Preventive Intervention Research.* Washington, DC: National Academy Press.

Mukherjee, Siddhartha. 2010. *The Emperor of All Maladies: a Biography of Cancer.* New York: Scribner.

Nadelmann, Ethan A. 2004. "Criminologists and Punitive Drug Prohibition: to Serve or to Challenge?" *Criminology and Public Policy* 3:441–450.

Nagin, Daniel S. 2013. "Deterrence: a Review of the Evidence by a Criminologist for Economists." *Annual Review of Economics* 5:83–105.

Nagin, Daniel S., Francis T. Cullen, and Cheryl L. Jonson. 2009. "Imprisonment and Reoffending." *Crime and Justice* 38:115–200.

Nagin, Daniel S., Alex R. Piquero, Elizabeth S. Scott, and Laurence Steinberg. 2006. "Public Preferences for Rehabilitation versus Incarceration of Juvenile Offenders: Evidence from a Contingent Valuation Survey." *Criminology and Public Policy* 5:627–651.

National Institute of Justice. 2004. "What Lessons Does It Take to Make Collaboration Work? Lessons Learned through the Criminal Justice System Project." *National Institute of Justice Journal* 251:8–13.

Navarro, Joseph A., and Jean G. Taylor. 1967. "An Application of Systems Analysis to Aid in the Efficient Administration of Justice." *Judicature* 51:47–52.

Nelson, Thomas E., Dana E. Wittmer, and Dustin Carnahan. 2015. "Should Science Class Be Fair? Frames and Values in the Evolution Debate." *Political Communication* 32:625–647.

Ney, Becki, and Peggy McGarry. 2006. *Getting It Right: Collaborative Problem Solving for Criminal Justice.* Silver Spring, MD: Center for Effective Public Policy.

Office of Justice Programs. 2010. *Criminal Justice Improvement and Recidivism Reduction through State, Local, and Tribal Justice Reinvestment.* FY 2010 Competitive Grant Announcement. OMB No. 1121–0329. Washington, DC: US Department of Justice.

Pacholke, Dan, and Sandy F. Mullins. 2015. *More than Empting Beds: a Systems Approach to Segregation Reform*. Washington, DC: Bureau of Justice Assistance.

Parsons, Talcott. 1977. *Social Systems and the Evolution of Action Theory.* New York: The Free Press.

———. 1951. *The Social System.* New York: The Free Press.

Perry, Rick. 2003. Gov. Perry Signs $117 Billion State Budget: Governor Uses Line-Item Veto Power to Eliminate $81 Million in Spending. Press release, June 22. Austin, TX: Office of the Governor.

Petersilia, Joan. 2016. "Realigning Corrections, California Style." *The Annals of the American Academy of Political and Social Science* 664:8–15.

———. 2003. *When Prisoners Come Home: Parole and Prisoner Reentry.* New York: Oxford University Press.

———. 1991. "Policy Relevance and the Future of Criminology." *Criminology* 29:1–16.

Petersilia, Joan, and Kevin R. Reitz, eds. 2012. *The Oxford Handbook of Sentencing and Corrections.* New York: Oxford University Press.

Peterson Foundation, The. 2016. *Per Capita Healthcare Costs: International Comparison.* New York: The Peterson Foundation. Available online (www .pgpf.org/chart-archive/0006_health-care-oecd).

Pew Charitable Trusts. 2012. *Time Served: the High Cost, Low Return of Longer Prison Terms.* Philadelphia, PA: Pew Charitable Trusts.

———. 2009. *The Long Reach of American Corrections.* Philadelphia: Pew Charitable Trusts.

Pfaff, John F. 2011. The Causes of Growth in Prison Admissions and Populations. Available at SSRN (http://ssrn.com/abstract=1884674).

Phelps, Michelle S., and Devah Pager. 2016. "Inequality and Punishment: a Turning Point for Mass Incarceration?" *The Annals of the American Academy of Political and Social Science* 663:185–203.

Piehl, Anne M., and Stefan F. LoBuglio. 2005. "Does Supervision Matter?" Pp. 105–138 in *Prisoner Reentry and Public Safety in America*, edited by Jeremy Travis and Christy Visher. New York: Cambridge University Press.

Platt, Anthony. 1977. *The Child Savers: the Invention of Delinquency.* 2nd edition. Chicago: University of Chicago Press.

Pratt, Travis C., and Jeff Maahs. 1999. "Are Private Prisons More Cost-Effective Than Public Prisons? A Meta-analysis of Evaluation Research Studies." *Crime and Delinquency* 45:358–371.

President's Commission on Law Enforcement and Administration of Justice. 1967. *The Challenge of Crime in a Free Society.* Washington, DC: US Government Printing Office.

Ramirez, Mark D. 2013. "Punitive Sentiment." *Criminology* 51:329–364.

Rand, Michael, and Shannan Catalano. 2007. *Criminal Victimization, 2006.* Washington, DC: Bureau of Justice Statistics.

Rapoport, Anatol. 1986. *General Systems Theory: Essential Concepts and Applications.* Cambridge, MA: Abacus Press.

Raudenbush, Stephen W., and J. Douglas Willms, eds. 1991. *Schools, Classrooms, and Pupils: International Studies of Schooling from a Multilevel Perspective.* New York: Academic Press.

Rawls, John B. 1971. *A Theory of Justice*. Cambridge, MA: Harvard University Press.

Reese, William J. 2013. *Testing Wars in the Public Schools: a Forgotten History*. Cambridge: Harvard University Press.

Regoeczi, Wendy, and Duren Banks. 2014. *The Nation's Two Measures of Homicide*. Washington, DC: Bureau of Justice Statistics.

Reich, Robert B. 1998. *Locked in the Cabinet*. New York: Knopf.

Reid, T. R. 2009. *The Healing of America: a Global Quest for Better, Cheaper, and Fairer Health Care*. New York: Penguin Press.

Reisig, Michael D. 2010. "Community and Problem-Oriented Policing." *Crime and Justice* 39:1–53.

Reisig, Michael D., and Travis C. Pratt. 2000. "The Ethics of Correctional Privatization: a Critical Examination of the Delegation of Coercive Authority." *The Prison Journal* 80:210–222.

Reynolds, Paul D. 2006. *A Primer in Theory Construction*. New York: Routledge.

Rhodes, William. 1990. *Models of the Criminal Justice System: a Review of Existing Impact Models*. Cambridge, MA: Abt Associates.

Ridgeway, Greg. 2013. "Linking Prediction and Prevention." *Criminology and Public Policy* 12:545–550.

Ridgeway, Greg, and John M. MacDonald. 2014. "A Method for Internal Benchmarking of Criminal Justice System Performance." *Crime and Delinquency* 60:145–162.

Roberts, Julian V. 1992. "Public Opinion, Crime, and Criminal Justice." *Crime and Justice* 16:99–180.

Roberts, Julian V., and Andrew Ashworth. 2016. "The Evolution of Sentencing Policy and Practice in England and Wales, 2003–2015." *Crime and Justice* 45:307–358.

Roberts, Julian V., and Mike Hough. 2005a. "The State of the Prisons: Exploring Public Knowledge and Opinion." *The Howard Journal* 44:286–306.

2005b. *Understanding Public Attitudes to Criminal Justice*. Maidenhead, UK: Open University Press.

Roberts, Julian V., and Loretta J. Stalans. 1998. "Crime, Criminal Justice, and Public Opinion." Pp. 31–57 in *The Handbook of Crime and Punishment*, edited by Michael H. Tonry. New York: Oxford University Press.

Roberts, Julian V., Loretta J. Stalans, David Indermaur, and Mike Hough. 2003. *Penal Populism and Public Opinion: Lessons from Five Countries*. New York: Oxford University Press.

Roberts, Marc J., William Hsiao, Peter Berman, and Michael R. Reich. 2008. *Getting Health Reform Right: a Guide to Improving Performance and Equity*. New York: Oxford University Press.

Roman, John K., Jeffrey A. Butts, and Caterina G. Roman. 2011. "Evaluating Systems Change in a Juvenile Justice Reform Initiative." *Children and Youth Services Review* 33:S41-S43.

Roman, John K., Terence Dunworth, and Kevin Marsh, eds. 2010. *Cost-Benefit Analysis and Crime Control*. Washington, DC: The Urban Institute Press.

Roman, John K., and Adele Harrell. 2001. "Assessing the Costs and Benefits Accruing to the Public from a Graduated Sanctions Program for Drug-Using Defendants." *Law and Policy* 23:237–268.

Rossi, Peter H. 1980. "The Presidential Address: the Challenge and Opportunities of Applied Social Research." *American Sociological Review* 45:889–904.

Rossi, Peter H., and Richard A. Berk. 1997. *Just Punishments: Federal Guidelines and Public Views Compared.* New York: Aldine de Gruyter.

Rossi, Peter H., Mark W. Lipsey, and Howard E. Freeman. 2004. *Evaluation: a Systematic Approach.* 7th edition. Thousand Oaks, CA: Sage Publications.

Rumsfeld, Donald. 2011. *Known and Unknown: a Memoir.* New York: Sentinel.

Sabol, William J. 1999. *Prison Population Projection and Forecasting: Managing Capacity.* Washington, DC: Office of Justice Programs.

Salamon, Julie. 2008. *Hospital: Man, Woman, Death, Infinity, Plus Red Tape, Bad Behavior, Money, God, and Diversity on Steroids.* New York: Penguin Press.

Sampson, Robert J. 2013. "The Place of Context: a Theory and Strategy for Criminology's Hard Problems." *Criminology* 51:1–32.

2012. *Great American City: Chicago and the Enduring Neighborhood Effect.* Chicago: University of Chicago Press.

2009. "Racial Stratification and the Durable Tangle of Neighborhood Inequality." *Annals of the American Academy of Political and Social Science* 621:260–280.

Sampson, Robert J., Christopher Winship, and Carly Knight. 2013. "Translating Causal Claims: Principles and Strategies for Policy-Relevant Criminology." *Criminology and Public Policy* 12:587–616.

Samuelson, Douglas A. 2006. "Back on the Beat: Two-Day Washington, DC, Symposium Reconnects O.R. and Criminal Justice." *Operations Research/ Management Sciences (OR/MS)* 33:36–40.

Sanders, Lisa. 2009. *Every Patient Tells a Story: Medical Mysteries and the Art of Diagnosis.* New York: Broadway Books.

Schaefer, Lacey, Francis T. Cullen, and John E. Eck. 2016. *Environmental Corrections: a New Paradigm for Supervising Offenders in the Community.* Thousand Oaks, CA: Sage Publications.

Sedgwick, Jeff. 2016. "Statistical Analysis Centers and the Justice Research and Statistics Association." *The Criminologist* 41:7–9.

Sevigny, Eric L., Harold A. Pollack, and Peter Reuter. 2013. "Can Drug Courts Help to Reduce Prison and Jail Populations?" *The Annals of the American Academy of Political and Social Science* 647:190–212.

Sherman, Lawrence W. 2003. "Misleading Evidence and Evidence-Led Policy: Making Social Science More Experimental." *The Annals of the American Academy of Political and Social Science* 589:6–19.

Sherman, Lawrence W., and Richard A. Berk. 1984. "The Specific Deterrent Effects of Arrest for Domestic Assault." *American Sociological Review* 49:261–271.

Sherman, Lawrence W., David P. Farrington, Brandon C. Welsh, and Doris L. MacKenzie, eds. 2002. *Evidence Based Crime Prevention.* London: Routledge.

Sherman, Lawrence W., Denise C. Gottfredson, Doris L. MacKenzie, John Eck, Peter Reuter, and Shawn Bushway, eds. 1997. *Preventing Crime: What Works, What Doesn't, What's Promising*. Washington, DC: Office of Justice Programs.

Siennick, Sonja E., Daniel P. Mears, and William D. Bales. 2013. "Here and Gone: Anticipation and Separation Effects of Prison Visits on Inmate Infractions." *Journal of Research in Crime and Delinquency* 50:417–444.

Siff, Scott, and David Mears. 1999. "The Mississippi River Basin: a National Treasure, a National Challenge." *Tulane Environmental Law Journal* 12:293–319.

Silver, Nate. 2012. *The Signal and the Noise: Why So Many Predictions Fail – but Some Don't*. New York: Penguin.

Simon, Jonathan. 2012. "*Mass Incarceration: from Social Policy to Social Problem.*" Pp. 23–52 in *The Oxford Handbook of Sentencing and Corrections*, edited by Joan Petersilia and Kevin R. Reitz. New York: Oxford University Press.

——. 2007. *Governing through Crime*. New York: Oxford University Press.

Skinner, Kiron K. 2011. "Qualitative Analysis for the Intelligence Community." Pp. 101–114 in *Intelligence Analysis: Behavioral and Social Scientific Foundations*, edited by Baruch Fischhoff and Cherie Chauvin. National Research Council's Committee on Behavioral and Social Science Research to Improve Intelligence Analysis for National Security. Washington, DC: The National Academies Press.

Skogan, Wesley, and Kathleen Frydl, eds. 2004. *Fairness and Effectiveness in Policing: the Evidence*. Washington, DC: National Academies Press.

Skoler, Daniel L. 1977. *Organizing the Non-system: Governmental Structuring of Criminal Justice Service*. Lexington, MA: Lexington Books.

Skolnick, Jerome. 1966. *Justice without Trial: Law Enforcement in Democratic Society*. New York: John Wiley and Sons.

Smith, Gary. 2014. *Standard Deviations: Flawed Assumptions, Tortured Data, and Other Ways to Lie with Statistics*. New York: Overlook Press.

Snell, Tracy L. 1993. *Correctional Populations in the United States, 1993*. Washington, DC: Bureau of Justice Statistics.

Sober, Elliott, and David S. Wilson. 1994. "A Critical Review of Philosophical Work on the Units of Selection Problem." *Philosophy of Science* 61:534–555.

Soled, Jay A. 2001. "Use of Judicial Doctrines in Resolving Transfer Tax Controversies." *Boston College Law Review* 42:587–617.

Sparks, Richard, Anthony E. Bottoms, and Will Hay. 1996. *Prisons and the Problem of Order*. Oxford, UK: Oxford University Press.

Spelman, William. 2009. "Crime, Cash, and Limited Options: Explaining the Prison Boom." *Criminology and Public Policy* 8:29–77.

——. 2008. "Specifying the Relationship between Crime and Prisons." *Journal of Quantitative Criminology* 24:149–178.

——. 2006. "The Limited Importance of Prison Expansion." Pp. 97–129 in *The Crime Drop in America*, edited by Alfred Blumstein and Joel Wallman. New York: Cambridge University Press.

1995. "The Severity of Intermediate Sanctions." *Journal of Research in Crime and Delinquency* 32:107–135.

Spohn, Cassia. 2013. "Racial Disparities in Prosecution, Sentencing, and Punishment." Pp. 166–193 in *The Oxford Handbook of Ethnicity, Crime, and Immigration*, edited by Sandra M. Bucerius and Michael Tonry. New York: Oxford University Press.

Stafford, Mark C., and Daniel P. Mears. 2015. "Causation, Theory, and Policy in the Social Sciences." Pp. 1–14 in *Emerging Trends in the Behavioral and Social Sciences: an Interdisciplinary, Searchable, and Linkable Resource*, edited by Robert A. Scott and Stephen M. Kosslyn. Hoboken, NJ: Wiley.

Steinmetz, Kevin F., Brian P. Schaefer, Rolando V. del Carmen, and Craig Hemmens. 2014. "Assessing the Boundaries between Criminal Justice and Criminology." *Criminal Justice Review* 39:357–376.

Stewart, Anna, Hennessey Hayes, Michael Livingston, and Gerard Palk. 2008. "Youth Justice Conferencing and Indigenous Over-Representation in the Queensland Juvenile Justice System: a Micro-Simulation Case Study." *Journal of Experimental Criminology* 4:357–380.

Still, Wendy S. 2016. "A Practitioner's Perspective on Realignment: a Giant Win in San Francisco." *The Annals of the American Academy of Political and Social Science* 664:221–237.

Stolz, Barbara A. 2002. *Criminal Justice Policy Making: Federal Roles and Processes*. Westport, CT: Praeger.

Sudnow, David. 1964. "Normal Crimes: Sociological Features of the Penal Code in a Public Defender Office." *Social Problems* 12:255–276.

Sullivan, Christopher J. 2013. "Computer Simulation Experiments and the Development of Criminological Theory." Pp. 65–89 in *Experimental Criminology: Prospects for Advancing Science and Public Policy*, edited by Brandon C. Welsh, Anthony A. Braga, and Gerben J. N. Bruinsma. New York: Cambridge University Press.

Sutton, John R. 1988. *Stubborn Children: Controlling Delinquency in the United States, 1640–1981*. Berkeley, CA: University of California Press.

Swanson, Richard A., and Thomas J. Chermack. 2013. *Theory Building in Applied Disciplines*. San Francisco: Berrett-Koehler.

Sykes, Gresham M. 1958. *The Society of Captives*. Princeton, NJ: Princeton University Press.

Taleb, Nassim N. 2012. *Antifragile: Things that Gain from Disorder*. New York: Random House.

Tanenhaus, David S. 2004. *Juvenile Justice in the Making*. New York: Oxford University Press.

Taxman, Faye S., ed. 2017. *Handbook on Risk and Need Assessment: Theory and Practice*. New York: Routledge.

Taxman, Faye S., and April Pattavina, eds. 2013. *Simulation Strategies to Reduce Recidivism: Risk Need Responsivity (RNR) Modeling for the Criminal Justice System*. New York: Springer.

Taxman, Faye S., April Pattavina, and Michael Caudy. 2014. "Justice Reinvestment in the United States: an Empirical Assessment of the Potential

Impact of Increased Correctional Programming on Recidivism." *Victim and Offenders* 9:50–75.

Texas Criminal Justice Policy Council. 1997. *Apples to Oranges: Comparing the Operational Costs of Juvenile and Adult Correctional Programs in Texas.* Austin, Texas: State of Texas.

Texas Department of Criminal Justice. 2015. *Texas Department of Criminal Justice Annual Operating Budget 2016.* Austin, TX: Texas Department of Criminal Justice.

Thielo, Angela J., Francis T. Cullen, Derek M. Cohen, and Cecilia Chouhy. 2016. "Rehabilitation in a Red State: Public Support for Correctional Reform in Texas." *Criminology and Public Policy* 15:137–170.

Thomas, Charles W. 2005. "Recidivism of Public and Private State Prison Inmates in Florida: Issues and Unanswered Questions." *Criminology and Public Policy* 4:89–100.

Tillyer, Rob, Robin S. Engel, and John Wooldredge. 2008. "The Intersection of Racial Profiling Research and the Law." *Journal of Criminal Justice* 36:138–153.

Tocci, Stephen L., Ian A. Madom, Michael P. Bradley, Phillip R. Langer, and Christopher W. DiGiovanni. 2007. "The Diagnostic Value of MRI in Foot and Ankle Surgery." *Foot and Ankle International* 28:166–168.

Tonry, Michael H. 2016. "Equality and Human Dignity: the Missing Ingredients in American Sentencing." *Crime and Justice* 45:459–496.

———. 2009. "Explanations of American Punishment Policies." *Punishment and Society* 11:377–394.

———. 2004. *Thinking about Crime: Sense and Sensibility in American Penal Culture.* New York: Oxford University Press.

———. 1997. *Intermediate Sanctions in Sentencing Guidelines.* Washington, DC: National Institute of Justice.

Travis, Jeremy. 2005. *But They All Come Back: Facing the Challenges of Prisoner Reentry.* Washington, DC: The Urban Institute Press.

Travis, Jeremy, and Sarah Lawrence. 2002. *Beyond the Prison Gates: the State of Parole in America.* Washington, DC: The Urban Institute.

Travis, Jeremy, and Christy Visher, eds. 2005. *Prisoner Reentry and Crime in America.* New York: Cambridge University Press.

Travis, Jeremy, Bruce Western, and Steven Redburn, eds. 2014. *The Growth of Incarceration in the United States.* Washington, DC: The National Academies Press.

Truman, Jennifer L., and Rachel E. Morgan. 2016. *Criminal Victimization, 2015.* Washington, DC: Bureau of Justice Statistics.

Ulmer, Jeffery T. 2012. "Recent Developments and New Directions in Sentencing Research." *Justice Quarterly* 29:1–40.

Unnever, James D. 2014. "Race, Crime, and Public Opinion." Pp. 70–106 in *The Oxford Handbook of Ethnicity, Crime, and Immigration*, edited by Sandra M. Bucerius and Michael H. Tonry. New York: Oxford University Press.

Unnever, James D., and Francis T. Cullen. 2010. "The Social Sources of Americans' Punitiveness: a Test of Three Competing Models." *Criminology* 48:99–129.

Unnever, James D., and Shaun L. Gabbidon. 2011. *A Theory of African American Offending: Race, Racism, and Crime.* New York: Routledge.

Van Gigch, John P. 1978. *Applied General Systems Theory.* 2nd edition. New York: Harper and Row.

Vanagunas, Stanley. 1987. "Crime, Justice, and Systems Analysis: Two Decades Later." *Criminal Justice Policy Review* 2:259–268.

Vanlandingham, Gary R., and Elizabeth K. Drake. 2012. "Results First." *Public Performance and Management Review* 35:550–563.

Visher, Christy A., and Jeremy Travis. 2003. "Transitions from Prison to Community: Understanding Individual Pathways." *Annual Review of Sociology* 29:89–113.

Von Hirsch, Andrew, and Andrew Ashworth, eds. 1992. *Principled Sentencing.* Boston: Northeastern University Press.

Walker, Samuel. 1992. "Origins of the Contemporary Criminal Justice Paradigm: the American Bar Foundation Survey, 1953–1969." *Justice Quarterly* 9:47–76.

Ward, Mike. 2006. "Plan to Revive Criminal Justice Policy Council: House Leader Asks Perry to Sanction Move, to Give Planning Assist." *The Austin-American Statesman*, June 7. Available online (http://sentencing.nj.gov/downloads/pdf /articles/2006/Jun2006/story18.pdf).

Weber, Max. 1978. *Economy and Society: an Outline of Interpretive Sociology,* edited by Guenther Roth and Claus Wittich. Berkeley, CA: University of California Press.

1949. *On the Methodology of the Social Sciences.* Translated and edited by Edward A. Shils and Henry A. Finch. Glencoe, IL: The Free Press.

Weinberg, Stephen. 2015. *To Explain the World: the Discovery of Modern Science.* New York: HarperCollins.

Weiner, Tim. 2012. *Enemies: a History of the FBI.* New York: Random House.

Weisburd, David, and John E. Eck. 2004. "What Can Police Do to Reduce Crime, Disorder, and Fear?" *The Annals of the American Academy of Political and Social Science* 593:42–65.

Welsh, Brandon C. 2016. "Making Sense of Crime Prevention Evaluation Research and Communicating It for the Public Good." *Criminology and Public Policy* 15:611–615.

Welsh, Brandon C., Anthony A. Braga, and Gerben J. N. Bruinsma, eds. 2013. *Experimental Criminology: Prospects for Advancing Science and Public Policy.* New York: Cambridge University Press.

Welsh, Brandon C., and David P. Farrington. 2012. "Science, Politics, and Crime Prevention: Toward a New Crime Policy." *Journal of Criminal Justice* 40:128–133.

Welsh, Brandon C., David P. Farrington, and B. Raffan-Gowar. 2015. "Benefit-Cost Analysis of Crime Prevention Programs." *Crime and Justice* 44:447–516.

Welsh, Brandon C., and Peter W. Greenwood. 2015. "Making It Happen: State Progress in Implementing Evidence-Based Programs for Delinquent Youth." *Youth Violence and Juvenile Justice* 13:243–257.

Welsh, Brandon C., and Rebecca D. Pfeffer. 2013. "Reclaiming Crime Prevention in an Age of Punishment: an American History." *Punishment and Society* 15:534–553.

Welsh, Brandon C., and Michael Rocque. 2014. "When Crime Prevention Harms: a Review of Systematic Reviews." *Journal of Experimental Criminology* 10:245–266.

Welsh, Brandon C., Michael Rocque, and Peter W. Greenwood. 2014. "Translating Research into Evidence-Based Practice in Juvenile Justice: Brand Name Programs, Meta-analysis, and Key Issues." *Journal of Experimental Criminology* 10:207–225.

Welsh, Brandon C., Christopher J. Sullivan, and David L. Olds. 2010. "When Early Crime Prevention Goes to Scale: a New Look at the Evidence." *Prevention Science* 11:115–125.

Welsh, Wayne N., and Philip W. Harris. 2016. *Criminal Justice Policy and Planning.* 5th edition. New York: Routledge.

Western, Bruce. 2006. *Punishment and Inequality in America.* New York: Russell Sage Foundation.

White, Ron, and Timothy E. Downs. 2014. *How Computers Work: the Evolution of Technology.* 10th edition. Indianapolis, IN: Pearson.

Wholey, Joseph S., Harry P. Hatry, and Kathryn E. Newcomer, eds. 2004. *Handbook of Practical Program Evaluation.* 2nd edition. San Francisco: Jossey-Bass.

Wilson, James Q. 1993. "The Problem of Defining Agency Success." Pp. 157–167 in *Performance Measures for the Criminal Justice System.* Washington, DC: Bureau of Justice Statistics.

Wilson, Reid. 2014. "Tough Texas Gets Results by Going Softer on Crime." *The Washington Post,* November 27. Available online (www.washingtonpost .com/blogs/govbeat/wp/2014/11/27/tough-texas-gets-results-by-going-softer -on-crime/).

Wortley, Richard, and Lorraine Mazerolle, eds. 2008. *Environmental Criminology and Crime Analysis.* New York: Routledge.

Wright, Kevin A., and Gabriel T. Cesar. 2013. "Toward a More Complete Model of Offender Reintegration: Linking the Individual-, Community-, and System-Level Components of Recidivism." *Victims and Offenders* 8:373–398.

Zane, Steven N., Brandon C. Welsh, and Gregory M. Zimmerman. 2016. "Examining the Iatrogenic Effects of the Cambridge-Somerville Youth Study: Existing Explanations and New Appraisals." *British Journal of Criminology* 56:141–160.

Zawitz, Marianne W. 1996. *Firearm Injury from Crime.* Washington, DC: Bureau of Justice Statistics.

Zegart, Amy. 2011. "Implementing Change: Organizational Challenges." Pp. 309–329 in *Intelligence Analysis: Behavioral and Social Scientific Foundations,* edited by Baruch Fischhoff and Cherie Chauvin. National

Research Council's Committee on Behavioral and Social Science Research to Improve Intelligence Analysis for National Security. Washington, DC: The National Academies Press.

Zimring, Franklin E. 2007. *The Great American Crime Decline.* New York: Oxford University Press.

2005. "Penal Policy and Penal Legislation: Recent American Experience." *Stanford Law Review* 58:323–338.

Index

Printed in the USA
CPSIA information can be obtained
at www.ICGtesting.com
LVHW041311051023
760094LV00005B/134